The President as World Leader

By the same author

American Freethought
Farthest Frontier: The Pacific Northwest

The President
as World Leader

by Sidney Warren

J. B. Lippincott Company
Philadelphia and New York

The concluding chapter of this book is based on the author's article, "How
Powerful Is the Presidency," in the July 21, 1962, issue of *The Saturday Review*,
whose editors have kindly given permission to use the material in this form.

TO

Sylvia
Glenn
Jessica

Preface

THE NATURE of the Presidency was profoundly affected when
the United States in the twentieth century achieved the status
of a world power. To the many constitutional roles of the chief
executive and those which had accrued to him over the years
was now added that of international leader. After World War
II his global influence vastly increased, and today his power
is unparalleled.

No previous study has focused primarily on this new and vital
function of presidential leadership. Using it as my central
theme, I have described and analyzed the achievements of the
Presidents from the time when they could no longer be concerned exclusively with domestic affairs to the present, when
their decisions may affect the future of all mankind.

It is, of course, beyond the capacity of any President to create
the kind of world he would wish the United States to inhabit.
In directing the course of American foreign policy, he is often
limited by factors entirely beyond his control. He is, however,
the nation's chief foreign policy maker, and is the most strategically placed of all government officials to influence the
nation's direction as a world power. The qualities and resources
which he possesses and the character of his statesmanship will
largely account for the success or failure of the nation in achieving its objectives. Accordingly, I have dealt with the background, personality, training, constitutional views of the office,
relations with Congress, ability to influence public opinion,

and political skill of the President as elements which have shaped his individual style of leadership.

I am deeply indebted to the many people who have assisted in making this book possible. The study had its origin in discussions with my very good friend Professor Samuel J. Konefsky, who encouraged me to undertake it, as did Professors Arthur Link, Thomas A. Bailey, Eric F. Goldman, Frank Freidel, James MacGregor Burns, William G. Carleton, and Allan Nevins. To Professor Thomas A. Bailey of Stanford University and also to my good friend Professor Martin Ridge of San Diego State College, I am extremely grateful for reading the manuscript and for offering many helpful comments and suggestions. Needless to say, I alone am responsible for any errors of fact or interpretation.

To Dr. William C. Rust, President of California Western University, I am especially grateful. He generously supported my undertaking throughout and extended every possible cooperation.

I want to express sincere thanks for the fellowship awarded me by the American Council of Learned Societies, the two grants by the American Philosophical Society, and the grant-in-aid by the Harry S. Truman Library.

Members of President John F. Kennedy's staff, including Theodore Sorensen and McGeorge Bundy, were most cordial and helpful during my visit to the White House, and I want to thank them here for the time they took from a very busy schedule to discuss with me some points relevant to this study.

I was extremely fortunate to have the opportunity of a long conversation with that great lady Mrs. Eleanor Roosevelt. Speaking as she always did with forthrightness and candor, she gave me some very illuminating insights into her husband's personality and career. Presidents Herbert Hoover and Harry S. Truman graciously consented to be interviewed and provided useful information not only about their own administrations but on presidential leadership.

Only those engaged in research can fully appreciate the extent to which the scholar is dependent on library personnel. The staffs of the Franklin D. Roosevelt Library and the Harry

S. Truman Library did everything possible to make my visits there not only profitable but pleasant. I also appreciate the assistance of the staffs at the libraries at the University of California at Los Angeles, Stanford University, and San Diego State College. My special thanks to Dr. Hazel Pulling, Librarian at California Western University, for her inexhaustible patience and expert assistance.

I cannot adequately thank Mrs. Harvey Furgatch, who gave unstintingly of her time and effort in ways too numerous to list. No author could wish for a more skilled or devoted aid.

Finally, to my wife I owe the greatest debt of all for her tireless involvement at every stage of the book.

SIDNEY WARREN

San Diego, California
March, 1964

Contents

The President as World Leader

Introduction

1. The Background

T HE tenure of the President is only four years, wrote John Adams, but his power during that time is greater than "a king of Poland . . . a king of Sparta. I know of no first magistrate in any Republican government, except England . . . who possesses a constitutional dignity, authority, and power comparable to his." While Adams was somewhat extravagant in his description, neither he nor any of his contemporaries could possibly have imagined the towering stature which the President of the United States was to attain in the future. By the twentieth century he would be elevated to global leadership, the single most important individual on earth, literally holding in his hands the fate of all mankind.

But that was far off in the future. The group of men who labored tirelessly through a steaming Philadelphia summer in 1787 to draw up a constitution for the new republic were concerned with providing an instrument of government that would serve not only for their own generation but for those yet unborn. Of all the items with which they grappled, none was regarded as more significant or debated more vigorously than the one which dealt with the office of the President. When agreement was finally reached, the result was a remarkable achievement. A tremendous range of power and maximum flexibility to make his leadership effective were provided for the chief executive, but at the same time checks and restraints were carefully built into the Constitution to prevent a dictatorial abuse of authority.

While the President is empowered to negotiate treaties with foreign governments, he must receive the advice and consent of the Senate before they can be ratified; his appointment of ambassadors and other high-ranking officials is likewise conditional on approval from that body. As commander in chief, he is circumscribed by the authority of Congress to establish armed forces, provide for their support, and declare war. In the broad field of legislation, he may propose but Congress can dispose. And in his role as chief administrator he is limited by the legislature's control over the purse strings.

At the same time, the President's independence of the lawmaking branch and his lofty status were assured by the provision for a fixed term in office without restriction as to re-eligibility and by providing for tenure dissociated from legislative majorities. Another structural device to enhance his position was to make his term in office distinct from that of members of the House and Senate. The method of election was designed to keep him above the influence of the public temper: The Constitution makers, aristocrats by birth or inclination, who distrusted the fluctuating moods of the masses, provided for an Electoral College, whose delegates, a select group chosen by the qualified voters, were expected to exercise independent judgment in deciding among presidential candidates. However, with the rise of the party system and universal suffrage, this method of election was reduced to a formality, and the President emerged as a popular leader, spokesman for all the people and exponent of the nation's will.

A highly controversial point at the convention was the single versus the plural executive. By deciding in favor of the former, the convention gave the presidency the enormous advantage of unity, especially in the conduct of foreign relations, where numbers represent weakness, not strength. A single executive would never become a house divided against itself, rendered helpless by the confusing babble of conflicting voices. Moreover, with speed and secrecy often essential, no one but the President was equipped to meet these conditions.

The presidential office uniquely combines the ceremonial

attributes of royalty with the democratic simplicities of the governing politician. Repository of both pomp and power, it represents the prestige of the monarch and the authority of the elected statesman. As head of the state the President reigns; as chief executive he governs.

Over the years the President's powers have expanded enormously. The steady accretion cannot be attributed solely to formal changes in the structure and processes of government. It has resulted largely from subtle and informal developments, most of all from the impact of the great Presidents who gave the office new dimensions, invigorated it, and provided a legacy that even weaker men could not dissipate.

The nation was fortunate, indeed, that a man of George Washington's stature was available to serve as the first President. Universally beloved and esteemed, he made the office a symbol of national unity. Thomas Jefferson, making political leadership an aspect of the presidency, used the party as an instrument for the exercise of power and as a tool to shape legislative policy. Andrew Jackson, the first President to be elected by truly popular choice, dispelled the Whig notion that the legislature was the sole guardian of the people's rights and liberties. "The President is the direct representative of the American people," he stated. "He possesses original executive powers and absorbs in himself all executive functions and responsibilities; and it is his especial duty to protect the liberties and rights of the people and the integrity of the Constitution against the Senate, or the House of Representatives or both together."

Abraham Lincoln, reacting boldly to the challenge of rebellion, not only enlarged the constitutional role of the presidency in times of crisis but invested the office with the attribute of moral leadership. Without waiting for legislative sanction, he ordered a blockade against southern ports, called out the militia, increased the size of the Army and Navy, suspended the writ of habeas corpus, disbursed public funds for unauthorized purposes, and barred the mails to material he considered treasonable. Justifying his use of executive prerogative in the absence of expressly granted authority, he declared, "No organic law can ever be framed with a provision specifically applicable to every question which may arise. The whole of the laws are being resisted and all will be destroyed if not protected. . . . I am to sacrifice one law in order to save the rest. . . . The Constitution is silent on the emergency." He had taken an oath to preserve the nation and the Constitution and therefore "measures, otherwise unconstitutional, might become lawful, by becoming indispensable to the preservation of the Union."

Historical forces prodded the nation's chief executives to enlarge their powers and add new roles in the exercise of leadership. As the country spread from coast to coast, as population soared, who but the President in a mass democracy could represent all the people? A congressman's constituency is local, and the legislator is often impervious to the needs of the people outside his own bailiwick. The President's constituency, on the other hand, is national, and his electoral strength drawn mainly from the industrial, urbanized sections of the country.

With the growth of democracy, a direct connection was established between leader and people, a relationship which was itself a significant instrument of leadership. In the twentieth century, the advent of the so-called positive state, with the government committed to policies of regulation and welfare, gave the President opportunities to enhance his strategic position. Possessing the advantage of corporate unity and singleness of purpose, he could draw upon his constitutional authority to recommend legislation and employ the great prestige of his office to press for its enactment. No one else was so ideally situated to serve as custodian of the people's welfare, once laissez-faire was abandoned as the guiding principle of government.

It is in the area of foreign relations, however, as chief diplomat and major foreign policy spokesman, that the President's influence has been most dramatically amplified. His authority, inherent in the second article of the Constitution, was never fully tapped as long as circumstances provided no occasion for its exercise. But with the emergence of the United States as a world power, with the experience of two major wars followed by prolonged and incessant crises, the President's leadership, prestige, and power have assumed a new magnitude.

In the early years, the chief executives considered it necessary and prudent to avoid entanglements in European rivalries and politics so that the nation might remain at peace, free to pursue an independent foreign policy, develop its internal resources, and engage in continental expansion. At the same time, they were not indifferent to world currents across the Atlantic but were ever alert to the ruptures and shifting alliances that could be used to the nation's advantage. By assiduously cultivating a policy of non-involvement in European affairs, the young republic succeeded in safeguarding its security throughout the formative period of its development.

George Washington's Farewell Address, emphasizing that the interests of the new nation were separate and distinct from those of Europe, set the tone for American foreign policy for more than a century. "The great rule of conduct for us in regard to foreign nations is, in extending our commercial relations, to have with them as little *political* connection as possible," he said. As the concerns of Europe were frequently productive of controversies essentially alien to the United States, "it must be unwise in us to implicate ourselves by artificial ties in the ordinary vicissitudes of her politics or the ordinary combinations and collisions of her friendships or enmities. Our detached and distant situation invites and enables us to pursue a different course." If the nation remained united under an efficient government, it would not be long before "we may take such an attitude as will cause the neutrality we may at times resolve upon to be scrupulously respected . . . when we may choose peace or war as our interest, guided by justice, shall counsel." Concluding his advice to his countrymen, Washington asked rhetorically, "Why forego the advantages of so peculiar a situation? Why quit our own to stand upon foreign ground? Why, by interweaving our destiny with that of any part of Europe, entangle our peace and prosperity in the toils of European ambition, rivalship, interest, humor or caprice?" No doctrinaire, he realized that a change in circumstances might justify a different response, that emergency situations might create the need for temporary alliances. His prescription was not to be taken as an immutable rule, but intended to enable the nation to control its own destiny as long as conditions permitted.

Thomas Jefferson's celebrated "Peace, commerce, and honest friendship with all nations, entangling alliances with none" reinforced Washington's view. It was echoed by statesmen of all political persuasions of that era, by Hamilton as well as Madison, and reflected the sentiment of the country at large. Extending the hand of "honest friendship," however, was not always uncomplicated. The problem soon arose of how to safeguard the nation's neutral rights when jeopardized by foreign wars, for along with non-entanglement, neutrality became a cornerstone of American policy. How to protect the commerce and trade vital to the country's growth and prosperity in the midst of turbulent international currents? The early leaders faced the issue by constructing a naval force, challenging French depredations on the high seas, dispatching naval expeditions to the Barbary Coast, and engaging in war against England in 1812. Both neutrality and isolationism were pursued to disengage rather than involve the nation in the vortex of European politics and to encourage rather than restrict its freedom of action.

When the United States was invited by Czar Alexander I of Russia to join the Holy Alliance, which he founded for the ostensible purpose of maintaining world peace, Secretary of State John Quincy Adams declined, stating that "the political system of the United States is . . . essentially extra-European. To stand in firm and cautious independence of all entanglement in the European system has been a cardinal point of their policy under every administration . . . to this day."

Great Britain's proposal, in 1823, that the United States join with her in protesting any move by the Holy Alliance to assist Spain in repossessing the newly independent Latin-American states, presented President James Monroe with the need to make a momentous decision. Should he follow Jefferson's advice that the offer be accepted? The aging former President reasoned that, as England was the one nation which could most effectively interfere with American interests, by agreeing to the request "we detach her from the band of despots, bring her mighty weight into the scale of free government and emancipate a continent at one stroke." While Monroe found this argument impressive, he yielded to Adams, his Secretary of

State, who said that he had already warned the Russians about interference in the Western Hemisphere and was prepared to serve a similar warning on any other European power. The United States, he was convinced, should act unilaterally, thereby preserving independence of action. Why "come in as a cockboat in the wake of the British man of war?" Adams pointedly asked, particularly as Britain in any case would be forced to support the United States since her interests in Latin America coincided with our own.

Later events were to justify Adams's astuteness. Deciding that the nation should take a stand on its own, President Monroe inserted into his 1823 message to Congress a declaration which has since been known as the Monroe Doctrine. The European nations were cautioned that any effort to extend their systems to the Western Hemisphere would be regarded by the United States as inimical to its peace and security. For its part, America would not interfere in the affairs of the continent. Thus, the concept of the inviolability of the Western Hemisphere was added to the existing one of non-involvement. Fortunately, throughout most of the nineteenth century, European preoccupation with revolutions, rivalries, wars, and the threats of war—combined with the indirect protection afforded by the British Navy in patrolling the Atlantic to promote a national interest which frequently coincided with America's—prevented a major challenge to the doctrine. Ultimately, the United States was itself sufficiently powerful to compel universal respect for the policy.

Thus an admonition made when the country was first established rapidly hardened into a national dogma. The ocean served as a gigantic moat to insulate the United States from embroilment in the quarrels and conflicts of Europe. Moreover, psychological and cultural attitudes soon evolved which reinforced isolationism. Enamored of the uniqueness of their national experience, Americans began to stress their distinctiveness from the rest of the world and to talk of setting an example for benighted lands to emulate. "Humanity with all its fears is hanging breathless on thy fate," wrote Longfellow. The torch of democracy, it was hoped, would light the way for all mankind, but the American people were prepared only to provide the illumination.

During the Greek struggle for independence in the 1820's, intervention, urged by sympathizers of the freedom movement, was opposed by Secretary of State Adams, to avoid, as he put it, involvement in wars of intrigue. It was fitting, he said, that the nation should give moral support, but "she goes not abroad in search of monsters to destroy. She is the well-wisher to the freedom and independence of all. She is the champion and vindicator only of her own." When the Hungarians were fighting for their freedom in 1848, the response was similar. While some Americans importuned the government for an alliance with republican movements and a number of senators urged diplomatic support, arguing that the nation now well out of its swaddling clothes need no longer be afraid of offending foreign powers, the prevailing sentiment was expressed by Senator Charles Sumner. He declared that while the United States should never close its ears to the cries of distress "or cease to swell with indignation at the steps of tyranny," the advice offered by George Washington should remain as a guide, and, like Washington when he addressed the Minister of the French Directory, "I would offer sympathy and God-speed to all, in every land, who struggle for Human Rights; but, sternly as Washington . . . against every pressure, against all popular appeals, against all solicitations . . . I would uphold the peaceful neutrality of the country."

For the remainder of the century, isolationist sentiments were continually reiterated by the nation's leaders. "To avoid entangling alliances has been a maxim of our policy ever since the days of Washington," President Buchanan said on taking office, "and its wisdom no one will attempt to dispute." In declining a French invitation in 1863 to join in urging the Russian Czar to adopt a more lenient policy toward the Poles, Lincoln's Secretary of State, William Seward, took the occasion to restate the position to which his country was committed. The policy of non-intervention, he declared, "straight, absolute, and peculiar as it may seem to other nations, has become a traditional one, which could not be abandoned without the most urgent occasion, amounting to a manifest necessity." Five years later, he rejected adherence to the Geneva Convention which established the International Red Cross, despite its humanitarian and non-political nature. It was unwise, he argued, for the United States to become a party to any instrument of a multilateral nature in the absence of an overriding necessity.

President Andrew Johnson underscored the isolationist credo, stating that the geographic situation of the United States combined with its economic resources make the nation "singularly independent of the varying policy of foreign powers and protect us against every temptation to 'entangling alliances.'" Twenty years later, President Cleveland in his inaugural address repeated the same tune. The needs of the people, he said, "and the attention which is demanded for the settlement and development of the resources of our vast territory dictate the scrupulous avoidance of any departure from that foreign policy commanded by the history, the traditions, and the prosperity of our Republic."

A policy of non-involvement based on abstention from political commitments in Europe never implied nor did it result in detachment from the outside world. Developments overseas that could be exploited for American advantage were quickly seized upon. The Napoleonic Wars, for example, provided the opportunity for the purchase of the vast Louisiana Territory and, by shaking loose Spain's imperial grip on Florida, enabled American statesmen to acquire that territory also. Eyes were turned to the Orient, where potentially rich trade with Japan and China beckoned. The Far East could provide an outlet for the nation's expansive, commercial spirit without jeopardizing the safety of the country, as the European powers were not strongly entrenched in the area, nor was the Pacific dominated by a single nation as was the Atlantic by Great Britain.

Avidity for oriental commerce spurred the United States to acquire California and Oregon, with Americans using a whole arsenal of ideological and moral rationalizations to justify economic goals. Commodore Perry "opened up" Japan with a message from the American President to the Japanese Emperor and a salesman's array of items produced by Western technology. Negotiations were also undertaken to expand trade with China, and an attempt was made in the 1850's to annex the kingdom of Hawaii.

Increasingly, the American flag became a familiar sight in Pacific waters, while the same spirit of "manifest destiny" pushed the boundaries of the country steadily toward the western ocean. Expansionist activities were temporarily halted in mid-century when the nation became successively absorbed with the problem of slavery, the threat of civil strife, the Civil War, and afterwards the Herculean and divisive task of reconstruction. Statesmen intermittently looked beyond their native shores, but their aspirations were peripheral to the main currents of American thought. The only extension of the country's domain during this period resulted from the acquisition by purchase of the Alaska Territory, derisively dubbed "Seward's folly" or "Seward's icebox" by critics.

During the postwar decades, the people flung themselves frenetically into the development of transportation, communication, industry, and finance. These were halcyon years for the nation which, safe behind two oceans, free from international intrigues, and with a land of boundless wealth to exploit, had little interest in foreign affairs. The isolationist spirit was further intensified by the immigrants who poured into the country. Millions of Europeans, impoverished and dispossessed, deserted the old continent with its perennial wars, conscription, social injustice, and regressive political institutions for the new land of hope and promise. Though retaining some ties with their former homeland, they shed their past in a more important sense: fearing that its evils might rub off on the land of their adoption, they desired to keep the Old World at a distance, and their reactions provided added strength to the feeling of separateness.

Americans, ignoring or unaware of the beneficent historical circumstances which made it possible for their country to pursue an independent course, acquired an overweening self-confidence. As Andrew Carnegie proclaimed, the old nations were creeping along at a snail's pace while "the Republic thunders past with the rush of an express," increasing in population, wealth, strength, and influence. Ironically, this very burgeoning robustness was to hurl the nation into the center of the international vortex. By the end of the century, the United States had become the leading manufacturing power of the world. Active participation in the arena of world politics was now inevitable.

The realization would come very slowly to most Americans that the transformed status of their country linked its destiny inextricably with the fate and fortune of other nations. The stakes of power would require the abandonment of aloofness and the assumption of novel responsibilities. Foreign relations would become increasingly important, the nation ever more intimately involved in the affairs of the world, and presidential leadership heavily challenged. A century and a quarter ago, Alexis de Tocqueville had presciently observed that the President's influence would increase in proportion as the country's foreign relations acquired a more active and continuing character. In the twentieth century, the President, as a leader in world affairs, would require the vision and talents of a statesman and the skill of a masterly politician.

Theodore Roosevelt

2. The Man and the Times Meet

SHORTLY after the turn of the century, an assassin's bullet ended the life of the placid, conciliatory President McKinley, catapulting into the White House a man who was his complete antithesis. The dynamic, ebullient Theodore Roosevelt, with his compulsive drive for power, was not only to enhance immeasurably the authority and prestige of the presidency but also to give the country a powerful thrust into world leadership.

Ironically, Roosevelt had been extremely reluctant to accept the nomination for the vice-presidency, regarding it as retirement into oblivion. This was a horrifying prospect for a man of his temperament, with the overwhelming need for ego gratification that only active leadership could satisfy. He would, he told Boss Platt of New York, "a great deal rather be anything, say professor of history, than Vice President." Nor were some of the party leaders happy about his choice, Mark Hanna vainly warning that only one life stood between "this madman" and the White House. Others, however, considered it the best way to cut off the obstreperous young man's political career. In the election campaign, Roosevelt should have taken a secondary place, but as Mr. Dooley expressed it, " 'Tis Teddy alone that's runnin', and he ain't a-runnin', he's gallopin'." Less than a year later, Roosevelt was "President by accident."

When he took the oath of office, Roosevelt declared that it would be his aim to continue "absolutely unbroken the policy of President McKinley." The pledge was little more than a conventional gesture, a token of respect for the memory of the fallen leader, in view of Roosevelt's ambitions for the nation.

For years, Roosevelt had been preoccupied with America's proper role in the international community. During the 1890's, he had been the most articulate and effective spokesman of a small but influential group of ardent exponents of "manifest destiny" which included political scientists, historians, and naval strategists. In their aim to make the United States a dominant power, they supported the doctrines of Captain Alfred T. Mahan, naval historian and geopolitical strategist. According to Mahan, control of the sea lanes was a decisive element in the struggle for power, and one with which the United States must be seriously concerned if the nation was to achieve greatness. He regarded as essential the expansion of foreign trade; acquisition of naval bases, refueling stations, and, if possible, colonies; and the development of a merchant fleet and a navy powerful enough to dominate the ocean highways and defeat any enemy. Furthermore, an isthmian canal under American control was indispensable, as was the possession of Hawaii and the establishment of bases in the West Indies, above all, in Cuba.

Neither Roosevelt nor any of Mahan's other disciples were primarily motivated by economic factors. Power and influence for the United States was their goal, and, in general, they expressed their sentiments in terms of "the white man's burden," national honor, national pride. Some were alarmed about the "yellow peril," advocating expansion to thwart Japan's growing influence. In the competitive struggle, the race would go to the strongest; power, boldly asserted, was the only alternative to national decay.

Through an endless flood of books and articles, the expansionists circulated their view widely, reaching both a popular and an elite audience. But as they became increasingly effective, as the drift toward imperialism became a swift current, many distinguished intellectuals became alarmed and, to confound the economic determinists, so did many business leaders and bankers who feared that foreign adventures would jeopardize commercial stability.

The expansionist crusade had received a new infusion in 1897 when Roosevelt was appointed Assistant Secretary of the Navy. He had eagerly sought the post, consumed by the desire to be in a position where he could influence the future course of the nation. Up to that point he had served in a variety of official but unspectacular capacities—New York State assemblyman for three terms, member of the federal Civil Service Commission, and police commissioner of New York City. Senator Henry Cabot Lodge, with whom Roosevelt had formed a devoted friendship that was to endure a lifetime, worked hard to secure the post for his friend. Aided by a number of other important men, he pressured every influential official. The tenacity of the group almost suggests a cabal by the expansionists to put one of their own into a key spot in Washington.

President McKinley, dubious all along about the impetuous young aspirant's views, soon found his misgivings justified. No sooner was Roosevelt in office than he began agitating to build up the Navy and urged an invasion of Cuba, which was then in revolt against its Spanish overlord.

To his countrymen, Roosevelt appealed for intervention in Cuba in the name of humanitarianism. While acknowledging that sugar, tobacco, and the country's proximity to the projected isthmian canal were important to the United States, he justified his views largely in terms of righteousness and good conscience. His major consideration was the people, groaning under the yoke of a despot, whose heroic movement for a "Cuba libre" was being savagely repressed. Tyrannical Spain, he insisted, must be driven from the Western Hemisphere. When the battleship Maine exploded in Havana Harbor in February, 1898, his efforts became almost frenzied. He importuned the President, conferred with Secretary of State William R. Day, and badgered his immediate superior, Navy Secretary John D. Long. The non-belligerent McKinley was resolutely seeking a peaceful solution, and, as Long commented, his assistant's "ardor sometimes went faster than the President or the Department approved."

Checked on all sides, Roosevelt wrote in deep frustration to a friend that "in the name of humanity and of national interest alike" the United States should long since have intervened in

Cuba. "The blood of the murdered men of the *Maine* calls not for indemnity but for the full measure of atonement which can only come by driving the Spaniards from the New World." He had spoken privately to everyone in authority, he continued, but could not, of course, make any public statements since he was "merely a minor official in the Administration."

While not a member of the top decision-making echelon, Roosevelt nevertheless managed to be very effective in preparing the country for the war he was convinced should and must come. As a member of the Naval War Board, he provided the impetus for the acquisition of matériel, the purchase of war vessels, and the completion of battleships. The elderly and cautious Long must frequently have felt that he was holding a wild bull by the tail. His poor health often kept him away from the office, and when he returned he would find members of the staff inundated by memoranda that Roosevelt had showered on them.

Once, when Long was absent, Roosevelt named George Dewey as commander of the Asiatic Fleet. Another time this "minor official" was in charge, "the very devil seemed to possess him," Long later reminisced, and he came "very near causing more of an explosion than happened to the *Maine*." Planning to be away for a few hours, the Secretary had left instructions that only routine matters be handled. No sooner was he out of the office than Roosevelt blew up a hurricane. He sent off messages to congressmen urging legislation on naval matters, instructed the European and Asiatic squadrons where to rendezvous in the event of hostilities, purchased large quantities of coal, authorized the enlistment of an unlimited number of seamen, had guns transferred from the Navy Yard in Washington to New York so that auxiliary cruisers could be armed, and, most important of all, sent secret instructions to Commodore Dewey to prepare for an attack on the Spanish fleet in the Philippines if war should be declared.

Secretary Long attributed Roosevelt's unprecedented behavior to his impulsiveness, unaware that his assistant had taken advantage of his absence to initiate war preparations that he and his friends had been discussing for months. A half year earlier, Roosevelt had written Lodge that "our Asiatic

squadron should blockade and, if possible, take Manila." From
then on, he endeavored to keep the fleet alerted. Since neither
Congress nor the President had made any decision along that
line, his initiative was largely responsible for enabling the fleet
to seize the Philippine Islands during the conflict. His directives on that February day may not have been as decisive as
they were later regarded by President Taft, who wrote that,
had it not been for Roosevelt's pressure on Congress to appropriate funds for the ammunition essential to "back any bluff we
might make with actual play," the country would not have
been in a position to declare war. But they helped make the
conflict brief and victorious. Dewey prepared his ships in the
weeks before the outbreak of hostilities, and when he entered
Manila Bay he demolished the Spanish fleet without suffering
any damage to his own.

When Roosevelt agitated for war he had no intention of
conducting maneuvers from behind a desk. In his personal
credo, courage was among the most exalted of virtues. War was
manly and exciting, peace effeminate and dull both for the
individual and the country. To prevent decadence, a nation
occasionally required an ordeal by fire. "The victories of peace
are great," he wrote, "but the victories of war are greater. No
merchant, no banker, no railroad magnate, no inventor . . . can
do for any nation what can be done for it by its great fighting
men." None of the qualities of a peaceful life "stand on a level
with those stern and virile virtues which move the men . . . who
uphold the honor of their flag in battle." That same year, in
1897, he wrote to a friend "in strict confidence" that he would
"welcome almost any war, for I think this country needs one."
William James observed that Roosevelt "treats peace as a condition of blubberlike and swollen ignobility, fit only for huck-
stering weaklings."

The moment war with Spain was declared, Roosevelt resigned his post to recruit men for a regiment which he would
lead. His daredevil tactics as commander resulted in long
casualty lists, and sometimes only luck saved the regiment
from total annihilation. But his courage in battle and his solici-
tude for his men earned him the undying devotion of the soldiers, and his exploits as leader of the famed Rough Riders

brought him national fame and led to the governorship of New York, to the vice-presidency, and then to the White House, the youngest President yet to hold office.

Roosevelt's temperament and outlook were very likely shaped by a sickly boyhood during which he had been deprived of the normal physical activities of youth. Extremely nearsighted, he stumbled around awkwardly until he was fitted with glasses at fourteen. Severely asthmatic, he was considered too frail even to attend private schools, and until he entered Harvard he was educated by private tutors. Having built up his body by rigid discipline and unremitting effort, he compensated in his adulthood for all he had missed in his youth by a heedless, boylike pursuit of adventure and strenuous activity. Boylike, too, was the way everything had to be done with exaggerated zest. "He killed mosquitoes as if they were lions," one biographer comments.

With the exception of Andrew Jackson, many of whose views on leadership he shared, no previous chief executive possessed Theodore Roosevelt's self-confidence, his dogmatic certitude, or the unshakable conviction that his course was best for the national interest. Both in foreign policy and domestic affairs, Roosevelt's exercise of power extended executive authority to the farthest limits permitted the President under the Constitution. He insisted that "the executive power was limited only by specific restrictions and prohibitions appearing in the Constitution or imposed by Congress under its Constitutional powers," and in the absence of these, presidential prerogative enjoyed wide latitude. Every executive officer, particularly those in high position, he felt, should be "a steward of the people bound actively and affirmatively to do all he could for the people." It was unnecessary for the President to rely on some specific authorization when a matter imperative to the nation had to be undertaken. "I did not usurp power," he wrote in later years, "but I did greatly broaden the use of executive power." According to his own analysis of what he called the Buchanan type of President, with its restricted view of the office, and the Lincoln type, representing the enlarged concept, he completely exemplified the latter.

Rather than fear controversy, he reveled in it. As his first

term was ending he wrote to his friend, George Otto Trevel-
yan, the British historian, that under the American system of
government the presidential office unfortunately tends to put a
premium on staying out of trouble rather than on achieving
results. As for himself, "I certainly would not be willing to hold
the Presidency at the cost of failing to do the things which
make the real reason why I care to hold it at all. I had much
rather be a real President for three years and a half than a
figurehead for seven years and a half."

It would have been impossible for Roosevelt at any time or
in any position to be a figurehead. A relative once remarked
about him, "When Theodore attends a wedding he wants to be
the bride, and when he attends a funeral he wants to be the
corpse."

Throughout his years as President, Roosevelt never left the
center of the stage, always performing with gusto to the great
delight of his nationwide audience. Expressing what was
undoubtedly a popular reaction, a national journal in 1906
wrote, "The scrapes he gets into, the scrapes he gets out of; the
things he attempts, the things he accomplishes, the things he
demolishes . . . his assumptions, presumptions, omnisciences
and deficiencies, make up a daily tale which those of us who
survive his tenure of the presidential office will doubtless miss,
as we might miss some property of the atmosphere we
breathe."

The excitement Roosevelt generated blinded many to the
fact that the dynamo was directed by a calculating, incisive
mind. Henry Adams once described him as being "pure act,"
but as important as physical activity to Roosevelt was the life
of the mind. He was the most cultivated President since
Thomas Jefferson, and his intellectual interests were equally
wide-ranging. His good friend Finley Peter Dunne wrote that
he was "more many-sided than any other man in my experience. To a student of government he was a statesman, to a
political reporter a crafty politician, to a man of letters an
author. He was an explorer, a hunter of big game, an orni-
thologist, a lover of poetry, a soldier, a historian." An omnivo-
rous reader, he was never without a volume close at hand.
While on a zoological expedition in Africa after he left the

White House, amid the hazards of jungle life when porters were dying of dysentery and sleeping sickness and being attacked by lions, he found time for varied reading, including a book of poems written by the son of Henry Cabot Lodge, about which he sent a detailed comment to his friend.

His courage became legendary. Whatever psychological reasons disposed him to court danger, his life was filled with incidents of valor and even reckless behavior. A dramatic, but not uncharacteristic, example was his reaction after an attempt on his life in Milwaukee during the campaign of 1912 when he was the presidential candidate of the Progressive Party. On his way to the hall to deliver an address, Roosevelt was shot in the chest by a would-be assassin. The wound might have been fatal had the bullet not been blunted by the manuscript and spectacle case which he was carrying in the upper pocket of his jacket. Bleeding, but not coughing blood, Roosevelt concluded that he would probably survive and, against the protestations of party leaders, insisted on making his speech. His voice feeble and halting, his balance unsteady, with men close at his side prepared to prop him up if he should fall, he continued to the end. Such intrepidity, combined with a superb talent for publicity, contributed greatly to Roosevelt's political appeal.

No previous chief executive had so assiduously cultivated the press or received as much newspaper coverage. As soon as Roosevelt took office, he established a press room in the White House and systematized procedures to disseminate news. He soon developed a coterie of trusted and sympathetic reporters to whom he generously extended the favors on which they depended. Aware that week ends, generally barren of official news, rarely produced headlines in the Monday editions, he proceeded to remedy that situation. Anything he could think of was grist for the mill—an executive pronouncement, some stricture on nature fakers, or an item on eugenics, all couched in vivid, forceful language.

Roosevelt's keen attention to the press was also motivated by his conception of the presidency as a "bully pulpit." For the first time, a President made a deliberate effort to use this medium of mass communication as a potent instrument for political leadership. In Jackson's day, several party newspapers were indirectly subsidized by the administration so that it could confidently rely on editorials supporting the policies in Washington. Roosevelt reached out for wider territory. As head of a democratic state, he never underestimated the importance of public support to carry out his programs. To obtain it, the American people would have to be informed. "Our prime necessity," he once said, "is that public opinion should be properly educated." On another occasion he stated, "I do not desire to act unless I can get the bulk of our people to understand the situation and to back up the action; and to do that I have to get the facts vividly before them."

Regarding himself as the spokesman of the people, he considered it his duty to counter any congressional effort to limit his power. "A strong people," he once said, "need never fear a strong man. . . . It is an admission of popular weakness to be afraid of strong public servants." While Roosevelt occasionally clashed with Congress, his relations with the legislative body, for the most part, were remarkably effective. Thoroughly seasoned in the art of practical politics, he never underestimated the usefulness of party organization, and his political experiences provided him with a valuable apprenticeship for higher leadership. He displayed a realistic awareness of the importance of the Speaker of the House, then enjoying unusually broad powers, as the instrument through whom executive direction over legislation might be exercised. He conferred regularly with him and with other legislative leaders, frequently inviting them to breakfasts and luncheons. Speaker Joe Cannon later recalled that Roosevelt discussed with him almost every major legislative recommendation before presenting it to Congress and requested that the leaders be first sounded out, "for he did not want to recommend legislation simply to write messages. He wanted results and he wanted to know how to secure results with the least friction." And, according to the veteran parliamentarian, Roosevelt was always prepared to settle for half a loaf if this seemed the only feasible prospect. Roosevelt, one writer commented, brought the presidency into an organic connection with Congress.

In legislative achievements, Roosevelt set a new record. He became, in the fullest sense of the term, the nation's chief legislator, the first President to initiate legislation and push for its enactment. In theory, he later wrote, the executive has nothing to do with legislation, but in practice he is or ought to be "peculiarly representative of the people as a whole. As often as not the action of the Executive offers the only means by which the people can get the legislation they demand and ought to have." A good executive, therefore, "must take a very active interest in getting the right kind of legislation."

To obtain his proposed measures, Roosevelt's messages to Congress were so constructed as to arouse the public to exert pressure on the legislative body. "People used to say to me that I was an astonishingly good politician and divined what the people are going to think," he wrote. "This really was not an accurate way of stating the case. I did not 'divine' how the people were going to think; I simply made up my mind what they ought to think, and then did my best to get them to think it."

Pragmatic rather than legalistic in his approach to presidential leadership, Roosevelt was influenced in his decisions by "the rule of necessity." He advocated a broad construction of the Constitution, convinced that the changing pattern of social and economic life in industrialized America required new responses by the government. "I am for popular rights," he once said, "and where they can best be obtained by the exercise of State rights, I am a good States'-rights man; and where they can best be obtained by the power of the nation, I am a nationalist."

A gifted speaker and prolific writer, he frequently expounded his views both from the platform and in print. The basic philosophy that guided his conduct in office, cogently summarized in his *Autobiography*, reveals that he was not a doctrinaire, wedded to any fixed constitutional dogma. "I believed in invoking the National power with absolute freedom for every National need; and I believed that the Constitution should be treated as the greatest document ever devised by the wit of man to aid a people in exercising every power necessary for its own betterment, and not as a strait jacket cunningly fashioned to strangle growth."

If strength, independence, and flexibility, in Roosevelt's

opinion, were essential for executive leadership in domestic affairs, they were even more vital to the proper conduct of the country's foreign policies. Unforeseen contingencies which might require quick and decisive action to defend the nation's interests could be handled adequately only by a man who possessed those attributes. Holding such a view, he was understandably disposed toward personal diplomacy, of which he became a consummate practitioner. The deplorable state of the diplomatic corps at the time impelled a man of his temperament and conviction to play an active role. A provincially minded Congress and a vicious spoils system had wreaked havoc on the once illustrious service. It had become hopelessly inefficient, filled with men who, for the most part, had not the slightest qualification for their positions. The consular service was especially notorious.

As no fundamental change was possible for the time being, Roosevelt gathered around him a small group of informal advisers, both public servants and private citizens. The select coterie was not confined to Americans. Three men whom he saw frequently and with whom he carried on a frank exchange of views about his own tasks of leadership and the broader aspects of international affairs were ambassadors from European countries: Jean Jusserand, Cecil Spring-Rice, and Hermann Speck von Sternburg. Often he exercised the functions normally handled by the Secretary of State, composing diplomatic messages and dispatches which were sent on to the State Department for transmission. On a number of occasions the department was not informed about matters of high policy, as when it was left in ignorance for two or three weeks that the Japanese government had asked the President to intercede in peace negotiations with Russia. For long periods, Mrs. Roosevelt was his only confidante in matters properly the concern of the State Department. It was not unusual for ambassadors abroad to communicate directly with the President, and important documents dealing with the government's foreign relations were sometimes kept out of the department's official archives.

Similarly casual and unorthodox were the President's relations with his Cabinet, which he rarely consulted as a body.

When he sought advice, he conferred with a member privately, and when he contemplated some action, he informed only the individual within whose province it fell. On the whole, he looked to his Cabinet for the administration of the respective departments and for confidential advice turned instead to his "Tennis Cabinet," an informal group of trusted friends. To those who valued compliance with rules and regulations, his highly individual style was disturbing and bewildering. Taft once said that Roosevelt demoralized his administration by dealing directly with subordinates, petty clerks, bureau chiefs, anyone who had the information he wanted, without bothering to channel his inquiries through responsible heads.

Less traditional in his methods than his predecessors, Roosevelt's broad exercise of power was nevertheless not unique. There had been other strong executives who extended the scope of the office. His leadership was distinctive because he was the first to be concerned with the enhancement of the power and prestige of the United States in world affairs.

Theodore Roosevelt

3. Extending the Nation's Power

ABSORBED by the goal of national power, Roosevelt regarded as illusory the notion that economic growth and riches alone could bring about its realization. Wealth was only a means to an end; the quality of the human resource was the crucial factor. As he told an audience in 1898, the people must be prepared to throw themselves selflessly, with Spartan dedication to their country's welfare, into the world struggle for supremacy. "The twentieth century looms before us big with the fate of many nations," he declared. "If we stand idly by, if we seek merely swollen, slothful ease and ignoble peace, if we shrink from the hard contests where men must win at hazard of their lives and at the risk of all they hold dear, then the bolder and stronger peoples will pass us by, and will win for themselves the domination of the world. Let us therefore boldly face the life of strife."

He deplored the pursuit of wealth for luxurious living and self-indulgence, agreeing with Brooks Adams that greed and acquisitiveness would lead to a degeneration of the nation's fiber, the corrosion of its creative vitality. Civilization itself would be endangered. American economic resources should be developed to aid the country in achieving strength, but kept subordinate to the higher values. He criticized the tendency to elevate economic man to paramount importance. The qualities that made for a meritorious individual—courage, honesty, moral responsibility, commitment to duty—were equally important for a nation. A great nation, he wrote to a friend, can remain so "only by doing a great work and achieving dangerous and difficult tasks."

A tough-minded, realistic approach lay at the core of Roosevelt's world view. Rivalry among powers was a factor of international life. The conflict of interests between France and Germany, between Russia and Japan, for example, could not be resolved by exhortations to universal peace and brotherhood. In the nineteenth century, the United States had been able to maintain itself without a substantial military force; in the twentieth, the emergence of new powers and America's own changing status were creating a new pattern of power relationships that required new responses. If the nation was to live in a world of fact and not fancy, it must recognize the role of force in achieving power and the necessity for constantly adjusting to situations created by power rivalries. Self-interest demanded that the United States, in conjunction with other advanced countries, employ its weight to promote stability abroad, forestall the abuse of power, and prevent eruptions that could lead to armed conflict.

The President's *Realpolitik* was startling to a people until then relatively insulated from world currents. Now Roosevelt was informing them that as a major power, "We have no choice as to whether or not we shall play a great part in the world. That has been determined for us by fate, by the march of events. We have to play that part. . . . All that we can decide is whether we shall play it well or ill." In articles and speeches he had long endeavored to make the nation aware that its growth and the increased interrelatedness of the world made an isolationist policy obsolete, its continued practice injurious. "We cannot avoid as a nation," he insisted, "the fact that on the east and west we look across the waters at Europe and Asia."

In 1903, Roosevelt told a San Francisco audience that the center of power keeps shifting from land to land and from sea to sea. The Atlantic Ocean was now as strategically important for the modern world as the Mediterranean once had been for the ancient world, and with the rise of Japan, the Pacific Ocean, in turn, was assuming a vital significance. To help maintain the balance of power in both Europe and Asia, a strong navy was indispensable.

Roosevelt saw two major weaknesses in the American naval situation. First, the 13,000 miles which separated the two seaboards made the Pacific virtually inaccessible from the Atlantic. During the war with Spain, it had taken the battleship *Oregon* sixty-eight days to complete the ocean-to-ocean voyage around the coast of South America, and that was regarded as a record-breaking time. Either a two-ocean navy or an isthmian canal was essential. Secondly, outposts in the western Pacific were inadequately defended, and unless the Navy was supreme in that area the United States would be helpless against a hostile power.

It was the President's intention that naval policy should be an integral instrument of American foreign relations. Shortly after he took office, he told Congress that "the Navy offers the only means of making our insistence upon the Monroe Doctrine anything but a subject of derision to whatever nation chooses to disregard it." If the American people did not support building and maintaining an adequate navy, they would have to accept "a secondary position in international affairs, not merely in political but in commercial matters." On another occasion he informed Congress that the country's foreign policy would be self-defeating unless accompanied by a sound attitude toward the Army and, even more so, toward the Navy. "It is as contemptible, for a nation, as for an individual," he declared, "to ... proclaim its purposes, or to take positions which are ridiculous if unsupported by potential force, and then to refuse to provide this force."

His objective, Roosevelt once said to Cecil Spring-Rice, was to keep the Navy in such fighting trim that an attack on the United States would be too dangerous and costly for any power to contemplate lightly. Should the British become too weak to maintain the European balance of power, then American preparedness would enable the United States to assume responsibility. In the Pacific, where the United States faced other newly emergent powers, the Navy could be an influential factor in promoting stability.

In 1907, Roosevelt undertook a demonstration of American

naval power to stir the American public, impress a burgeoning rival in the Far East, and strengthen the nation's position in the Pacific—a fourteen-month, round-the-world cruise by the battleship fleet. It was entirely a Rooseveltian undertaking; he consulted neither the Congress nor his Cabinet, arranging the venture in secrecy. The elaborate preparations required for coal-burning vessels were made by him directly with the naval commanders. Overruling the admirals, he decided that the smaller vessels of the torpedo destroyer class should form part of the expedition. Later he wrote, "No single thing in the history of the new United States Navy has done so much to stimulate popular interest and belief in it as the world cruise." Moreover, strained relations with Japan made it "the most important service that I rendered to peace." Many people, he said, feared that the expedition would be regarded as a threat, but "if there were any feeling on the part of Japan . . . that very fact rendered it imperative that the fleet should go." For his part, he did not so consider it, but if he were mistaken, and it was so construed, then an aggressive action by Japan would be met by a nation fully prepared, and the policy of the United States would have been completely vindicated. He regarded it an effective coordination of military power with foreign diplomacy, a highly successful exhibition of naval strength, and a demonstration that "our fleet could and would at will pass from one to the other of the two great oceans."

Willing support for the President's naval expansion program came from steel manufacturers, congressmen eager to promote employment in their districts, and professional patriots. Few, however, shared his awareness of its implications for the nation's defense requirements. Traditionally, Americans had regarded the oceans as formidable, even impregnable barriers; Roosevelt tried to make them see that modern technology had transformed them into international highways.

To achieve national magnitude, not only was an adequate navy essential, but a vigorous program of overseas expansion. In the active struggle for empire among the European powers and Japan, the United States, Roosevelt was convinced, could refrain from participating only at the peril of its future. As an apostle of imperialism, he believed that the world fell naturally into the categories of the rulers and the ruled, with the white race dominant, since it had distinguished itself industrially and militarily.

For individual members of any racial group, Roosevelt could have the highest regard, judging them solely on their personal merits, but he was contemptuous of the so-called backward peoples whose movements for independence he considered lawless and proof of their irresponsibility, since in his eyes they were incapable of self-government. On the other hand, if they remained passive, this demonstrated their backwardness. Either way, they were damned by Roosevelt's imperialist logic.

He approached colonialism with a sense of duty and mission. The superior talents of the civilizing nation imposed an obligation to raise the level of the dominated peoples to the point where they would be ready for self-government. Patronizingly, he ignored native aspirations for self-determination; the decision for self-government or independence was exclusively the prerogative of the colonial power. Imperialism, Roosevelt was convinced, had made a positive and lasting contribution to civilization, and English rule in Asia and Africa was especially beneficent. "Every expansion of a great civilized power," he declared, "means a victory for law, order and righteousness." His indiscriminate endorsement of imperialism was later qualified when he became aware that some expansionist nations threatened stability, and that while the United States might share a common interest with a power, in one area, it could be menaced by the same nation in another.

Roosevelt's deep commitment to imperialism enabled him to shut his eyes to the grossest injustice. After the ghastly suppression of the Chinese Boxer uprising in 1900, in which American troops participated, he told a Boston audience that the United States had simply "done its part in a bit of international police duty." American "gallantry was unstained by murder and cruelty." Yet he knew that William Rockhill, the American Commissioner in China, had reported that the "police action" could be compared to a Mongol invasion during the thirteenth century. From the seacoast to Peking, he wrote, hardly a single house was spared looting and burning; Peking itself was "pillaged in the most approved manner, and from the General down to the lowest camp follower, from the Ministers of the Powers to the last attaché . . . everyone has stolen, sacked, pillaged. . . ."

Roosevelt's forceful leadership made the sharpest impact in the Caribbean. If a strong navy was to act as the shield for American power, then an interoceanic canal had to be constructed and its approaches safeguarded. He opposed the arrangement made with Great Britain in 1850 that neither power would exercise exclusive control of any canal built in the region, for unless the United States could have sole rights, the defense purpose would be defeated. Even before he became President, he wrote Mahan, "I do not see why we should dig a canal if we are not to fortify it so as to insure its being used for ourselves and against our foes in time of war." He advocated the abrogation of the commitment with Great Britain. Should the British prove obdurate, he was prepared to urge unilateral renunciation of the treaty, a prerogative he considered a nation might exercise in pursuit of its own security. To Lodge he wrote that he would have the treaty revoked only as a last resort and not until after "I had counted the cost and unless I was prepared to back up words by deeds. . . ." He would continue to build up the Navy and strengthen the Army to a formidable expeditionary force. "In short I wish to see us act upon the old frontier principle 'Don't bluster, don't flourish your revolver, and never draw unless you intend to shoot.' " Britain yielded, and Roosevelt now had a free hand to push his scheme.

From its inception until the end, the canal project was handled almost entirely by the President himself. As he told an audience in 1911, "I am interested in the Panama Canal because I started it." If he had acted in the traditional manner, Roosevelt said, he would have "submitted a dignified state paper of probably two hundred pages to the Congress and the debate on it would be going on yet; but I took the Canal Zone and let Congress debate, and while the debate goes on the canal does too."

How he "took" the Canal Zone is a classic example of Roosevelt's tenacity in pursuing a goal. Unexpectedly, Colombia became a stumbling block in his path when its senate rejected a treaty signed with the United States granting territory for the construction and use of a canal. Enraged, Roosevelt denounced the Colombian officials as "homicidal corruptionists" and their president as that "contemptible little creature in Bogotá." To Mark Hanna he wrote, "It might be well to warn those jack-rabbits that, great though our patience has been, it can be exhausted." That those "bandits" should frustrate the great United States was intolerable.

Conveniently, just at that point, Panama, then part of Colombia, made a bid for autonomy. Within a matter of hours, Roosevelt issued orders to the commanders of the cruisers *Marblehead* and *Boston* to "prevent landing of any armed force . . . with hostile intent at any point within fifty miles of Panama." Similar instructions went out to the commanders of two other ships. Roosevelt consulted neither Secretary of State Hay nor Secretary of War Root, nor even the Congress, for "a council of war does not fight, and I intended to do the job once for all," he later wrote to a friend. In the same letter he commented on how the Panamanians rose up in unison against their oppressors, striking a blow simultaneously for liberty and for the canal. Had they not revolted, he continued, he would have urged Congress to take possession of the isthmus by force of arms. As it was, he prevented needless bloodshed, he claimed, by using the Navy to forestall Colombian efforts at suppressing the insurrection.

Almost before it had begun, the bloodless revolt was over. With deep emotion, the president of the new republic greeted his troops. "The world is astonished by your heroism! . . . Long live the Republic of Panama! Long live President Roosevelt!" Recognition was promptly accorded the new government and a treaty concluded giving the United States a perpetual lease on the Canal Zone on the same terms refused by Colombia.

The whole affair had the overtones of a comic opera. The "spontaneous" uprising had been organized in Room 1162 of the Waldorf-Astoria Hotel in New York City, headquarters for the projected republic. A declaration of independence and a constitution were also drafted there. In that room, the commander of the rebel forces was selected and funds raised to pay men fifty dollars in gold for joining the army. The planned date of the revolution had to be postponed one day to allow time for the *U.S.S. Nashville* to reach the Atlantic side of the isthmus.

Whether or not Roosevelt had actually incited the revolt will probably never be known, but he was able to present Congress with a *fait accompli* when it met. A more cautious President probably would have reopened negotiations with Colombia to explore ways of satisfying objections based largely on insufficient financial compensation. The imperious Roosevelt, however, would not even have considered this approach, as it would have meant delay and required more patience than he was willing to exercise. Nor could a great power permit itself to be thwarted by the petty politicians of a tiny country bickering for a few extra dollars. He was not alone in his sentiments. Many Americans would have regarded it as debasing to submit to prolonged negotiations. Of seventy newspapers polled at the time by the *Literary Digest*, fifty-three endorsed Roosevelt's action in concluding the treaty with Panama.

Never at a loss to rationalize in accents of righteousness whatever policy he chose to follow, Roosevelt declared that he had supported the rights of collective civilization. In the course of his negotiations, he asserted, he had followed "the highest, finest, and nicest standards of public and governmental ethics."

Even before the Panama episode, Roosevelt was concerned about protecting the area around the future canal from European encroachment. A serious challenge occurred in 1902 when Germany, Italy, and England attempted to compel Venezuela to pay debts owed their nationals, and a German warship bombarded a fort and surrounding territory. Roosevelt had not objected when the three nations established a blockade; in fact, he had stated the year before that the United States "does not guarantee any state against punishment if it misconducts itself, provided that punishment does not take the form of the acquisition of territory by any non-American power." But military action was excluded from the permissible forms of chastisement. He demanded that the issue be arbitrated. According to Roosevelt's account years later, Germany was the major culprit by refusing to yield, and only an ultimatum backed up by his action in mobilizing the fleet in the Caribbean persuaded the

Kaiser's government to capitulate. No contemporary records support his claim about an ultimatum, but one can be given without blustering. Roosevelt had a statesman's perception of the necessity, at times, to provide a government with an opportunity to save face, and he was capable of exquisite tact when handling sensitive situations. Throughout the two-month period while he was dealing with the German government, the public was unaware even that a crisis existed.

Two years later, he was provided with another opportunity for direct and vigorous diplomacy when a similar situation developed in Santo Domingo. To forestall pretexts for the seizure of territory by European creditor nations, he used his annual message to Congress to announce what has since become known as the Roosevelt Corollary to the Monroe Doctrine. The United States, he said, had no intention of interfering with any nation which keeps order and pays its obligations. However, if "chronic wrongdoing . . . results in a general loosening of the ties of civilized society, . . . intervention by some civilized nation" might be required. Adherence to the Monroe Doctrine "may force the United States, however reluctantly, . . . to the exercise of an international police power" in the Western Hemisphere.

When the European governments threatened to collect their debts forcibly, Roosevelt arrogated the "police power" to himself. He proceeded to put the Dominican finances in order by compelling Santo Domingo to accept a receiver-general whom he appointed to collect customs receipts and make disbursements. Since he had made the arrangements without consulting the Senate, that body retaliated by refusing to ratify the protocol. The President figuratively shrugged his shoulders and ordered the American agents in Santo Domingo to proceed as instructed, later commenting that the Senate is "a helpless body when efficient work for good is to be done," and in regard to treaty making "wholly incompetent."

As in some other cases, Roosevelt's practical remedy was effective. In a little over two years foreign debts were paid and graft and corruption suppressed, the income from customs receipts proving adequate for normal governmental needs. He was vindicated when the Senate some time later ratified a treaty embodying the provisions to which it had previously objected. As Roosevelt recorded in his *Autobiography,* "We secured peace; we protected the people of the islands against foreign foes, and we minimized the chance of domestic trouble." There were additional consequences. His benevolent interference in the affairs of another country extended the scope of the Monroe Doctrine by setting a pattern for unilateral action by the United States to dominate weaker states in the hemisphere. And it widened the range of formal executive prerogative in the conduct of foreign policy.

Aggressive diplomacy by the President was not intended to encourage economic imperialism or turn the Caribbean into an American lake to promote investments, but those were the results. To extend the influence of American power in the region, Roosevelt pointed to the advantages for private investors of a strong hand by government. Annexation of land in the area merely for the sake of territorial gain he regarded as pointless. During the Santo Domingo affair, he wrote that he had about the same desire to acquire the island "as a gorged boa constrictor might have to swallow a porcupine wrong-end to." Some imperialists, like his friend General Leonard Wood, advocated taking over Cuba. Roosevelt, however, prided himself on having ended American armed occupation of the island, though he fully endorsed the Platt Amendment under which Cuba was tied to the United States as a protectorate and made subject to military intervention for a variety of reasons. In 1906 he did send Marines to Cuba to put down an uprising, but only with extreme reluctance and after exploring all other possibilities.

Probably no chief executive in the years following the war with Spain, when Americans were intoxicated with "manifest destiny," could have reversed the trend toward increasing domination of an area that even earlier had been of special interest to the United States. Roosevelt began with an aspiration to strengthen the Navy and the nation's strategic defenses by constructing an isthmian canal. He could not foresee, nor most likely, would he have cared, that economic imperialism and political domination would inevitably result, leaving a legacy of ill will. His leadership in Caribbean and Latin-

American affairs both reflected and helped to shape America's new role as a world power. The United States, which in its early years was considerably dependent on British sea power to help uphold the Monroe Doctrine, now, under the President's vigorous direction, assumed exclusive responsibility for its enforcement.

National self-interest also demanded attention to Asia. In the fifty years since Commodore Perry had penetrated Japan, the ancient feudal empire of the Mikado had become a formidable power. While America, too, had undergone a transformation during the same period, with population and commerce booming along the Pacific slope, and trade with China increasing, politically the country kept its back toward Asia until Roosevelt reversed the position. He was among the few to recognize the impact on the United States of power rivalries in the Far East, and he also believed that American involvement in European politics was closely linked to events in Asia. Occurrences there might spark a chain reaction that would not only endanger the nation's interests in the Pacific but also have repercussions on European stability that, in turn, would entangle the United States.

At the beginning of the century, exports to China and Japan were already far in excess of those to South America. At the same time Britain, Germany, Japan, and Russia were engaged in fierce competition for commercial hegemony in China. It appeared to Roosevelt that short of force the only way to maintain Chinese territorial integrity, guarantee equality of opportunity for all nations, and protect American interests— objectives sought by John Hay's Open-Door Policy—was to preserve the balance of power in the region. Japan and Russia, having already carved out slices of China, were now facing each other with bared fangs, and the President tried strenuously but unsuccessfully to have them negotiate their differences.

When war broke out in 1904, Roosevelt hoped they would fight until "both are fairly well exhausted and that then peace will come on terms which will not mean the creation of either a yellow peril or a Slav peril." If Japan won, he wrote, "it may possibly mean a struggle between them and us in the future." On the other hand, if Russia were victorious, she "would be so intolerable as to force us to take action . . . she will organize northern China against us."

With Japan's unexpected victories at Port Arthur and Mukden presaging Nipponese domination, Roosevelt embarked upon a course of personal diplomacy in an effort to retain some degree of equipoise in the Far East. Believing that both sides wished him to act but realizing that neither would want the other to know it had taken the initiative, he sent them identical notes offering to serve as an intermediary in bringing about a meeting between their representatives. In separate communications he advised the Japanese that a prolongation of hostilities would cost them more than they could hope to receive in indemnities; he warned the Russians that if they stubbornly persisted in fighting they would be driven out of Siberia. At the same time he tried to persuade Britain and Germany to apply pressure on the belligerents to negotiate a peace, but the European nations, with their own axes to grind, refused to cooperate.

Japan and Russia, each still believing that a complete victory was possible, were not immediately receptive. Roosevelt persisted, acting alone and in secrecy; neither Cabinet nor Congress nor even the State Department was kept informed of his series of skillful, intricate maneuvers. Among other things, the American ambassador to Russia was replaced by a close personal friend. In Washington, Roosevelt dealt directly with Kogoro Takahira, the friendly Japanese ambassador, and with the influential Baron Kentaro Kaneko, who had been a Harvard classmate. He engaged the help of personal friends in the foreign diplomatic corps. Finally, with Russian funds exhausted and revolutionary upheavals threatening, with Japan on the verge of financial collapse, Roosevelt was able to arrange for a peace conference at Portsmouth, New Hampshire.

Throughout, the President's diplomacy had been masterly, and he continued to make his good offices available at the conference. When Russia threatened to walk out unless Japan's demands for a large monetary indemnity and all of Sakhalin Island were withdrawn, he persuaded the Japanese to relinquish the former and accept half of the latter. The Open Door in Manchuria, which he had earlier requested as a condition for his mediating efforts, was guaranteed, and Russia acknowledged Japan's "paramount" interests in Korea. Several months prior to the peace settlement, in a memorandum since known as the Taft-Katsura Agreement, the United States had approved Japan's suzerainty over Korea and the Japanese disavowed any aggressive designs against the Philippines. In this way, Roosevelt hoped to safeguard American interests in the far Pacific.

The Treaty of Portsmouth, signed on September 5, 1905, was hailed as a magnificent victory for Roosevelt. He had become, one journal wrote, "the most popular man in the world." For his efforts, the President was awarded the Nobel Peace Prize the following year. The Japanese people, however, who had not been informed by their rulers that the desperate financial plight of the nation prohibited a continuation of the struggle, were bitterly disappointed with the treaty. They were convinced that the United States had betrayed them, and their resentment was to have serious effects on the future relations of the two countries.

Roosevelt was pleased with the settlement, which, he said, left Russia still an Asiatic power "face to face with Japan so that each may have a moderative action on the other." As he told Senator Eugene Hale in 1906, while his primary motive in mediating the war was to end the bloodshed, "I was also interested in the desirability of preventing Japan from driving Russia completely out of East Asia." But in his efforts to redress the balance, Roosevelt helped establish Japan as a world power, and the repercussions would be felt decades later. Moreover, China would be enfeebled by the replacement of Russia by Japan as the major threat to her independence. It was, however, beyond Roosevelt's vision or that of most men to look so far ahead in time. He succeeded in ending a war, managed to hold the conference on American soil free from the pressures of European powers, and obtained probably the best settlement possible under the circumstances.

The international situation was too complex and fluid for any balance of power to have stability. Two years after Portsmouth and again in 1910, Japan and Russia concluded a secret treaty dividing between them spheres of influence over most of North China, Mongolia, and Korea, from which they hoped to exclude all other nations.

While Roosevelt was trying to douse the fire in the Far East, another continent began to smolder over control of Morocco. With France's ally, Russia, involved in her own war, the Germans decided to challenge France's hegemony in the North African sultinate, demanding an Open Door and a conference to effectuate it. Tension mounted, and Roosevelt became apprehensive that the German army might actually march across the French border where the British fleet would be unable to exert a countervailing influence. Conflict in Europe might not only jeopardize the prospect of completing negotiations in the Far East but, if the formidable military power that was Germany should be victorious, the United States would be compelled to prevent its domination of the continent. When the Germans asked him to intervene, Roosevelt agreed to help, at the same time urging them to moderate their demands.

Calling in his old friend, Ambassador Jusserand, Roosevelt told him, "I know your government will consider that I am meddling in its affairs," but since war between his country and Germany would threaten world peace, "I feel justified." Moreover, he was greatly concerned about France, which would inevitably suffer defeat in a war with Germany, and "It would cause me anguish if any misfortune" overtook his country. "You know," he continued, "what I think of humiliating oneself in the face of a threat. None the less, there are concessions that can with honor be made to avert a conflict, and I should not hesitate."

Characteristically, Roosevelt's correspondence and discussions with the Germans and the French were kept secret from all but a very few trusted friends. Even Secretary of State John Hay was not informed, presumably because his anti-German sentiments would hamper negotiations; nor were the ambassadors to France and Germany advised.

By adroitness and subtlety, Roosevelt was instrumental in arranging the Algeciras Conference of January, 1906, attended by thirteen nations. He planned the agenda, sent American diplomats to participate in the proceedings, offered to mediate at a critical juncture, and broke a serious deadlock, persuading Germany to compromise by recalling the Kaiser's promise to support any decision which Roosevelt considered fair if the Germans and French disagreed.

This unprecedented intervention in a foreign dispute precipitated an avalanche of criticism from Congress and the press. Senator Bacon of Georgia, leader of the Democratic minority, introduced a resolution deploring United States participation as a departure from the traditional policy of non-involvement in the politics of the European continent. Newspaper editorials charged that since the nation had no interest, either political or economic, in Morocco, Roosevelt was attempting the role of a "World Caesar."

At Algeciras, as at Portsmouth, Roosevelt sought to preserve the balance of power. He instructed the American delegate, Henry White, to acknowledge France's special interests in Morocco by virtue of proximity, but at the same time to work for a settlement that provided for unrestricted commerce and an Open Door. The peace of the world and the best interests of the United States rested on continued entente between England and France, he informed White, and "we do not wish to contribute towards any estrangement between those two countries." But White was also cautioned to keep in mind that America was friendly to Germany and wished to remain so. In general, the United States supported Anglo-French interests, with the result that the agreement gave France virtual control over Morocco.

By instructing the American delegates to sign the treaty, Roosevelt broke with a pattern of non-involvement in European affairs. The Senate, however, fearful of the implication, approved the agreement only after appending a reservation to the effect that the United States had participated solely to benefit American trade, and disavowing any intention to settle European political questions. But this gesture could not obscure the fact that a President of the United States had played a leading part in resolving an international crisis. A major embroilment was postponed for eight years. Considering the nature of the European power struggle, however, nothing Roosevelt did or failed to do could have made the peace achieved at Algeciras more lasting. Recalling the events several years later, Roosevelt revealed his motive for intervention to Herman von Eckardstein, who had been German Ambassador to Great Britain at the time: "I certainly would have found myself compelled to interfere if Germany attacked France." So long as England was successful in preserving the balance of power "not only in principle, but in reality, well and good." If, for any reason, she failed, "the United States would be obliged to step in at least temporarily" in order to restore it, regardless of which country or group of countries would have to be opposed. Prophetically he concluded, "In fact, we ourselves are becoming, owing to our strength and geographical situation, more and more the balance of power of the whole world."

The insights which Roosevelt revealed to intimate friends were not apparent in his public declarations. He would have regarded it as most imprudent to express in public what he told von Eckardstein. Well aware that the American people were not yet prepared to emerge from the cocoon of their isolationism, to accept the fact that any war in Europe or Asia would involve them, he fed them glittering moralistic generalities. The requirements of collective civilization, peace through justice, and righteousness were his themes.

Repeatedly he reverted to his favorite subject, the exertion of power through continued armed readiness. For the nation to achieve flexibility in world affairs, it must rely on its "own preparedness and resolution, and not upon the good will of any outside nation," he wrote a friend. England was sincerely friendly, he continued, but "even this English friendliness would be a broken reed if we leaned on it, unless we were entirely able in addition to fight for our own land." Inoffensiveness would not save the country from aggression. Aided by a powerful navy, and dealing equitably with foreign nations, the United States could hope to maintain friendly relations with all.

He scorned "professional peace demagogues," regarding them as well-intentioned but misguided idealists whose "egotistical lunacy" produced much wicked nonsense. The Navy, he insisted, had accomplished more for peace than all the peace societies put together. Had it not been for the condition of

naval strength during the past few years, he wrote Charles
William Eliot in 1906, the country would have been "within
measurable distance of war" with either one European or one
Asiatic power. Either "would grin with entirely unaffected en-
joyment at the thistledown arguments" of the pacifists.

At the same time, he enthusiastically supported the Hague
Peace Conference of 1907 as an expression of the nation's desire to supplement military force with multilateral agreements
for reduction of arms, a Permanent Court of International Justice, and codification of international law. Such goals were
congenial to most Americans, since they did not require abandoning the isolationist principle of non-commitment in world
politics. Roosevelt hoped for an agreement that would limit the
size of battleships, but, as he wrote Andrew Carnegie, it would
be a mistake to rely on disarmament. To strip the free nations
of the world to a level of impotence while leaving the military
despotisms armed to the teeth might well be catastrophic. The
idealistic vagaries of the Russian Czar who was ardently
championing the Hague conference should not be taken seriously, he said, for his professions of peace were designed to
cloak policies promoting the interests of those nations threatening international stability.

The conference produced little of a tangible nature to mitigate the factors leading to war. It was unable to reach any
agreement on the limitation of armaments. Mr. Dooley expressed the prevailing skepticism when he said that most of the
time had been spent discussing "how future wars shud be
conducted in th' best inthrests iv peace."

Endorsing the principle of arbitration as a method for settling disputes, the President promoted a number of treaties
with other nations. He was proud of having been responsible
for bringing two altercations in the Western Hemisphere before the Hague Tribunal, one involving Venezuela and the
other Mexico. In accepting the Nobel Peace award for his
mediation in the Russo-Japanese War, he made an eloquent
plea for developing and strengthening that judicial body. But
he advocated arbitration only within limited areas of what he
regarded as practical applicability. In his opinion, minor disputes could be arbitrated, provided that an equilibrium of

strength existed between the adversaries. He was firmly opposed to arbitration where the issues in dispute involved a
nation's honor or vital interests. The factors customarily responsible for wars, especially those resulting from an imbal-
ance of power, could not, he believed, be mediated. If a nation
did not possess the capacity to protect itself or did not intend
to mobilize power at a critical moment, neither peace treaties,
nor conventions, nor arbitration pledges would avail.

Whether brandishing the big stick or cajoling foreign rulers,
Roosevelt thoroughly relished the practice of diplomacy. What
sometimes proved frustrating, however, were the obstructions
created by federal-state relations within the American constitutional system, the problems of coping with public behavior
inimical to the national interest but outside the scope of the
national government's jurisdiction. When California in 1906
exacerbated already strained relations between the United
States and the Japanese government, he was constitutionally
prevented from taking direct action. Acutely sensitive about
the western attitude toward race, the Japanese were infuriated
by the action of the San Francisco School Board to segregate
children of their nationals in the public schools. Such exclusion
because of race, they declared, was "an act of discrimination
carrying with it a stigma and odium which it is impossible to
overlook." Roosevelt himself was furious with his fellow citizens. "The infernal fools in California, and especially in San
Francisco, insult the Japanese recklessly," he told his son, "and
in the event of war it will be the Nation as a whole which will
pay the consequences."

Pointedly directing his remarks to the people of California in
his annual message to Congress in December, 1906, he declared that barring Japanese children from the common schools
was a "wicked absurdity." The country, he pointed out, had
much to learn from Japan, which had made notable contributions to civilization, and no nation was fit to teach unless it was
also willing to learn. He warned that federal power would be
used unhesitatingly to protect lives and property, in the event
of violence, and urged that state's rights be exercised in a responsible manner. "Good manners should be an international,
no less than an individual attribute."

This international outlook failed to impress the Californians, who vehemently denounced him, the *San Francisco Chronicle* storming that he was "an unpatriotic President who united with aliens to break down the civilization of his own countrymen."

Roosevelt exerted his considerable personal influence, sending a Cabinet member to San Francisco to put pressure on the local authorities and bombarding the governor and legislators with messages. The mayor and the school board were then invited to Washington, where he succeeded in persuading them to repeal the exclusion ordinance. Aware, however, that this was only a temporary respite as long as antagonism to Japanese immigration continue to cause eruptions on the West Coast, Roosevelt sought for an arrangement to limit the entry of Japan's nationals. After a series of notes exchanged in 1907 and 1908 with the Japanese ambassador in Washington, an executive accord, since known as the Gentlemen's Agreement, was worked out, whereby Japan would not issue passports to laborers and the United States would refrain from any legislative prohibition of Japanese immigration.

While recognizing that the Japanese were justified in their anger, Roosevelt felt that a demonstration of power might be salutary. He decided to send the battleship fleet on a world cruise, including a visit to the port of Yokohama, ignoring vociferous protests from many Americans who feared that this might provoke war instead of preventing it. On the eve of departure, the President personally reviewed the fleet and presented the commanding officer with sealed orders. Later he boasted, "Every particle of trouble with the Japanese government and the Japanese press stopped like magic as soon as they found that our fleet had actually sailed and was obviously in good trim."

On the West Coast, however, anti-Japanese feeling remained, the hostile atmosphere producing periodic flare-ups which made Roosevelt fearful that a serious incident might some day provoke armed conflict. He confessed to Senator Eugene Hale his feeling of impotence because "our federal form of government, with all its advantages, has very great disadvantages when we come to carrying out a foreign policy, and it would be a most difficult thing to prevent mobs and demagogs in certain parts of the country from doing a succession of acts which will tend to embroil us with the Japanese." Another crisis occurred in 1909 with the proposal for an anti-alien land law in California, obviously aimed at barring the Japanese from owning land. Roosevelt later confided that he was more concerned over this development than any of the other stormy episodes during his incumbency. Once again real trouble was averted by his forceful action, but the measure was defeated only by the narrowest margin.

Apart from the possibility of direct conflict, Roosevelt was apprehensive that the edifice he had so carefully erected at Portsmouth might collapse as a result of the inflamed atmosphere on the West Coast. Regarding Japan as a bulwark against Russia, he believed that maintenance of friendly relations with the island kingdom was essential. Moreover, as he wrote on the eve of his retirement, "There is no more important continuing feature of our foreign policy" than relations with Japan. Dealings with the Orient, he felt, were certain to become increasingly important. He did not believe that war was likely, but there was always the possibility, and although he thought the United States would win, "There is at least a chance of disaster."

The other significant factor in Far Eastern politics was relations between the United States and Russia. By 1904, Roosevelt had come to feel that the Czar's government, traditionally friendly, was menacing the Anglo-American entente which he had been forging in the Far East. Russian behavior was sufficiently disturbing for him to ask the Navy to formulate plans of action should it become necessary to bottle up the Vladivostok squadron. His experience as mediator in the Russo-Japanese conflict caused him to distrust the Russians. "They are utterly insincere and treacherous; they have no conception of truth, no willingness to look facts in the face, no regard for others of any sort or kind, no knowledge of their own strength or weakness, and they are helplessly unable to meet emergencies." He was not at all certain that Russia might not make another effort to challenge Japan in a renewed attempt to achieve hegemony over Asia.

In the ever-shifting international scene, Roosevelt was confident that one element would remain stable—Anglo-American friendship. Even before he entered the White House, Roosevelt, who appreciated the shield of British sea power more than most Americans, denounced the Anglophobes who would have been pleased to see Britain weakened. If that came to pass, he said, it could very well be "that within a few years we shall be face to face with the question of either abandoning the Monroe Doctrine and submitting to the acquisition of American territory by some great European military power, or of going to war." As the threat of German power became ever more palpable, as England came to value America's burgeoning strength, and as the United States became increasingly aware of the community of interests shared with Great Britain, the two nations began to minimize their differences and concentrate on cooperation. A common heritage provided the additional cement. "Fundamentally our two nations are very much alike," Roosevelt wrote an English friend in 1901. Britain demonstrated a growing attitude of conciliation, yielding in the Hay-Pauncefote negotiations over the Panama Canal and two years later supporting the United States in the dispute with Canada over the Alaskan boundary. "The settlement of the Alaskan boundary settled the last serious trouble between the British Empire and ourselves as everything else could be arbitrated," Roosevelt wrote Mahan some years later.

When the British were negotiating a treaty with Japan, they sent the President the draft copy. Anglo-American cooperation at Algeciras further indicated the solidity of the relationship between the two countries. "I never even take into account war with England," Roosevelt said in 1905. "I treat it as out of the question." Years before the outbreak of World War I, he commented that if England should suffer disaster, the United States would be fighting for its national life within five years. Despite his strong convictions on the limited uses of arbitration, he remarked in 1911 that the only country with which he would consent to sign a total arbitration agreement was Great Britain.

As in other matters where Roosevelt felt the substance to be the cardinal element, he considered it unnecessary to arouse popular prejudices by seeking to enter into any formal arrangements with the British. He had tried to awaken the public to an awareness of their new world role and their new responsibilities, but they were not yet prepared to discard old dogmas for the new imperatives. "We are as naturally insular as ever the English were in the old days when compared with the rest of Europe," he wrote to Henry White a year before retiring from office. "The same feeling that made England believe that it did not have to take part in any European concert . . . makes this country feel that it can be a law for itself."

Without illusions that he was bringing about an ideological transformation, he was satisfied to exercise vigorous leadership in meeting specific problems with specific responses, drawing the nation, through the back door as it were, ever closer to the center of the world stage. Always concerned with the strategic implications for American power, Roosevelt never shrank from making decisions that he felt would serve his purposes. Yet, contrary to the impression he sometimes conveyed, he rarely acted on impulse. His decisions were arrived at after thoughtful deliberation, with the possible alternatives carefully evaluated and the action chosen with due consideration to possible consequences.

Roosevelt was fully conscious of the restraints imposed on his freedom of action by the interests of other nations, the constitutional processes, the power of public opinion. At the same time, the nature of international society in his day permitted the bold leader a degree of freedom impossible for the statesman of a later generation. His choices were uncomplicated by such considerations as explosive nationalism, the need to preserve cohesion within an alliance, or the task of harmonizing national policy with the preponderant sentiment of a world organization. Nor did the threat to employ force or its actual use have the portentous implications that it would have in a later period.

A basic rule of Roosevelt's diplomacy was never to bluff or take a position that he would be unable to back up. If he felt that intimidation would serve in a particular situation, he first made certain that he could implement his words, if necessary, and that the requisite action would be approved by the American people. Generally, he received public approbation, since he symbolized and reflected the prevalent national attitude. The expansionist spirit which he exalted was shared by both conservatives and progressives. It might not have been implemented to the same extent by a less forceful President, but Roosevelt never abandoned his principle that a leader should lead.

An egotistical self-righteousness, however, led him to an exaggerated regard for the rectitude of his actions. Those Americans who dissented, as in the Panama Canal affair or the intervention in Santo Domingo, he dismissed as sentimentalists, ignoring the fact that their views represented a legitimate difference of opinion.

So comprehensively did he fill the role of foreign policy leader that for the first time an American President became the peer of the powerful rulers of ancient Europe in the councils of world affairs. It was entirely consistent with his temperament and outlook that Roosevelt greatly admired the strong men of history: Frederick the Great, Napoleon, Bismarck. In an autocratic society, he might readily have followed in their footsteps.

To Roosevelt's great credit, his commitment to democratic institutions and traditions impelled him to relinquish the power he coveted and which he could have had for another four years. "I should like to have stayed on in the Presidency," he commented during the 1908 campaign, "and I make no pretense that I am glad to be relieved of my official duties." But his view of the office—"I think the President should be a very strong man who uses without hesitation every power that the position yields"—made it mandatory, as he himself said, that it should not be held too long by any one man. Moreover, he had pledged in 1904 that he would not stand for re-election, and he would not break his promise.

Roosevelt had only to say the word, for as late as the summer of 1907, Senator Allison of Iowa declared that he would be renominated again unless he "positively" refused. Believing that he would be drafted, unless he chose a successor well in advance of the party convention, Roosevelt selected his Secretary of War, William Howard Taft, and for two years worked strenuously on his behalf. Taft's victory over his Democratic opponent, William Jennings Bryan, was regarded by political commentators as more of a triumph for Roosevelt's activities than of the candidate's, whose campaign, as one Republican paper observed, was "loaded with calm." It was a portent of the new administration, for no two men could have been more diametrically opposed in personality and in their views of the presidency than the outgoing chief executive and the new head of state.

William Howard Taft

4. A Restricted View of Office

WILLIAM HOWARD TAFT entered the White House with a dual handicap. A huge man of some three hundred pounds, slow-moving, easy-going, with little political skill and few qualities of leadership, he followed one of the most vigorous and magnetic Presidents ever to occupy the office. Moreover, he had never yearned for the strenuous life of a President. Detesting competitiveness, crowds, the glare and demands of public office in general, he wrote his wife, "Politics, when I am in it, makes me sick."

As President, he conscientiously struggled to take an interest in his many duties, but lacking zest for his job he sometimes had to drag himself away from a bridge game to return to work. At the same time, he complained to an aide that there was too much to do and not enough time in which to do it. He detested that major activity of the political leader, delivering speeches—and even more, preparing for them—because, as he once admitted, he did not know "exactly what to say or how to say it." Required to make an important tour before the election of 1908, he left without a single prepared address and with "a barrenness of ideas" that made him turn pale at the prospect of appearing on a platform.

While Taft longed for the cloistered serenity of the Supreme Court, Helen Herron Taft's ambition for her husband triumphed. When he was offered the position of Associate Justice in 1906, she begged Roosevelt to prevail on him to reject it.

The President was extremely persuasive, writing Taft that he was "the man who is most likely to receive the Republican presidential nomination and who is, I think, the best man to receive it, and under whom we would have the most chance to succeed." Wistfully Taft told his wife, "If the Chief Justice would retire, how simple everything would become!"

Until he became President, Taft's life had been smooth and untroubled. Reared in a peaceful little town in Ohio, in a warm and loving home atmosphere, he developed into a placid, good-natured youth. Even his obesity, against which he struggled from time to time, seems to have troubled him little. His progression up the economic and professional ladder was steady and sure. Entering politics after graduation from Yale Law School, he was promptly appointed to the State Superior Court to fill an unexpired term and was elected the following year. Later, he was contentedly carrying out his duties as a judge of the Federal Circuit Court when Roosevelt, who had a high regard for his abilities, appointed him head of the Philippine Commission to study the situation in the newly acquired archipelago. Promotion to Governor General followed and then the Cabinet post, where, as Secretary of War, his administrative skill earned him Roosevelt's confidence and esteem.

The party leaders who pushed Taft's nomination were influenced by his outstanding performance in the Philippines. They overlooked the fact that on the island he had been the supreme ruler, answerable to no one; that he did not have a Congress, a literate public, or an opposition party to contend with. Above all, his placid nature craved tranquility. A letter he wrote to Roosevelt several months after his inauguration reveals an astonishing humility and lack of self-confidence. A truly remarkable communication by a President, it deserves lengthy quotation:

If I followed my impulse, I should still say "My dear Mr. President." I cannot overcome the habit. When I am addressed as "Mr. President," I turn to see whether you are not at my elbow. When I read in the newspaper of a conference between the Speaker and the President, or between Senator Aldrich and the President, I wonder what the subject of the conference was, and can hardly identify the

report with the fact that I had had a talk with the two gentlemen. . . .

I want you to know that I do nothing in the Executive Office
without considering what you would do under the same circumstances and without having in a sense a mental talk with you over
the pros and cons of the situation. I have not the facility for edu-
cating the public as you had through talks with correspondents, and
so I fear that a large part of the public will feel as if I had fallen
away from your ideals. . . . I can never forget that the power that I
now exercise was a voluntary transfer from you to me, and that I am
under obligation to you to see to it that your judgment in selecting
me as your successor and in bringing about the succession shall be
vindicated according to the standards which you and I in conversation have always formulated.

With the best will in the world, Taft could never have followed in his predecessor's footsteps. Taft's training in the law,
his years as a law professor and a magistrate, his entire background disposed him to a restricted, conservative, legalistic
approach to government. Since the President's powers are derived exclusively from the Constitution, he believed that he
should not be regarded as a political chieftain or expected to
exercise political leadership.

Taft's narrow view of the office never changed. In a lecture,
"The Presidency," which he gave in 1915 after the years of
stress were happily behind him, he stated that "the President
can exercise no power which cannot be fairly and reasonably
traced to some specific grant of power or justly implied and
included within such express grant as proper and necessary to
its exercise." Only the Constitution or a legislative statute, he
pointed out, can provide that specific grant, as no "undefined
residuum of power" existed which could be wielded merely
because the public interest seemed to require it. This limited,
formalistic concept of executive prerogative inevitably restricted the scope of the presidency which Roosevelt's broad,
expansive interpretation had enlarged. Taft was convinced that
his predecessor had played fast and loose with the Constitution
and rationalized his arbitrary use of power.

He also disagreed that it was the President's duty to assume
the role of chief legislator, as he had "no initiative in respect to

legislation given him by law except that of *mere recommenda-tion* and *no legal or formal method* of entering into argument and discussion of the proposed legislation while pending in Congress." Executive power was limited to actions required to protect the public welfare in time of emergency or when the legislative branch neglected its clearly defined obligations.

Taft's theories, which inhibited presidential leadership, coupled with his political ineptitude, were disadvantages enough in dealing with Congress. Unfortunately for the President, a revolt by Republican insurgents early in his administration stripped the Speaker of much of his power, leaving a vacuum in leadership on Capitol Hill, where under Roosevelt an "organic connection" had been maintained. Although few Presidents came to office with greater prestige, the "monarch" himself having bestowed his mantle on him, Taft soon aroused irritation and resentment. His amateurishness was glaringly apparent in the way he handled the knotty tariff question and the Ballinger-Pinchot controversy.

Having called Congress into special session to enact a lower tariff, Taft failed to intervene or use his patronage powers, despite urgent pleas by the Progressives, when congressmen began to succumb to the temptations of lobbyists and logrollers. Equally fatal was his snubbing of the powerful midwestern Progressives because he found them personally objectionable. After signing the Payne-Aldrich Tariff Act, which clearly discriminated against the Midwest, stronghold of Republican insurgents, he tactlessly told an audience in Minnesota during a speaking tour that "on the whole, the Payne bill is the best bill that the Republican Party ever passed." The rest of the journey, one reporter wrote, was "a polar dash through a world of ice."

Next he forfeited the good will of the Roosevelt followers in the Northeast and Far West by placing himself in the position of seeming to be a tool of anti-conservationist interests. When his Secretary of the Interior, Richard A. Ballinger, was publicly accused by Chief Forester Gifford Pinchot, an ardent exponent of conservation, of confirming doubtful claims to Alaskan coal land by the Morgan-Guggenheim syndicate whose attorney he formerly had been, the President stubbornly supported the former and dismissed the latter from office. Public wrath com-

pelled Ballinger to resign, and, although Taft replaced him
with a dedicated conservationist, the whole affair was disastrous to his image. Through lack of political astuteness, Taft
had alienated a vital segment of his party's following.

He was a hard and conscientious worker, but his passive approach, and perhaps most of all his lack of that indispensable
flair for engaging the public's emotions, produced one failure
after another. Outwardly cheerful and expressing satisfaction
with the progress of his regime, to Theodore Roosevelt alone
he confided his inner despondency. "It is now a year and three
months since I assumed office and I have had a hard time," he
wrote the ex-President. "I do not know that I have had harder
luck than other presidents but I do know that thus far I have
succeeded far less than have others." He was dutifully trying to
carry out his mentor's policies, he continued, but his methods
had failed.

Taft's "ultimate defeat," writes his principal biographer, "was
caused in no small measure by . . . repeated, incessant headlines
which, try as he might, he could not guide or control." The
President was utterly incapable of making effective use of the
press, that vital tool of a chief executive for molding public
opinion. Relationships with the correspondents when he was
Secretary of War had been mutually pleasant and satisfactory,
but this changed completely when he entered the White House.
In his efforts to maintain the dignity of his office, he became
overly cautious with his statements, and because of his guarded
approach and his feeling that presidential press feeding was unseemly, the stream of news, which under Roosevelt had been a
torrent, soon dried up. Within a month, reporters were complaining that the President was withholding news, to which
Taft replied, when he heard this, that he "could not talk to the
newspapermen." As the drought continued, newsmen naturally
sought information elsewhere, and they obtained it in abun-
dance from opponents of the administration. Aloofness became
two-sided, the situation feeding upon itself, so that before his
first year was out Taft wrote, "I see very few newspapermen."

With his Cabinet, Taft's relations were administratively
proper. Henry L. Stimson, who served as his Secretary of War,
wrote approvingly of Taft's style in his *Memoirs*, recalling that

every administrative function in the entire government was directed by one of the nine Cabinet posts and funneled to the President via the department head. By dealing with his departments through the Cabinet, he inculcated a sense of responsibility and security to the constitutional officer involved, Stimson stated. Orderly and reliable, the President never bypassed officials in favor of personal confidantes or displayed partiality to a trusted lieutenant. Yet, it is the consensus that the personal touch, that indefinable spark of leadership, was absent.

His judicial training and background, combined with his pacific nature, led Taft warmly to espouse the peace movement's campaign to end war through one formula or another. The Hague conferences of 1899 and 1907 had generated hope that conflicts could be averted by legal tribunals and international treaties containing provisions for settling disputes by juridical or other means. An increasing number of Americans, denounced by those of the Roosevelt or Mahan persuasion as "mushy philanthropists," "visionaries," and "mollycoddles," were endorsing world disarmament movements or international peace conferences. They were repelled by the ex-President's strident nationalism, objected to his preoccupation with preparedness, and opposed his "big stick" diplomacy.

As a program, the arbitration of international disputes was not dramatic enough to activate a mighty crusade. But in 1910, it was the one major goal to which all who sought to prevent future wars subscribed. It was especially appealing because no departure from the traditional policies of isolation or neutrality or the Monroe Doctrine was required. Taft and Secretary of State Philander C. Knox made arbitration treaties with as many nations as possible a key element of their foreign policy. In promoting his program, the President went beyond accepted practices by endorsing arbitration even of those disputes which involved "national honor" or affected the vital interests of the parties concerned. If these treaties are to be of value, he maintained, they must be made to apply to the issues that provoke war. As a question of national honor is usually at stake, he proposed to make the treaties meaningful by taking this into account. In the past, observed Taft, arbitration treaties contained provisions to negotiate "everything that is highly unimportant. We leave out the questions which, when they arise, are likely to lead to war."

On August 3, 1911, the United States signed all-inclusive arbitration treaties with Great Britain and France, and Taft hoped similar arrangements could be concluded shortly with six other countries. Andrew Carnegie, elated by this achievement, wired Taft, "You have reached the summit of human glory. Countless ages are to honor and bless your name."

The celebration was premature. Senate approval was required, and that body quickly objected to Clause III, which empowered a joint commission representing the signatory nations to refer the dispute to the Hague Tribunal for arbitration, if in its opinion the issue was justiciable. The Senate felt that, by subscribing to this clause, the United States would surrender its traditional freedom of action. Taft argued that if America had the exclusive privilege of determining the justiciability of an issue, it could conveniently refer for arbitration only those about which it could be assured of a favorable outcome. The whole effort, he maintained, would be reduced to a sham if questions dealing with vital interests and national honor were excluded.

Hoping to "set a fire under the senators which may change their views," Taft set out across the country on a speaking tour. He had to fight every step of the way against his old friend Theodore Roosevelt, who attacked the treaties in articles and speeches, accusing the President and his supporters of lack of moral courage. "Righteousness," Roosevelt declared emphatically, was more important than peace. Stung by this indictment, Taft was moved to reply that preferring to submit questions to arbitration instead of fighting implied no lack of personal courage. The United States, he said, was a powerful and wealthy country "afraid of no nation in the world so far as battle is concerned," and since it was not involved in entangling alliances it should set an example of leadership in a world plagued by such involvements.

Roosevelt argued that the treaties would destroy the historic prerogatives of the chief executive to conduct an independent course in foreign policy. In one talk he denounced the entire peace movement as hypocritical. Are we honest in signing such treaties, he demanded, when we really know that in a matter of vital interest we could not and would not commit ourselves to arbitration? On the merits of the controversy, while the President could be credited with high-mindedness and lofty aspirations, logic undoubtedly rested with Roosevelt.

The loyal, unassuming Taft was bewildered and shaken by the vituperation of the man whom he still regarded as his friend, although he had had intimations of Roosevelt's cooling off since the Ballinger-Pinchot affair. "It is very hard to take all the slaps Roosevelt is handing me at this time, Archie," he confided to his secretary. Everyone was urging him, he said, to return verbal blow for blow. "If it were anyone else I would know just what to do, but I can't get into a public row with him. He knows that, and he has me at a disadvantage." He simply did not understand what Roosevelt was trying to do, he lamented, except make his way more difficult. Obviously he could not ask the ex-President's advice on all questions, he continued unhappily, or subordinate his administration to him and still retain his self-respect, "but it is hard, very hard, Archie, to see a devoted friendship going to pieces like a rope of sand."

When the treaties were acted on by the Senate, they were crippled by so many amendments that, as Taft later commented, their own father would not have recognized them. The European powers requested renegotiation, but the President was soon to be caught up in the 1912 election campaign. The matter was dropped, not to be revived again during his administration.

Despite the enthusiasm with which Taft had championed the abortive arbitration treaties, he made a *volte-face* on the desirability of arbitration not too long after, leading one journal to remark that the "great cause of arbitration . . . will be set back for unreckonable years." The issue arose when Congress was considering a bill to exempt American coastwise shippers from paying tolls when using the newly completed Panama Canal. Britain protested that the United States was violating its commitment under the Hay-Pauncefote Treaty, whereby the terms would be equal for all nations, and urged that the question be adjudicated. Taft flatly refused to concede that this was a matter for arbitration because "all Europe will be interested and all their representatives will be against us. . . ." Congress agreed with the President and passed the bill.

Pledged to follow Roosevelt's foreign policies, Taft struggled along, but he possessed neither his predecessor's skill nor his understanding of the dynamics of international rivalries. Roosevelt, for example, would have been alert to the possible danger of an attempted purchase by a Japanese syndicate of a large parcel of land near Magdalena Bay in Baja California. Taft was completely unconcerned. Senator Lodge, apprehensive that the purchasers might be a blind for the Japanese government, introduced a resolution prohibiting the sale of strategic tracts in the Western Hemisphere to non-Americans unless authorized by the United States. This so-called Lodge Corollary to the Monroe Doctrine was passed by the Senate, but the President dismissed it with the statement that, since the legislative body had no authority to make foreign policy, he would not consider it binding on his future actions.

When a second Moroccan crisis in 1911 again threatened the peace, Taft, in marked contrast to the role performed by Roosevelt six years earlier, announced that the United States had no interest, direct or indirect, in what he referred to as a strictly European affair. Nor did he show any concern or awareness of the implications of the Italo-Turkish War and the Balkan Wars, which were localized conflicts but significant precursors of the 1914 holocaust. It was unnecessary, he thought, to become involved in any way in those far-off disputes, nor did he appreciate the importance of contributing the weight of American power and influence to achieve international stability.

Taft also felt no compulsion to enhance America's status in the world arena, and in the Caribbean his policies emphasized economic rather than strategic and political reasons for intervention. With his active encouragement and that of Secretary of State Knox, commercial relations and investment opportunities in the area were greatly extended. Replying to some critics who denounced the partnership of government and private capital in foreign affairs, the President defended the practice that had come to be designated as "dollar diplomacy." "The theory that the field of diplomacy does not include in any degree commerce and the increase of trade relations is one to which Mr. Knox and this administration do not subscribe. We believe it to be of the utmost importance that while our foreign policy should not be turned a hair's breadth from the straight path of justice, it may be well made to include active intervention to secure for our merchandise and our capitalists opportunity for profitable investment."

Rationalizing financial imperialism as altruistic, Secretary Knox declared that the American dollar was being used to ameliorate the lot of downtrodden people. But the bankers who extended loans to foreign countries were not motivated by selfless ideals, and the government had no means of insuring that interest rates would not be grossly excessive, which they often were. And when obligations were not met, it was invariably demanded that the United States collect the debt. American diplomatic representatives abroad assumed the role of salesmen, the success of their mission often being measured by the quantity of orders they were able to obtain.

The Taft-Knox policy led to the establishment of firm military, political, and economic control over several Central American republics. Through arrangements made by Knox, American bankers established a financial receivership in Honduras. Marines were dispatched to Nicaragua to assist revolutionaries, supported by an American mining company, in their efforts to overthrow a government hostile to the company's interests. When the treaty Knox negotiated with the new administration failed to be ratified by the Senate, he urged American bankers to move in. Financial domination by the northern colossus aroused such fierce resentment that within three years a revolt broke out, which was promptly crushed by Marines again dispatched by Taft. The result of the administration's enlargement of "opportunity for profitable investment" was a legacy of acute distrust, even hatred, of the United States throughout Latin America.

Yet, in Mexico, when a revolution overthrew the dictator Porfirio Díaz and replaced him with a regime hostile to the United States, Taft refused to intervene even when Americans and American property were attacked. He ordered both the Army and the Navy to exercise caution to avoid provocative acts which might possibly cause retaliation. When shots were fired across the southern border, he requested the authorities of the Arizona border towns to ask their citizens temporarily to withdraw to places where they could not be struck by bullets. He was determined, it seems, not to meddle in Mexico's domestic situation.

In the Far East, Taft and Knox attempted to promote dollar diplomacy and revive the Open Door. To secure opportunities for American capital, they challenged the control of Japan and the European banking "consortium" of Britain, France, and Germany by insisting on the right of American bankers to invest in Chinese railroad projects and make loans to the government. After four years of effort, the United States was finally admitted to the combine, but no large-scale investments materialized. American bankers were reluctant to risk their capital, particularly as they were resented by the other financial interests already there. The President described the administration's attempts in his annual message to Congress in 1912 as a policy which subsituted "dollars for bullets." By promoting American investments and protecting the independence of China, he declared, international tensions would be eased. His policy could not have succeeded even if the financiers had cooperated, for he failed to grasp that investments alone could not create a strong, autonomous China, that an aggressive commercial policy must be linked with political action.

Just as Taft lacked comprehension of the dynamics of power relationships, he was equally unresponsive to the changing character of his own country. He clung desperately to principles and ideas that the American people were rapidly discarding, having "neither the will to return to the past nor the inclination to disturb the present," as one historian so aptly put it. Within his own party, rumblings of discontent with his conservatism in domestic legislation erupted into a full-scale revolt in 1911 when insurgents organized the National Progressive Republican League, a split in the ranks which was to prove fatal to Taft's chances for re-election.

Roosevelt's vigorous championship of social and economic reform made him the natural leader of the new group, although at first he refused to consider another bid for the presidency. Then, in February, 1912, he announced his intention to seek the nomination because, as he charged, Taft in league with the Old Guard had scuttled "my policies." It was one of the ironies of American politics that the man who so ardently endorsed Taft in 1908 as the best choice for President should as passionately denounce him four years later and strive to gain the nomination for himself.

The primary battle was a shabby exhibition, with Roosevelt roaring that the President was feeble and incompetent and Taft abjectly apologizing for attacking his former idol, for "even a rat in a corner will fight." Still the popular hero, Roosevelt triumphed easily over his opponent in the primaries, even winning Taft's home state. But as the party machinery in the various states supported Taft, a preponderance of delegates at the convention gave him their vote. Roosevelt and his followers stalked out of the convention and founded the Progressive Party. In the ensuing three-cornered fight, the Democrats captured the White House. With Woodrow Wilson, the hiatus in presidential leadership fortunately came to an end.

Woodrow Wilson

5. Scholar in the White House

FEW men came to the presidency as well equipped for their responsibilities from a theoretical and practical standpoint as did Woodrow Wilson. An academic background in political science made him knowledgeable in the complexities and subtleties of government and politics. His experience as a university president and state governor provided administrative and executive skills, and perhaps equally important was his overriding desire for leadership.

Even as a youth Wilson aspired to the role of statesman, to a place in public life where he could influence the course of national affairs. So consuming an ambition did this become that when he was not yet thirty he wrote in deep frustration to his fiancée Ellen Axson, that for some time he had had "a 'lurking sense of disappointment and *loss,* as if I had missed from my life something upon which both my gifts and inclinations gave me a claim'; . . . I have been shut out from my heart's *first*—primary—ambition and purpose, which was, to take an active, if possible a leading part, in public life, and strike out for myself, . . . a *statesman's* career." He had to submerge a strong instinct for leadership, an "unmistakably oratorical temperament," and "content me with the sober methods of the scholar and the man of letters." If only he could inspire "a great movement of opinion," impelling the masses to high political achievement, he would be "complete."

As an undergraduate student at Princeton, Wilson had already begun to examine in depth the nature of the American government. In an article entitled "Cabinet Government in the United States" which he published in the *International Review,* a scholarly journal edited by Henry Cabot Lodge, he made a critical evaluation of the British and American systems, finding the latter much inferior. In America, as the legislature is sovereign, the President is rarely able to exercise leadership and is merely the executor of the laws. Cabinet officers are little more than chief clerks in the executive department. Worse still, "Congress is a deliberative body in which there is little real deliberation; a legislature which legislates with no real discussion of its business." With major matters handled by committees, an individual congressman is seldom able to exert any influence. Many of these serious shortcomings could be corrected by adopting some features of the British system.

The article foreshadowed a broader criticism in his doctoral dissertation, *Congressional Government,* published several years later in 1885. Here he indicted the control of government by irresponsible congressional committees, lauding the system of party responsibility prevailing in the British Parliament where the Prime Minister heads the House of Commons, from which body he was selected.

Absorbed with the problems of leadership, Wilson concentrated on those structural barriers in the American system which he felt prevented even the able leader from functioning effectively. Writing at a time of virtually absolute congressional supremacy, when Presidents were captives of congressional and party machines and not distinguished by brilliance or initiative, he deplored the dearth of leadership in American public life. "The prestige of the Presidential office," Wilson lamented, "has declined with the character of the Presidents. . . . That high office has fallen from its first estate of dignity because its power has waned; and its power has waned because the power of Congress has become predominant. . . . [Except for his veto power] the President might, not inconveniently be a permanent officer; the first official of a carefully graded and impartially regulated civil service system, through whose sure series of merit-promotions the youngest clerk might rise even to the chief magistracy."

His assessment of the President's role was shared by that astute observer James Bryce, who stated in *The American Commonwealth,* published about the same time, that the main duties of a President were to see that the laws were duly executed and to maintain the public peace. Knowledge, profoundity of thought, and imagination might help him gain an influence over the nation, but were not really necessary, since "four-fifths of his work is the same in kind as that which devolves on the chairman of a commercial company or the manager of a railway." The qualities which the country chiefly required were "firmness, common sense, and most of all, honesty."

Two decades later, however, when the forceful Theodore Roosevelt was in the White House, Wilson began to modify his views. Although still regarding the parliamentary system as superior, he observed from the President's vigorous exercise of power that the office contained tremendous potential even within the existing framework. Roosevelt's dominant role in legislative affairs and in foreign policy, his guidance of public opinion, had reinvigorated the presidency, demonstrating that the Constitution provides more than adequate scope for a strong leader. Wilson concluded that a fundamental revision of the governmental system was unnecessary. A strong President could make the office serve the needs of the country despite structural impediments in the constitutional system.

In a series of lectures given at Columbia University in 1907 and published the following year under the title *Constitutional Government in the United States,* Wilson now saw the President "as the unifying force in our complex system, the leader both of his party and the nation." The method of selecting a candidate at national conventions bestows on the President the role of party leader, the representative of the party's controlling ideals and principles. And, declared Wilson, he can dominate the party by being an effective spokesman for the sentiments and aspirations of the country.

As only the President is elected by all the people, Wilson believed that he could become as commanding a figure as the British Prime Minister through skillfully exercising party and national leadership. If he wins the admiration and confidence of the country, Wilson stated, "no other single force can withstand him, no combination of forces will easily overpower him. His position takes the imagination of the country. He is the representative of no constituency, but of the whole people." He could be the leader of his party and the leader of the nation, or he might be one or the other. If he leads the nation, his party could not resist him. "His office is anything he has the sagacity and force to make it."

The only limitation on presidential leadership Wilson now maintained was the President's own restricted view of the Constitution. Those Presidents who denied themselves power which they might legitimately exercise were theorists unsuited for statesmanship, unable or unwilling to comprehend that the flexible nature of the Constitution gave adequate scope for the broad exercise of power. "The President is at liberty both in law and conscience to be as big a man as he can," he stated. "His capacity will set the limit, and if Congress be overborne by him, it will be no fault of the makers of the Constitution—it will be from no lack of constitutional powers on its part, but only because the President has the nation behind him, and Congress has not."

Wilson had his first opportunity to satisfy his craving for leadership as head of Princeton University. In the process of trying to shape the university to his concept of an institution of higher learning, he became embroiled in controversies that made him a national figure. The most acrimonious of these feuds involved the construction of a graduate residence hall. Dean Andrew West insisted upon a site isolated from the main stream of campus life, and Wilson insisted just as firmly that the building be located where it would be an integral part of the university community.

As the debate progressed, the opposing views were championed with mounting passion by the faculty, the student body, and the board of trustees. Personalities and issues became blurred; even old friendships dissolved. A proffer of a generous financial benefaction in aid of Dean West's plan for a graduate school further embittered the dispute. To enlist the support of the alumni, Wilson in 1910 undertook a speaking campaign across the country.

What had begun as an intramural rivalry on differing educational philosophies was transformed by Wilson into a crusade
against the status quo in the colleges, the churches, in fact, in
the nation at large. Democracy, he asserted, was the real issue,
and the stakes were far larger than Princeton. As the churches
in their pursuit of wealth were lowering the standards of Christian service, the universities in their search for financial support were relegating community service to a minor place. The
colleges must be reconstructed from the foundations up as part
of a wider program of reform throughout the country. Everywhere the people were seeking leadership to help effect
change, and he urged the Princeton alumni to become the
vanguard of the movement.

At that point in 1910, the country was caught up in a mood
of progressive reform. Wilson's frequent references to the need
for restraining privileged groups opposed to the general welfare made him the object of widespread attention. This role of
progressive gladiator was new. A lifelong Democrat, he had always been fairly conservative. Only a half dozen years earlier
he had flayed William Jennings Bryan for his "radicalism,"
which he charged was corrupting the Democratic Party and had
even demanded his expulsion. Now, although he made no
specific legislative recommendations, he fully supported the
liberal indictment of social, economic, and political inequities of
American life. In public addresses he denounced the domination of the great corporate interests, their immunity from public
control, and the consequent erosion of representative government. Special privilege, he said, undermined the general welfare.

At the same time, his thoughts were turning to a political
career. In 1909, replying to a friend's suggestion that he enter
the political lists, he confided his embarrassment: "It is mani-
festly undesirable that the head of a university should seek a
prominent part in party contests." An active effort to obtain
political office would be unseemly, but if an invitation should
be extended to him from a leading and responsible political
figure, he would feel obliged to give the matter his very earnest
consideration.

The graduate school affair ended in complete defeat for

Wilson, and when he was approached by New Jersey party leaders to run for governor he accepted without hesitation. The politicians had long had their eye on him. They not only believed he could win, but they were sure that this "politically innocent academician" would be easy to manipulate. When Wilson informed them that he would make no commitments of any kind, they smiled politely, dismissing his statement as a stock gesture.

His election as governor of New Jersey gave Wilson the opportunity for political leadership. For the next two years he was immersed in the art of practical politics. To the dismay of the political bosses, the academician proved to be more adept at political leadership than if he had served a long apprenticeship. Soon after he took office, he plunged into open warfare against them. By his direction, one of the legislators introduced a bill which provided for regulating primary and general elections and prevented the rigging of slates. His next step was to exert pressure directly or through his secretary, Joseph Tumulty, to have the bill passed. He talked with legislators individually and in groups. Against all precedent, he attended a caucus meeting at which the opponents of the measure hoped to kill it secretly. Challenged by a legislator for unwarranted interference with the legislative process and with breaking down the separation of powers, he replied that by electing him the voters acknowledged his leadership of the party. And the party leader, he felt, should participate directly in policy making. "You can deprive me of office and turn away from me, but you cannot deprive me of power so long as I steadfastly stand for what I believe to be the interests and legitimate demands of the people themselves." For two hours the governor held the floor, demonstrating an agility and firmness that would have done credit to the most seasoned politician. The bill was passed. The political scientist had succeeded in translating his theories of leadership into practice.

Wilson thoroughly delighted in the political life. The zest with which he approached his tasks, his grasp of detail and knowledge of issues, his command of strategy, and his ability to deal with men plainly marked him as a natural leader. With an enviable record in his legislative program, the intensity with which he fought for liberal measures augmented his national reputation as a reformer.

The next logical step was the White House, and the road was cleared for him by that strange Texan, Colonel Edward M. House, and by a reconciliation between Wilson and his erstwhile ideological opponent, William Jennings Bryan.

Colonel House, who came to know President Wilson intimately, was often baffled by what impressed him as a most contradictory personality. In his diary he records that Wilson told him he was nervous when speaking in public. "I had thought that he was entirely free from it, and yet he said that if he had to walk across a crowded stage with an audience in front of him, he always wondered whether he would drop before he reached the speaker's stand." The confession astonished House since Wilson was an extremely effective platform speaker: poised, dynamic, highly articulate. During the election campaign, all his addresses were delivered extemporaneously, generally from a brief outline on a single sheet. Another contradiction House found was in Wilson's political approach. The President, he wrote, described himself as being a Democrat like Jefferson but with aristocratic tastes. "Intellectually, he said, he was entirely democratic, which in his opinion was unfortunate for the reason that his mind led him where his taste rebelled."

The renowned sculptor Jo Davidson related that neither Wilson nor his wife were pleased with a bust which he had made of the President. He greatly admired Wilson, he said, yet he had been unable to portray his subject as a warm human being. His presence was impressive, but he was cold. Like God, suggested Davidson, he could be feared and respected, but he could not evoke affection.

Writing of the President-elect, Franklin K. Lane, who was to become Secretary of the Interior, said, "The fact is, I think he is apt to prove one of the most tremendously disliked men in Washington that ever has been here. He has a great disrespect for individuals, and so far as I can discover a very large respect for the mass."

What Lane and undoubtedly many others took for disdain appears to have been a lack of self-confidence in face-to-face encounters which Wilson did not experience when addressing a group. "I have a sense of power in dealing with men collectively," he had once written to his fiancée, "which I do not feel always in dealing with them singly. . . . One feels no sacrifice of pride necessary in courting the favour of an assembly of men such as he would have to make in seeking to please one man."

Wilson could charm audiences, inspire and persuade them, but with rare exceptions, and these were mainly women, he could not establish intimate relationships with individuals. It was not that he scorned friendships. On the contrary, Wilson had an almost obsessive need for friends, but he feared close ties. He might have been describing himself in an article he wrote on Edmund Burke where he relates his break with Charles Fox: "His passion for the principles he served was deeper than the passion for his friend. A shallower man for whom public questions were less like the very essences of life and thought and action might have kept his friend without giving up his opinion. But for Burke no such divided comradeship and allegiance was possible."

His intense need for ego gratification compelled him to reject the friendship of anyone who could not completely share his views. He equated disagreement on matters of public policy with personal antagonism, and unquestioning compliance with loyalty. He could sometimes grudgingly accept advice, but criticism was intolerable. On issues which to his mind involved principle, no room existed for an honest difference of opinion. There was a right side and a wrong side and he was never in doubt as to who was right. As few men can or are willing to maintain a relationship on these terms, even with a President, Wilson turned to women who could admire him uncritically. An associate of his New Jersey years wrote that Wilson "felt all opposition to be merely irritation, and that if he needed any human associations they must be with people who either lauded him and made it their business to agree with him on everything, or else with people who were uncomfortable because they didn't understand what he was talking about or were not particularly interested. This accounted for his fondness for women's society."

Wilson once unburdened himself to a female friend about

the dissolution of a deep and cherished friendship. "Why is it that I was blind and stupid enough to love the people who proved false to me and cannot love, can only gratefully admire and cleave to, those who are my real friends by the final, only conclusive proof of conduct and actual loyalty, when loyalty cost and meant something? . . . Perhaps it is better to love men in the mass than to love them individually!"

With his compulsive need for unquestioning loyalty, Wilson had the good fortune to win the friendship of a man who was prepared to be a self-effacing alter ego. Colonel Edward Mandell House—the title was an honorary one bestowed for political favors—had picked Wilson, then governor of New Jersey, as "the best man who can be nominated and elected" President. After an exchange of letters, Wilson went to see the Texan, and almost immediately House became Damon to Wilson's Pythias.

The gears of both personalities meshed as though designed for each other. House, passionately eager to be involved in politics but unable to participate actively because of his health, was content to be the invisible power behind the scenes. Seeking nothing but to be permitted to serve, he soon completely won the confidence of Wilson, who had once remarked that "If I make an intimate of a man in politics it isn't long before he wants me to do something which I ought not to do." Well informed, an intuitive artist in human relations, with a keen, perceptive intelligence, House became an ideal and invaluable companion. When he differed with his friend, he could argue so subtly that he did not offend. He knew when to keep silent, how to listen, how to flatter and encourage. He was completely and absolutely devoted. Yet, in the end, even this friendship was shattered against Wilson's inflexible will.

Some of Wilson's other characteristics often became tragic flaws of leadership at moments of crisis. While his egotism, his unbending will, his dogmatic certitude served him well at times, on other occasions they were destructive to him or the cause he espoused. Robert Lansing, who became his Secretary of State, thought that he relied on intuition rather than reason in reaching conclusions. "Even established facts were ignored if they did not fit in with this intuitive sense, this semi-divine power to select the right."

Like his father and his grandfather, both of whom had been Presbyterian ministers, Wilson believed in the Calvinist doctrine of predestination: the righteous would ultimately be rewarded, and the wicked punished. He was convinced that a moral law governed the universe, and that the fate of nations, like the fate of individuals, was subject to a providential grand design, to the immutable decrees of an omnipotent God. In Wilson's moral universe, man was a lonely soul whose duty it was to seek for the truth, to follow the dictates of his conscience. In that endeavor, reason and intellect had their limitations. "My life would not be worth living if it were not for the driving power of religion, for faith, pure and simple," he wrote. "I have seen all my life the arguments against it without ever having been moved by them. Never for a moment have I had one doubt about my religious beliefs. There are people who believe only so far as they understand—that seems to be presumptuous and sets their understanding as the standard of the universe. . . . I am sorry for such people." His deep commitment to Christian revelation endowed him with a strong moral fervor and a driving conscience. From it stemmed his sense of justice, his sense of duty, and his sense of destiny. To placate his conscience, he often found it necessary to rationalize policies in terms of high moral purpose.

Beneath a calm, poised façade lurked devils of restiveness, discontent, violent temper. Seemingly confident of his purpose and fixed in his determination, Wilson was frequently plagued by qualms and doubts. Although reserved, even aloof in his official contacts, he was warm and charming to his family and those in his intimate circle. Publicly austere and humorless, he could delight a party with his lighthearted abandon and entertain them with mimicry and a storehouse of jokes.

Though Wilson had been immersed in the academic environment and devoted most of his life to scholarly pursuits, his intellectual interests were narrow. What little literature he read consisted almost exclusively of the English romantic poets and novelists of the early nineteenth century. His knowledge of science and technology was meager, and he was little interested in philosophical thought or in the pursuit of intellectual theories for their own sake. But his mind was sharp, and his ability to absorb ideas, to cut through a maze of irrelevancies to the essence of a problem, impressed both friend and foe.

Although Wilson had been in the public eye for some years before he entered the White House, and was respected as a scholar, he remained a mystery. Even his warmest supporters and admirers expressed uncertainty about him. Walter Hines Page, later to be appointed Ambassador to the Court of St. James's, confided to his diary that nobody seemed to know Wilson and "I wonder if he quite knows himself. Temperamentally quite shy, having lived too much alone and far too much with women (how I wish two of his daughters were sons!) this Big Thing having descended on him before he knew or was quite prepared for it. . . . And he talks—generalities to the public. Perhaps that's all he can talk now. Wise? Yes. But does he know the men about him? Does he really know men? Nobody knows." Taft had grave apprehensions about this "schoolmaster" whose "opportunism and dictatorial manner" he feared would push the Democratic Party to radical extremes. To his brother he speculated that "With the Senate and the House Democratic, and the schoolmaster a marplot in the White House, and a gentleman who knows it all, the toboggan that the Democratic sled will strike will give it a swiftness of movement in some direction that will set the people aghast, whether such movement will be successful or not."

With a crusader's zeal, Wilson resolved to set a new tone in Washington of uncompromising honesty, hoping thereby to establish a pattern for all government agencies. It was a noble aim, but the hard facts of political life made for inevitable compromise. In the first place, it was impossible for the President personally to supervise the more than fifty thousand patronage jobs that were available. But even more important, he realized almost at once that he could never hope to achieve the legislative program to which he was committed unless he shut his eyes to the distribution of the loaves and fishes. Thus Secretary of State Bryan undermined the foreign service which his predecessor had built up so laboriously by filling it with incompetent party hacks appointed for political reasons. Wilson did succeed, however, in placing some distinguished and competent men in ambassadorial posts.

The feeble political leadership during the preceding President's four years reinforced Wilson's determination to shape his own presidency along the lines of his Columbia University lectures on constitutional government. Having abandoned the British cabinet system as his model, he now envisioned a combination of the British prime ministership and the American presidency. Shortly before his inauguration, when Congressman A. Mitchell Palmer requested that Wilson endorse a plank in the Democratic Party platform advocating an amendment restricting the presidency to a single term, Wilson replied that the President must be a prime minister, "as much concerned with the guidance of legislation as with the just and orderly execution of law." As the nation's spokesman, even in the most consequential dealings with foreign nations, he must sooner or later be made answerable "to the Houses whom he seeks to lead, either personally or through a cabinet, as well as to the people for whom they speak." But that, he felt, would be worked out at some future date. In the meantime, as long as the President is commanded to lead, "he is surely entitled to . . . all the power he can get from the support and convictions and opinions of his fellow countrymen." If a limitation were to be placed on the President's eligibility, his power in the people's behalf would be "immensely weakened. . . . I believe that we should fatally embarrass ourselves if we made the constitutional change proposed. If we want our Presidents to fight our battles for us we should give them the legitimate means. . . . Strip them of everything else but the right to appeal to the people, but leave them that." While attempting in every way to extend the people's power, as regards the presidency we "fear and distrust the people and seek to bind them hand and foot by rigid constitutional provision."

From the very beginning, Wilson assumed the role of party leader and enlarged the legislative leadership that had been asserted by Theodore Roosevelt. He was the first President since John Adams to deliver a message to Congress in person. The revival of the practice after more than a century, and in the face of legislative resentment against a "speech from the throne," indicated his resolution to breach the barrier between the two branches of government. He was unremitting in his demands for legislation, consulted frequently with leaders of the Democratic Party in both Houses, and was instrumental in determining the priority of measures to be considered. The minutest details of bills pending before Congress received his closest scrutiny. Often he mediated between opposing factions in the party when his program appeared to be threatened. To maintain discipline and bring dissidents into line, he used the party caucus in both House and Senate, nor did he hesitate to wield the patronage club to bolster his legislative objectives.

Until 1917 he managed to keep the Democratic Party under tight control, serving as its spokesman in national affairs. A combination of factors favored his efforts: workers, farmers, and other distressed groups were demanding government help; the Republican Party was torn by schism and revolt; dethronement in 1910 of the potent Speaker of the House had left a power vacuum, which Wilson, unlike Taft, turned to his advantage; a large crop of freshmen in Congress looked to the President; and he was further aided by an impressive Democratic majority. He made effective use of the public platform and the press. In his first great legislative battle, which was for tariff reform, he routed a powerful lobby by forcefully denouncing it to the newspapers. Under ceaseless pressure from the White House, the legislative mill kept grinding for the immediate enactment of a broad social and economic program.

Wilson's role in the currency reform issue which led to the Federal Reserve Act illustrates his active legislative leadership. He began with a message to Congress in June, 1913. For the next six months he pursued his objective relentlessly. He consulted with House and Senate leaders, with members of the appropriate committees, and even with Republicans, cajoling, flattering, importuning. He received delegations of bankers. He conferred frequently with William Jennings Bryan to insure support from congressmen who were still under the Commoner's influence. He kept in constant touch with Secretary of the Treasury McAdoo and arranged for important amendments. He blocked plans for congressional adjournment, even though it meant that Congress must swelter through a Washington summer. When the caucus, despite strenuous efforts, failed to control all party members by December, it voted unanimously to forgo a holiday adjournment unless the bill was passed before the twenty-fourth. This was absolutely unprecedented behavior. Commented the *New York Times*, "To-day's action of the party conference is a striking illustration of the discipline the President has instilled into the party ranks."

With the passage of the currency reform measure and other victories which followed, many who had been skeptical about Wilson began to feel that a lack of conventional political training was, in his case, no handicap to effective leadership. Those who recalled his inflexibility in the Princeton graduate school fracas were surprised at his ability for skillful compromise. The fact remained, however, that he was prepared to compromise only on relatively minor matters where the basic objective remained unaffected. On what he considered large principles, he was unbending, ready to stake his prestige and leadership on the outcome. In one instance, with regard to a congressional act where he felt principle was involved, he stated flatly, "Nor should the question be compromised as some have suggested; in fact, it will not be compromised. It will be repealed." And so it was. When he was charged with bad faith because he was in opposition to a plank in the party platform of 1912, he replied, "I feel that no promise made in a platform with regard to foreign affairs is more than half a promise. It cannot mean that if the foreign elements in the situation are beyond our control we will undertake to control them."

For all his skill as a parliamentary tactician, and for all his emphasis on the President as leader of his party, he was unable to realize his prime ministerial aspiration. He could not fashion an enduring party structure in Congress that would have the unity he admired in the British system. Authority over the party could be maintained only so long as the public at large supported him, but with a change in the popular mood, the President lost his capacity to bend legislators to his will.

Wilson's philosophy of presidential leadership was shaped partly by mature, intellectual conviction, but undoubtedly it was also an outgrowth of his personality pattern. His driving urge to dominate men and situations, his inward or outward fury when he was blocked, his craving for uncritical admiration, his moral certitude all probably stemmed from a boyhood spent in the shadow of a domineering, demanding father in a stern, Calvinist atmosphere. Might there not be a psychological explanation for Wilson's selection of Robert Lansing as Secretary of State to succeed Bryan? While few trained men outside of the department were available, the nature of House's recommendation to Wilson is significant: "I think the most important thing is to get a man with not too many ideas of his own and one that will be entirely guided by you without unnecessary argument, and this, it seems to me, you would find in Lansing."

Temperamentally, Wilson was disposed to be his own Secretary of State, and to dominate the scene in other areas of executive activity. Franklin K. Lane wrote of Wilson to a friend, "My own ability to help him is very limited, for he is one of those men made by nature to tread the wine press alone. The opportunity comes now and then to give a suggestion or to utter a word of warning, but on the whole I feel that he probably is less dependent upon others than any President of our time."

Cabinet members were regarded by Wilson as primarily administrators rather than political advisers. He counseled with very few of them concerning problems outside their own departments. Even on matters as important as his war message to Congress in 1917, the Cabinet was not consulted. When Colonel House asked him why he had not done so, he replied that if he had, every man would have offered some criticism and suggestion. He preferred to have the entire responsibility on his own shoulders.

The press, for Wilson, was a vehicle to reach the people and obtain their support for his policies. At the beginning he hoped to effect a partnership with the newspapermen for what he termed a "common counsel." But he was soon irritated with them over what he felt were transgressions of propriety, having expected a greater degree of responsibility than a free press in a democratic society is capable of exercising. His attempt to regularize press conferences (the first President to do so) similarly failed. For about a year he met with the press twice a week. Questions and answers were spontaneous; the only restriction was that the President's remarks could not be quoted without his consent. But reporters had the impression that Wilson was trying to match wits with them. He was "sensitive" and they were "ill at ease." He needed "comprehension, if not actual agreement," to draw him out. Bitterly he wrote to George Creel that when he came to Washington he anticipated close and cordial relations with the press. "I prepared for the conferences as carefully as for any lecture, and talked freely and fully on all large questions of the moment." The group had a few brilliant men, he continued, but the majority were interested only in the personal and trivial rather than in principles and policies. However, he won the respect of a group of influential editors and correspondents, and with Frank I. Cobb of the New York *World* maintained a cordial and continuing relationship.

Often he was annoyed by the way the press handled policy statements that he had transmitted to reporters. "Since I came here," he wrote to Charles W. Eliot, "I have wondered how it ever happened that the public got a right impression regarding public affairs, particularly foreign affairs." For a while he considered establishing a national publicity bureau, a sort of clearing house for all government information, but, probably realizing that it would be regarded unfavorably by newspapermen, dropped the idea. Later, when America entered the war, the Committee on Public Information headed by George Creel was based on his plan. Nevertheless, the newspapers provided him with a forum. What might he have accomplished if today's media of mass communications, enabling a leader to project voice and face throughout the land, had been available to him?

Wilson entered office at the juncture between an old and a new era. Domestic concerns would begin to recede into the background as foreign entanglements came to the fore. The partial insulation the country had enjoyed for so many generations would soon vanish, and, except for brief interludes, the American people would never again experience the luxury of tranquility.

Woodrow Wilson

6. Ordeal of Neutrality

"IT would be the irony of fate," Woodrow Wilson told a friend shortly before he left for Washington, "if my administration had to deal chiefly with foreign affairs." Neither in his theoretical studies of government nor as governor had he been concerned with foreign relations. In his campaign speeches and later in his inaugural address, he had been virtually silent on the subject. This omission reflected both a state of relative international calm and Wilson's own preoccupation with domestic affairs.

Nevertheless, Wilson was keenly aware of the new direction America was taking, set for it by the nature of the twentieth century international environment, and of the President's responsibility in guiding the nation. As early as 1900 he had written that the war with Spain resulted in "greatly increased power and opportunity for constructive statesmanship given the President by the plunge into international politics and into the administration of distant dependencies. . . . The President of the United States is now . . . at the front of affairs, as no President, except Lincoln, has been since the first quarter of the nineteenth century."

Two years later, in his Princeton inaugural address, he had declared that the nation had reached maturity, that the period of American isolation was over. A shift in focus together with a return to presidential influence was now required. With the United States more sensitive than ever to currents from abroad, the President and his advisers "stand upon our chief point of observation." And in 1907 he had said with prophetic insight that the President can "never again be the mere domestic figure he has been throughout so large a part of our history." The country had developed to the top rank in power and resources. "The other nations of the world look askance upon her, half in envy, half in fear, and wonder with a deep anxiety what she will do with her vast strength. . . . Our President must always, henceforth, be one of the great powers of the world, whether he act greatly or wisely or not." He could never again be a mere domestic officer, the mere executive he was in the thirties and forties. "He must stand always at the front of our affairs, and the office will be as big and as influential as the man who occupies it."

Providing the framework for Wilson's world view, as well as for his approach to all public questions, was a set of moral and ethical values, a sense of righteousness derived from his religious background. A nation was "a moral essence" which should be guided by the same standards of moral conduct as applied to individuals and held equally accountable for any immoralities. As the United States was destined to be a leader among the nations of the world, it was her responsibility to "go to the ends of the earth carrying conscience and the principles that make for good conduct."

The right of peoples to control their own political fortunes was one of his articles of faith, though he also believed that those countries which were not prepared to insure political stability would have to submit to the tutelage of the more advanced nations. Not until all peoples had developed a political consciousness, a mature system of law, respect for the dictates of morality, and an allegiance to ideals that transcended material interests, would self-government and democracy be universal. America's mission was to promote the democratic cause everywhere. This could be done only by setting an example for right conduct at home and by supporting movements for freedom and progress abroad.

Foreign policy under Wilson took on a new character, owing to this cast of mind. Rooseveltian realism and self-interest were replaced by standards of national honor, Taft's dollar diplomacy by a new kind of moral interventionism. Secretary of State William Jennings Bryan coincidentally shared this evangelical approach. He wanted to go even further in his eagerness to implement the principles of Christian love in foreign policy. He desired to renounce the use of force as an instrument of national power, have the United States proclaim its opposition to war, and declare that there were no disputes which could not be submitted for arbitration to an international tribunal. A statement of this kind, Bryan felt, would not only eliminate the danger of attack but give the nation a moral pre-eminence among the world powers.

The President and his Secretary of State were essentially missionaries. They would teach men everywhere how to govern themselves and persuade nations that democracy was best for them. When Sir William Tyrol, who was returning to England in November, 1913, said to Wilson, "I shall be asked to explain your Mexican policy. Can you tell me what it is?" The President confidently replied, "I am going to teach the South American republics to elect good men."

At that point Wilson had already spent several months as schoolmaster to the Mexicans. Shortly before his inauguration, the head of the army, Victoriano Huerta, had seized control of the Mexican government and several days later had had the deposed president assassinated. Taft, soon to retire from office, left the matter of recognizing the new regime to the incoming administration. For more than a year, Wilson was completely absorbed with the Mexican problem. Throughout he dealt with its complicated ramifications virtually alone, but he was totally unprepared to handle the delicate diplomatic involvements and ignorant of the internal situation. He assumed that Mexico was fully prepared for democracy in the American manner although it was less advanced than the United States. The differences between the two nations, he believed, were superficial rather than fundamental. All that was required was to schedule free elections and adhere to constitutional practices.

To begin with, Wilson issued a public statement that the United States had no sympathy with those in Latin America who seek to "seize the power of government to advance their own personal interests or ambition." Though directed at

Huerta, it was widely interpreted to mean that Wilson would regard with disfavor any efforts by Latin-American revolutionists to overthrow existing governments, and in effect it announced a new recognition policy for the United States. The traditional policy, of recognizing *de facto* governments, had been cogently expressed by Secretary of State Buchanan in 1848 when he declared, "We do not go behind the existing Government to involve ourselves in the question of legitimacy. It is sufficient for us to know that a government exists, capable of maintaining itself; and then its recognition on our part inevitably follows." In time the requirement was added that a government comply with its international obligations and provide protection to foreign interests. Recognition carried no implication of approval.

Wilson proposed to reverse this settled policy by reserving for the United States the right to inquire whether the new regime was adhering to its own constitution and, even beyond that, whether the rulers had been motivated by personal interests and ambition or by a sincere desire to eliminate despotism. To Wilson the test of constitutional legitimacy seemed reasonable and honorable; to the Latin Americans it was meddling in their internal affairs. As events in Mexico and elsewhere were to show, his test was unworkable because it could not be applied arbitrarily in all situations. Furthermore, he encountered strong opposition from European governments which did not wish to have their own relations jeopardized by Wilson's peculiarly rigid standards.

In due course Venustiano Carranza, the governor of a northern province, started a movement to depose Huerta and restore constitutional government. Wilson was delighted and offered to mediate, but in a manner which would accomplish the defeat of Huerta. As his personal intermediary to fill this delicate assignment, he appointed John Lind, a Democratic chieftain from Minnesota, who knew no Spanish, nothing of the country, and as little of diplomacy. Lind's mission was doomed from the start. Huerta flatly rejected his strong terms as conditions for mediation and recognition.

Wilson then attempted to isolate Huerta from the European nations who had been furnishing his provisional government with money and arms in keeping with traditional practice. He first sought to persuade the British government to withdraw recognition and join with the United States in a boycott of the Huerta regime, as these actions might influence other nations to follow suit, but a diplomatic note proved entirely unavailing.

Incensed, Wilson dashed off a biting memorandum on his own typewriter. The United States, he said, was the nation with the greatest responsibility to Mexico. Huerta's illegal regime could not have survived without financial aid from those nations who extended recognition contrary to American wishes, but it could not continue in power without the consent of the United States. Would other governments cooperate or was it their intention to "antagonize and thwart us and make our task one of domination and force?" It was an extraordinary document, but never sent. John Bassett Moore of the State Department, requested by Wilson to put the statement into "as strong and direct language as the courtesies and proprieties of pacific diplomacy permit," instructed the President on international manners. All nations possessed the sovereign right to extend or withhold recognition in accord with their national interests and need not ask permission from the United States.

A genuine concern for the welfare of the Mexican people moved Wilson. "My ideal is an orderly and righteous government in Mexico," he explained to a journalist, "but my passion is for the submerged eighty-five per cent of the people of that Republic who are now struggling toward liberty." His sympathies, he said, were with the masses who were striving to obtain their rights in the land. He sharply excoriated the hidalgos and others who were exploiting the economy for their selfish purposes. "They want order—the old order; but I say to you that the old order is dead. It is my part, as I see it, to aid in composing those differences so far as I may be able, that the new order, which will have its foundations on human liberty and human rights, shall prevail."

As his motives were exemplary, he was astonished when Carranza's "Constitutionalists," as they called themselves, not only refused his offer of arms and men but declared that they would oppose entry of American troops into Mexico. All they desired was the right to purchase arms and ammunition from the United States and be permitted to work out their national destiny in their own way. Chagrined, Wilson withheld aid until it became obvious that the Constitutionalists could never overthrow Huerta until they had more war matériel.

During the next four years, Wilson's insistence on helping the unwilling Mexicans almost precipitated war on two occasions. The first occurred in April, 1914. When news was received that a German merchant ship with a cargo of ammunition for the Huerta government was due to arrive in Vera Cruz, the President ordered the fleet to occupy the city and prevent the ship from unloading its cargo. Carranza immediately denounced this as wanton aggression and threatened war if American troops attempted to penetrate any further into Mexico.

Huerta abdicated in July, 1914, but civil war broke out again when Carranza's general, Francisco "Pancho" Villa, broke with his chief. Wilson and Bryan, ignoring the fact that Villa was ignorant, completely unfit for political leadership, and commanding many of the worst elements in Mexico, decided to support him because they felt he would be more amenable than Carranza to American control. Villa was defeated in his struggle for power, whereupon Wilson and his new Secretary of State, Robert Lansing, sought the aid of the leading Latin-American states to force Carranza's removal and the creation of a new provisional government. Only preoccupation with the German submarine controversy in the summer of 1915 caused the administration to abandon plans for intervention, an action which might very well have resulted in conflict as Carranza by then had consolidated his power.

The second crisis occurred in April of the following year. Several months previously, Villa had removed seventeen Americans from a train at Santa Ysabel and shot all but one; then in March he raided Columbus, New Mexico, burning the town and killing nineteen inhabitants. A punitive expedition was dispatched across the Mexican border to pursue Villa; within two weeks or so it had penetrated more than 300 miles. Mexican leaders became alarmed, fearing that the United States intended to occupy the northern part of their country permanently. Then, on April 12, forty Mexicans were killed in a skirmish between American and Mexican troops. Carranza demanded the prompt withdrawal of the expedition and, when Washington refused, ordered his commanders to resist the Americans if they moved in any direction but toward the border. Wilson replied on June 20 with a warning that any attack on American soldiers would lead to "the gravest consequences." After another incident involving the troops of both countries almost resulted in war, Carranza's proposal that a Joint High Commission be appointed to investigate and make recommendations for settling the difficulties was approved by Wilson. But as the Americans insisted on discussing the protection of oil interests in Mexico, while the Mexicans demanded immediate withdrawal of the expedition, the commission could not reach an agreement and disbanded in 1917. An armed clash was averted only because American involvement in the European war now seemed inevitable. The President had no choice but to accede to Carranza's demand for prompt evacuation of American troops and on March 13, 1917, accorded *de jure* recognition to his regime.

Wilson failed in Mexico because he stubbornly insisted on being the Moses who would lead an oppressed but proud people into the land of Canaan, whether or not they wanted to be led by him, and because he failed to realize that ideas no matter how worthy cannot be imposed by force or good intentions.

In the Caribbean, as in Mexico, Wilson was motivated by lofty ideals. The United States, he believed, should employ its power to promote democracy, justice, and peace. "It is a very perilous thing," he told an audience in Mobile, Alabama, in October, 1913, "to determine the foreign policy of a nation in terms of material interest. . . . We dare not turn from the principle that morality and not expediency is the thing that must guide us and that we will never condone iniquity because it is most convenient to do so." But these moral preachments failed to herald the inauguration of a bold, new policy.

Considerations of national security, pressure from financial interests demanding government protection for their property abroad, and Wilson's own belief in the need for economic expansion overseas made a continuation of the Rooseveltian policy in the Caribbean inevitable. In fact, Wilson's administration was responsible for more interventions than had been undertaken by both Roosevelt and Taft. His rationale emphasized popular democracy and economic welfare for the Latin Americans rather than the self-interest of the United States, but in effect little distinguished his moral imperialism from the military and economic interference of his predecessors. His interventions were equally unpopular.

In the summer of 1915, when Haiti defaulted on its debts, American Marines were sent down and the republic was compelled to accept a treaty which made it a virtual protectorate. Later, when the dictator president was murdered by a vengeful mob, the Marines stayed on to preserve order and constitutional processes. In the Dominican Republic, a revolutionary uprising in the summer of 1914 resulted in a state of anarchy. Marines were promptly dispatched to control the country, and a military government was established which remained for years; customs receipts were turned over to the American military governor, whose rule was as complete as though he were president. Cuba, as on previous occasions, was occupied by American Marines in 1916 when a disputed election resulted in civil war. The situation in Nicaragua was particularly ironic. Withdrawal of American troops stationed there would have been a signal for civil war and the overthrow of a regime detested by the people. But as the elements seeking power would have been violently hostile to the United States, a situation that could not be permitted in an area so close to the canal, the occupation and support of a dictator continued. Intervention in these Central American countries produced fiscal reforms and some progress in education and sanitation, but they left a heritage of bitter resentment.

Despite the interventions and occupations, a few notable achievements were scored in mitigating suspicion and hostility. Congress in 1912 had exempted American ships engaged in the coastwise trade from paying canal tolls, contrary to the Hay-Pauncefote Treaty. Wilson considered this action immoral. He conferred with congressional leaders, then went before a joint session and in the strongest terms urged repeal of the measure, even threatening to resign his office: "In case of failure in this matter, I shall go to the country, after my resignation is tendered, and ask it to say whether America is to stand before the world as a nation that violates its contracts as mere matters of convenience, upon a basis of expediency." The clause was repealed.

Seeking to rehabilitate America's moral position, the President attempted to make amends to Colombia for the loss of the Panama Canal Zone during the Roosevelt administration, regarding the manner in which it was acquired as nothing less than "petty larceny." Wilson and Bryan negotiated a reparation treaty with the Colombian government providing for an indemnity of twenty-five million dollars, together with free use of the canal. Furthermore, the United States expressed "sincere regret that anything should have occurred to interrupt or mar the relations of cordial friendship that had so long subsisted between the two nations." When Theodore Roosevelt learned of the treaty, his violent denunciations of this "belated blackmail" reverberated throughout the country. Despite Wilson's pleas that "this nation can afford to be just; even more, it can afford to be generous in the settling of disputes, especially when by its generosity it can increase the friendliness of the many millions in Central and South America with whom our relations become daily more intimate," Roosevelt supporters in the Senate succeeded in blocking ratification. The President's attempt to offer an apology was a unique gesture for the time. That a powerful nation would publicly acknowledge a wrong to a weak and helpless country impressed many, especially in the lands south of the border.

To reverse the course of Taft's dollar diplomacy in the Far East, Wilson decided to withdraw American participation from the European banking consortium for investment in Chinese railroad projects which his predecessor had approved. Following a discussion with his Cabinet, the President announced in March, 1913, that it would be "obnoxious to the principles upon which the government of our people rests." The proposed loan seemed "to touch very nearly the administrative independence of China itself," and the United States would use only fair means to promote the trade of its citizens with that country. While the Chinese were grateful and the action morally commendable, the result was an unhappy one. Wilson's failure to consider the political realities of the Far East, including China's weakness, served to encourage the ambitions and expansionist program of the one power in the Far East which threatened the interests of the United States.

Tension with Japan, temporarily eased by Theodore Roosevelt's forthright action in the West Coast school and land issues, flared up again in April, 1913, when the California legislature enacted a law barring Japanese from owning land. Ignoring Wilson's public appeal and Secretary of State Bryan's personal plea, the governor signed the measure. In Japan, indignation rapidly turned to wrath. A vehement protest was sent to the State Department, and so explosive did the situation become that in May the Joint Board of the Army and Navy warned the President that war with Japan was "not only possible, but even probable," urging him to transfer American warships to the Philippines to prevent a surprise attack.

For the next year the two countries exchanged notes, until in June, 1914, Baron Kato abruptly terminated negotiations. Once again relations were dangerously exacerbated, until the outbreak of war in Europe drew Japan's attention to China. Taking advantage of the European powers' involvement and their fear that she might withdraw from the conflict unless they acceded to her wishes, Japan, in January, 1915, presented China with Twenty-one Demands that would have reduced the country to the status of a satellite. The United States was in no position to thwart Japan by force, but a note was sent declaring that the government could not recognize any agreement "impairing the treaty rights of the United States and its citizens, the political or territorial integrity of the Republic of China, or the international policy relative to China commonly known as the open door." This diplomatic intervention succeeded in modifying a few of Japan's demands.

Disturbed by the American protests, the growing diplomatic influence of the United States in Peking, and the number of American loans to China, Tokyo in 1917 sent a special ambassador, Viscount Kikujiro Ishii, to Washington for clarification of policy on Japan's role in China. After weeks of negotiation, the Lansing-Ishii agreement was signed in November. It recognized that geographical proximity gave Japan a special interest in China but stated that China's "territorial sovereignty . . . remains unimpaired," and both nations promised to adhere to the Open-Door Policy. A number of ambiguous phrases were later to cause considerable difficulty, but the defeat of Germany was paramount and Wilson wished to avoid prolonged wrangling.

Where Roosevelt used power to protect American security, Wilson attempted to establish correct rules of conduct among nations for the same purpose. In this spirit, Secretary Bryan presented, in the summer of 1914, an ambitious plan for peace through conciliation based on the hope that wars could be avoided if opportunities were created for calm and reasonable discussion. Treaties providing for permanent commissions to investigate all disputes, even those involving the honor and vital interests of a nation, were signed with more than thirty countries. The signatories agreed not to increase their armaments for one year, and to allow a "cooling off" period of one year for the issue to be examined before engaging in war.

To symbolize the new atmosphere of cooperation, Bryan presented a memento to each diplomat who signed for his country. This was a nickeled paperweight made out of a melted-down saber designed like a ploughshare with a line from Isaiah on the blades—"They shall beat their swords into ploughshares"—and a sentence on each beam by Bryan—"Nothing is final between friends" and "Diplomacy is the art of keeping cool."

Unhappily for the world, Bryan's triumph was short-lived. The paperweights had hardly been put to use when the uneasy peace of Europe was shattered. One by one the major powers responded to their commitments as members of alliances, and their armies began the march of death.

When the headlines in the press shrieked the horrifying news, Americans, long indifferent to diplomatic crises overseas, were stunned. Wilson's ambassadors had been assuring him that there was no danger of war, but he was uneasy. Several months before the outbreak of the conflict, he had dispatched Colonel House to Berlin and London for talks with civilian and military leaders in the hope of persuading them to reach some *détente.*

On August 4, the President issued the routine proclamation of neutrality. Fifteen days later he appealed to the people to exercise self-restraint, pointing out that the effect of the war on the United States would depend on what Americans said and did. Those who really loved their country, he continued, "will act and speak in the true spirit of neutrality, which is the spirit of impartiality and fairness and friendliness to all concerned." The temper of the nation would be determined by the tenor of public meetings, newspaper and magazine articles, sermons from the pulpit. He solemnly warned "against that deepest, most subtle, most essential breach of neutrality which may spring out of partisanship, out of passionately taking sides. The United States must be neutral in fact as well as in name. . . . We must be impartial in thought as well as in action, must put a curb upon our sentiments as well as upon every transaction that might be construed as a preference of one party to the struggle before another."

The plea was admirable but highly impractical. Most Americans heartily agreed that the nation should remain neutral about a conflict in which they felt they had no stake. But to expect Americans to remain impartial in thought while bound by ideology and national origin to one or the other of the belligerent camps was clearly unrealistic. Wilson's own background and heritage made him sympathetic to the British and French. He confided to House that a German victory would affect the course of civilization and compel the United States to become a military nation. At the same time, he realized that the causes of the conflict were complex. Germany alone was not responsible, he told a reporter shortly after the outbreak of war in an off-the-record interview, and consequently, "I think that the chances for a just and equitable peace that will be lasting will be happiest if no nation gets the decision by arms."

Almost immediately Wilson sought to bring about a negotiated peace, turning to Colonel House to represent him in this effort. He believed, and the Colonel agreed with him, that a limited British victory which would eliminate the threat of a revival of militarism in the future was preferable to having

Germany decisively crushed. In December, House was sent abroad as Wilson's personal representative on a mission to explore the possibility of peace discussions by the belligerents. He found both sides so confident of victory that their price to lay down arms was far too high. "Everybody seems to want peace," he wrote, "but nobody is willing to concede enough to get it."

Wilson tried again in December, 1915, encouraged by Sir Edward Grey's assurances that England would agree to a negotiated peace if the United States would consent to join a postwar league of nations. Following discussions in the capitals of the belligerent powers, the House-Grey Memorandum was drawn up in London on February 22, 1916. It stipulated that whenever England and France considered the time "opportune," Wilson would call a peace conference. Should the Allies accept and Germany refuse to participate, "the United States would probably enter the war against Germany." The word "probably" was added at Wilson's request.

Actually, armed intervention was not being considered by either Wilson or House. Both felt that diplomatic pressure would be effective in persuading the combatants to negotiate. But within a few months, the Allied military position improved, all talks of peace ended, and Wilson was still faced with the problem of safeguarding the nation's neutral rights while keeping it out of war.

From the beginning, maintaining neutrality presented the greatest challenge to leadership ever to confront a President. Wilson had his own views, but on so momentous a question he could hardly overlook the judgment of his advisers or the opinions of influential persons throughout the country. To whom should he assign the greatest weight? To Secretary of State Bryan, who vehemently argued for rigid impartiality toward the belligerents? To Robert Lansing, counselor for the State Department, whose legal dicta hardly concealed his pro-Allied bias; or to Walter Hines Page, Ambassador to Great Britain, who was sometimes more militantly British than the Prime Minister himself? Or to Colonel House, the hardheaded realist, to whom discretion was always the better part of valor? To whose voice should he listen—Americans sympathetic to Germany or to Britain, pacifists, militarists, bankers, merchants, farmers? The country, like Wilson, was overwhelmingly pro-Allied, but it was also firmly resolved to stay out of the conflict.

In keeping with the rights of a neutral nation, the government made no effort to embargo shipments of arms to the belligerents. Secretary of State Bryan explained to the chairman of the Foreign Relations Committee that "the duty of a neutral to restrict trade in munitions of war has never been imposed by international law or municipal statute," and that the United States never prevented shipments except during civil strife in Latin America. Inconsistently, however, he regarded the lending of money to belligerents as incompatible with true neutrality, and when the firm of J. P. Morgan requested permission on August 15, 1914, to float a loan to France, it was turned down. This policy, though, was soon abandoned after economic involvements made it untenable.

Great Britain's successful blockade and the effective controls imposed upon neutral trade with the Central Powers reduced commerce with Germany to a mere trickle. Trade with England, on the other hand, soared, and it was soon apparent that extensive credits would be necessary to finance the heavy war purchases. When the British pound sterling sagged dangerously under the tremendous burden of war financing in the summer of 1915, the American business community became alarmed. Secretary of the Treasury William McAdoo urged an immediate loan of $500,000,000 to Great Britain to insure continuation of the prosperity resulting from the export trade. He was joined by Bryan's successor, Secretary of State Robert Lansing. If the Allies were unable to pay for their war purchases and were compelled to stop buying, then the United States, Lansing warned, was headed for "industrial depression . . . financial demoralization, and general unrest and suffering among the laboring classes. Can we afford," asked Lansing, "to let a declaration . . . of neutrality . . . stand in the way of our national interest which seems to be seriously threatened?" On September 7, 1915, the President agreed to permit a group of New York bankers to float the loan.

While trade practices and the extension of credits to the

Allies discriminated against the Central Powers, the range of realistic alternatives open to Wilson was exceedingly narrow. Even if he were not convinced that a German victory would be a threat to American security, he was helpless with regard to the British maritime controls and blockade. Both Germany and England unquestionably had violated international law, the former by overrunning Belgium, the latter by the restrictions which control of the Atlantic enabled her to impose. During the early period of the war, Wilson's problems were mainly with the British, who were seizing American ships transporting noncontraband to neutral destinations. Repeatedly, he remonstrated with them, yet he felt that there were limits to the pressure he cared to exert on behalf of unimpeded trade with Germany. "I have gone to the very limit in pressing our claims upon England," he confided to Joseph Tumulty. "War with England would result in a German triumph. No matter what may happen to me personally in the next election, I will not take any action to embarrass England when she is fighting for her life and the life of the world."

Once Germany embarked on a campaign of submarine warfare in February, 1915, to counter British maritime control, Wilson's problem of maintaining neutrality was made infinitely more complex. The U-boats were highly vulnerable to a single shot from a merchantman, so that they dared not risk giving a warning before firing a torpedo. Accordingly, the traditional rules of search and guarantees for the safety of passengers on enemy vessels were abandoned. The President warned the Germans that they would be held to "strict accountability" for destruction of American lives and property. When in March, 1915, the British ship *Falaba* was sunk and one American was lost, Wilson was in a dilemma. He had not yet decided what steps to take when the British passenger liner *Lusitania* was torpedoed and 128 Americans went down. A shock of horror and outrage swept the country, but with the people as a whole firmly against involvement there was no outcry for war. All eyes turned to Wilson for his reaction.

To forbid Americans to travel on armed merchant ships or deny clearance to belligerent vessels carrying American citizens, as Bryan urged, would run counter to the rights of a neutral nation. Wilson concluded that he would rest his case on the high ground of humanity and insist that the Germans abandon their policy of unrestricted warfare. An exchange of notes between the President and the Imperial Government ensued. Submarines, Wilson insisted, must warn their intended victims and make provision for the safety of passengers and crew. A repetition of the *Lusitania* incident, he warned, would have grave consequences. To Secretary Bryan this approach risked war with Germany, and after a note had been dispatched to Berlin he resigned in protest.

Despite Bryan's fears, the Imperial Government shrugged off the warning, for in August the British liner *Arabic* was sunk with two American fatalities. This time Wilson and Secretary Lansing decided to force the issue even at the risk of a diplomatic break. The Germans agreed to abandon unrestricted submarine warfare against passenger vessels, promising that ships which did not resist would first be warned and proper provision made for passengers and crew.

The *Lusitania* disaster roused many Americans, previously indifferent, to advocate preparedness. Until then such sentiment in the country had been confined to a small but vocal minority, enabling the President to state in his annual message to Congress on December 8, 1914, "We shall not alter our attitude because some amongst us are nervous and excited." Now Wilson kept vacillating, uncertain whether an armament build-up would strengthen neutrality or propel the country into war. At the same time, with the Republicans leading the preparedness movement, he was concerned that opposition might be politically disastrous to the Democratic Party by causing it to be stigmatized as cowardly or weak. Reluctantly, in the summer of 1915, he directed his Secretaries of War and the Navy to study the matter. In November, he announced the government's intention to undertake an armaments program and shortly thereafter submitted his requests to Capitol Hill.

Many progressives and pacifists in Congress and throughout the country viewed this change in the President's position as a betrayal. Their distrust of Wilson was heightened when the administration took a stiff line toward Germany after that country announced, in violation of her pledge, that beginning on February 29, 1916, all armed merchant ships would be sunk on sight. Lansing informed the Imperial Government that the United States would not warn its citizens against traveling on armed vessels. Wilson, for his part, appealed desperately to Britain through House: "Germany is seeking to find an excuse to throw off all restraints in under-sea warfare. . . . If the English will disarm their merchant ships she will be without excuse and the English will have made a capital stroke against her. We are amazed the English do not see this opportunity to gain a great advantage without losing anything." The plea, of course, was futile.

Swelling tension with Germany, the preparedness drive, and the administration's stand on the rights of neutrals created alarm in Congress that the President was plunging the nation into war. On February 17, 1916, Jeff McLemore, Democrat of Texas, introduced a resolution into the House warning Americans against travel on armed belligerent ships. Outraged by this challenge to the executive prerogative in the conduct of foreign policy, Wilson struck back through a letter to the chairman of the Senate Foreign Relations Committee, which he made public. "The honor and self-respect of the nation is involved," he stated. "We covet peace and shall preserve it at any cost but the loss of honor." It would be deeply humiliating if, through fear, citizens were forbidden to exercise their rights, and it would be an abdication of America's position as spokesman "for the law and the right." Once a single concession was made, "the whole fine fabric of international law might crumble under our hands, piece by piece. What we are contending for in this matter is of the very essence of the things that have made America a sovereign nation. She cannot yield them without conceding her own impotency as a nation and making virtual surrender of her independent position among the nations of the world."

When the McLemore resolution was followed by a similar one introduced into the Senate by Oklahoma's Thomas Gore, the President exploded, "It is with such a——outfit as that that I am supposed to act and achieve nationally for America!" Immediately he went into action to demonstrate that the President, not Congress, directed foreign policy. He took the unprecedented step of writing to the ranking members of the Rules Committees to ask for a prompt vote on the two resolutions. Reports had come to him, he said, that "divided counsels in Congress in regard to the foreign policy of the government are being made industrious use of in foreign capitals." To his secretary he expressed the fear that the proposed legislation, dealing with a matter that fell within the President's province, would produce an unfortunate cleavage in the country. He would not be rushed into war, but neither would he be intimidated into abandoning the country's defense of neutral rights. Wilson had his way. In early March, the measures were tabled.

When several weeks later a German U-boat attacked without warning the unarmed *Sussex*, a small French steamer, and several Americans were injured, Wilson had to make a crucial decision. House and Lansing urged a strong stand, but the President hesitated. He was still loath to take any step that might hasten intervention. Finally, after three weeks of anguished deliberation, he dispatched a virtual ultimatum to the German government warning that unless the policy of unrestricted submarine warfare against passenger and freight-carrying vessels was abandoned, diplomatic relations would be severed. The Germans yielded, and for a time the situation was relatively calm.

Antagonism was now directed against England. Americans were incensed over the intensification of maritime restrictions, censorship of American letters and seizure of parcels, denial of coaling facilities unless shipowners submitted to stringent controls, but probably most of all by the publication of a "black list" of United States firms and individuals suspected of doing business with Germany and with whom the Allies forbade their subjects to trade. The President was angered by the persistent refusal of the British to carry out the promise contained in the House-Grey Memorandum. By the fall, he was so inflamed over British behavior that he could even conceive of the possibility of war with the Allies.

In the meantime, popular attention was focused on the election campaign of 1916. The Republicans, requiring a candidate and a platform to appeal to the conservative East and also attract the progressive and peace-minded elements of the Midwest and Far West, chose Charles Evans Hughes, an Associate Justice of the Supreme Court. The Democrats returned with enthusiasm to Wilson.

At the Democratic convention, the politicians played on the strong desire of the American people to avoid involvement in the European struggle. "He kept us out of war" soon emerged as the campaign slogan. Wilson was greatly disturbed by its quick, popular appeal. "I can't keep the country out of war," he wrote to Josephus Daniels. "They talk of me as though I were a god. Any little German lieutenant can put us into the war at any time by some calculated outrage." Yet during the campaign he indirectly encouraged the popular feeling by warning that a Republican victory would mean almost certain war with Germany.

For the Republican candidate it was a difficult campaign. Not wishing to alienate either the large number of German-Americans on the one hand, or the interventionists on the other, and afraid that an attack on his opponent's record on domestic reform might make his position appear reactionary, Hughes evaded the large issues. Hopefully he concentrated on the President's Mexican policy and administrative inefficiency, but he had not counted on Theodore Roosevelt. The Rough Rider took off on his own, violently attacking Wilson for cowardice and demanding an unflinching defense of American rights. In general, he beat the war drums so effectively that he estranged the very groups Hughes was trying to reach and which he needed for victory.

Wilson won re-election by the slimmest of margins. On election night, with the returns showing that Hughes had carried the entire Eastern seaboard, Wilson went to bed privately conceding defeat. Headlines for Hughes had already been prepared by the newspapers. The West and Midwest turned the tide. The final result, however, was in doubt for several days, as it hinged on California. Wilson carried that state by only a few thousand votes. His hairline victory was partly due to the endorsement of his reform leadership by progressives and socialists, but mainly to the widespread hope that he would keep the country out of the European carnage.

Increasingly concerned that unless the war ended the United

States would be drawn in, Wilson decided to attempt a final peace effort. Both belligerents professed to favor a just and durable peace, disclaiming any intention to impose vindictive terms, he told House, yet neither had ever made it plain what it was fighting for. Wilson would not offer to mediate, as he had done previously, but ask them to clarify their objectives, as a preliminary move, he hoped, toward peace. Although Lansing and House believed this approach entirely too impartial in tone, a note was dispatched on December 18.

As might have been expected, the response was totally negative. The Allies resented the implication that theirs was not a loftier cause and plainly indicated their intention to exact huge reparations from the Central Powers. Germany, with the military tide then in her favor, refused to stipulate the minimum demands she would be willing to consider. It was obvious that neither side was interested in Wilson's objective, and that each would settle for nothing less than a victor's peace.

Addressing a joint session of Congress on January 22, 1917, the President called for a peace without indemnities, without reprisals, without humiliation. In eloquent terms, he pleaded, "Victory would mean peace forced upon the loser, a victor's terms imposed upon the vanquished. It would be accepted in humiliation, under duress, at an intolerable sacrifice, and would leave a sting, a resentment, a bitter memory upon which terms of peace would rest, not permanently, but only as upon quicksand. Only a peace between equals can last." His forebodings were to be confirmed by the tragic course of events in the postwar world.

Wilson told a friend, "The real people I was speaking to were neither the Senate nor foreign governments, but the people of the countries now at war." Yet, however passionately the people desired an end to the holocaust, it is doubtful whether after all the blood-letting they would have permitted the enemy to escape what they regarded as retribution. Their rulers, having expended a vast treasure and with their leadership at stake, were certainly not disposed to surrender the prospects of victory. On January 31, several days after Wilson's address, the Germans presented completely unacceptable territorial demands, accompanying them with the announcement that beginning the following day all ships, belligerent and neutral, would be sunk without warning in a wide zone around Britain, France, and Italy.

No alternative seemed to remain for the President but to sever diplomatic relations. Still hoping to avoid war, however, he told a joint session of Congress that he could not believe the Germans intended to carry out a policy which would result in the destruction of American lives and ships. But the Germans were not bluffing. Shipping companies were unwilling to risk their vessels, and as merchandise began to pile up on docks and in warehouses the President was besieged with demands to arm merchant vessels. He resisted until the British turned over to him a note by the German Foreign Minister, Alfred Zimmermann, to the German minister in Mexico, which they had intercepted and decoded: if the United States should enter the war, he was to try to persuade Mexico to join the Central Powers, for which it would be rewarded with the "lost territory" of Texas, New Mexico, and Arizona.

Outraged, the President immediately asked Congress for approval to arm merchant vessels and employ any other measures he deemed necessary for protecting maritime rights. Although no overt act has as yet occurred, he said, conditions might change and he wished the freedom to act after Congress adjourned. Then on March 1 he made public the text of the Zimmermann note. Not since the *Lusitania* disaster had the American people been so shocked and infuriated. A bill to arm merchant vessels was approved promptly by the House, but when it reached the Senate it was filibustered to death by a dozen senators under the leadership of Robert La Follette and George Norris. Wilson was furious. "A little group of wilful men, representing no opinion but their own, have rendered the great Government of the United States helpless and contemptible," he stormed. Drawing on his powers as commander in chief, he proceeded to have guns placed on the ships so that by month's end armed merchantmen were moving through the war zones.

The drift toward involvement became a current as the submarine began to exact a toll of American lives on American ships. When three unarmed cargo vessels were sunk without warning on March 18, Secretary Lansing urged Wilson to have Congress declare war. He was supported by the entire Cabinet at a meeting on March 20, at which Postmaster General Albert Burleson read a sheaf of telegrams demanding action. Despite great pressure, the President still hesitated. At last, after three days of mental agony, he bowed to the inevitable.

About one o'clock in the morning of April 2, 1917, the day he was to appear before Congress to ask for a declaration of war, Wilson confessed to his old newspaper friend Frank Cobb that he had never been so indeterminate about anything in his life. The consequences of intervention terrified him. "Once lead this people into war and they'll forget there ever was such a thing as tolerance. To fight you must be brutal and ruthless, and the spirit of ruthless brutality will enter into the very fibre of our national life." Freedom of speech and assembly, he prophesied, would suffer, legal and moral restraints would be relaxed, profiteering would become rampant. It would take a generation for the nation to recover its balance. "If there is any alternative, for God's sake, let's take it."

Gaunt, haggard, he stood before Congress that evening to deliver the message which only Colonel House and Mrs. Wilson had seen. Quietly but firmly, he declared "the recent course of the Imperial German Government to be in fact nothing less than war against the government and people of the United States" and asked Congress to recognize the state of war "which has thus been *thrust* upon it." The American people, their President stated, were being asked to fight in defense of their rights. German aggression had left them no alternative, and "we will not choose the path of submission." This was a position which most could understand and accept. But for Wilson there had to be an additional, a loftier, motive for pouring a nation's blood and wealth into the jaws of Moloch. It was provided by the Russian Revolution in March, which placed a liberal provisional government in power. Wilson was now able to present the war as a clear-cut struggle between the democracy of the Allied nations and the autocracy of the Central Powers. We shall fight, he declared, "for the ultimate peace of the world" and to make the world "safe for democracy." In entering this crusade, the President asserted, the United

States disavowed any goals of domination or conquest or indemnity. Its objective was to promote democracy, champion
the right of people to govern themselves, and to defend the
interests of small nations everywhere.

The applause which rocked the hall was not quite unanimous. Opponents of intervention bitterly attacked the President for partiality toward England in his neutrality policy.
They regarded as untenable his distinction between property
rights and human rights. If the submarine took lives, so in its
own way did the British blockade. Thundered Senator Norris,
"We are going into the war upon the command of gold!"

Even many who supported the war declaration did not share
Wilson's idealistic aspirations. A portent of things to come was
Senator Borah's statement that there was "but one sufficient
reason for committing this country to war, and that is the
honor and security of our own people. . . . I join no crusade; I
seek no alliances; I obligate this Government to no other
power. I make war alone for my countrymen and their rights,
for my country and its honor." The irrepressible Theodore
Roosevelt asserted that America's decision for war was amply
justified by self-interest and national right without resorting to
embellishments.

The American people, however, were passionately caught up
in the Great Crusade. Ironically, Wilson's idealism was to be
responsible for the corrosive postwar disillusionment and the
bitter debate which would rage for years over the reasons for
entry into the conflict and whether the nation should have
gone in at all. Yet once the Germans embarked on unrestricted
submarine warfare, did the President have any alternative? To
submit at that point would have constituted a repudiation of
his own emphasis on freedom of the seas and defense of neutral
rights. From a practical standpoint, it would have had a devastating effect on the American economy. Moreover, the possibility of a German victory would have been enormously increased,
and neither Wilson nor, apparently, the American people were
willing to accept this as the price of peace. As Henry Cabot
Lodge said about a month before the fateful decision, the President did not want war, but "he is in the grip of events."

Wilson's prodigious efforts to preserve neutral rights were

doomed both because of America's position in the world economy and the nature of modern warfare. Once he was compelled to abandon traditional neutrality, whatever course the nation followed would inevitably abet one side at the expense of the other. Impaled upon the horns of a dilemma, the President concluded that his actions should be motivated by what was best for his country.

In the final analysis, then, it was German submarine warfare that provoked American intervention. The submarine was responsible for the death of American citizens, arousing violent passions which broke down the resistance of Americans toward entering the conflict. The assault was direct, immediate, and visible. Anything less tangible would not have produced the kind of response the people were asked to make for a distant nation separated by the barrier of a wide ocean.

Woodrow Wilson

7. *Liberator in Europe*

ONCE committed to intervention in the European conflict, President Wilson's painful dilemma was to reconcile winning the war with preparing the country for a peace without vengeance or aggrandizement. Before the era of the citizen army, when wars were fought by professional soldiers or paid hirelings, it was not necessary to induce hatred of the enemy; fighting was a job like any other, and men performed it well or ill according to their natures. But in modern times, at least in democratic states, the passions of the citizen-warrior must be aroused if he is to perform effectively. Wilson tried to resolve his quandary by constantly making a sharp distinction in his speeches between the Imperial German Government, led by militarists, and the helpless people compelled to do its bidding. But his efforts were as futile in 1917 as they were in 1914 when he asked for "neutrality in thought." Almost overnight the country vibrated with frenzied execrations of the Germans. To convince the American people, to say nothing of the Europeans, that only a peace without victory was worth fighting for would be a formidable task.

Nevertheless, Wilson was not pessimistic even after he learned about secret treaties among the Allies which distributed the spoils of the German Empire and provided for huge indemnities. England and France do not share America's views about the peace, he wrote House, but "when the war is over we can force them to our way of thinking because by that time they will, among other things, be financially in our hands." He spoke in a similar vein at a Cabinet meeting in the fall of 1917. The nation, he was confident, would emerge from the war so strong financially that by her power to extend or withhold credits she would be able to enforce her views on Europe.

Almost at once, Wilson began preparing for the peace in anticipation of the complicated territorial, economic, and other problems that were bound to arise. He wished to set forth in specific terms the aims for which America was committing her blood and treasure, to clarify for people everywhere the real nature of the struggle. At his request, Colonel House assembled a group of experts, later designated the "Inquiry," to whom he could turn for information and recommendations. With their assistance and House's collaboration, he drew up a statement which has since come to be known as the Fourteen Points.

The address was delivered to Congress on January 8, 1918, timed to take advantage of a temporary disruption in the Soviet-German peace talks. Negotiations by the Bolsheviks for an armistice with the Central Powers had begun at Brest-Litovsk in December, a month after they had seized power. Trotsky had submitted his terms to the Allies, inviting them to join the negotiations, but when no reply was forthcoming, he agreed to a cease-fire with the Germans to be followed by a peace treaty. The Bolsheviks' denuciation of the war as a capitalist-imperialist venture, their exposure of the secret treaties entered into by the Allies, and their appeal to the masses to rise up against their oppressors demanded a counterthrust.

Wilson hoped to remove the label of "imperialist" from the Allied nations, provide a response to the challenge of the Bolsheviks' social revolution, persuade Russia to return to the Allied cause, and arouse a world-wide demand for a lasting peace. He began with a discussion of the proceedings at Brest-Litovsk and praised the Soviet leaders for their insistence on open peace negotiations "in the true spirit of modern democracy." Then he enumerated the objectives for which the war was being waged. The first five principles were of universal interest: the end of secret diplomacy, freedom of the seas in war and peace, removal of international trade barriers, reduc-

tion of armaments, and an equitable adjustment of colonial
claims. The next eight dealt with territorial adjustments and
the achievement of self-determination. Foreign troops should
be withdrawn from Russian soil and the government welcomed
"into the society of free nations under institutions of her own
choosing;" Belgium and France evacuated and Alsace-Lorraine
returned to the latter; autonomy accorded to the diverse
peoples of Austria-Hungary; Italian frontiers adjusted along
nationality lines; the Balkan peoples given their freedom; an
independent Poland with free access to the sea established;
autonomous development for nationalities under Turkish rule
and free passage through the Dardanelles for ships of all nations insured. The fourteenth point called for "a general association of nations" to guarantee political independence and territorial integrity to all nations.

House declared that this "declaration of human liberty" was
the most important statement the President had ever made.
Liberal and labor groups hailed it as the harbinger of a new
era. Many Americans who were either lukewarm or opposed to
the President's policies praised it. Senator Henry Cabot Lodge,
however, cynically commented that the call for open covenants, freedom of the seas, disarmament, and an association of
nations exemplified the platitude that virtue was better than
vice. In official circles abroad reaction was mixed, each nation
responding in terms of its own interests. The British applauded
the speech but had strong misgivings about the demand for
freedom of the seas. The Italians saw in the call for self-
determination an attempt to deprive them of non-Italian territory in the Northern Adriatic that had been promised them
by the secret Treaty of London. The Russians were not impressed, and several months later they signed a separate peace
with Germany. In practical terms, the net result was slight, but
it did raise Allied morale at the front and established the President as a spokesman for a peace based on justice.

Wilson's war leadership confirmed Colonel House's observation that the President was "something of an autocrat by
nature." Impelled to have his hand on every string, he required
that all communications from the State, War, and Navy Departments and from his confidential advisers he delivered to him

unopened. The documents were read carefully and then sent to the appropriate personnel. He jealously guarded the executive prerogative against any attempted infringement by Congress. When one senator proposed a joint congressional committee to assist him in the war effort, Wilson stated that legislative interference in executive matters would produce much discussion but little efficiency. A resolution introduced by another senator to widen the scope of the Military Affairs Committee in order to permit supervision of the conduct of the war met with vehement disapprobation. If it passed, declared the President, he would regard it as a lack of confidence in his administration. It was "an attempt . . . to interfere in the most serious way with the action of the constituted executive. I protest most earnestly against the adoption of any such action."

Criticism of the war effort, or of any of his policies, Wilson considered a personal affront or as leading to disorder. To prevent "civil discord," he told Cecil Spring-Rice, was the President's task. Equating discord with dissent, he tacitly encouraged repression of any nonconformity, with a resulting loss to individuals and groups of constitutional liberties. Aided by George Creel and the Committee on Public Information, he swept the nation into an almost hysterical support of the national effort.

An unusually high degree of political unity characterized the early months after America's entry into the conflict. In time, however, Republican politicians attacked the administration for seeking partisan advantage from the war and began to demand a voice in policy making. They were supported by many newspapers which suggested that such distinguished Republicans as Theodore Roosevelt and Elihu Root replace Secretary of the Navy Josephus Daniels and Secretary of War Newton D. Baker, the two men most disliked by the opposition party. Although many notable Republicans were serving in administrative capacities, the President refused to consider a bipartisan coalition cabinet.

Party rivalry festered, and Wilson's handling of the armistice negotiations subjected him to acrimonious criticism. On October 3, 1918, with its army in retreat and facing certain disaster, the German government, under pressure from the military, appealed to Wilson to take measures to end hostilities on the basis of the Fourteen Points. Wilson replied, on October 8, that France and Belgium must first be evacuated, that stringent guarantees must be given that fighting would not be resumed, and that the Fourteen Points be accepted without qualification. He also insisted on dealing only with the civilian leaders. The Germans responded with a request for a mixed commission to arrange for evacuation of their troops. Wilson flatly rejected this, stating that evacuation must be left to the Allied command. In an exchange of notes with Prince Max of Baden, the German Chancellor, the President made it clear that he would agree to nothing less than submission to the absolute supremacy of the American and Allied armies. For days the Chancellor wavered, but finally, on October 20, he informed the President that his conditions would be accepted, that his government agreed to surrender on the basis of the peace outlined in the Fourteen Points.

Persuading the Allies to concur on armistice terms Wilson found even more difficult than prevailing upon the Germans. Allied leaders objected to the "freedom of the seas" clause of the Fourteen Points, and to others which they knew would conflict with the territorial provisos of their secret treaties. Clemenceau and Lloyd George were also reluctant to tie their hands by concluding an agreement with the enemy.

Discussions among the "friends" became so strained that Wilson cabled House, whom he had sent to Europe on his fourth wartime mission, "If it is the purpose of the Allied statesmen to nullify my influence force the purpose boldly to the surface and let me speak of it to all the world. . . . [The] League of Nations underlies freedom of the seas and every other part of peace programme so far as I am concerned." House informed the Allied leaders that unless they came to terms, the President would seriously consider concluding a separate peace. Accord was finally reached and on November 11, 1918, in a railway car in Compiègne Forest, the Armistice was signed.

Later, a myth gained currency among the Allies that Wilson had imposed a premature peace and thus deprived them of total victory. Actually, Wilson's diplomacy saved countless lives by making unnecessary a struggle to the bitter end. But perhaps, in the light of subsequent events, the world would have fared better had Germany been invaded and her armies vanquished. For a German myth also sprang up, which was to serve Hitler's iniquitous purposes, that the army had been stabbed in the back by civilians. The fact was that General Erich von Ludendorff urged the government to seek a armistice because, as he informed the Kaiser, "the situation is daily growing more acute" and delay would be disastrous. Although the army was not decisively beaten at that point, defeat was inevitable, and had the Germans not capitulated, they would have been pulverized.

In the weeks prior to the Armistice, Wilson had to contend with attacks from Congress and a segment of the American public. As he had predicted, many in the nation had become intolerant and vengeful. Partly this was his own fault for failing to check the extravagant "beast of Berlin" and "hang the Kaiser" propaganda with which Creel's organization had saturated the country. Congress once again attempted to challenge the Executive's conduct of foreign affairs by introducing a series of resolutions condemning negotiations with Germany and calling for unconditional surrender. Henry Cabot Lodge stated in the Senate that "the only thing now is to demand unconditional surrender. I would leave this to Marshal Foch and the General of the Armies." Theodore Roosevelt jumped into the fray with both feet, excoriating the President. He urged the Senate to repudiate the Fourteen Points and sent a public telegram to Republican leaders: "Let us dictate peace by the hammering guns and not chat about peace to the accompaniment of the clicking typewriters."

Wilson once told a newspaperman that the best way to deal with Roosevelt was to ignore him, but now his fulminations and the Republican onslaught rattled the President and led him to make a serious blunder. Convinced that "if it can be subtly enough managed" the opposition sought to "take the direction of the war out of the hands of the administration and place it where the Republicans can control it more directly," and pressured by Democratic leaders, he entered the contest in the bitterly disputed congressional elections. On October 25,

1918, the day after Roosevelt's telegram, he appealed to the voters to return a Democratic majority to Congress. "I have no thought of suggesting that any political party is paramount in matters of patriotism," he stated. However, in such perilous times it was "imperatively necessary that the Nation should give its undivided support to the Government under a unified leadership" and a Republican Congress would divide the leadership. Europe would interpret the capture of either Chamber by Republicans as "a repudiation" of his leadership; therefore, he pleaded, let voters unmistakably express their mandate "by returning a Democratic majority" to both Houses of Congress.

Wilson's appeal was not unprecedented and was one which as leader of the party he was entitled to make. Nevertheless, his strategy was inept. There were Republicans in Congress who had consistently supported him and there were Democrats who had as consistently opposed him. An appeal for the election of those who shared his views regardless of party would have been far wiser. To stake his prestige on the outcome of hundreds of contests that would in many instances be decided on purely local issues was singularly foolhardy.

The Republicans captured both Houses of Congress for reasons that, on the whole, had nothing to do with Wilson's leadership. People were resentful about high taxes and irritated over wartime controls, farmers were discontented with government price ceilings on their crops, and there was the usual opposition strength in mid-term elections. The President's tactic, however, provided his critics with ammunition to say, as Roosevelt did on November 26, that "our allies and our enemies and Mr. Wilson himself should all understand that Mr. Wilson has no authority whatever to speak for the American people at this time. His leadership has just been emphatically repudiated by them." Whether or not his leadership had in fact been repudiated, the failure of the appeal was to handicap his subsequent peacemaking.

In mid-November, Wilson startled the American public by the announcement that he would attend the peace conference in Paris. No President had ever traveled abroad or participated personally in peace negotiations. Wilson did not reach his decision impulsively. The pre-Armistice haggling, faithfully reported by Colonel House, convinced him that a face-to-face confrontation with his European counterparts was essential. "I want to tell Lloyd George certain things I can't write to him," he said. He balanced the need for his presence at home during the trying period of transition from war to peace against the danger that, without his presence in Paris, the Allies would impose the kind of peace that could only breed future wars. The preoccupation with vindictive reparations and selfish territorial adjustments must be counteracted. He would be the voice speaking for humanity.

Opinions on the President's decision were mixed. Robert Lansing, Bernard Baruch, and Herbert Hoover were among those who felt that he should not go abroad and so advised him. Colonel House had serious reservations, lacking confidence in Wilson's talents as a negotiator. Nevertheless, he refrained from expressing his doubt for fear of conveying the impression that he was pushing himself forward as head of the delegation. Deliberately ambiguous, he cabled from Paris, "My judgment is that you should . . . determine upon your arrival what share it is wise for you to take in the proceedings." Frank Cobb, who had been assisting House in Paris, probably expressed a widely held viewpoint when he suggested, in a memorandum to the Colonel, which was transmitted to the President, that the moment Wilson sat down at the council table he would lose all the power derived from distance and detachment. "Instead of remaining the great arbiter of human freedom he becomes merely a negotiator dealing with other negotiators;" by remaining in Washington, he would have the ear of the whole world and speak "from a place of commanding eminence." He must fight for peace and freedom on his home ground and "not upon the diplomatic soil of Europe . . . whose combatants are skilled in the ways of maneuver and intrigue."

Most members of the Cabinet, on the other hand, regarded Wilson's presence in Paris as not only desirable but absolutely essential. Secretary Lane felt that the very success of the conference depended on the President's heading the delegation. From Paris, General Tasker Bliss wrote to Secretary of War Baker, "I wish to God that the President could be here for a week. I hear in all quarters a longing for this. The people who want to get a rational solution out of this awful mess look to him alone. . . . In this dark storm of angry passion that has been let loose in all quarters I doubt if anyone but he can let in the light of reason."

Whether or not Wilson's role as a peacemaker would have been more effective had he remained at home and negotiated from a position of "commanding eminence" can never, of course, be determined. On balance, and from the perspective of hindsight, it does not seem likely. For one thing, facilities for communication had not yet advanced sufficiently to permit instantaneous contact—the telephone cable across the Atlantic was not yet laid—nor could planes cross the ocean, and without radio the President's voice could not be carried abroad. The overwhelming public acclaim he received when he arrived in Europe surely had a somewhat tempering effect on the other diplomats, and only his dogged persistence day in and day out thwarted a completely Carthaginian peace.

One unmistakable blunder was the composition of the American delegation. Wilson ignored the Senate completely, as well as any important member of the opposition party. He appointed Colonel House, Secretary of State Lansing, General Bliss, and, to almost everyone's astonishment, Henry White, a career diplomat and only nominally a Republican. In the past, White had served very ably in a number of European capitals—Roosevelt called him "the most accomplished diplomatist this nation has ever produced"—but he had been retired since 1909 and had no influence either in Congress or with his party. In view of Senator Lodge's chairmanship of the Foreign Relations Committee, his appointment would have been logical, but since a mutual antagonism between him and the President ruled that out, political wisdom should have suggested the desirability of other outstanding Republicans such as William Howard Taft, Elihu Root, or Charles Evans Hughes. To each of these men Wilson had some objection. He regarded Taft highly but thought his amiability would be a weakness at the bargaining table. Hughes he considered too inexperienced and Root too closely identified with dollar diplomacy, "a hopeless reactionary" who "would discourage every liberal element in the world."

An equally serious error was Wilson's failure to consult either formally or informally with members of the Senate, his indifference to the fact that they would want to share in the peacemaking. That the Republicans had their own views was indicated by the resolution introduced by Senator Knox on December 3, which would have prevented Wilson from carrying out his most cherished aim if it had passed. It declared that since the nation entered the war in defense of maritime rights and to destroy the German menace, the peace settlement should be confined to those purposes, and the creation of an international organization should be left to a future conference of all states, belligerent and neutral.

Early in December, President Wilson, members of his delegation, and several hundred technical advisers and assistants embarked for Europe on the *George Washington*. During the voyage, Wilson assembled the group in his cabin to present his views and outline his proposals for the peace conference. He hoped, he said, that by maintaining a standard of justice, America would win the world's esteem and thereby be accepted as an umpire. "The men whom we are about to deal with, do not represent their own people." This naïve observation was first of all factually incorrect. At that moment the election campaign in England gave every indication that Lloyd George would receive, as indeed he did, an overwhelming popular mandate. Clemenceau also had great popular support as the four-to-one vote of confidence he received in the French Chamber a few days later revealed. Secondly, by implying that the desires of the people were different from those of their rulers, Wilson overlooked the primitive urge for vengeance which he himself had said war arouses. And, finally, he ignored his own recent devastating experience when his appeal to the people for the return of a Democratic Congress was decisively repudiated.

Wilson's faith in his power as spokesman for the people was reinforced by the delirious reception given him during his four-week tour of France, Italy, and England on his arrival in Europe. In Paris, the ride from the quay to his residence would have turned any man's head. The route was a solid mass of people waving flags, cheering wildly, weeping for joy. "Le grand Américain," the press called him, allotting more space to him than it had ever accorded to kings; "le pur champion du droit et de la justice, le Christophe Colomb d'un nouveau monde." Similar accolades were repeated wherever he went. Ray Stannard Baker, press secretary for the American delegation, recalled an incident which illustrates the tremendous confidence the people of Europe placed in his leadership. One morning he found in his office two Polish peasants, accompanied by a French-speaking priest, who came from a tiny mountain settlement in northern Austria slated for incorporation into the new nation of Czechoslovakia. They had heard that the American President who was in Paris had said that people should have the right to determine how and by whom they were to be governed. Desiring to be part of Poland, they had walked hundreds of miles to Paris to appeal to the President to set things straight.

The Europe that Wilson confidently hoped to resuscitate was in an agony of upheaval. Germany was torn by revolution. The once mighty Austro-Hungarian empire was disintegrating. In Russia a bloody civil war raged in the wake of the Bolshevik Revolution. Independent countries were emerging out of the wreckage of empires. The "stable" countries, the victors in the great slaughter, were polishing their axes. Englishmen were clamoring for vengeace and "blood"; the French were demanding retribution and iron-clad security; the Italians, territorial aggrandizement at the expense of Austria in compensation for losses suffered. People everywhere wanted help of some kind—the Koreans, the Armenians, the Albanians, the Swedes.

Against this background of turmoil and clamor, the statesmen assembled at Paris early in January, 1919. The guns of battle had been silenced; now the clash of conflicting purposes would resound in the conference hall. Only the idealist from the new world was intent on a just peace and the creation of a system of collective security. The victorious Europeans came to redraw the map of Europe, insure their security, and extract as much compensation as possible from the defeated enemy.

Little effort had been made by the Allies during the war to achieve political coordination, and leaders on both sides of the Atlantic frequently thought at cross-purposes. As late as September, 1918, House had cabled Wilson suggesting that the vital assistance being provided to the Allies be used as leverage to compel acceptance of the American position.

Not only issues but personalities contributed to the wide divergence. One young career diplomat, Joseph Grew, foresaw the difficulties Wilson would have with Allied leaders: "Lloyd George, Clemenceau and Orlando do not like the President. They are frankly jealous of the President's role . . . can the President force the Allies to permit him to control the kind of peace that is to be made? The Allies individually and collectively are making strenuous efforts to take the leadership away from the President." If they were jealous then, Wilson's triumphal tour of Europe could only have intensified the emotion. Lloyd George later recalled that Clemenceau followed the movements of the President like an old watchdog "keeping an eye on a strange and unwelcome dog who has visited the farmyard and of whose intentions he is more than doubtful." His own sentiments toward Wilson were inclined to be arctic. Acidly he remarked that Wilson was like a missionary as he lectured his fellow statesmen on right being more important than might, and justice more eternal than force. "He was," he observed, "the most extraordinary compound I have ever encountered of the noble visionary, the implacable and unscrupulous partisan, the exalted idealist and the man of rather petty personal rancours."

Moreover, the reactions of both men were fortified by the relentless opposition to Wilson of powerful congressmen. Several days before the President arrived in Paris, Senator Henry Cabot Lodge, chairman of the Foreign Relations Committee, demanded on the floor of Congress that heavy indemnities be imposed on Germany and the country be reduced to impotence. Gratuitously he advised the Allies that they need pay no attention to Wilson's theories about boundaries, for such matters were not his proper concern. And most important, all plans for a League of Nations should be postponed until after a German peace settlement had been reached. "Every day the

Republicans tell Lloyd George, Orlando, and Clemenceau that I do not and cannot speak for America," Wilson bitterly confided to Creel, "and that my one function is to act as their rubber stamp."

Lloyd George, secure in his popular mandate, took full advantage of the situation. At a secret meeting he informed the British delegation that the President was politically infirm at home and that his pledges might not be honored. "His occasional threats to appeal to American public opinion, when he did not get his way at the Conference, conveyed no real menace. There was no assurance that his country would support him in a break with the Allies on any issue."

The President also had to contend with his own staff. A number of Americans, openly sympathizing with the victims of German aggression, frequently made Wilson's advocacy of a "just" peace appear ignominious. At one point Clemenceau accused the President of pro-German leanings on an issue in which the latter was opposed by his own experts. Secretary Lansing disagreed with the President on fundamental questions. Hostile to the entire concept of a League of Nations as contrary to the American isolationist tradition, he tried to block Wilson before discussions on the organization began. At a meeting with the American members of the commission assigned to draft a League covenant, the Secretary pressed for a resolution that would restore peace immediately, proclaim the general purpose of the League, and leave the details of the covenant for later consideration. Although this idea was categorically rejected by Wilson, Lansing the next day went over his superior's head to repeat his proposal at a session of the Council of Ten, leaders of the major powers, where the President could not oppose him without exhibiting to the world that the American delegation was divided.

Since he could not depend on his Secretary of State, the President virtually ignored him and turned to Colonel House. Yet even his devoted friend did not fully support his views. House's fervent desire to promote the establishment of a League made him willing to sacrifice almost any of the other parts of the President's program. To enlist the support of the other powers, he was prepared to acquiesce in their claims for territories and indemnities. His eagerness to be conciliatory led Henry White to comment that House had become the unwitting ally of European nations, and Wilson, time after time, found himself resisting the concessions that the Colonel kept urging on him.

Before the conference was over, the unique friendship between the two men was badly strained. Upon his return to Paris from a brief visit home to attend to domestic matters, Wilson found articles in the press lavishly praising the Colonel's activities at the conference and intimating that progress had been made because he had not been hampered by the presence of the President. Mrs. Wilson, who had always distrusted the Colonel, suspected that the newspaper stories were inspired by House's own staff and so informed her husband. At first the President firmly defended his friend, but he had been infected with doubt. House seemed unusually friendly to Clemenceau . . . he was fond of stage managing . . . the concessions he advocated to the Allies. . . . According to Mrs. Wilson, when the President learned of certain arrangements made during his absence, he was furious, storming that House had given away everything he had won before he left Paris. "He has compromised on every side, and so I have to start all over again and this time it will be harder, as he has given the impression that my delegates are not in sympathy with me." The following year, when Wilson was battling with the Senate for acceptance of the League of Nations, his daughter Margaret tried to patch up the rift, but the President could not accept House's explanation that he had acted out of concern for the League and for his friend's political future.

Undercurrents of discord, personal pique, petty incidents charged the atmosphere at Paris. For example, the French wanted Wilson to tour the devastated regions, hoping that he would "see red" and thus be more amenable to imposing heavy reparations on Germany. He refused at first, because of reports that rehabilitation of devastated areas had been deliberately postponed to impress him, but was finally impelled to yield after Lloyd George informed the conference that *he* had been to the battlefields near Château-Thierry. Wilson insisted, however, that if all France were a shell hole, he would not change his approach to the peace settlement.

The first of the Fourteen Points, "open covenants openly arrived at," occasioned a sharp attack upon the President. Expecting that complete details on what transpired in the council chamber would be made available, American reporters were indignant when the official four-line report of the session was released on the opening day. They presented a formal protest to the President. From Washington, Joseph Tumulty, Wilson's secretary, cabled frantically that Wilson should leave the conference if necessary rather than be a party to secrecy. Explanations to the journalists about the danger of releasing information before any final decisions had been taken made no impression on men normally suspicious of diplomats. Moreover, his public relations were impaired, for he alone among the leaders refused to meet with the press after one newsman had betrayed a confidence. He also kept silent about his strenuous efforts to obtain a freer dissemination of news.

With few details available, rumors began to fly and "leaks" became commonplace. The situation provided fuel for the President's political opponents at home, who charged that something sinister would be foisted on the American people. Members of the Senate kept complaining throughout the proceedings that they were being kept in the dark.

In the conference rooms, the bickering went on interminably. The European statesmen pawed around in the pot with greedy fingers, determined to pull out the best plums for their countries. Wilson's staff complained that "the French are talking us to death." The President himself sometimes despaired of pinning Clemenceau down. After a long disputation the wily Frenchman would seemingly concede an important point, only to reverse himself the next time the subject was reopened.

At the end of March the deliberations bogged down. On April 3, the American experts who came to report to Wilson that the Allies "were acting like the Devil," found him ill in bed. He appeared to be suffering from a severe cold, but the present-day medical view is that he had a vascular occlusion. Discouraged and debilitated, Wilson indicated his intention to return home and requested that the *George Washington* be made available. Tumulty hastily cabled that everyone would regard his leaving as petulant behavior and Americans would call it desertion.

The President remained, and the haggling continued. Wilson worked harder than any major figure at the conference. Even Lloyd George wondered how he survived from day to day. His schedule was grueling. As one of his biographers records:

After an eight o'clock breakfast, he did in two hours what in normal times might be thought a day's work at his desk. Then a conference or two before the morning meeting of the inner council; guests at lunch and sometimes at dinner; sessions all afternoon— sometimes two at once in adjoining rooms, with the President going back and forth and carrying in his mind the threads of argument. In the evening a daily talk with Baker, then dinner—for which he no longer took time to dress—and afterwards another conference or study of maps and reports to prepare for the business of the morrow.

After almost four months of bitter wrangling which left Wilson physically and emotionally drained, the treaty was finished. The clacking of the tongues ceased, but the end was not yet. On May 7, the document was presented to the Germans. For almost two months they refused to sign the "dictat" but at last yielded to the inevitable, and on the afternoon of June 28, in the Hall of Mirrors at Versailles, the signatures were affixed. For a pitifully brief period the President basked in the warmth of approval. When the three top-hatted statesmen came out of the Hall, crowds burst through the cordons of troops, shouting "Vive Clemenceau!" "Vive Wilson!" "Vive Lloyd George!" At the station to say farewell, Clemenceau clasped Wilson's hands and with Gaelic emotion told him, "I feel as though I were losing one of the best friends I ever had." The train moved out . . . and murmurings about Wilson as a "betrayer," begun some weeks before, shortly rose to a crescendo.

The disillusionment of liberals on both sides of the Atlantic with the Treaty of Versailles was acute. John Maynard Keynes, technical adviser to the British delegation, resigned and poured out his disgust with the treaty in *The Economic Conse-*

quences of the Peace, which became a best seller in Europe and America. It was Clemenceau, he asserted, who had triumphed at Paris. Wilson, that "blind and deaf Don Quixote" uttering pious platitudes, had been duped by the crafty European statesmen. Keynes was acrimonious about what he regarded as Wilson's surrender of the principles embodied in the Fourteen Points, attributing his dereliction to the fact that the President was bemused by the League of Nations as a panacea for all international problems.

William C. Bullitt, later to become first ambassador to the Soviet Union, and two other young men on the American staff, resigned in protest. George Herron, an American professor who performed valuable liaison work for Wilson in an unofficial capacity, reflected the dismay. With American intervention and Wilson's leadership, he wrote, he had been persuaded that this would be the last war, that "the nations of the world would become one fold and one family." All the pledges had been violated by the Peace Commission. "The peoples of the world were duped."

Wilson himself was largely responsible for the disenchantment. The leader of a nation must have confidence in his capacity to influence events, but he must also be conscious of the limits of his power in a given situation. Wilson had underestimated the operating force of power politics and overestimated his ability to change the world. Failing to recognize that insuperable difficulties might block him from achieving his objectives, he proclaimed them with a certainty that raised false hopes. His lofty moral tone encouraged a widespread belief that Germany's defeat would be followed by a new universal order bringing peace to mankind. People everywhere came to see him as a modern St. George, and he suffered the fate of all heroes when their worshipers discover that they are mortal, that magic swords exist only in myths.

Still he might have forestalled some of the attacks had he expressed himself honestly about the treaty. Battle-scarred and weary after it was concluded, his first reaction had been, "If I were a German, I think I should never sign it." Later, he told his delegation that "though we did not keep [the British and French] from putting irrational things in the treaty, we got very serious modifications out of them. If we had written the treaty the way they wanted it, the Germans would have gone home the minute they read it. Well, the Lord be with us." Instead of making a similar judicious statement to the American public, he cabled that if the treaty were ratified, it would "furnish the charter for a new order of affairs in the world. . . . There is ground here for a deep satisfaction, universal reassurance and confident hope."

The Versailles Treaty was largely the creation of Clemenceau and Lloyd George, whose political realism persuaded them that if they were too yielding, if they failed to bring back the spoils, their leadership would be repudiated. But it also bore the marks of Wilson's influence. The decision to incorporate the League into the treaty, and the agreement to assign mandate status to the former German colonies rather than transfer possession to the victors, were examples of the President's achievements at Paris. Compromise made the treaty possible. The end result was a combination of good and bad.

Wilson's great hope for a "peace without victory" was lost in the clamor for revenge not only of the Europeans but of many Americans. "If Germany can be made safe only by hunger and torment and relative poverty," thundered the *Philadelphia Evening Ledger,* "then it is better for the rest of the world that she be made to endure hunger and torment and poverty." Wilson could not prevent having Germany stamped with guilt for the war and saddled with the entire cost of the conflict.

The boundary decisions were appallingly involved. Austria-Hungary had fallen apart before the conference opened and *de facto* national governments were ruling the pieces. Poland and Rumania could not have been dislodged from the areas they had seized except by force. The Central European populations were a hopeless mixture, making self-determination along strictly ethnic lines an impossibility. Any kind of settlement inevitably would have created a minorities problem, and the various treaties with all their faults were the closest approximation to an ethnographic arrangement that had ever been achieved.

One of Wilson's gravest failures, and the one which was to

have the most serious consequences in the years to come, was
with respect to Russia. He not only acquiesced in excluding the
Bolsheviks from the conference, despite the sixth of his Fourteen Points, but ordered American participation in the invasion
of Russia. At first he tried to exert a moderating influence upon
the European leaders. When Winston Churchill on February
14, 1919, asked the Supreme Council to send troops and
munitions in support of the White Russians, Wilson urged that
all foreign troops be withdrawn from the strife-torn country.
He demonstrated good intentions by sending William Bullitt
shortly thereafter on an unofficial mission to Moscow. Bullitt
returned to Paris on March 17, convinced that the Communists
wanted peace. He brought back a plan by Lenin, who he felt
was in firm control, for an immediate armistice and amnesty on
all sides. The Bolshevik proposals were never given serious
consideration. Wilson joined the Allies in sending material aid
to Admiral Kolchak, then fighting west of the Urals and hoping
to advance upon Moscow.

On the vexing Shantung issue, Wilson was able only to scale
down somewhat the Japanese demands. His sypathies were
with the Chinese, but Japan's threat to boycott the League
forced him to recognize her economic suzerainty over the
area. In any case, it was highly doubtful that Japan could have
been eliminated either politically or economically from China,
especially since none of the nations were prepared to go to war
solely to keep her out of Shantung.

As Wilson reluctantly made one concession after another, he
clung to the belief that whatever the deficiencies of the peace
settlement, whatever the injustices, these could all be corrected
by the "collective conscience" of mankind operating through
the League of Nations. The world organization was his last
great hope for a lasting peace.

Woodrow Wilson

8. Triumph and Tragedy

THE concept of an international organization to prevent war was not original with Woodrow Wilson, but his driving force was to be instrumental in creating and shaping such a body. Almost as soon as the shrapnel exploded over Europe in the summer of 1914, he began to reflect about a world body. An association of nations must be created, he told his brother-in-law, which would have the means to exert force against any power that attempted to violate the peace.

A group of Americans with a similar idea organized the League to Enforce Peace in 1915, headed by William Howard Taft. Its purpose was to urge the establishment of a world body that would use military or economic measures against any nation which went to war instead of submitting its grievances for adjudication. On May 27, 1916, the President and Senator Henry Cabot Lodge were invited to address the league at a banquet at which both eloquently endorsed its aim. Unhappily, as it turned out, Lodge's enthusiasm was to be short lived.

Wilson's speech, which marked the beginning of his public advocacy of an international organization, represented a revolutionary innovation in American foreign policy. As House commented, it was "the turning point in our international relations and in our old-time non-interference policy." For the first time a President openly subscribed to the principle of collective security. Peace can be maintained, he said, only if the

nations of the world pledge to submit their disputes to an international body.

Three days later, at a Memorial Day address, Wilson amplified his ideas. "I shall never myself consent to an entangling
alliance," he stated, "but I would gladly assent to a disentan-
gling alliance . . . which would disentangle the peoples of the
world from those combinations in which they seek their own
separate and private interests and unite the people of the world
to preserve the peace of the world upon a basis of common
right and justice."

Encouraged by a favorable reception to his talks, Wilson had
the Democratic Party insert a statement into the platform of
1916 that it was the duty of the United States to enter any
reasonable association which would protect small nations,
promote self-determination, and uphold neutral rights. In his
"peace without victory" address to Congress in January, 1917,
he emphasized that a new community of power must replace
the old balance of power, and he repeated an earlier assertion
that where a concert of nations exist there can be no entangling
alliances.

In the months that followed, Wilson speculated about the
structure of a world organization but decided not to present
any specific plan. As he wrote to J. St. Loe Strachey of the
London Spectator in the spring of 1918, "I have thought only
of a mutual guarantee of political independence and territorial
integrity; and also, as you suggest, of the binding and sacred
force of treaty agreements." Domestically it would be politically imprudent, he told House, to fix the precise authority or
be too specific in defining the jurisdiction of a body such as a
league, and abroad, a premature elaboration of details might
arouse needless friction among the European powers. Any
planning during the war was unwise, he felt, as divergent
approaches could split the Allies.

To clarify their own ideas, Wilson and House in the summer
of 1918 prepared a number of drafts for a league covenant.
House questioned the advisability of a universal organization
in which small nations would enjoy equal status with the large
powers. Though too poor and weak to make the financial and
military contributions that might be required for the punish-

ment of aggression, the former would collectively constitute a numerical majority and be able to dominate the policies of the organization. Wilson countered that restricting membership would violate universality, the cardinal principle on which the proposed league ought to be based. Perhaps at the beginning the organization might be limited to the participating nations at the peace conference and, in due course, others admitted.

To lay the groundwork for acceptance of a world body, Wilson during the war continually made references in vague terms to the general idea. In September, 1918, he delivered a major address to an assemblage at the Metropolitan Opera House in New York. Declaring that a league covenant should be made part of the peace treaty, he emphasized that it must be the most essential part and not postponed until after the peace conference. The United States, he said, would not enter into any special arrangements with particular nations but was "prepared to assume its full share of responsibility for the maintenance of the common covenants and understandings upon which peace must henceforth rest."

At the end of the conflict, Wilson had to translate a nebulous idea into a concrete reality. As chairman of the Commission on the League of Nations at the Paris conference, he was chiefly responsible for drafting the covenant. He worked tirelessly and doggedly to have the League accepted as an integral part of the peace treaty. On this, as on so many other issues, he had to combat the formidable resistance of Clemenceau. The Tiger of France was not opposed to a league, but he was insistent that it be so constructed as to protect his nation's security. To him this meant an organization possessing a strong general staff at the head of an effective police force, with power to recruit and train men and inspect the military establishments of the member nations. To Wilson, Clemenceau's concept was untenable, for it would substitute international for national militarism. Not only did the United States Constitution forbid international control of American armed forces, but opponents of a league in the Senate were already voicing apprehension that the nation's troops might be required to fight in remote places. In Wilson's judgment, the aroused conscience of mankind would provide the League with its greatest source of strength.

Wilson prevailed, but, with the French still insistent on having their need for security satisfied, he joined Lloyd George in pledging armed assistance to France in the event of unprovoked aggression by Germany. Only his desperate eagerness to win acceptance of the League could have led him to ignore that sacred cow in the nation's tradition, the principle of no entangling alliances. The proposed security pact was never even considered by the Senate.

After six weeks of deliberation and debate, agreement upon a covenant was finally reached, and on February 14, 1919, Wilson stood before a plenary session of the conference to deliver his report. It was a day of superlative triumph, for the age-old dream that the world might be rid forever of the curse of war now appeared possible of fulfillment. His voice charged with emotion, Wilson declared, "A living thing is born, and we must see to it that the clothes we put upon it do not hamper it. . . . I think I can say of this document that it is at one and the same time a practical and humane document. There is a pulse of sympathy in it. There is a compulsion of conscience throughout it. It is practical, and yet it is intended to purify, to rectify, to elevate."

The President was exultant, but he had little doubt that the real fight for the League was yet to begin. He did not expect that senators opposed to involving America in a world organization would readily approve a treaty of which the League Covenant was an integral part. To Wilson, "advise and consent" meant that the Senate's role in the treaty-making process began only *after* negotiations had been completed. Constitutionally he was correct, with ample precedent to support his view, but considering the extraordinary issue involved and the known views of the opposition, political wisdom would have dictated continuous consultation with Senate leaders while the treaty was being formulated. Wilson's studied indifference to the Senate, his failure to conduct a vigorous educational campaign on behalf of the League, is all the more remarkable in view of the many ominous signs of dissension prior to the Peace Conference.

On the day the American peace delegation embarked for Europe, Senator Lodge handed Henry White a detailed memo-

randum which stated that "under no circumstances" should the
League be made part of a peace treaty, for "Any attempt to do
this would not only long delay the signature of the treaty of
peace . . . but it would make the adoption of the treaty, un-
amended, by the Senate of the United States and other ratify-
ing bodies, extremely doubtful." He asked White to show the
note in confidence to Clemenceau, Balfour, and Nitti, all of
whom he knew personally, so that they could be informed of
"what I believe to be the real feeling of the United States and
certainly the Senate of the United States. This knowledge may
in certain contingencies be very important to them in strengthening their position." White, however, never showed the memorandum to any of the Allied leaders.

Six weeks before the conference opened, Lodge announced
on the floor of the Senate that the Allies must know that "the
Senate can and often has rejected treaties. Others the Senate
has refused to ratify and held without action. Many others
have been vitally amended." His address was the opening salvo
in a battle between the Senate and the President—more especially, between the senator from Massachusetts and the President—that was to reverberate throughout the world. His
antagonism to Wilson, which was both personal and political,
went back to the time when, following the sinking of the *Lusitania,* Wilson, resisting pressure for militant action, declared
that a nation might be "too proud to fight." "That phrase . . .
destroyed my confidence in him," Lodge wrote, "because he
had shown himself destitute of the strength, patriotism, courage and unselfishness which were so sorely needed at that precise moment in any man who was called upon to stand at the
head of the American nation."

A substantial number of other Republicans in the Senate
disliked the President with varying degrees of intensity and for
a variety of reasons. After sixteen years of unbroken Republican domination, they could not become accustomed to a
Democrat in the White House. Wilson's re-election (by the
narrowest of margins) embittered them further. Not since
Andrew Jackson had a Democrat been returned to office for a
second, consecutive term. They were incensed by the manner
in which he drove Congress and were outraged by the labor,

tariff, income tax, and reform measures he succeeded in pushing through.

Even if the world organization had not become identified as "Mr. Wilson's League," it would have generated opposition. While many Republicans were not isolationists and did not object to foreign involvements if they augmented the nation's strategic requirements or enlarged its political and economic influence, membership in the League was another matter. They believed it would not only necessitate involvement in world affairs without promoting American power, but could even be responsible for weakening the nation, since its resources might be enlisted to support causes that Wilson's idealism favored. Moreover, they were convinced that the League would restrict America's freedom of action, embroil her in European quarrels, and impair sovereign authority over such matters as immigration policies, the tariff, the Monroe Doctrine, and the disposition of troops. Wilson was to destroy himself in attempting to overcome this formidable opposition.

In the meantime, the President sailed for home to attend to urgent domestic matters. The day after his ship docked, on February 24, 1919, he addressed an audience of eight thousand at Mechanic's Hall in Boston. With characteristic self-confidence and complete lack of political discretion, he condemned the "narrow, selfish, provincial purposes" of those who opposed the League, warning, "I have fighting blood in me and it is sometimes a delight to let it have scope, but if it is challenged on this occasion it will be an indulgence." Only the united forces of the civilized world could guarantee the maintenance of peace, he declared. "Any man who thinks that America will take part in giving the word any such rebuff and disappointment as that does not know America. I invite him to test the sentiments of the Nation."

The gauntlet having openly been flung down before the world, the opposition could do no less than pick it up. Moreover, Wilson, by discussing the Covenant in public before he presented it to the Senate, enraged Lodge and other Republicans, particularly since they had honored his request to refrain from public debate until he had spoken to them. A week later, circulation of a round robin by Lodge netted signatures of thirty-seven senators and two senators-elect, who went on record in opposition to "the constitution of the League of Nations in the form now proposed" and called for the conclusion of the peace treaty as the first order of business. Released to the press, the resolution indicated that the forces opposed to Wilson could muster that magic one-third plus one necessary for defeating a treaty.

Wilson's reply that same day in New York was resolute and defiant. In a speech at the Metropolitan Opera House, he declared that when the treaty came back, "gentlemen on this side will find not only the Covenant in it, but so many threads of the treaty tied to the Covenant that you cannot dissect the Covenant from the treaty" without destroying the entire edifice. "The structure of peace will not be vital without the League of Nations, and no man is going to bring back a cadaver with him."

But the President did take into account some of the major criticisms that were leveled at the League, for when he returned to Paris he arranged to have the Covenant amended along lines suggested by Taft, Hughes, Root, and some Democrats. He obtained the consent of the European leaders to a number of changes which he hoped would disarm the opposition: domestic questions such as tariff and immigration were exempt from League jurisdiction, the Monroe Doctrine was given special status which placed it outside of League authority, and member nations were given the right to withdraw from the League on two years' notice. Lodge, who had been asked by Henry White to submit proposals of his own, replied tersely that the proper procedure was for Wilson to ask the Senate formally for its advice. He had already carefully begun to lay his plans.

The Republicans were split into three groups: at one extreme were the "irreconcilables" or "bitter-enders," headed by William E. Borah of Idaho and Hiram Johnson of California, who were opposed to League membership under any conditions; at the other extreme were those favoring the organization, but with mild reservations; and in the center were those with strong reservations that would substantially reduce American commitments. To maintain maximum effectiveness, the

Republican majority in the Senate had to unite these divergent factions and prevent Wilson from pulling into his camp the mild reservationists whose support he needed for approval. The President had strong backing within his own party. Only four of the forty-seven Democrats opposed the treaty, but this was still far short of the required two-thirds majority.

When Wilson appeared before the Senate on July 10, 1919, to urge treaty acceptance, the League had wide public support, and with enough mild reservationists responding to this sentiment a prompt vote might have been favorable. Lodge, an astute politician, knew that this enthusiasm would inevitably evaporate as the shock of the conflict wore off, patriotic sentiment faded, and the prejudices of various interest groups throughout the country were revived. The most advantageous strategy, therefore, was to delay and procrastinate, which could be effected in numerous ways. He read the 264-page treaty word by word to the members of the Senate Committee. It took a fortnight. Then, on July 31, public hearing began which stretched over a six-week period. The Committee on Foreign Relations listened to Americans of Persian, Egyptian, Hindu, Chinese, Irish, and Italian extraction, to any group that might have a grievance against the Paris peacemakers. When the President was asked whether he would testify, he gladly consented. The interrogation at the White House centered on the controversial Article X which obliged each nation to respect the territorial integrity and political independence of every other; but in general Wilson was subjected, according to the New York *Tribune,* to "probably the most searching inquiry ever directed, for a public record, at any President of the United States or any other head of a great power." Wishing to embarrass the President, Senator William E. Borah asked him when he had learned about the Allies' wartime secret treaties (which were clearly inconsistent with the principles of the Fourteen Points). Wilson disavowed having had any knowledge of them at the time he left for the Peace Conference. The reply amazed his interrogators, who were not aware that Wilson's memory was often faulty. It also appeared incredible to the American public, since the treaties had been exposed by the Bolsheviks and published in the newspapers.

For several weeks, Wilson met almost daily with Republicans who were more or less friendly to the League. Nearly all made it clear that they favored some kind of reservation. They assured him that if he accepted reservations the treaty would be ratified promptly, but if he remained obdurate, the Senate would obtain them anyway after what would probably be a long and bitter fight. Wilson refused to yield, insisting that to attach reservations would require reconsideration of the treaty, with all the complications involved in renewing acceptance by each of the signatory governments, including Germany. He would consent only to reservations of an interpretative nature, provided they were not embodied in the treaty.

At the beginning, the President believed that he could persuade the Senate to abandon its demands because public opinion strongly favored the League. But as the hearings dragged on and the opposition kept monopolizing the headlines with distortions impossible to combat, he was aware that the tide of sympathy was ebbing. One last recourse remained—a direct appeal to the people. If they had the facts, he was confident they would rally to his standard. He would set out on a month-long speaking tour of the western states. Joseph Tumulty and his physician, Dr. Cary Grayson, as well as Cabinet members and friends, were appalled. The strain would be intolerable on a man who suffered from daily attacks of indigestion, headaches, and a neuritis in his shoulders. They pleaded with him not to go, Grayson warning that no doctor could be responsible for the outcome. Wilson was adamant. "I promised the soldiers that it was a war to end wars," he said. "If the treaty is not ratified by the Senate, the war will have been fought in vain and the world will be thrown into chaos."

The President left Washington on September 3, 1919. Within the next twenty-two days he traveled 8,000 miles, delivering thirty-four addresses, granting innumerable interviews, participating in scores of parades, and making dozens of rear-platform talks. Anger at his opponents led Wilson at times to become injudicious and intemperate. He compared them to the Bolsheviks or characterized them as "absolutely ignorant," or "absolute, contemptible quitters." These verbal blasts could only solidify their hostility, but the huge crowds which turned out everywhere to hear him cheered his impassioned oratory.

Indefatigably Wilson pleaded that America's participation in the League was vital not only for Europe but for herself. Peace had become indivisible, and aggression could not be curbed unless every great power supported the organization. Recent experience had shown that the country could not avoid being dragged into a major conflict. As to Article X, against which critics were fulminating, it would, contrary to their statements, greatly reduce disputes among nations and thereby help prevent wars. Congress would not be shorn of its authority. The United States would remain free to defend itself if necessary. And in disputes to which the nation was not a party, it could exercise a veto in the council. Above all, he warned, "I can predict with absolute certainty that within another generation there will be another world war if the nations of the world do not concert the method by which to prevent it." In such a struggle, "not a few hundred thousand fine men from America will have to die, but as may millions as are necessary to accomplish the final freedom of the world."

It was Wilson's last appeal; at Pueblo, Colorado, on September 19, after days of racking pain, the President's dwindling physical reserves, which he had used to the limits of endurance, gave out. He could not continue his tour and, in complete despondency, returned to Washington. Four days later he suffered a thrombosis which left him a semi-paralyzed invalid.

Until his partial recovery several months later, Mrs. Wilson served as "regent," a buffer between the President and his public duties. She and Dr. Grayson determined what business should be brought to his attention. "Woodrow Wilson was first my beloved husband whose life I was trying to save, fighting with my back to the wall," she later wrote. "After that he was the President of the United States." Diligent and efficient, she transmitted to the President résumés of important matters that required his attention. "I studied every paper sent from the different Secretaries or Senators," she recalled. "I tried to digest and present in tabloid form the things that despite my vigilance had to go to the President. I, myself, never made a single decision regarding the disposition of public affairs. The only decision that was mine was what was important and what was not." But the "only decision" was the most vital one. Frequently the President was left uninformed or misinformed on matters of public policy. Papers submitted to the President were usually returned with notations written by Mrs. Wilson. Many responsibilities of the chief executive, which only he is constitutionally authorized to discharge, were abdicated by default. Twenty-eight bills, for example, became law without presidential action during this period.

The doctors advised against suggesting that Wilson resign, fearing the effect it might have on the invalid. For weeks the President was kept isolated, and not even Cabinet members or others in key administrative posts were informed as to the nature of his disability. "No one is satisfied that we know the truth," wrote Secretary Lane to his brother, "and every dinner table is filled with speculation. Some say paralysis, and some say insanity. Grayson tells me it is nervous breakdown, whatever that means." Meanwhile, he continued, the Cabinet was running things.

Secretary Lansing called the Cabinet meetings, for which Wilson never forgave him, regarding it as an unwarranted usurpation of power. Yet Lansing, who was denied access to the President, actually served him well. The publicity given to these meetings probably forestalled congressional inquiries as to whether the President was able to discharge his duties, or as to the whole question of his disability and continued tenure.

To what extent Wilson's illness affected the outcome of the League battle can never, of course, be determined, but from September 26 until the Senate acted for the second and last time the following March, his party supporters in the legislature were deprived of his leadership. In a major address to the Senate in September, Lodge objected to the League Covenant mainly because it would endanger the sovereignty and independence of the nation. "I think now, as I always have thought and believed," he declared, "that the United States is the best hope of mankind and will remain so as long as we do not destroy it by mingling in every broil and quarrel that may desolate the earth." Under his direction, the Foreign Relations Committee drew up no less than forty-five amendments and four reservations to the treaty. The amendments were de-

feated, but the four reservations were expanded to fourteen, all
of which were unacceptable to Wilson. One, providing that the
United States could withdraw from the League simply by
concurrent resolution of Congress, would deprive him, the
President felt, of a voice in the decision, consequently undermining his authority in foreign affairs. Two others would grant
the United States the option of deciding whether or not an
issue was domestic and whether or not it came within the pur-
view of the Monroe Doctrine, which in both cases would
exempt it from League jurisdiction. Still others permitted the
nation to increase armaments, regardless of any limitations
agreement, and to withdraw consent to the Shantung settlement in the Versailles Treaty.

Of all the reservations, the one against which the President
was most adamant dealt with Article X. It stated that the
United States would assume no obligation to preserve the territorial integrity or political independence of any other country
or employ its armed forces for such an objective unless authorized by Congress. Wilson felt strongly that if the League
Council recommended action against an aggressor, member
states were morally obliged to go to the aid of the victim.

Before he had left on his western tour, the President gave his
Senate leader, Gilbert Hitchcock, a list of four reservations
that he would accept if absolutely necessary. The most important of these dealt with Article X—that a Council vote to use
armed force was only a recommendation, leaving each member
free to act as he saw fit. Unfortunately, this list was not made
public, nor did Wilson attempt to use it to win support of the
mild reservationists. At the time, he was still confident that he
could gain acceptance of the treaty without any change, and
after his collapse on his return to Washington it was too late.
Hitchcock was able to see the President twice briefly, before
the first vote in November but could not bring himself to tell
his stricken leader that not only public opinion but even some
of his supporters in the Senate were moving toward acceptance
of the League with reservations.

On November 19, with voting but hours away, Senator
Hitchcock rushed to the White House to tell Mrs. Wilson that,
unless the administration accepted the Lodge planks, the

treaty would be beaten. Mrs. Wilson relates that she pleaded with her husband to accede, but he insisted that he had no moral right to consent to changes without expecting other nations to do the same. The country's honor was at stake. "Better a thousand times to go down fighting," he told her, "than to dip your colours to dishonourable compromise!" The President dictated a note for Senator Hitchcock: "In my opinion the resolution in that form [embodying the reservations] does not provide for ratification but rather for nullification of the Treaty. . . . I trust that all true friends of the Treaty will refuse to support the Lodge resolution."

If any of his Cabinet members or political lieutenants had been able to reach Wilson and bring him up to date on the alignment of forces as it had finally take shape, perhaps he might not have been so adamant. As it was, the Democrats in the Senate, under standing instructions issued by the President, joined the "bitter-enders" to vote down the Lodge reservations, thereby causing defeat of the treaty and the League with it. Thus ended the first round in the struggle. A week later Colonel House, writing to a friend, raised some pointed questions. Had the President received the numerous letters and petitions from his supporters in the League battle urging him to accept the reservations, some of which had recently been modified, and what was the date of the President's letter urging the Democratic senators to vote against the treaty in any form but the original one? But most important, "Who was the President of the United States during these crucial weeks when decisions vital to the security of our country, and to the peace of the world, had to be, and certainly were, made? Who acted in his name in the days and weeks when the President was not in touch with his constitutional advisers?"

In January, 1920, Wilson sent a letter to party members at the Jackson Day Dinner that, if there was any doubt as to how the people felt about the League, "The clear and single way out is to submit it for determination at the next election to the voters of the nation." Later that month he contemplated making a public appeal. The memorandum for his proposed speech indicates that Wilson failed utterly to grasp the political realities involved in the League struggle, possibly as a result of his illness and seclusion. He considered proposing a national referendum. All senators who had voted against the treaty were to resign and stand for immediate election. If all or a majority were re-elected, he would resign from the presidency, as would the Vice President and the Secretary of State. The post of the Secretary would be filled by a Republican who, in the order of succession, would be elevated to the presidency. This unrealistic idea never went beyond the draft stage.

To the bitter end, Wilson remained obdurate. Shortly before the Senate was to vote for the second and last time, he informed Senator Hitchcock that the United States should enter the League wholeheartedly and unreservedly, accepting its responsibilities for world leadership, or it should not enter at all. Every one of the Lodge reservations, he insisted, represented a sweeping nullification, and those who supported them were nullifiers of the treaty whether or not they realized it. This was his last word for the guidance of the Democrats in the Senate.

On March 19, 1920, the rancorous battle came to an end. Forty-nine senators voted for the treaty with the Lodge reservations, and thirty-five irreconcilables and administration supporters voted against. A number of Democrats broke ranks to vote for the reservations, but not enough. Had seven more deserted their leader in the White House, the treaty would have had a two-thirds majority. The following day Hitchcock wrote to the President that it had required "the most energetic efforts" on his part to prevent a majority of the Democrats from deserting to Lodge.

The tragic irony was that so little separated Wilson's interpretative amendments from Lodge's reservations and that effective participation in the League would have been little restricted by the reservations. William Howard Taft, who felt that almost any concession was worth making to save the treaty, wrote bitterly that Lodge and Wilson "exalt their personal prestige and the saving of their ugly faces above the welfare of the country and the world."

Thus the treaty and the League were ground between the millstones of Wilson's ego and Lodge's desire for partisan advantage, with their personal vendetta providing additional power. On Wilson's part the "supreme infanticide," as one writer put it, was due to his pride, his stubbornness, his self-righteousness. Therein lay the failure of the President's leadership. Lodge understood Wilson's weakness and played the President as a fisherman plays a trout. In his own account of the League battle, Lodge writes that he was convinced the President would prevent acceptance of the treaty with reservations if he possibly could. "I based this opinion on the knowledge which I had acquired as to Mr. Wilson's temperament, intentions and purposes." And he concludes, "I made no mistake in my estimate of what President Wilson would do under certain conditions."

The evidence suggests that Lodge intended to defeat the League and used the reservations to accomplish his purpose. While Wilson was still in Paris, Lodge had discussed strategy with Senator Borah. It would be impossible, he said, to defeat ratification of the treaty if a straight vote were taken in the Senate immediately, and the best thing to do, therefore, was to engage in a prolonged discussion of amendments and reservations. Senator James E. Watson of Indiana, one of the irreconcilables, recounts a conversation with Lodge before the vote in March, 1920. According to Watson, who expressed concern that Wilson might accept the reservations, Lodge replied confidently that Wilson's hatred of him was so intense that "never under any set of circumstances in this world" could he be induced to do so. When Watson said that this seemed a slender thread on which to hang so great a cause, Lodge cried, "A slender thread! Why, it is as strong as any cable with its strands wired and twisted together."

A deeply partisan Republican, Lodge was willing to sacrifice almost anything for party advantage. If the Republicans were to score an electoral triumph in 1920, the Democrats, whose prestige was at its height in the wake of military victory, would have to be discredited. What better way than to put the onus for defeat of the League on Wilson's head?

Nevertheless, it was not the senator but the President who had the ultimate responsibility of securing approval of the treaty. Wilson kept insisting that concessions to the opposition would only result in further demands and that major changes would necessitate renegotiation with the European powers. However, the European powers might have accepted the reservations; if they had refused, then the senator would have borne the odium for the debacle.

Another of Wilson's weaknesses which produced a failure of leadership was his unshakable conviction that the people would rise to his defense. Apparently he had learned nothing from his experiences during the peace negotiations. When he found that he could not sway the Senate, he clung to the belief that his cause would be vindicated in a "solemn referendum" in the November election. His expectation was not fulfilled nor, realistically, could it be, for only one-third of the Senate was seeking re-election. At the same time, Lodge was expressing wishful thinking when, after the Republican landslide in 1920, he jubilantly proclaimed, "We have torn up Wilsonianism by the roots." Both the Republican platform and the Republican candidate were ambiguous on the League, muddling the issue and confusing the voters. Moreover, a number of domestic factors which affected the nation more directly conspired to defeat the Democrats.

Wilson's confidence that eventually the American people would reconsider remained unshaken. In his last public address, on Armistice Day, 1923, the ex-President declared, "I am not one of those that have the least anxiety about the triumph of the principles I have stood for. I have seen fools resist Providence before, and I have seen their destruction. That we shall prevail is as sure as that God reigns." He told a friend that he had "not the shadow of a doubt" of the ultimate acceptance of the League, for "the world will not commit suicide."

Wilson spent the remaining few years of his life after he left the White House as a private citizen in relative seclusion. He wrote an article and made one public address. Although a semi-invalid, he sought for some way of again exerting leadership. For a while he thought of a seat in the Senate, but he rejected it as an inadequate forum from which to exert world influence. He told a New Jersey reporter whom he had known for many years that, from the messages he kept receiving, "I realize that I am everywhere regarded as the foremost leader of the liberal thought of the world, and the hopes and aspirations of that liberal thought should find some better place of expression than in the Senate. . . . Think of the people of Poland and of Czechoslovakia and the other countries whose freedom we gave them—they know that they owe their very national existence to me, and they are looking to me to lead them." There was only one place where he could be sure of effectively asserting that leadership. He had cherished hopes for the presidential nomination in 1920 and, even as his strength and life were ebbing away, still hoped to be his party's choice again.

At the end of January, 1924, he failed alarmingly, and Dr. Grayson was hastily summoned. On Sunday, February 3, the end came quietly. Services were held in the house on S Street which Wilson, with the aid of friends, had purchased after retiring from office.

Because of his position as Republican leader, Senator Lodge was appointed a member of the congressional committee to attend the funeral. As soon as Mrs. Wilson learned of this she wrote to the senator, asking him not to come as his presence would only embarrass him and be unwelcome to her. He replied that "nothing would be more distasteful to me than to do anything which by any possibility would be unwelcome to you." This exchange of messages was a fitting conclusion to one of the most rancorous political feuds in America history. If it could have been checked, if the United States had joined the League, the world possibly might have avoided a purgatory of appalling dimensions.

Woodrow Wilson's career as President of the United States combined elements of greatness with shortcomings imposed by his personality. A leader of men, he was often a poor judge of individuals. For all his high-mindedness, he was stubborn, headstrong, and intolerant, finding it impossible to yield graciously or sometimes even at all. Burning with the flame of moral passion which his religion fanned, he approached men with a rigidity that made him regard as enemies those who differed with his version of principle, and principle to him was inviolable.

His romantic faith in the people made him confident that their instincts would persuade them to take the proper course. But in summoning them to high purpose, he neglected to pay sufficient heed to the requirements of practical politics; nor did he provide enlightenment on the realities of international politics and on the challenge to the country's national interest. In offering the possibility of a world at peace through the repudiation of old practices, he was, to the world's misfortune, far ahead of his age. His magnificent vision, however, assures him a place for all time among the great leaders of mankind. Without his indefatigable labors, the world's first effort at collective security, the League of Nations, would not have come into existence.

Under Wilson the presidency was elevated to an international institution with a world-wide constituency. Theodore Roosevelt sought to enhance the power of the United States by winning respect for its strength. Woodrow Wilson's aim was to win admiration for its ideals. The former wished to involve the nation in world affairs through an assertion of its power position; the latter desired world leadership to be based on moral position. To achieve his goal, Roosevelt addressed himself primarily to the chancelleries of the world and incidentally to the American people. Wilson appealed to all mankind.

Both leaders recognized that the emergence of the United States as a great power provided new opportunities for world leadership, but Wilson was no more successful than Roosevelt in jolting the American people out of their traditional isolationism. Not for several decades and only after the most devastating cataclysm in history would the popular response be transformed.

Warren G. Harding and Calvin Coolidge

9. Hiatus in Leadership

A REPUBLICAN came to power in 1920 primarily, as Mark Sullivan said, because for many Americans the outgoing President had become "the symbol of the exaltation that turned sour, personification of the rapture that had now become gall, and sacrificial whipping boy to the present bitterness." Farmers were resentful because Wilson had removed price supports, working men were antagonistic because of runaway prices, and management was incensed because of his alleged coddling of labor. In the final analysis, however, the nation wanted, in Warren G. Harding's apt words, "not heroics but healing, not nostrums but normalcy, not revolutions but restoration, not surgery but serenity."

Temperamentally and philosophically, candidate Harding was prepared to allow executive leadership to revert to the Whig concept of congressional supremacy which prevailed during the post-Civil War decades. He would acknowledge Congress to be the primary source of national policy, refrain from using the party as an instrument of leadership, preside over but not dominate the executive branch, and above all reflect rather than seek to influence public attitudes.

"Normalcy" and "serenity" were the magic words, and Harding epitomized both. With unconscious irony, a leading journal wrote during the election campaign that whatever might be the defects of the nominee as a world statesman, he was "an exceedingly courteous gentleman." If he were elected, "good

139

nature, both to political friends and to political enemies,"
would once again prevail in the White House. "The Senator's
speeches may be properly criticized for their vagueness, for
their lack of original thought, for their occasionally conflicting
character . . . but they are certainly not lacking in the decen-
cies of political controversy. And this is another case where
style is the man." Good nature, it seemed, was considered an
adequate substitute for leadership for the candidate aspiring to
the highest office in the land.

A minority viewed the prospect of a Harding in the White
House as little short of calamitous, concurring with the *New
Republic*'s denunciation of the Republican Party for nominating "a party hack, without independence, without knowledge of international politics, without any of those moral and
intellectual qualities which would qualify him" for the presidency.

Harding's major asset was his appearance—he looked like a
President. Tall, well built, gray-haired and dignified, he would
easily have been singled out as a man of consequence even in a
gathering of notables. His charm and affability made him
appealing to both men and women. He spoke well and, when
reading from a prepared text, could produce the oratorical
flourishes reminiscent of a nineteenth-century solon. The content of his addresses was another matter. William Gibbs
McAdoo described them succinctly and colorfully when he
said that the speeches "leave the impression of an army of
pompous phrases moving over the landscape in search of an
idea; sometimes these meandering words would actually capture a straggling thought and bear it triumphantly, a prisoner
in their midst, until it died of servitude and overwork!"

The son of a small-town homeopath of limited means, Harding attended an academy which he left a year before graduation. He began to study law but soon abandoned it. After brief
efforts at teaching school and selling insurance, he ventured
into the publishing business by buying an interest in the local
newspaper with $300 which he had earned by playing the alto
horn in the town's cornet band. He was pushed into state politics both by his wife and his friend, Harry Daugherty, a politically influencial Ohio lawyer. From county auditor he shortly

rose to the state senate and then served a term as lieutenant governor, creating hardly a ripple in any of these posts. In 1914 he won a seat in the United States Senate where he remained until his election to the presidency. His six-year record was notably undistinguished. He did not sponsor a single measure of any significance. Whenever possible he avoided committing himself on any major public issues, and he never hesitated to reverse his position if public opinion or party politics required it. This unflagging party loyalty was rewarded by membership on several important committees. Senator Lodge placed him on the vital Foreign Relations Committee; he knew little of foreign affairs, but he was pliant, subservient, and dependable.

It was Harry Daugherty's decision that made a President of the man who would have been completely content as an unimportant cog in the legislative wheel for as long as his constituents would have him, and then would have returned happily to the anonymity of Marion, Ohio, to play poker on Saturday night, go to church the next morning, join in a game of bridge, and play tuba in the town band. Daugherty brought Harding to the attention of party leaders throughout the country, and when the Republican nominating convention at Chicago deadlocked, he persuaded the Old Guard in control that Harding was an ideal "dark horse." Harding, he said, had many friends and no enemies, had voted for the Lodge reservations, and, most important, would be an unassuming and popular figurehead who could easily be dominated by the congressional leadership. Early on the morning of June 12, after hours of discussion in a "smoke-filled" room at the Blackstone Hotel, the political bosses settled on his candidacy. Their choice was speedily ratified by the convention.

Unlike the Democratic candidate, James M. Cox, who traveled indefatigably up and down the country, Harding never stirred out of Marion. His backers had been advised "to keep Warren at home" for "if he goes out on tour somebody's sure to ask him questions, and Warren's just the sort of damned fool that will try to answer them." Whereas Cox unequivocally stated his position, Harding made conciliatory and ambiguous speeches from his front porch, either straddling the controversial issue of the League of Nations or contradicting himself. In pompous and hackneyed addresses, he sometimes spoke vaguely about "a new association of nations" in place of the League; at other times he suggested joining with reservations. On the one hand he espoused straightforward isolationism, while on the other he favored a full-fledged assumption of American responsibility in world affairs. Prominent leaders of the internationalist wing of the party, after a visit with the candidate, came away confident that he endorsed their wishes for qualified entrance into the League. Arch-isolationists in the party were equally convinced that he championed their approach to world affairs.

When a peace crusader asked him for a definite statement of his views, he replied that he had a very clear idea of what the nation could and should do in working out an international agreement, "but as a candidate of a party I do not want to make my plan an issue in a campaign" as he believed that "international agreements ought to be made a concerted agreement of the executive and the Congress." Harding's equivocal and noncommittal stance reflected, perhaps, a native shrewdness not credited to him but more likely expressed his concept of the nature of the presidential office. He regarded the chief executive in terms of a small-town mayor: he should be the guest of honor at conferences, cornerstone layings, and ceremonies dedicating public buildings. Legislation was the business of Congress, administration the concern of the department heads who comprised the Cabinet, policy the affair of the party caucus. The President's main function was to provide a sense of harmony and be the presiding officer who sees that the governmental machinery runs smoothly.

That he was unqualified for the presidency, Harding was well aware. "I am not fit for this office and should never have been here," he told Nicholas Murray Butler. He had been maneuvered into accepting the nomination as throughout his life he was manipulated by people who used him to serve their own ends. Harding recognized his weakness and once made an admission that is both a poignant and devastating commentary on the man who occupied the nation's most eminent position. Addressing the National Press Club in 1922, he related that his father once told him, "Warren, it's a good thing you wasn't born a gal. Because you'd be in the family way all the time. You just can't say No."

With his background and personality, Harding was understandably overwhelmed by the tasks and problems with which he had to deal, often complaining pathetically to friends about their magnitude and complexity. On one occasion his secretary found him sitting at his desk looking helplessly at a report in front of him. He looked up and then burst out, "I don't know what to do or where to turn in this taxation matter! Somewhere there must be a book that tells all about it, where I could go to straighten it out in my mind. But I don't know where the book is, and maybe I couldn't read it if I found it! And there must be a man in the country somewhere who could weigh both sides and know the truth. . . . My God, but this is a hell of a place for a man like me to be."

At the beginning of his term, Harding scheduled biweekly press conferences when questions could be spontaneously asked and answered. The President was easily flustered, and after a *faux pas* which caused considerable embarrassment to the State Department this arrangement had to be abandoned. Henceforth, written questions were submitted in advance.

With Congress, Harding maintained his distance. A genial and affable companion with other politicians, he found it difficult to develop a proper official relationship with congressmen, and his restricted view of executive prerogative precluded a vigorous and commanding leadership of the legislative body. He merely proposed measures occasionally, and, since he did not avail himself of any of the formal or informal machinery for the employment of pressures and sanctions, Congress disposed at its pleasure.

In foreign affairs, Harding immediately decided against exercising personal command. When as President-elect he announced at a press conference the appointment of Charles Evans Hughes as his Secretary of State, a reporter questioned him on the foreign policy he planned to pursue. "You must ask Mr. Hughes about that," he replied, and then added, "That is going to be another policy of the next administration. From the beginning the Secretary of State will speak for the State Department." The most that can be said for Harding's role in foreign policy is that he chose an able man to conduct it. During his tenure, the ideas and the initiative came almost entirely from Hughes, who was accorded wide latitude and discretion and to whose judgment the President deferred.

In his inaugural address, President Harding set the tone for America's attitude towards international relations: "Confident of our ability to work out our own destiny and jealously guarding our right to do so, we seek no part in directing the destinies of the Old World. We do not mean to be entangled. We will accept no responsibility except as our own conscience and judgment may determine." Some leading State Department officials were aware, however, that the peace of the United States depended on peace in Europe and that the only way to insure it was active cooperation with the European powers. But they were unable to channel policy in view of apathy or hostility on the part of the public, isolationism in the Senate, and lack of support from the White House. When a separate peace treaty was concluded with Germany, the Senate appended a proviso that the United States should not be represented on any body or commission without specific authorization by Congress.

Almost as soon as the guns had ceased firing, the leading powers had initiated plans for rearmament. With a naval race in prospect, action was deemed imperative by the United States, which instigated the Conference on Limitation of Armaments. Attended by representatives of the five major naval powers, the United States, Great Britain, Japan, France, and Italy, it met in Washington on November 12, 1921. President Harding made the opening address, but Secretary Hughes conducted the negotiations. A series of agreements included: a five-power naval pact which provided for a ratio in capital ship tonnage; a four-power treaty pledging Britain, America, Japan, and France to respect each other's possessions in the Pacific; and a nine-power treaty which pledged the signatories with interests in the Far East to respect the sovereignty, independence, and territorial integrity of China, to maintain the Open Door, and to refrain from seeking special rights or privileges. In effect, an Anglo-American understanding replaced the

Anglo-Japanese alliance in the Far East, and Japanese naval expansion was checked for a projected ten-year period.

The effort to achieve naval arms control was supported both by internationalists and isolationists. While cooperation with foreign powers was involved, the United States could remain free of "entangling alliances" and any system of collective security. Membership in the Permanent Court of International Justice or World Court also had wide appeal, because compliance with its decisions was not obligatory and it was not an organic part of the League structure. Nevertheless, when the issue of membership arose in 1923, Harding was indifferent. Hughes's campaign to win support in the Senate was vehemently attacked by such bitter-enders as Senators Lodge, Borah, and Johnson on the basis of the Court's tenuous connection with the League. But with seventy-three senators in favor of membership, nine opposed, and thirteen doubtful, vigorous action from the White House might have disarmed the opposition. In June the President called for a total separation of the Court from the League and went on to say that while he still favored ratification of the Court Protocol, he would not fight for it. "I shall not attempt to coerce the Senate of the United States," he declared. "I shall make no demand upon the people. I shall not try to impose my will upon any body or anybody. I shall embark on no crusade."

Harding's desire to please rather than to lead, to placate rather than arouse, to be tolerant and amiable are qualities that make for good fellowship but are serious defects in a head of state. They were disastrous to the President. His pathetic need for friendship at any price and his trusting nature blinded him to the way his "friends" were using him for their own debased purposes. If he had not died suddenly on August 2, 1923, the shameful corruption that riddled the government, which was exposed shortly thereafter, undoubtedly would have destroyed him.

Vice President Calvin Coolidge learned of Harding's death while visiting the family farm in Vermont where he was born. His father, a notary public, administered the presidential oath in "the sitting room by the light of the kerosene lamp." To modern and urban Americans, this tender scene evoked a nos-

talgia for the "good old days" of the rural past, and for millions
Coolidge became at once the embodiment of old-time virtue.

In appearance and demeanor, Coolidge contrasted sharply
with Harding. An observer wondered how a man of his "unim-
pressive physique, his reticence, his lack of florid speech, his
utter want of social attributes, his entire aloofness" could ever
have been elected even to a municipal council. Yet, beginning
in 1899 with his election to the city council of Northampton,
Massachusetts, he moved steadily upward to city solici-
tor, mayor, member of the state House of Representatives, state
senator, lieutenant governor, governor, Vice President. Beneath
his unprepossessing exterior was a politician of uncommon
shrewdness. He acquired a national reputation while Governor
as a result of his action in breaking the Boston police strike of
1919. His famous statement, "There is no right to strike against
the public safety by any body, any time, any where," made him
a symbol of law and order and propelled him into national
politics. Coolidge achieved success by studiously avoiding controversial issues, by a highly skillful identification with the
public interest in the broadest terms, by the use of the glittering generality and the cliché, by being all things to all men.

Throughout the years of his public service, the image Coolidge projected was that of a man consummately devoted to his
job. When he was a member of the Massachusetts legislature,
the local paper wrote, "He attends to his duties diligently . . . is
always looking out for the details of his bills and not letting
anything slip by him which ought to go in, or omitting anything which should not be left out." Later, when he presided
over the state senate, the same journal described his administration as "business-like and without any fireworks." The
identical statement could have been made about his administration in the White House.

Like his predecessor, Coolidge voluntarily abdicated the
leadership which the Constitution intended that the chief executive should exercise, including responsibility for foreign
policy, which was turned over to the Secretary of State. He
conceived his role to be that of titular head of an organization
supervised by a competent staff. He would reign, not rule.
Several years after Coolidge retired, he made a revealing state-

ment in justifying his refusal to take a stand on a certain issue pending before Congress. "I wouldn't take it," he wrote. "The situation had not developed. Theodore Roosevelt was always getting himself in hot water before he had to commit himself upon issues not well defined." Administrators would get along better, he went on, if they would "restrain the impulse to butt in or be dragged into trouble. They should remain silent until an issue is reduced to its lowest terms."

Coolidge's reluctance to commit himself was coupled with a resistance to change, which stemmed partly from a devotion to the laissez-faire principle and partly, no doubt, from a phlegmatic disposition. As he put it in an address to the nation, "Our most important problem is not to secure new advantages but to maintain those which we already have." Since legislation produced change, Coolidge disliked legislation. "Don't be in a hurry to legislate," he once declared.

President Coolidge considered his constitutional duty fulfilled when he reported to Congress on the state of the Union and recommended measures for its consideration. Congressmen, after all, had been sent to Washington to represent their constituents, and he was not obliged to persuade or coerce. He rarely held conferences either with groups of congressmen or with individual members on key committees to exert executive influence for pending legislation. To promote cordial personal relations, legislators were frequently invited to White House breakfasts, but at these informal gatherings discussions on policy matters were taboo. Coolidge made a virtue of avoiding any conflict with the legislative branch. As he failed to press hard for any program, his wishes, more often than not, were ignored. Although he was highly popular with the American people, the Republican Congress to an unusually large degree passed laws that he opposed, overrode laws that he vetoed, and failed to enact legislation that he advocated.

The election of 1924 was another three-cornered race, with Coolidge the popular nominee of the Republican Party, the conservative John W. Davis heading the Democratic ticket, and "Fighting Bob" La Follette the choice of progressives who were dissatisfied with the status quo proclivities of the major parties. Aside from the progressives who supported the third party, little popular interest was taken in the campaign, and Coolidge was returned to office in a landslide. He had campaigned very little, remaining quietly at his desk in the White House and carefully avoiding any semblance of partisanship. The majority of the voters were obviously pleased with his record and with the homely philosophy he expressed when accepting the nomination: "In the commonplace things of life lies the strength of the nation. It is not in brilliant conceptions and strokes of genius that we shall find the chief reliance of our country, but in the home, in the school, and in religion. . . . The people want a government of common sense."

This reverence for the commonplace, which was a complete measure of the man, produced a pitifully inadequate statesmanship during years when forceful, informed leadership might have made a difference to the future of the world. That the war had basically altered the international economic pattern seemed beyond Coolidge's comprehension. With Europe on the verge of bankruptcy and the United States the chief creditor nation, he endorsed raising tariff walls, thereby making it impossible for the debtors to discharge their obligations in the only way available to them—with their goods. And the President's response to the knotty problem of the war debts was his now famous, "They hired the money, didn't they?"

Coolidge's narrow vision precluded an awareness of the forces already brewing abroad that were to turn Europe into a cauldron of despair in a little over a decade. The President reinforced the ostrichlike attitude of most Americans by pouring out a steady stream of platitudes about non-entanglement, while tossing a soporific to the internationalists by supporting participation in the World Court and expressing a willingness to cooperate in the non-political work of the League of Nations.

The President's recommendation, twice made, to affiliate with the World Court was ignored by the isolationists. When the Senate did take up the matter, participation was approved but with five reservations. The majority of the member nations were willing to accept four but balked at the fifth, which denied the Court the power "without the consent of the United States [to] entertain any request for an advisory opinion touching any dispute or question in which the United States has or claims an interest." Coolidge refused to reopen negotiations and also turned down a request from twenty-one nations to discuss the reservation informally with American leaders in the hope that some formula could be worked out. He took the position that the Court would have to accept the Senate's terms or not at all. "The situation has been sufficiently developed," he stated, "that I do not intend to ask the Senate to modify its position." He did not think the legislative body would take favorable action, "and unless the requirements of the Senate resolution are met by other interested nations I can see no prospect of adhering to this Court."

Americans, it seemed, were unwilling to become part of any international arrangement that in any way restricted the nation's freedom of action, but all—isolationists, internationalists, moderates—were agreed that the United States must help to maintain peace. The only problem was how. At last it appeared that a formula was found on which all could agree: a universal pledge to outlaw war and to settle disputes only by pacific means. A proposal embodying these features had been outlined in 1918 by Salmon O. Levinson, a Chicago attorney. It attracted little attention until Senator Borah picked it up and in February, 1923, introduced a resolution into the Senate substantially incorporating the Levinson plan. To the isolationist from Idaho, its virtue lay in the absence of a commitment by the United States to use force or become politically involved in any security system. Nothing came of his efforts. Then, in 1927, French Foreign Minister Aristide Briand, after discussing the subject with Nicholas Murray Butler and James T. Shotwell, both of the Carnegie Endowment for International Peace, proposed a bilateral pact renouncing war.

At first the President and Secretary of State Frank B. Kellogg were unreceptive, for such a treaty conjured up visions of an alliance. The latter suggested instead a multilateral agreement and, by the end of the year, began negotiations with other governments. On August 27, 1928, at Paris, the representatives of fifteen nations signed the Pact of Paris, or the Kellogg-Briand Pact, as it came to be known, and eventually almost every sovereign state in the world subscribed to it. The treaty piously pledged the signatories to renounce war but imposed absolutely no obligations on any nation to assist in checking aggression. It was widely acclaimed in the United States, as it supposedly would help maintain the peace without the vexations, frustrations, and vicissitudes resulting from the involvement of American power in world politics. The President hailed it in glowing terms. Had an agreement of this kind existed in 1914, he said, "there is every reason to suppose that it would have saved the situation and delivered the world from all the misery which was inflicted by the great war. It holds a greater hope for peaceful relations than was ever before given to the world." Senator Carter Glass expressed the conviction of the few realists when he said that the pact was "worthless, but perfectly harmless." Abroad it was generally regarded as a futile and meaningless moral gesture.

Perhaps one reason for Coolidge's enthusiasm was the failure of the Naval Disarmament Conference at Geneva a year earlier. He had sponsored the gathering in an attempt to halt the race among the five naval powers in building cruisers, destroyers, and submarines which threatened to upset the fine balance of naval strength so carefully constructed in 1922. The French and Italians refused to participate, and after six weeks of futile discussion the conference adjourned without reaching any agreement.

In the Caribbean, the administration's foreign policy made substantial progress. Ironically, the business-oriented Harding and Coolidge administrations began a reversal of the interventionism which took place under the idealistic Wilson. With the approaches to the Panama Canal secured against any possible threat, the process of troop withdrawal from Nicaragua, Haiti, and Santo Domingo was gradually set in motion. A climate was created in which friendly relations with Mexico could again be resumed, and steps were taken to repudiate the Roosevelt Corollary. In 1923, Secretary Hughes stated that the Monroe Doctrine was exclusively a policy of self-defense, not intended to justify interference by the United States in the affairs of neighboring countries or to infringe on their independence. A State Department memorandum five years later underscored this point in greater detail.

On the whole, Calvin Coolidge's "reign" was a peaceful one. The country was experiencing an unprecedented prosperity and, while some mutterings of discontent could be heard, these were in a minor key. This was the era of the "roaring twenties," of the "great experiment" which turned the bathtub into a still for making the forbidden drink, of the skyrocketing stock market. The American people and their President were blithely heedless that the world was beginning to slide toward economic disaster. Coolidge's task, states his biographer, "was to keep the Ship of State on an even keel before a favoring wind— not to reconstruct the hull or install motive power or alter the course. He was a safe pilot, not a brilliant one. Under him the nation was not adventurous, but it was happy. He won no battles, challenged no traditions, instituted few reforms."

One of the most popular Presidents the nation ever had, he could unquestioningly have obtained the nomination for the asking if he had wished to run for a second term in 1928, and he would have achieved a sweeping triumph at the polls. What was there about this withdrawn, colorless man, who looked "as though he had been weaned on a pickle," with his bone-dry humor, ascetic tastes, and Puritanical outlook, that would appeal to masses of people? Even his biographer, who tried to add some warmth to his portrait, could create only a one-dimensional figure, an abstraction of a human being. The net impression is of a bodiless mind, mediocre but calculating. The man himself is a shadow—possessing not one of the interests that add richness to life, without vitality, incapable of joy, lacking any appreciation of beauty whether in nature or in art, and without even a single petty vice to make him seem more human.

Coolidge was the beneficiary of a period when the people needed a symbol of the virtues they had been taught to revere and which they had abandoned with nagging feelings of guilt. The ascetic in the White House stood for everything they felt they should be but were not. He represented a rock-ribbed stability in a society shifting and altering at a feverish pace. Moreover, since a leader is generally identified with the state of the nation, the President profited from the general prosperity. He believed in letting well enough alone, and the majority of the people gratefully and heartily echoed his sentiments.

It was not necessary for Coolidge to create a popular image. He was exactly what he appeared to be. All he had to do was to keep himself in the public eye to insure his popularity. Assiduously, "silent Cal" deluged the nation with a torrent of statements. During his tenure he probably supplied more wordage to the press than Theodore Roosevelt and Woodrow Wilson combined. This outpouring was facilitated by a generous and systematic use of ghost writers, who had become a fixed part of the President's staff during the previous administration.

For the most part, Coolidge's pronouncements consisted of sermonettes on American history and the American way of life. He inveighed against wastefulness, radical experiments, foreign entanglements, and the garden variety of iniquities. His homilies lauded honesty, industry, and thrift. He paid homage to sobriety and peace and the Golden Rule. In short, he used the mass media of communication, including the latest recruit, radio, not to shape and influence public policy or as a lever on Congress but as a vehicle for personal popularity.

In their attitude toward the presidency, both Harding and Coolidge belonged more to the nineteenth than to the twentieth century, the last of the chief executives to preside during a relatively untroubled era. The nation would never again be able to afford the luxury of quiescence in the White House.

Herbert Hoover

10. Victim of Crises

PROSPERITY in the twenties was resting on a foundation as tenuous as cobwebs, but most dazzled Americans saw only steel girders. "My God, How the Money Rolls In!" was a national theme song, and the ticker tape machines clattered merrily on, showing prices spiralling into the stratosphere. The sounds of rejoicing almost drowned out the voices of two groups to whom prosperity was a meaningless word: farmers of the Midwest struggling against sagging prices and the unorganized workers crushed by pitifully small wages.

In the election campaign of 1928, a Republican slogan was "A Chicken in Every Pot, a Car in Every Garage." Accepting the nomination, Herbert Hoover intoned, "We in America today are nearer to the final triumph over poverty than ever before in the history of any land." The general affluence, for which the Republicans claimed credit, combined with euphoria to offer the Democrats little chance even with a candidate who possessed all the political virtues. As it was, Alfred E. Smith was marked for defeat at the outset. He was a Catholic and, as a product of the East Side of New York, had acquired accents, mannerisms, and habits of dress distasteful to middle-class, rural, and small-town America. Moreover, he was a "wet" when a great many Americans paid at least lip service to prohibition and, though personally honest, was tainted by his association with the notorious Tammany machine. Finally, since the party platforms revealed no basic differences on issues, to abandon the custodians of the national prosperity seemed pointless to most voters. The Republican candidate won by a landslide.

Herbert Hoover's life was the classic prototype of the American success story. Born of poor Quaker parents on an Iowa farm, he was orphaned at the age of nine. He put himself through school and college, receiving a degree in mining engineering from Leland Stanford University in 1895. By the time he was forty, he had already achieved an outstanding reputation in his profession, having directed vast engineering projects and served as consultant to governments all over the world. He had also accumulated a fortune that permitted him to retire. To a successful private career was added a distinguished record of public service in Europe and the United States. After the outbreak of hostilities in Europe, he directed Belgian war relief; when America entered the war, he served at home as Food Administrator. During the period of armistice, he headed the Supreme Economic Council and afterward the American Relief Administration.

Without partisan affiliation, and with a reputation for disinterested patriotism and integrity, Hoover was appealing to both parties in 1920; each considered recruiting him as its presidential candidate. Secretary Lane wrote with unqualified enthusiasm that not only could Hoover give the country wise leadership, but he enjoyed the confidence of the people on both sides of the Atlantic. "It would not surprise me to see him nominated on either ticket, and I believe I will vote for him now as against anybody else."

Once Hoover declared himself a Republican, he was a favorite with the crowds at the party convention. But few delegates and none of the bosses supported him, and he spent the next eight years as Secretary of Commerce, in which post he achieved national prominence.

Mark Sullivan observed after Hoover's election that he was the first President truly qualified by education and training for leadership in the age of modern science. In addition, his humanitarian activities during and after the war would make him a force for peace and "justify looking upon his inauguration as a landmark." One historian prophesied that "Hoover the engineer would be the symbol of the coming age of material fulfillment, as Jefferson had been of democracy and Lincoln of emancipation."

These and other astute observers overlooked Hoover's lack of essential qualifications for presidential leadership: he had no practical experience in politics, had never held an elective office, and was totally unfamiliar with the legislative process. That these would prove to be handicaps became apparent after he entered the White House. His political ineptitude made it difficult for him to secure cooperation from Congress. Accustomed to giving orders, he could not adjust to the basic give and take of the political process. Personally cold, reserved, and unimaginative, he was unable to arouse any public response in support of his programs. Visitors often found him unapproachable. An excessive sensitivity to criticism frequently deterred him from acting. "I do wish," Secretary of State Henry L. Stimson confided to his diary, "he could shield himself against listening to so much rumor and criticism. . . . He wastes an enormous amount of nerve tissue and anxiety on these interruptions." His touchiness also affected his relations with the press, which steadily deteriorated throughout his tenure.

When he took office, Hoover was completely sanguine about prospects for the future, both domestic and foreign. He hoped to accomplish some reforms at home and to direct foreign relations "into a greater cooperation for advancement of peace and international progress." It seemed to him, he wrote to his Secretary of State, that "there is the most profound outlook for peace today" unmatched during the last half century. The dangers of war "during the next six or ten years . . . are inconceivably less than they have been at any period since the Great War." Like so many other of the nation's leaders during the twenties, Hoover regarded American entry into that struggle as an unfortunate aberration not likely to recur. Europe had to be helped to maintain peace, and America need only employ its great moral force to contribute to that objective.

Even before his inauguration, Hoover decided to improve the tone of hemispheric relations by undertaking an unprecedented good-will tour of Latin America. Although the bonds of political domination by the United States over Central America had been loosened during the Harding and Coolidge administrations, resentment against "Yankee" imperialism was still widespread. Intervention, the President-elect concluded, would have to be abandoned. In the twenty-five speeches he delivered during his ten-week tour of the major South American countries, he repeatedly used the phrase "good neighbor" to suggest the spirit that would guide his administration.

Officials in the countries he visited greeted him warmly, and American newspapers hailed his tour as a diplomatic triumph. The Latin-American people, though, were markedly unenthusiastic. They wanted policies, not slogans. Their mistrust was justified in 1930 when the President signed the Smoot-Hawley Tariff Act which deprived his "good neighbors" of a substantial part of their market in the United States. As the great depression had already shattered their economies, this helped complete their economic ruin, leaving millions on the edge of starvation.

At the same time, efforts were made to institute a fresh approach to Latin America. *De facto* recognition was granted to a new regime as soon as it demonstrated effective control and indicated an intention to honor international obligations. The onus of meddling, by contrast with Wilson's missionary diplomacy, was thus avoided, but when a more or less democratic regime was superseded by an oppressive dictatorship, the United States, by its prompt recognition, risked alienating the people. Intervention and the Roosevelt Corollary, which sanctioned it, were repudiated. To place an official stamp on the new attitude, a memorandum, prepared by J. Reuben Clark, Under Secretary of State in the Coolidge administration, was disinterred from the files where it had reposed for several years and issued as a public document. According to the memorandum, the United States henceforth would not assume any responsibility to preserve order and protect property in Latin America, or to act as an international policeman. This was a great stride forward in eradicating the image of Yankee imperialism, preparing the way for implementation of the good neighbor approach in the next administration. In these, as in all other aspects of foreign policy, Hoover's Secretary of State played at least as active a role as the chief executive, if not the dominant one.

The perennial issue of World Court membership arose once again in 1930. Hoover asked the Senate in December of that year to ratify the Protocol of the Court subject to the modifications already secured by Elihu Root. The isolationists remained obdurate, despite the President's assurance that the United States would be free to withdraw at any time and that membership would not entangle it in the diplomacy of other nations. Under the circumstances, it is doubtful whether even strong pressure by Hoover would have brought the nation into the Court.

Another matter that came up periodically and was quickly disposed of was recognition of the Soviet Union. Senator Borah, a persistent advocate, stated in one of his major Senate addresses in March, 1931, that "there can be no disarmament . . . until Russia is brought into the family of nations, and amicable relations and clear understanding with all other powers are established." Hoover, like his predecessors, was adamant and unrealistic in his opposition. He compared the Soviet Union to a wicked and disgraceful neighbor whom no one attacked, but neither was he invited into the homes in the neighborhood. The Communists, he stated, were carrying on propaganda for the overthrow by violence of the United States government, "but denial of recognition kept their potency from being serious." Yet, during all the years that America ignored the fact of Soviet existence, hundreds of the nation's business firms were engaged in active trade with Russia. And the pariah, which the United States alone of all the major powers refused to recognize, had become an increasingly important factor on the world scene.

Within eight months after Hoover entered the White House, the economic structure of the world began to crumble disastrously and with terrifying rapidity. Preoccupied with their own economic survival, the American public became even less concerned with international affairs than during the preceding complacent administrations. The President, however, could not remain indifferent. By 1931, Germany and Austria, on the verge of complete bankruptcy, were obviously unable to meet their reparations commitments. The Allies, also teetering on the edge of catastrophe, would face financial ruin if they attempted war debt payments to the United States without these funds. A Europe in shambles might mean the permanent loss of billions of dollars in private investments abroad.

On June 20, 1931, Hoover announced a moratorium on all war debts and reparations for one year. Stimson, more realistic, had urged complete cancellation, but the President regarded the debts as a solemn obligation. Congress concurred with Hoover's view expressing in a joint resolution late in 1931 not only its opposition to cancellation but even to reduction of the war debts. This unyielding position was shown to be futile when, in 1932, five nations, including France, defaulted completely; by mid-1934 all the others except Finland had followed suit. For more than a decade American Presidents had insisted on the fiction that war debts were not related to reparations. Now the whole sorry business reached an inevitable conclusion.

Throughout this period, Hoover was actively interested in disarmament. Like many other Americans he sought the advantage of security without the accompanying responsibility of binding obligations. After consultations with Prime Minister Ramsay MacDonald, who visited Washington in the fall of 1929, a five-power naval conference was scheduled to meet in London in the hope that an arms limitation accord would effectively implement the moral pledges of the Kellogg Pact. The United States delegation, which consisted of Secretary Stimson, Secretary of the Navy Charles F. Adams, one influential senator from each party, and three ambassadors, was as eminent a roster as could be assembled. Wishing to avoid the failure of 1927, Hoover persuaded France and Italy to attend, but their cooperation could not be enlisted at the conference.

After weeks of the usual wrangling, a treaty was finally concluded on April 22, 1930. The three major naval powers agreed to suspend construction of battleships until 1936 and established a series of ratios for smaller vessels. An "escalator clause" permitted modifications if other governments built beyond their relative strength at the time of the treaty. The rapid build-up of the German and Italian navies after 1933 activated this clause, and as a result the agreement became meaningless.

At the time, however, the President acclaimed the treaty as an alternative to mutual suspicion, hate, and ultimate disaster. When the Senate adjourned without taking action on it because some members felt it would prevent a desired reduction in taxes and others believed the Navy had not been granted adequate strength, Hoover called the Senate back into special session. A number of senators, perhaps influenced by charges in the Hearst press that the United States had been hoodwinked by Britain and Japan, demanded the confidential papers relating to the negotiations. The President refused, vigorously defending the executive prerogative in foreign policy. These papers, he said, were given to him in confidence. To maintain good relations with other nations, to protect future negotiations, the executive must not be guilty of a breach of trust by betraying these confidences. He did, however, permit individual senators to consult the files, and after much heated debate the treaty was finally approved by a vote of 58 to 9.

Rejoicing at the victory, Hoover declared that the agreement would inspire a greater faith throughout the world in the effectiveness of peaceful negotiation as opposed to force; it was a step toward general world disarmament which would promote world peace; and best of all, from the point of view of the United States, the country would be adequately protected without a burdensome military budget. He neglected to mention that the financial burden would be considerable if the United States constructed vessels up to its quota.

In the spring of 1932, President Hoover dispatched Hugh Gibson to Geneva to represent the United States at a disarmament conference on land and air weapons held under the aegis of the League of Nations. With him he sent a plan that was as excellent as it was visionary. He proposed that all land armies be reduced to the size required to preserve internal order, that bombers and all arms used for offensive purposes be abolished, and that the tonnage of all naval vessels be reduced by one-third. No provision for inspection and control was included, as Hoover felt that violations could not be kept secret and insistence on inspection might risk defeat of the plan. The demand of the European nations for more security through arms blocked any action. Two years later, with the rise of the Nazi dictatorship, the conference disbanded.

How thin a reed to depend on were naval pacts or other disarmament accords for maintaining peace was demonstrated in the fall of 1931. On September 18, Japan invaded Manchuria in direct violation of three treaties to which she was a signatory: the League Covenant, the Nine-Power Treaty, and the Paris Peace Pact. China promptly appealed to the League to act under Article II and to the United States, as sponsor of the Kellogg Pact, to take steps to uphold "the principle of peaceful settlement of international disputes."

Hoover and Stimson were shocked by the aggression, but as the attack had been perpetrated by Japanese militarists in defiance of the civil authorities, Stimson hoped that in time the Wakatsuki cabinet would check the army and end the affair. He informed the Chinese government on October 8 that "we have not attempted to go into the question of right and wrong. . . . we are not taking sides. . . . we are 'playing no favorites.'" That some day, the Japanese bombed the temporary Chinese capital at Chinchow. Far from curtailing their operations, the Japanese seemed to be planning to swallow the entire province.

A League Council meeting was scheduled for October 13 to consider the situation. Stimson persuaded Hoover to allow the American consul general at Geneva, Prentiss B. Gilbert, to attend the proceedings. After Japan and China were formally reminded of their obligations under the Paris Peace Pact, Stimson cabled both governments that the United States concurred in the resolution.

The Japanese, figuratively thumbing their noses at the Council, plunged deeper into China. Deciding against forceful action, the President instructed Stimson to advise Japan that the conquest of Manchuria would not be recognized. On January 7, 1932, a document, since known as the Stimson Non-Recognition Doctrine, was dispatched to both Japan and China. The American government, it declared, would not acknowledge any treaty or agreement between the disputants which might "impair the treaty rights of the United States . . . in China . . . [or] the sovereignty, the independence, or the territorial and administrative integrity . . . of China, or the inter-

national policy . . . commonly known as the open-door policy;
and that it does not intend to recognize any situation, treaty, or
agreement which may be brought about by means contrary to
the convenants and obligations of the Pact of Paris. . . ." Undeterred by this verbal diplomacy, Japan attacked Shanghai at
the end of January. By the following month Manchuria had
been organized into a puppet state under the name of Manchukuo and formally recognized by Japan in the fall.

To believe, as Hoover did, that a threat as feeble as non-
recognition could stop the aggressors was to fly in the face of
reality. Stimson considered the Doctrine a prelude to further
action, not a final step. He was convinced that the only way to
deal with the aggression was to apply economic and, if necessary, military sanctions against Japan, but the President would
not hear of this. He believed, as he stated at a Cabinet meeting,
that the Nine-Power Treaty and the Kellogg Pact were "solely
moral instruments based upon the hope that peace in the
world can be held by the rectitude of nations and enforced
solely by the moral reprobation on the world." The Manchurian
affair, he believed, was primarily a controversy between China
and Japan, and the United States had never set out to preserve
peace among other nations by using force. Furthermore, a dis-
passionate approach should take into account Japan's point of
view. Suffering economically from the chaotic situation in
China, the Japanese might well say, "Either the signatories of
the Nine-Power Pact must join with us to restore order in
China or we must do it as an act of self-preservation." The
United States was not obliged to go to war over this question,
since neither its freedom nor economic future was imperiled.
While America was cooperating with other countries to employ
"moral pressure," he said, it would not engage in "sanctions
either economic or military, for these are the roads to war."

The President both shared and reflected the view of the
majority of Americans whose traditional isolationism was intensified by the depression. England's role was equally unhe-
roic, but the British might have pressed for bolder action by
the League if assured of United States support. And Japan,
cognizant of the American position on sanctions, could ignore
all the palaver at Geneva. After the Lytton Commission, sent

by the League to investigate the situation, published its report condemning the invasion but recommending no action, the Japanese withdrew from the League to spend the next few years preparing for a real adventure in horror. The Manchurian incident was a green light to any would-be aggressor, since he was assured that the great powers were incapable of uniting to preserve peace.

While preoccupied with events in the Far East in the winter of 1932, the President was already looking ahead to the election. He would like, he said, "to get out" of international affairs temporarily and concentrate on domestic problems. But his approach to urgent matters at home antagonized most of the nation, weakening his political influence. Unfortunately, Hoover's philosophy of "rugged individualism" prevented him from accepting the principle of direct federal relief to the millions in desperate need or from undertaking a large public works program to relieve unemployment. As the American people prepared to vote in November, the economic crisis reached its nadir. In his depressingly dignified way, Hoover pleaded that world conditions over which the American government had no control were responsible for the calamity. This factual explanation made little impression on people struck by disaster; they required action, not diagnosis. Nor could they take seriously his warning that if his Democratic opponent were elected "the grass will grow in the streets of a hundred cities, a thousand towns; the weeds will overrun the fields of millions of farms."

By contrast, the ebullient Franklin D. Roosevelt, radiating confidence and charm, conducted a vigorous and animated compaign. "Every man has a right to life; and this means that he has also a right to make a comfortable living," he declared in one address. In another, he struck a responsive chord when he declared that the "princes of property" must safeguard the public welfare by exercising "the responsibility which goes with . . . power," or else "the government must be swift to enter and protect the public interest." The promise of a "new deal" and the hope which he inspired swept Roosevelt into office by the overwhelming popular vote of almost twenty-eight million and an electoral vote of 472.

Up until the very end of his tenure, Hoover was dogged by

crises. Three months before he was to leave office, the moratorium granted the debtor nations was due to expire, and their alarming financial position required prompt action by the administration. Several of the governments informed the United States that they would be unable to meet their obligations. As a lame-duck President, Hoover sought to consult with the President-elect to work out a joint policy on this and other pressing foreign policy matters. Roosevelt, however, felt that the responsibility rested "upon those now vested with executive and legislative authority" and refused to bind the new administration in any way to the old. "For me to accept any joint responsibility . . . might well be construed by the . . . other nations . . . as a commitment, moral even though not legal, as to policies and courses of action," he declared. In more or less normal times, the period of transition between the outgoing and incoming administrations does not present a grave problem, but in the crucial period from November, 1932, to March, 1933, the policy of drift was catastrophic.

Both in domestic and world affairs during a critical era in the nation's history, Hoover's leadership was inadequate. Had he been fortunate enough to preside during tranquil times, he might have left the White House in a glow of appreciation. As it was, he was wedded to an ideology not only useless but ruinous as a guide for the times, and he was too inflexible to divorce himself from it. Experimentation and innovation, which were essential at that point, were alien to his nature. Serious, reserved, and inclined towards pessimism—Stimson commented that he always managed to inject a dark note into discussions—he kept individuals at a distance and left the masses unmoved. His intentions, which were admirable, and his sense of responsibility, which was great, were poor substitutes for the bold and affirmative action which the White House should have undertaken.

The Hoover administration represented two distinct phases of presidential leadership. On the one hand, it was part of the hiatus of the twenties when weak chief executives, dominated in foreign affairs by their secretaries of state, were passive in all their approaches to governmental responsibility. Their orientation suited the mood and circumstances of the times. On the other hand, Hoover was also the President of the thirties, a new age when recurring crises were becoming commonplace and during which the White House was to reflect the atmosphere of stress. Starting in one era and almost immediately plunged into the second, Herbert Hoover, by nature and philosophy, found it impossible to make the transition.

11. Shaping of a Leader

IT was a gray, bleak, and dreary morning on that fourth day in March, 1933, when Franklin D. Roosevelt took the oath of office, and the weather matched the mood of the people. Despondency hung like a pall over a nation floundering blindly and hopelessly in a suffocating depression for the past three years. But the resonant voice delivering the inaugural address which was being carried into millions of homes rang with confidence, and the words sent a thrill of hope into millions of hearts. "This great Nation will endure as it has endured, will revive and prosper," the President declared. "So . . . let me assert my firm belief that the only thing we have to fear is fear itself . . . which paralyzes needed efforts to convert retreat into advance."

The poised, serene man who addressed "My friends" from the White House podium, standing erect despite his useless legs, had been intimately acquainted with fear and once had come close to despair. Eleven years before, at thirty-nine, he thought for a time that all hopes and ambitions were ended forever. Strikingly handsome, intelligent, of a wealthy and patrician background, he was sailing through life as smoothly as on one of his beloved sailboats when an attack of poliomyelitis left him paralyzed from the waist down. Grimly refusing to accept a life of invalidism, he taught himself to walk with braces and cane after years of gruelling effort. When he was asked at one time how he managed to stand the crushing strain of the presidential office during the most cataclysmic period of the nation's history, he replied, "Once I spent two years lying in bed trying to move my big toe. That was the hardest job I ever had to do. After that, anything else seems easy."

Roosevelt came to the White House rich in political experience. After briefly practicing law, he began his public career in 1910 as a member of the New York state senate. Even then he already gave intimations of the magnetism and political skill which the American public later were to acknowledge so overwhelmingly. Just barely squeaking through in a district that had not sent a Democrat to the state capitol in more than a half century, he was returned to office two years later by a large majority of his Dutchess County constituents. As a member of the legislature, he aligned himself with the progressive faction battling for political reform, attracting considerable attention even outside his state by a successful challenge of the Tammany machine's time-honored practice of dictating the choice of a candidate for the United States Senate. His humanitarianism and concern for the underprivileged were already apparent in his vigorous championing of such measures as a workmen's compensation law and an act limiting the hours of labor for children.

An ardent Wilson supporter working actively for his nomination at the 1912 convention, Roosevelt was rewarded with an appointment as Assistant Secretary of the Navy, a post he filled with distinction. Influential in achieving the expansion and modernization of the fleet, he was largely responsible, after America's entry into the war, for the mine barrage across the North Sea from Scotland to the Norwegian territorial waters. When he resigned in 1920 to accept the nomination for Vice President, he had achieved a national reputation and acquired valuable contacts with key political leaders throughout the country. Defeat of the Democrats sent him back to his law office. He did not try for a public position again until 1928 when, though doubtful about his health, he was persuaded by Alfred E. Smith to run for governor of New York in the hope that he would strengthen the ticket in that pivotal state. While Smith lost the state by more than 100,000 votes, Roosevelt piled up a majority of 25,000 and two years later was re-elected by the greatest majority ever won up to that time by a gubernatorial candidate.

At Albany, Roosevelt once again demonstrated his liberal inclinations, pressing for the adoption of old-age pensions, state unemployment insurance, a forty-eight-hour work week for women and children, and other labor reforms. With the onslaught of the depression, he moved swiftly and decisively to cope with its ravages. In the summer of 1931, addressing the legislature, he expressed the credo that had already come to inform his leadership. "Modern society, acting through its Government," he said, "owes the definite obligation to prevent the starvation or the dire want of any of its fellow men and women who try to maintain themselves but cannot. . . . To these unfortunate citizens, aid must be extended by Government, not as a matter of charity, but as a matter of social duty."

His successful record as governor, his popular leadership of a strategic state, and his strong political ambition made the nomination for the presidency the next logical step. But it did not come easily. Powerful forces in the Democratic Party opposed him, and many of the party leaders had their own favorites. Some were alienated by Roosevelt's declared commitment to internationalism. As the vice-presidential candidate in 1920, Roosevelt had urged American participation in the League of Nations. In 1928, at the request of the editor of the influential journal, *Foreign Affairs,* he contributed an article dealing with the position he believed the Democrats should take on foreign policy. He paid glowing tribute to the statesmanship of Woodrow Wilson, denouncing the Republican retreat into isolationism which, he said, caused the nation to forfeit the opportunity to assume world leadership. He reminded his readers of Wilson's lasting contribution in obtaining world support for a League of Nations that even without American participation had become the "principal agency for the settlement of international controversy." In conclusion he urged an internationalist approach, but cautiously refrained from endorsing any new effort to bring the United States into the League.

The arch-isolationist, William Randolph Hearst, who carried substantial weight in the Democratic Party, decided that Roosevelt's internationalism made him unsafe. In a radio broadcast on January 1, 1932, he announced that he was giving his support to John Nance Garner of Texas. Shortly thereafter the newspaper headlines of his vast publishing empire charged that Roosevelt had supported American entry into the League of Nations. The people, Hearst declared, were entitled to know just where the presidential aspirant now stood on the issue. With the country as a whole fearful of any ties with Europe, Roosevelt became alarmed and made a public recantation, dismaying veteran supporters of the League. At a meeting of the New York State Grange in February, he stated that United States participation in the world organization "would not serve the highest purpose of the prevention of war and a settlement of international difficulties in accordance with fundamental American ideals." He was therefore opposed to joining, suggesting instead "a national policy which will make us an example of national honor to other nations." Hearst, however, did not come to his support until the nominating convention, when he realized that, unless the votes committed to Garner were released, the beneficiary would be either of the other two contenders, to whom he was even more strenuously opposed.

To some Roosevelt appeared to be an opportunist with no sense of principle. Probably the most stinging attack was made by Walter Lippmann, who warned in 1932 that Roosevelt's progressivism was not to be taken seriously. He accused the presidential aspirant of carrying water on both shoulders, "indulging in platitudes with the intent of holding on to both right-wing and left-wing supporters," of having no real convictions and lacking a firm grasp of public affairs. He was, he said, "an amiable man with philanthropic impulses, but he is not the dangerous enemy of anything . . . no crusader . . . no tribune of the people . . . no enemy of entrenched privilege. He is a pleasant man, who, without any important qualifications for the office would very much like to be President." An editorial in the Scripps-Howard press characterized him as irresolute, favoring delay, prone to generalize. "In Franklin Roosevelt we have another Hoover."

Within a few months his detractors were to learn that they had been wrong on every count. Among other things, they underestimated his talent as a political tactician. As Roosevelt wrote to a Wilson supporter during the Hearst affair, he was still completely loyal to the ideals of Woodrow Wilson, but there was a difference between ideals and the methods of attaining them. The former remain fixed but methods continue to change with changing circumstances. "I am looking for the best modern vehicle to reach the goal of an ideal while they [the Wilsonians] insist on using a vehicle which was brand new and in good running order twelve years ago. Think this over! And for heaven's sake have a little faith." Since Hoover probably could be beaten by almost any opponent, why risk the nomination over an issue on which the party was split, and which, in any case, lacked any sense of immediacy for the electorate?

At the same time, this pragmatist, ever ready to experiment with means, to discard one plan when another seemed more workable, who never sacrificed opportunity to principle, was also an idealist. Throughout his presidency he held aloft his grand objectives and endeavored to keep the attention of the public focused on them. During the Second World War, those who sneered at his lofty aspirations as "crazy altruism" or "starry-eyed dreaming" earned sharp rebuke. "I get everlastingly angry at those who assert vociferously that the four freedoms and the Atlantic Charter are nonsense because they are unattainable. If those people," he declared, "had lived a century and a half ago they would have sneered and said that the Declaration of Independence was utter piffle. If they had lived nearly a thousand years ago they would have laughed uproariously at the ideals of the Magna Carta. And if they had lived several thousand years ago they would have derided Moses when he came down from the Mountain with the Ten Commandments."

One of the most complex individuals ever to have occupied the White House, Franklin Roosevelt seems to have been a mystery even to those who knew him most intimately. An extrovert, exuberant and cordial, he maintained an inpenetrable reserve. The warmth and geniality of his manner masked an inner detachment. Seemingly accommodating and affable, he was shrewd and calculating; on occasion, ruthless. He genuinely liked all kinds of people and was well aware of the effectiveness of his charm. "He is wholly conscious of his ability to send callers away happy and glowing in agreement with him and his ideas," wrote Raymond Moley, "and he particularly enjoys sending people away who have completely forgotten under his spell the thing they came to say or ask." Although he found it difficult to say "no" to loyal aides, he could be relentless to those who stood in his way, and in the pursuit of an objective almost everyone could be expendable.

In the struggle to master his crippling disability, pity would have been fatal, and so he cultivated cheerfulness so assiduously that it became part of him. An inherent self-assurance and optimism were confirmed by triumph over his illness. "I have never heard him say there was a problem that he thought it was impossible for human beings to solve," Eleanor Roosevelt once said. "He often recognized the difficulty of a problem and readily admitted that he did not know the answer, but was completely confident that there was an answer and somewhere a man could be found who knew the answer."

When asked about his philosophy, he is said to have replied, "Philosophy? I am a Christian and a Democrat—that's all." His faith was a simple one, unencumbered by any theological complexities, nor was he subject to the spiritual probings and soul searchings that were Wilson's torment. Free of self-doubt, untroubled by an oppressive conscience, he approached life simply and directly. Arthur Schlesinger, Jr., has written that at bottom Franklin Roosevelt "was a man without illusions, clearheaded and compassionate, who had been close enough to death to understand the frailty of human striving, but who remained loyal enough to life to do his best in the sight of God."

A deep and sincere compassion for a floundering humanity was combined with confidence in the ordinary man's common sense. People, he believed, were basically rational and decent, possessing a well-developed moral sense and a desire to do the right thing. Sometimes they had to be shown the right way, which was the purpose of education, the obligation of leadership in a democratic society.

While Roosevelt's own education was obtained at the best schools in the country—Groton, Harvard, Columbia Law

School—he showed little interest in or familiarity with the creative arts or literature or the speculations of philosophy. His bent was toward naval studies, geography, American politics, history, biography. A fertile imagination and an intuitive understanding of people, coupled with a capacious memory for facts of all kinds and an ability to "pick brains," were among his invaluable assets.

During the election campaign of 1932, Roosevelt gathered around him a group of personal advisers whose academic background produced the appellation, "brain trust." The composition of the group varied over the years, including at one time or another Raymond Moley, Rexford G. Tugwell, Adolf A. Berle, Jr., Samuel I. Rosenman, Felix Frankfurter, Thomas G. Corcoran, and Harry L. Hopkins. Originally summoned to research current issues and to help draft Roosevelt's speeches, they stayed on either as technical experts or policy advisers.

Although Roosevelt had never seriously studied constitutional theory or made a systematic inquiry into the governmental process, he agreed with his cousin Theodore that the presidency was a pulpit for providing leadership. A President, he said in 1928, when placing Alfred E. Smith's name in nomination at the Democratic convention, must have that "rare ability to make popular government function, . . . to reverse the present trend towards apathy and arouse in the citizenship an active interest—a willingness to reassume its share of the responsibility for the nation's progress." Shortly after his election he declared that "the Presidency is not merely an administrative office. That's the least of it. It is more than an engineering job, efficient or inefficient. It is pre-eminently a place of moral leadership. All of our great Presidents were leaders of thought at times when certain historic ideas in the life of the nation had to be clarified." Past occupants of the White House like Washington, Jefferson, Jackson, Lincoln, Cleveland, Roosevelt, and Wilson, he suggested, had been strong executives precisely because they had fulfilled this function.

The national emergency, with a bewildered people turning to the President for hope and a rudderless Congress turning to the White House for direction, provided the challenge to which Roosevelt was temperamentally and intellectually prepared to respond. His leadership during the early days of his tenure has become legendary. The legislative triumphs he scored during his first "hundred days" were unparalleled in American history. In rapid-fire succession, the Seventy-third Congress was bombarded with a series of bills designed to bring about relief and recovery. All were promptly enacted, for no one on Capitol Hill doubted the enthusiastic and over-whelming mass support that Roosevelt enjoyed.

Regarding administration as a minor aspect of presidential leadership, and impatient with administrative detail, Roose-velt's approach was sometimes erratic, his methods never quite conventional or predictable. Guided by what Rexford Tugwell calls the "rule of responsibility," and placing great value on his role as policy maker, he not infrequently departed from ac-cepted patterns in order to strengthen his authority. An activist in the fullest sense, he expected that all matters of any impor-tance be submitted to him for approval. Frequently two or more men were assigned to a similar project, each deliberately kept ignorant of what the other was doing. Though this might later cause resentment, it had the effect of encouraging a competition of ideas and made control over subordinates more effective.

Partly to hold the reins of policy making, and partly to cut the red tape that had ensnarled the regular executive depart-ments, Roosevelt encouraged the creation of many new agen-cies and bureaus whose chiefs were permitted to bypass exist-ing channels for direct access to the President. Secretary of State Cordell Hull resented Roosevelt's failure to respect duly constituted lines of command. He objected to his tendency to communicate directly with the Under Secretary and was par-ticularly offended whenever special emissaries abroad reported directly to the White House instead of going through the regu-lar departmental channels. An example of Roosevelt's unortho-doxy was the assignment in 1933 of preparing the way for recognition of the Soviet Union to his friend, Secretary of the Treasury Henry Morgenthau, because he had more confidence in him than in the conservative bureaucracy of the State De-partment.

Secretary of War Stimson was similarly piqued. He regarded

Roosevelt as the poorest administrator under whom he had ever worked, complaining that a vast number of administrative posts had been needlessly created and placed in charge of inexperienced men who, in many instances, were appointed because of personal favoritism. These officials reported directly to the President and, Stimson lamented, often enjoyed easier access to him than Cabinet officers.

On the other hand, Raymond Moley found the President a superb administrator whenever his political fortunes were at stake. On such occasions he would make the fullest use of his skills. "It is astonishing," he wrote in words that were echoed by few others, "that Roosevelt so ordered the various divisions of his political activity, so sharply delegated authority, and so clearly maintained personal contact with each of us, that there was never the semblance of conflict and never an overlapping of functions." While Moley exaggerated, considering the known rivalry within the official family and the duplication of duties, it is true that Roosevelt assigned a far greater importance to the art and skill of political leadership than to the narrower, administrative aspects of the presidency. Therein lay his strength.

Those close to Roosevelt have commented on his reluctance to dismiss subordinates. According to Robert Sherwood he called himself a "softie" about this. The President could be thoroughly ruthless towards those whom he found disloyal, but he was extremely loath to take action against the merely incompetent or even recalcitrant. Similarly, his loyalty sometimes strained the limits of political expediency, as when he flouted public sentiment by appointing Edward J. Flynn, political boss of the Bronx, New York, as ambassador to Australia, or antagonized powerful elements in the party, as when Jesse Jones was dropped as Secretary of Commerce in favor of Henry Wallace.

Roosevelt's unprecedentedly long tenure in office and his talent for leadership often produced exaggerated and distorted notions of his skill as a politician. His supporters tended to regard him as a political wizard; his detractors accused him of dictatorship. The myths originated in the months following his first election, when Congress's compliant behavior made it appear to be a rubber stamp legislature. Neither supporters nor critics reflected that Roosevelt had carried all but six states and swept into office with him a preponderantly Democratic Congress more than eager to cooperate with him. Moreover, Roosevelt used patronage skillfully and had a close working relationship with the hardheaded leadership of both Houses.

But Roosevelt's success in dominating the Congress was short-lived. For the most part he had to fight for every goal, and lacking the power of the magician or the despot, he sometimes fumbled and he sometimes failed. Just after the Seventy-fourth Congress convened in 1935, Senator Key Pittman, Chairman of the Foreign Relations Committee, wrote to the President expressing concern over the absence of political leadership and to urge stronger direction over Congress. "It is apparent that there is no Democratic Party in the United States Senate," he declared, although nearly two-thirds of the members were registered Democrats. The fault was lack of confidence in the success of the administration and "discontent with regard to patronage." There were complaints "that the administration is responsible for the lack of Democratic solidarity," that the Democrats had won a victory, but "the Republicans hold office . . . that there is no leadership . . . that defeat is inevitable; and every man must take care of himself. . . . May I beg of you to lay all administrative matters aside until you have your legislative matters straightened out."

Relations with Congress deteriorated despite Roosevelt's landslide victory in 1936, as increasingly he asked for legislation without first consulting its leadership. Then he committed a serious political blunder when he intervened in the selection of the Senate's Majority Leader after the death of the incumbent. By exerting heavy pressure, he managed by one vote to win the post for Alvin Barkley, but he lost his influence over the Senate. He was equally clumsy about the Court Reorganization Bill, and his veto of the wartime tax bill provoked Senate Majority Leader Barkley to resign in protest.

With the American people Roosevelt's influence and prestige remained substantially undiminished until the end. Regarding personal appearances as essential not only to gauge public sentiment but to enhance his popularity, he traveled more than eighty thousand miles by rail across country during his first term in office, visiting all but three states. He was the first chief executive to employ a systematic technique for gathering and evaluating individual opinions on public questions. A staff carefully examined the thousands of letters that poured into the White House each day. More than a concern with public sentiment, this attention to the opinions of citizens was in keeping with his concept of "moral leadership." The presidency, he once declared, should become a "great clearing house for exchange of information and ideas, of facts and ideals affecting the general welfare."

Radio talks, which became known as "fireside chats," were utilized by Roosevelt not only to clarify significant public issues but to mobilize public support behind his legislative program. Unrivaled in the use of this medium, Roosevelt, as one reporter put it, was "the best showman" the White House had ever had. He had the unique ability of creating the kind of relationship that he once described as "a subtle bond which makes him [the President] their champion and makes them enthusiastically trust him with their loyalty and their love." He possessed all the personal attributes to help establish that bond: warmth, buoyancy, optimism, and a confidence that was instantly communicable. Moreover, he had that other invaluable quality of leadership, a flair for phrasemaking and the ability to arouse and inspire, through an eloquent but intimate oratory that made each individual feel as though he personally was being addressed. In 1932, with his ringing injunction against fear, he jolted out of their torpor a people numbed and bewildered by a disaster they could not comprehend. He later drew his countrymen into the battle against privilege by assailing "economic royalists" and asserting that "the flag and the Constitution stand for democracy." He engaged them in the struggle against social injustice with the declaration, "We cannot afford to accumulate a deficit in the books of human fortitude." He was the prophet of the Old Testament: "Divine Justice weighs the sins of the coldblooded and the sins of the warmhearted in different scales." He was the embattled crusader: "It is a war for the survival of democracy," and "I am enlisted for the duration."

With the press Roosevelt at once established a highly satisfactory rapport, flattering the White House correspondents with his frequent "off the record" remarks, encouraging them to ask questions freely. Under his capable direction, the press conference was revitalized, becoming an effective instrument for enlightening the public, influencing Congress, creating a favorable image of the administration with "background" stories, and communicating his views to the world. One Washington reporter observed that the President had transformed the press conference into "a distinctively American device for informing the nation of what the President is contemplating and the President of what the nation is thinking." His radio talks were generally followed by a meeting with the press, then, after an interval, by a message to the Congress outlining the need for some specific legislation.

No amount of formal training or adherence to a particular theory could have provided the skill to exercise the role of popular leader and schoolmaster to the American people. A master politician, he used all the tools available in a democratic society. He always attempted to obtain a wide base of public support, to win the cooperation of any powerful group with which he had to deal, and to keep from antagonizing any cohesive national, religious, or racial blocs. To secure universal approbation, he knew, was of course impossible—a few powerful enemies or hostile symbols could even be a political asset—but he never failed to concentrate on those groups whose support was essential to the success of a particular program.

The variety of tactics he employed to achieve his political objectives, the way he balanced his means and ends, led critics to accuse him of contradictions and inconsistencies. Roosevelt, in the introduction to his *Public Papers*, readily conceded that the charge was valid. Those who seek inconsistencies in these volumes, he wrote, will find them. There were "inconsistencies of methods, inconsistencies caused by ceaseless efforts to find ways to solve problems for the future as well as for the present. There were inconsistencies born of insufficient knowledge. There were inconsistencies springing from the need of experimentation. But through them all, I trust that there also will be found a consistency and continuity of broad purpose." Rexford Tugwell, who had observed him at close range, commented that no leader had ever been more determined to achieve his objective, or more flexible about the means he employed.

Franklin Delano Roosevelt

12. Retreat to the Storm Cellars

THE period of the thirties marks a point in history when the tempo of the world suddenly began to accelerate, never to return again to the old jog trot. In the interim between Roosevelt's election and inauguration, Adolf Hitler came to power, transforming Germany into an armed leviathan spewing hatred and menacing world order. In Asia, Japan, unmistakably hostile to the Western nations, persisted with her military and imperialist program.

While Roosevelt was fully preoccupied with internal affairs, as head of a world power he could not ignore his international responsibilities. Using the war debts question as a springboard for discussion, he initiated a series of bilateral talks with the leaders of other states. Dealing at first with economic matters, the talks were soon expanded to a far wider scope. The parade of diplomats to the White House and State Department in these "get acquainted" sessions began late in April, 1933, and continued on through May. At the meeting with Prime Minister Ramsay MacDonald, it was agreed to convene a World Economic Conference in London on June 12, to seek a way out of the deadly economic morass into which the world was sinking ever more deeply. Roosevelt also promised MacDonald to continue American support of the disarmament conference then in progress, to which the Prime Minister had just presented a plan for dealing with the Hitler threat.

Shortly thereafter, in a fireside chat on May 7, the President informed the nation that he had discussed with the foreign leaders who visited Washington plans to reduce armament costs, scale down trade barriers, and stabilize currency. "I want to emphasize to you that the domestic situation is inevitably and deeply tied in with the conditions in all of the other Nations of the world." Unless world conditions were sound, he said, prosperity would never return to the United States. A world economic conference was scheduled, he told his listeners, and it was vital that it succeed. "The future of the world demands it and we have each of us pledged ourselves to the best joint efforts to this end."

In acknowledging the influence which such world-wide factors as trade barriers and currency stabilization might have on the domestic economy, he thus publicly expressed for the first time the thesis that the European element in the equation was decisive. His position greatly encouraged the internationalist Secretary of State, Cordell Hull, who headed the American delegation. The members of the group setting out for London were in disagreement about the merits of currency stabilization. Moreover, they had received no specific instructions from the President as to the nature of the United States position, because he himself was not sure what the best course should be. After the gold standard had been formally abandoned in April, the dollar began to fall in relation to foreign currencies, stimulating American exports and a rise in prices. Stabilization, Roosevelt feared, might halt this desirable trend.

At the conference, the European powers themselves were divided between those led by France, who favored the stabilization of foreign exchange through a return to the gold standard, and the others who preferred to concentrate on the domestic price structure. A tentative agreement was reached which set the dollar-sterling rate at about four dollars to the pound and, in effect, would prevent the President from using his discretionary power to alter the gold content of the dollar. When rumors of the agreement reached the United States, stock and commodity prices began to sag, and the entire price structure seemed imperiled. Inflationists in Congress raised a shout of protest. On June 17, Roosevelt cabled Hull, "We must retain full freedom of action . . . in order to hold up price levels at home."

Shortly thereafter, Raymond Moley, who had gone to London with the latest instructions from the President, submitted an alternative plan which would not seriously bind the United States. But Roosevelt, apparently convinced by now that stabilization of any sort would adversely affect recovery at home, soon withdrew this mild proposal. Furthermore, it appeared to him that preoccupation of the conference with currency had caused it to lose sight of the larger issues affecting international stability. On July 3 he sent a cable which has since become known as the "bombshell" message, in view of its impact abroad. "I would regard it as a catastrophe amounting to a world tragedy," he stated, "if the great Conference of Nations, called to bring about a more real and permanent financial stability and a greater prosperity to the masses of all Nations, should, in advance of any serious effort to consider these broader problems, allow itself to be diverted by the proposal of a purely artificial and temporary experiment affecting the monetary exchange of a few Nations only."

Many Americans strongly backed the President, but Europeans were enraged. The gold block delegates declared that they would go home at once. Hull sprang into action. By strenuous efforts he prevented the conference from disbanding, but it only survived for another three weeks. While Roosevelt often has been accused of "torpedoing" the conference, the reason for its failure was far more complex. One of the Swedish delegates, an economist, stated afterward that the gold countries dictatorially demanded that all others submit to their rule and "finally refused to take part in any monetary discussions if their terms were not accepted. It was this imperative attitude that at last wrecked the conference." Equally adamant was the United States, representing those nations eager to affect the domestic price level by means of a managed currency. The gap was simply too great to be bridged. As Roosevelt later declared, "We were engaged at home in a great program of rehabilitation . . . which called for the raising of values—and . . . no human being could, at that moment, determine exactly where even a temporary stabilization point should be fixed for the dollar, franc, or pound." That those countries which pleaded so urgently for stabilization to keep from going off the gold standard had been needlessly agitated was confirmed by the fact that two or three years later they were still on gold. To protect his own program of raising prices through currency inflation, Roosevelt practiced economic nationalism, but his approach was pragmatic rather than doctrinaire as was demonstrated by the complete support he later gave Hull's program of tariff reduction under a system of reciprocal trade agreements.

Earlier that same year, at the Geneva World Disarmament Conference, Hitler was threatening to walk out and launch an intensive rearmament program. In March, Ramsay MacDonald submitted a plan providing for the use of economic sanctions against any nation identified as an aggressor. Roosevelt was doubtful whether he could obtain Senate approval to participate in such collective action. However, he instructed Norman Davis, his representative at the sessions, to give informal assurance that the United States could at least be counted on not to obstruct any joint measures against an aggressor. Since even this negative assistance would involve some departure from traditional neutrality and therefore require legislation, Roosevelt and Hull revived Hoover's request to the lame duck Congress for authority for the President to bar arms shipments to aggressors.

The conference limped along, hobbled by the usual conflicting interests, and in May virtually came to a dead halt. Germany was becoming increasingly belligerent. On May 12, Hitler's announcement that he would make an important policy address to the Reichstag seemed to signal the end of all attempts at disarmament. But Roosevelt would not yet concede defeat. Just before the anticipated harangue, he sent a message to the heads of fifty-four nations appealing for a drastic reduction and eventual elimination of all land armaments, support of the MacDonald plan, and a proposal for a multilateral non-agression pact. Whether or not this had any influence on the Fuehrer, his speech was surprisingly moderate.

Then on May 22, with the President's authorization, Davis formally announced to the conference that the United States would agree to the reduction of all armies to the level of police forces (a revival of the Hoover proposal), would cooperate in the establishment of an inspection system, accept the Mac-

Donald plan, consult with other countries in the event of a threat to the peace, and, finally, refrain from any measures which would interfere with the application of sanctions by other nations. To Roosevelt's and Hull's astonishment, the proposals were coolly received in Europe. France regarded them as an inadequate commitment to European security, while other nations quibbled about the distinction between "offensive" and "defensive" weapons or how to define aggression. At home, on the other hand, the isolationists in the Senate became so agitated that the arms embargo resolution under consideration by the Senate Foreign Relations Committee was amended to ban shipments to *all* parties in a dispute, making it completely ineffective for stopping an aggressor. The President decided not to press the matter. Endeavoring just then to win support from Congress for some essential domestic legislation, he feared to risk antagonizing the legislators.

Hitler withdrew from the conference and from the League of Nations in October. Still unresigned, Roosevelt made another attempt at arms control by proposing a limited agreement to supervise and curb the manufacture and sale of munitions. Formal discussions followed, but the conference soon bogged down in the customary endless debate, and when the Third Reich instituted military conscription the following spring, the disarmament conference adjourned. It was never to be reconvened.

For the first time in many years, Roosevelt's natural optimism deserted him. An arms race not only menaced peace, but the vast sums poured into non-productive steel would further drain the almost bloodless nations. Moreover, social justice and the improvement of economic conditions were possible only if the world was free from the threat of aggression. He was disgusted with England. While Hitler's policies were the immediate cause of the breakdown of the disarmament discussions, Great Britain, he privately charged, bore a definite share of the responsibility by refusing "to accept detailed publicity as to armament orders on the ground that it would prejudice their armament trade. . . . The present British government is not sincere in seeking legislation or reduction of present world armaments or present world trade in war-like weapons."

It was also disturbing that preoccupation with the German challenge was causing Britain to become indifferent to the alarming trends in the Far East. With the Japanese seeking to further their military ambitions by achieving parity in naval vessels, only joint Anglo-American action, Roosevelt felt, could stabilize the situation. He even suspected that England was secretly wooing Japan. While the disarmament conference was still in session, he directed Davis to warn the British Foreign Office discreetly but firmly that if any signs pointed to England's "preferring to play with Japan to playing with us, we shall be compelled, in the interest of American security, to approach public sentiment in Canada, Australia, New Zealand, and South Africa in a definite effort to make these Dominions understand clearly that their future security is linked with us in the United States."

Influenced partly by the threatening policies of Japan and Germany, Roosevelt initiated negotiations in 1933 for recognition of the Soviet Union, personally handling many of the details. Resumption of diplomatic relations had been openly urged long before. In August, 1932, Republican Senator Borah, who had been pressing the matter, wrote to the Secretary of State about information he had received from a friend in Tokyo that a treaty was being negotiated between Japan and Russia. "Viewing Japan's policy . . . and looking at her program . . . I feel more strongly than ever that our relationship with Russia ought to undergo a change. I am satisfied that by proper steps taken upon the part of our government any close relationship between Russia and Japan could be avoided." Moreover, Roosevelt, in common with many members of the business community, hoped that recognition would stimulate large-scale trade with the Soviet Union. Senator Hiram Johnson stated that there were "billions of dollars worth of future orders in Russia for American workers to fill." Negotiations proceeded smoothly, and the day after they were concluded the President told a Savannah, Georgia audience that "Mr. Litvinov and I believe that through the resumption of normal relations the prospects of peace over all the world are greatly strengthened."

Friendly relations with the countries of the western hemisphere Roosevelt considered of major importance. In his inaugural address he had reiterated the Hoover administration's disclaimer that the United States possessed the right of intervention in the internal affairs of the Latin-American nations. To implement his position, his first step was to conclude an agreement on August 7, 1933, with the president of Haiti, providing for the withdrawal of all remaining Marines. Then, in a talk on December 28, he stated, "The maintenance of constitutional government . . . is not a sacred obligation devolving upon the United States." Maintaining law and order "in this hemisphere is the concern of each individual Nation within its own borders" and should orderly processes break down, "it becomes the joint concern of a whole continent in which we are all neighbors."

At the seventh Pan-American Conference at Montevideo that month, the United States gave positive evidence of intent to cooperate with its neighbors on an equal basis. The major accomplishment, for which Secretary Hull was largely responsible, was a policy statement known as the Convention on Rights and Duties of States. It dealt with such questions as the equality of states, recognition of *de facto* governments, sovereignty of states in their relations with foreign nations, and inviolability of territory. For the first time a pledge of nonintervention by the United States was incorporated into a multilateral agreement, and throughout Roosevelt's administration the pledge was honored. When the conference ended, Roosevelt could truthfully say that "a better state of feeling among the neighbor Nations of North and Central and South America exists today than at any time within the memory of this generation."

Latin Americans were pleased and impressed when the United States made no move to intervene during a series of uprisings in Cuba in 1933, sending naval vessels only to protect American lives and property. On May 28, 1934, the Platt Amendment, which for more than three decades had given the United States the right to interfere in Cuba, was abrogated, and the island ceased to be a protectorate. At about this time, Panama, too, was "liberated" from its protectorate status after a series of conferences.

Under Roosevelt, the traditional policy of intervention to

protect property rights was abandoned never to be resumed. In 1935, Under Secretary of State Sumner Welles outlined the American position when Cuba was experiencing another upheaval. The question may be raised, he stated, as to what the United States would do if domestic violence in a country threatened the lives of American citizens and American investments. As funds invested abroad generally yielded a higher return than at home, investors should be prepared to assume greater risks, and one of these is "the possibility of domestic violence which may cause damage to capital invested." As for the protection of American nationals, the government's action indicates "the future course of our policy in this respect." American warships were sent to Cuban ports only to evacuate American citizens if the situation made this necessary, "but no Marines were landed."

After a truce had been arranged in 1935 between Bolivia and Paraguay, which had been carrying on a particularly sanguinary war for three years over some disputed land, President Roosevelt proposed a hemisphere meeting to prevent the repetition of a similar situation. When the Inter-American Conference for the Maintenance of Peace convened at Buenos Aires on December 1, 1936, he was so anxious for the success of the meeting that he made the long trip to deliver the opening address. The objective, he stated, was not "to form alliances, to divide the spoils of war, to partition countries, to deal with human beings as though they were pawns in a game of chance," but "to assure the continuance of the blessings of peace."

During the course of an amicable three-week session, eleven treaties and sixty-two resolutions were approved which, in essence, reaffirmed the Montevideo declaration of a hands-off policy in the affairs of other nations and provided, among other things, for the peaceful settlement of differences and united action against any internal or external threat to the peace. Two years later, the Pan-American Conference held at Lima, Peru, was equally successful. A declaration reaffirmed the principles agreed to at previous gatherings and provided that, in the event of an external threat of aggression, the foreign ministers would meet to consider such cooperative action as might be necessary to deal with the challenge to the hemisphere.

The good neighbor policy was put to a major test in 1938 when the Mexican government expropriated American oil holdings. No economic or military pressure was exerted by the United States, and the companies involved reached their own financial settlement with Mexico. Roosevelt's course, based on the concept of juridical equality among the states, elevated relations between the United States and its neighbors to the south to the highest point they had ever reached. One reason for the President's success was his personal appeal to Latin Americans. They responded to his anti-imperialist attitude, to his New Deal program for social and economic reform, and regarded him as a champion of the oppressed everywhere.

Despite the lack of opposition to Roosevelt's cooperation with the League in the Bolivia-Paraguay dispute, the powerful isolationist sentiment of many Americans compelled him to move cautiously with regard to a more basic relationship with that organization. While the nation collaborated in many of the League's non-political activities, he could see no possibility for membership. But three of his predecessors had urged joining the World Court. He also raised the issue in 1935, and like them he was defeated. With apparently little effort the isolationists, led by Father Coughlin, a demagogue with a tremendous radio following, and William Randolph Hearst, were able to mobilize sentiment so rapidly and effectively that Capitol Hill was inundated with telegrams. If Roosevelt desired to measure the intensity of the isolationist temper, he was provided with a barometer. Deeply disappointed, he wrote to Henry L. Stimson that "these are not normal times; people are jumpy and very ready to run after strange gods. . . . I fear common sense dictates no new method for the time being—but I have an unfortunately long memory and I am not forgetting either our enemies or our objectives." Yet, during the fight over the World Court, the President apparently did not consider the issue important enough to make a radio appeal to the country.

Roosevelt saw unmistakable manifestations that the world was hurtling toward catastrophe, and the information he continually received from abroad heightened his apprehension. As

early as June, 1933, the consul general in Berlin informed him
that some of the leaders of the new German government were
"capable of actions which really outlaw them from ordinary
intercourse," that no peace would satisfy them unless they
achieved their fullest ambitions. The commercial attaché at the
American Embassy in Berlin the following year warned that no
confidence could be placed in Nazi assurances of peaceful
intentions. They were determined to eradicate the memory of
1918 "by inflicting humiliations in particular upon the French,
the Poles, the Czechs and anybody else they can get their
hands on. . . . Let us repeat this fact and let it sink in, the
Nationalist Socialist movement is building a tremendous military machine . . . [which] lies in the hands of narrow, ignorant
and unscrupulous adventurers who have been slightly touched
with madness from brooding over Germany's real or imagined
wrongs, as well as the slights and indignities thrown in their
own individual way as they attempted to organize the movement." The Nazis, he went on, were determined to secure more
power and territory, and they would not hesitate to use force in
achieving their aims. Word also reached Roosevelt that same
year from other sources of an impending military alliance
between Germany and Japan.

From 1934 on, Ambassador Long in Italy reported on the
intensive war preparations and the fanatical devotion to Benito
Mussolini of large segments of the Italian people. "Italy is irrevocably determined to proceed in Africa," he wrote, and warned
that unless this ambition was checked European peace would
be menaced for the next generation. He also commented on
a growing rapprochement between Italy and Germany.

The situation in the Far East was equally ominous. Ambassador Grew wrote from Tokyo of Japanese ambitions "to obtain
trade control and eventually predominant political influence in
China, the Philippines, the Straits Settlements, Siam and the
Dutch East Indies, the Maritime Provinces and Vladivostok,
one step at a time . . . pausing intermittently to consolidate and
then continuing as soon as the intervening obstacles can be
overcome by diplomacy or force." He warned that the United
States would be "reprehensibly somnolent" if it placed its hope
and reliance on the restraining power of treaties.

In private communications and discussions, Roosevelt expressed his deep concern and his feeling of helplessness. To Colonel House he wrote in April, 1935, that he had thought over "two or three different methods by which the weight of America could be thrown into the scale of peace and of stopping the armament race. I reject each in turn for the principal reason that I fear any suggestion on our part would meet with the same kind of chilly, half-contemptuous reception on the other side as an appeal would have met in July or August, 1914." Germany had just announced a rearmament program, in violation of the Versailles Treaty, and he hoped that England, France, and Italy then meeting at Stresa could agree to impose a land and sea blockade against the Reich. If the blockade were effective, then the United States could cooperate by recognizing it. In this way, sanctions could be employed, though under another guise. "I advance this thought because rumor has come to me that something along this line may be discussed at Stresa."

No agreement was reached on a policy of counterthrust, and Roosevelt's "methods" were confined to the realm of private speculation. The European powers seemed incapable of collective action, and at home there were the isolationists. Of the latter, he wrote again to House in September that they belong to a "very large and perhaps increasing school of thought" which believes that it is possible and desirable to withdraw from all but the most perfunctory relationships with Europe. Disgustedly, he went on, "They imagine that if the civilization of Europe is about to destroy itself through internal strife, it might just as well go ahead and do it and that the United States can stand idly by."

Yet, during the critical mid-thirties, Roosevelt made no attempt to counter the isolationists with a forthright expression of his views. In view of the importance which he attached to the President's role as schoolmaster, the only explanation must be that he thought it would be futile. In a democratic society, the head of a nation can change popular attitudes only when they are superficial and unstable or when the opposition is poorly organized and ineptly led. None of these conditions prevailed. Isolationism was deeply ingrained and widely prevalent. Americans clung tenaciously to a belief in the uniqueness of their country's institutions and the wisdom of keeping out of the involvements of a corrupt Europe. Their spokesmen were numerous, influential, and articulate. Even the mildest attempt at collective security created an uproar. Thus, for example, when Roosevelt offered in May, 1933, to participate in joint consultation if a disarmament plan was adopted, John Bassett Moore, a leading authority on international law, denounced it as "the gravest danger to which the country had ever been exposed, a danger involving our very independence."

A reinterpretation of history fed the postwar disillusionment and was in turn fed by it. Wilson's idealism was disparaged as naïve, the Allied nations were considered to have been equally responsible with Germany for the war, and American policy makers were condemned either for not having been absolutely neutral or for having capitulated to the war profiteers.

The conviction that American entry into the war had been reprehensible was fortified by the disclosures of the Nye Committee. In April, 1934, the Senate approved a resolution submitted by the arch-isolationist senator from North Dakota, Gerald P. Nye, authorizing an investigation of war profiteering in the munitions industry. Nye was appointed to head the inquiry. The hearings themselves, and later the published report about the bribing of politicians, evasion of taxes, fantastic profits from the sale of munitions, patents shared with the enemy powers, collusion in not bombing enemy munitions plants, sent a wave of revulsion over the country. "Merchants of Death," referring to those parasites who lured the nation into war and grew sleek and fat on the blood of the boys dead in the trenches, was a book title that became a household phrase. Plays and movie films graphically depicted the horrors of battle, while an endless stream of anti-war books and pamphlets poured off the presses. *Road to War* by Walter Millis, published in 1935, which had a wide circulation, dealt with the nation's economic ties to the Allies and the influence of British propaganda. The dust jacket urged the reader to learn how "a peace-loving democracy, muddled but excited, misinformed and whipped to frenzy, embarked upon its greatest foreign war. . . . Read it and blush! Read it and beware!"

To convince the public that the appalling facts exposed by the Nye Committee were unrelated to the fundamental issues that brought America into the war would have required an educational program of heroic proportions. Moreover, Roosevelt regarded it as politically inexpedient to engage the powerful isolationists in the Senate, among whom were progressives like Borah, Nye, La Follette, and Wheeler. He could not risk their desertion of the New Deal program by whipping up a storm over foreign policy.

An equally potent consideration was the inability of the European powers to effect a coalition in defense of their own interests, wrangling bitterly among themselves while the lighted fuse was steadily growing shorter. The Hoare-Laval Pact accepting the conquest of Ethiopia was only one of the unhappy indications of European division and duplicity. It reinforced the isolationists' belief in the validity of their position.

Even before Mussolini began to destroy the hapless little kingdom of Ethiopia with tanks and poison gas, the combination of heightening tension abroad and the revelations of the Nye Committee induced a demand for measures to insulate America from European wars. In the summer of 1935, a neutrality law was drafted. One of its provisions made it mandatory for the President to proclaim an arms embargo against any belligerent in a conflict. Roosevelt opposed this section on two counts: first, by depriving him of discretionary authority, it would undermine the executive's traditional control over foreign policy; and secondly, it would have the undesirable effect of injuring the victim of aggression.

Roosevelt and Hull favored legislation giving the President discretionary authority to withhold shipments from the invader as a possible deterrent. The isolationists countered with the argument that an embargo could only result in dragging the nation into foreign disputes. Senator Key Pittman, chairman of the Foreign Relations Committee, cautioned Roosevelt that he would be "licked" if he insisted on "designating the aggressor in accordance with the wishes of the League of Nations." The only concession the White House was able to obtain was a six-months' time limit on the mandatory feature, after which it was hoped the question would be reconsidered.

When Congress, by a virtually unanimous vote, enacted the legislation, Roosevelt, agreeing with much of its purpose and substance, signed the measure. But he did so with a warning message that was considerably stronger than a draft prepared by Hull. Although it was the policy of the government to avoid being drawn into the wars of other nations, he stated, "no Congress and no Executive can foresee all possible future situations. . . . It is conceivable that situations may arise in which the wholly inflexible provisions . . . of this act might have exactly the opposite effect from that which was intended. . . . [They] might drag us into war instead of keeping us out."

Increasingly pessimistic reports from abroad reduced to the vanishing point Roosevelt's faint hope that peace would be maintained. Early in 1936 he wrote to Ambassador William C. Dodd in Berlin, "All the experts here, there and the other place say 'There will be no war.' They said the same thing all through July, 1914. . . . In those days I believed the experts. Today I have my tongue in my cheek." And to Jesse I. Straus in Paris: "There are those who come from England and France and Germany who point to the fact that every crisis of the past three years has been muddled through with a hope that each succeeding crisis will be met peacefully in one way or another in the next few years. I hope that point of view is right but it goes against one's common sense."

In March, 1936, the Germans brazenly reoccupied the Rhineland in clear violation of the Versailles Treaty. The action went unchallenged by England and France, the latter falling back on British irresolution as a pretext for her own failure to move decisively. The French Foreign Minister asked Ambassador Straus to request a public statement from the President or his Secretary of State denouncing the immorality and illegality of Germany's unilateral action. "It was his belief," wrote the ambassador, "that the President's words would have wide attention, and real effect, particularly in England." But in transmitting the memorandum to the President, Hull appended a note in which he indicated that no action was called for as the peace treaty between the United States and Germany had not been violated. Roosevelt remained silent.

On another occasion the following year, the cautious

Hull dissuaded the President from exercising international leadership to halt the drift to war. Under Secretary of State Sumner Welles had proposed that all the governments be invited to send high-level representatives to the White House, where Roosevelt would attempt to galvanize the moral conscience of the world on behalf of peace and declare America's readiness to support any efforts to prevent war. He would urge subscription to a set of principles covering international conduct, effective methods for reducing and controlling armaments and promoting the economic security and welfare of all nations through equal access to raw materials. The President would also invite the nations to select a small number of governments, representing the various geographical areas, to constitute an executive committee which would prepare a detailed agenda for later consideration by a world-wide conference. Welles hoped that the proposal would strengthen British and French resolution in the campaign to check aggression.

Roosevelt was impressed with the idea and planned to assemble the world's statesmen on Armistice Day, 1937, but Hull objected. The Secretary contended that the aggressors would naturally pay lip service to the goal of peace and, by their seeming concurrence, lull the democracies into a false sense of security. Moreover, the timing was bad, as the United States was seeking to increase its defense capacity. The meeting might also influence Congress against adopting a more internationalist position. In any case, he urged that the British be consulted first. Swayed by all these considerations, Roosevelt temporarily abandoned the plan, but two months later communicated secretly with the British Prime Minister about it. As the British were then in the process of negotiating with Hitler and planning to accord *de jure* recognition to Mussolini's conquest of Ethiopia, Chamberlain rejected the whole idea.

In the meantime, the headlong rush toward catastrophe continued. Civil war erupted in Spain in July, 1936, when the Republican coalition government was attacked by the Fascists under the leadership of General Francisco Franco, who planned to establish a dictatorship. In the fall, Hitler joined with Mussolini in a Rome-Berlin axis that soon developed into a comprehensive political and military alliance. When shortly thereafter the Germans entered into an anti-Comintern pact with the Japanese, the union of the three militarist powers was complete. In the summer of 1937, Japan launched a full-scale invasion of the Chinese mainland.

Casting about for some way to use his influence, Roosevelt asked his ambassador in Berlin to ascertain, if possible, Hitler's foreign policy objectives for the next ten years. Would the Chancellor be willing to make a public statement concerning his maximum ambitions? Would he be willing "to state whether or not he would have any sympathy with a general limitation of armaments proposal"?

Finally, the President decided to see if he could arouse the American people out of their dangerous indifference and perhaps put some steel in the spine of the European diplomats. On October 5, 1937, in a Chicago address, he declared that a reign of terror and international lawlessness was sweeping across the globe, threatening the very foundations of civilization, and warned, "let no one imagine that America will escape . . . that this western hemisphere . . . will continue tranquilly and peacefully to carry on the ethics and arts of civilization." Then, turning as it were to Europe, he declared, "The peace-loving nations must make a concerted effort in opposition to those violations of treaties and those ignorings of human instincts which today are creating a state of international anarchy and instability from which there is no escape through mere isolation or neutrality."

When an epidemic occurred, he went on, the community "joins in a quarantine of the patients in order to protect the health of the community against the spread of the disease." War is a contagion which can travel to places remote from its origins. "We are determined to keep out of war," he said, "yet we cannot insure ourselves against the disastrous effects of war and the dangers of involvement . . . we cannot have complete protection in a world of disorder in which confidence and security have broken down. . . . America hates war; America hopes for peace. Therefore, America actively engages in the search for peace."

Reaction from the isolationists was prompt and violent: warmongering, they shrieked, some congressmen even clamoring about impeachment. While a number of newspapers responded favorably, the majority attacked the President's position as a dangerous departure from the neutrality designed to keep the nation out of foreign wars. According to his intimate advisers, Roosevelt was surprised by the volume and intensity of the attacks. He was also disheartened that some Cabinet members and congressional leaders failed to speak out publicly in support of his stand.

Afraid that he had overreached himself, Roosevelt attempted to pull back on the limb the next day. When asked at his press conference whether his "quarantine" speech implied a repudiation of neutrality, Roosevelt replied that it might even represent an enlargement of the neutrality policy. Were any economic sanctions contemplated? "No, not necessarily," he replied. "Look, sanctions is a terrible word to use. . . . Let's not call it that. Let's call it concert of action on the part of peace-loving nations." Was that going to be brought into play? "I can't tell you what the methods will be. We are looking for some way to peace, and by no means is it necessary that that way be contrary to the exercise of neutrality."

A public opinion poll taken shortly after the address revealed widespread concern that if the President were permitted to exercise initiative and discretion he might drag the nation into the conflict. As between tighter neutrality regulations and the President's judgment, sixty-nine per cent of those polled expressed greater confidence in the former. Roosevelt later told his friend, Samuel Rosenman, "It's a terrible thing to look over your shoulder when you are trying to lead—and to find no one there." To the Reverend Endicott Peabody, his old Groton schoolmaster, he wrote that he was battling a public psychology of long standing, and to Colonel House he expressed the hope that with time people could be made to realize that "war will be a greater danger to us if we close all the doors and windows than if we go out in the street and use our influence to curb the riot."

Convinced that to press the campaign for collective security which he had launched in his quarantine speech would be both inexpedient and futile, Roosevelt retreated, but to an extent that he was later to regret. The arms embargo provision of the

Neutrality Act had been applied to Spain, and throughout the long, savage struggle he refused to have it lifted against the Loyalist government even when it became clear that the rebel forces were being given massive assistance by Germany and Italy. Britain and France had adopted a "non-intervention" program intended to localize the conflict by barring assistance to both sides, but it served only to keep the legitimate government from receiving aid. The ambassador to Spain, Claude G. Bowers, informed the administration that the embargo was of incalculable aid to the dictators, but when the Spanish government asked the United States to condemn the large-scale military assistance Germany was providing the Fascists, Secretary Hull replied that "this government is primarily interested in keeping out of war."

Some members of the administration were gravely concerned about the prospect of a Fascist victory. Harold Ickes, for one, bitterly characterized America's policy as "shameful." Even a number of prominent isolationists favored lifting the embargo, the effect of which they regarded as unneutral, Senator Nye himself introducing a resolution to do so in the spring of 1938. Roosevelt, whose sympathies were entirely with the Loyalists and who recognized that Spain had become a testing ground for the dictatorships, kept vacillating even while the rebel forces were hammering at the gates of Madrid. In January, 1938, when the Spanish Loyalist cause seemed all but lost, Henry L. Stimson publicly urged that the prohibition of arms be rescinded, warning that a law intended to keep the nation at peace was imperiling the country by easing the path of the dictators.

With a substantial segment of popular opinion in both Europe and America favoring the legitimate Spanish government, the embargo conceivably might have been lifted had Roosevelt taken the lead. But he was deterred by considerations of internal politics. He was wary of further jeopardizing his political influence, which had plummeted since his abortive efforts to "pack" the Supreme Court and "purge" conservative Democrats by campaigning against them in the primaries. The Democrats in Congress would oppose him, he was told, and also it "would mean the loss of every Catholic vote next fall."

"This was the cat that was actually in the bag," Secretary of the Interior Harold Ickes, who had tried to persuade him to act, fumed in his diary, "and it is the mangiest, scabbiest cat ever. This proves up to the hilt what so many people have been saying, namely, that the Catholic minorities in Great Britain and America have been dictating the international policy with respect to Spain." Not too many months later, according to Ickes, Roosevelt was to confess that he made a grievous error in not attempting to have the embargo lifted.

Considering the commitment of the Germans and Italians to a Franco victory, Roosevelt probably could not have influenced the outcome of the Spanish struggle, but if he had acted more courageously, the democratic nations across the Atlantic might have responded to his moral leadership.

In the meantime, the assault upon the ever more fragile peace continued. In March, 1938, Nazi tanks and troops crossed the border into Austria, and within a few hours that country's life as an independent nation was snuffed out. Czechoslovakia became the next target, Hitler raving that the Sudeten minority had to be liberated from an intolerable situation, and that he had thirty-six divisions ready to see that they received "justice." The crisis reached a boiling point in September. Once again, and probably at the most fateful moment of the twentieth century, the Western powers were pathetically irresolute and also stubbornly unwilling to seek the cooperation of the Soviet Union for a collective stand against aggression. Panicked by Hitler's threats, Prime Minister Neville Chamberlain flew to the Fuehrer on September 22 to plead with him to take the Sudeten area peacefully. Now confirmed in his belief that the democracies were spineless, Hitler raised his demands. Shocked at this duplicity, and probably also guilt-ridden, Britain and France balked at further appeasement.

For several days war appeared imminent as Chamberlain ordered air-raid shelters dug in London and mobilized the Royal Navy. At that point, President Roosevelt stepped in. Without endorsing any particular proposals, on September 26 he personally appealed to all the heads of state involved "not to break off negotiations looking to a peaceful, fair, and constructive settlement of the questions at issue." The following day he

responded to Hitler's reply—a tirade about the sufferings of
the Sudeten Germans—by stating that the Fuehrer could
render "an outstanding service to humanity" by exercising
moderation. He also privately communicated with Mussolini,
urging him to exert his influence. After a few more nerve-
wracking days, Chamberlain, Daladier, Mussolini, and Hitler
met at Munich on September 30 and disposed of Czechoslovakia. The democratic leaders abjectly conceded to all of Hitler's previous demands and some new ones in return for his
"sacred" promise that he would make no more territorial claims.

While Britain and France were primarily responsible for allowing the dismemberment of Czechoslovakia, the United
States was not guiltless. By failing to remonstrate against the
sordid infraction of law and justice, it shared in the culpability.
But almost everywhere people were hysterical with relief, and
Chamberlain was hailed as a hero for having pulled the world
back from the abyss. Roosevelt expressed the American reaction in a letter to Canada's Prime Minister, MacKenzie King:
"We in the United States rejoice with you, and the world at
large, that the outbreak of war was averted." Personally, however, he was gravely disturbed. To William Phillips, ambassador to Italy, during that fateful September, he wrote pessimistically that any arrangement between Chamberlain and
Hitler might merely postpone what appeared to be an inevitable conflict "within the next five years." Prime Minister
Chamberlain's "peace in our time" was regarded with despair
by a small number of people in both Europe and America.
Winston Churchill called it "a total and unmitigated defeat."
Harold Ickes was highly doubtful that it would insure peace,
"Hitler being the maniac that he is."

The rejoicing over the Munich accord was pathetically brief.
The German dictator was soon calling for additional armaments on the ground that Chamberlain's promises of cooperation were valid only so long as he remained in office; he might
be replaced at any time by men like Winston Churchill or
Alfred Duff Cooper. From Ambassador William Bullitt in
France, Roosevelt received pessimistic reports which confirmed his own doubts of the viability of the settlement.

In a radio address to the *Herald Tribune* Forum on October

26, 1938, the President expressed his apprehension. "It is becoming increasingly clear," he said, "that peace by fear has no higher or more enduring quality than peace by the sword. There can be no peace if the reign of law is to be replaced by a recurrent santification of sheer force. There can be no peace if national policy adopts as a deliberate instrument the threat of war." He made his reference to Hitlerism explicit by stating further that there could be no peace if national policy caused millions of people to wander homeless over the world, or if men were denied freedom of thought, expression, and religion. The United States was willing, he continued, to join in disarmament efforts, but lacking "greater reassurance than can be given . . . for example, by actual discussions, leading to actual disarmament," it was compelled to increase its own military and naval establishments.

Even before Munich, Roosevelt recognized the implications of the Nazi threat for American defense. At Queen's University, Ontario, where he went to receive an honorary degree in August, 1938, he warned the dictators in words that he himself inserted in the State Department draft: "The people of the United States will not stand idly by if domination of Canadian soil is threatened by any other Empire." With this pledge he gave notice that his country's obligation under the Monroe Doctrine included the defense of Canada. After Munich, Roosevelt announced plans for a tremendous expansion of the Air Force, not only to strengthen the security of the United States and the Western Hemisphere but to provide a necessary supplement to the British and French air capacity. Moreover, he hoped that perhaps Hitler might be deterred if he saw that America was seriously engaging in a preparedness program.

Another warning by Roosevelt to the dictators that the nation would not remain indifferent to the menace of war, and one of his most eloquent statements, was the annual message to Congress of 1939. Disturbances and trends abroad, he declared, threatened three institutions vital to the American way of life: religion, democracy, and international good faith. "There comes a time in the affairs of men," he said solemnly, "when they must prepare to defend not their homes alone but the tenets of faith and humanity on which their churches, their governments, and their very civilization are founded." While the United States refrains from taking military measures to check aggression, he went on, it cannot ignore aggression. "Words may be futile, but war is not the only means of commanding a decent respect for the opinions of mankind. . . . There are many methods short of war, but stronger and more effective than mere words, of bringing home to aggressor governments the aggregate sentiments of our own people. . . . Once I prophesied that this generation of Americans had a rendezvous with destiny. That prophecy comes true. To us much is given; more is expected. This generation will nobly save or meanly lose the last best hope of earth."

The words were stirring and the voice rang with sincerity, but the President had stopped short of elucidating what "short of war" and "rendezvous with destiny" actually meant. He had not yet engaged himself in a campaign of public enlightenment to clarify the real nature of the threat to American security. His reluctance was understandable. When he was alleged to have remarked at a conference with some senators that America's frontier lay on the Rhine, the isolationists kicked up a furor. Roosevelt denied the statement, but he later explained what had actually happened to Ambassador John Cudahy. "I did point out that there are fifteen or sixteen independent nations in Europe whose continued independent political and economic existence is of actual moment to the ultimate defense of the United States." Furthermore, he had told the senators that if the Baltic states went the way of Czechoslovakia, the position of the United States would be weakened even more than it had already been by the Munich settlement.

As the dictators continued to chalk up one victory after another, even Chamberlain was compelled to acknowledge the failure of appeasement. In April, 1939, the British and French pledged themselves to guarantee the independence of Poland. They had arrived at a point from which there was no turning back. Should Hitler ignore the commitment, as every indication suggested that he would, war was inevitable. Roosevelt, under no illusion as to the eventual position of the United States if Europe went up in flames, dispatched a message to Hitler on April 14, soliciting him to demonstrate the sincerity of his oft-repeated disclaimer of warlike intentions. He asked for assurance that for at least ten years no attack would be made against any of thirty-one independent states that he specified. This period would provide an opportunity to negotiate outstanding issues, and the United States would promise to help achieve settlements. As soon as a favorable response was received, two basic problems would be given immediate consideration: methods for obtaining relief from the crushing burden of armaments, and the opening up of international trade to give every nation equal access to raw materials and the opportunity to buy and sell in the world market.

The reaction from Germany and Italy was obscene. Goering, who was then visiting Mussolini, said that the message indicated an incipient brain disorder; Il Duce disagreed—it sounded more like a case of creeping paralysis. Hitler delivered a harangue before the Reichstag. None of the states named by Roosevelt felt any need for non-aggression pacts, he proclaimed, and ended with his "assurance" that he had no designs on the United States. His reply was both cunning and biting. Isolationists crowed that Hitler had outmaneuvered the President. "He asked for it!" Nye exulted. But many on both sides of the Atlantic felt that Roosevelt's message to some degree had aroused the American people to the imminence of danger and provided a clear statement of America's stake in the preservation of peace.

Roosevelt could think of only one remaining step that might just possibly be a deterrent to the dictators: a demonstration of willingness to extend material assistance to the democracies and, in the event of war, aid to the victims of aggression. Revision of the neutrality law would be required, extending the "cash-and-carry" provision to include the sale of arms. Under the existing statute, belligerents were permitted to obtain goods other than arms if they paid for them and transported the cargo on their own vessels. The proposed change would enable the British, with their financial and shipping resources, to obtain needed matériel, pay for it, and transport it on their own ships. For months the White House pressed for congressional action, but without success. On July 14, Roosevelt sent a detailed memorandum to the Senate in which he pointed out that

amending the act "in no conceivable sense could breed trouble
but . . . to a far greater extent than the present act would both
aid in making less likely a general war and, while keeping
strictly within the limits of neutrality, reduce as far as possible
the risk of this nation being drawn into war if war comes."
Hull, in a message to the Senate endorsed by the President,
argued that the issue was too critical for partisanship and
pleaded for collaboration between executive and legislative
branches. The administration was flatly turned down. An appeal to the House was similarly rejected.

When the Foreign Relations Committee voted to postpone
consideration until the next session of Congress in January,
Roosevelt made one final effort to obtain action from the
Senate. He summoned to the White House Vice President
Garner and Senate leaders of both parties for a "no-holds-
barred" conference. Recounting his endeavors to maintain the
peace, which was now acutely threatened, he said, "I've fired
my last shot. I think I ought to have another round in my belt."
He pleaded for support of the democracies before it was too
late. When Borah said calmly that there would be no war, that
the hysteria was manufactured, Hull begged him to come to
his office and read the cables. "I have sources in Europe that I
regard as more reliable than those of the State Department,"
Borah retorted disdainfully.

Vice President Garner polled those present to ascertain the
possibility of success on the Senate floor. "Well, Captain," he
said finally, turning to the President, "we may as well face
the facts. You haven't got the votes, and that's all there is to
it." Quietly Roosevelt told the group that the responsibility
would be theirs. He repeated his statement at a press conference early in August: "If we have another serious international crisis they have tied my hands, and I have practically
no power to make an American effort to prevent such a war
from breaking out . . . it is perfectly obvious who will be responsible—a solid Republican minority plus twenty to twenty-
five per cent of the Democrats." He felt that if Germany knew
that great quantities of war matériel would be made available
to England, there was an outside chance that the Nazis would
hesitate to set off a conflict.

Unlike the British and French leaders, Roosevelt was not blind to the possible danger of an unholy alliance between the Soviet Union and Germany. On August 1, he warned Stalin that if he teamed up with the Nazis, Hitler would attack Russia after he had destroyed France. Later that month the Russians and Germans signed a non-aggression pact, and with his right flank insured Hitler prepared to march on Poland. Roosevelt made a last despairing effort to avert catastrophe with a message to Hitler that Poland had accepted his offer to mediate and pleading that he do so, too. The Fuehrer did not trouble to reply. One week later, on September 3, 1939, German legions, striking with a panoply of the latest instruments of destruction, began to pulverize Poland from the ground and from the air. Chamberlain had no choice but to honor his government's pledge. The holocaust had begun.

That evening the President went on the air to alert the nation. "When peace has been broken anywhere, the peace of all countries everywhere is in danger," he said. Although the conflict was thousands of miles away, "we are forced to realize that . . . every ship that sails the sea, every battle that is fought, does affect the American future." Unlike Wilson, he did not suggest that the people refrain from taking sides. "This nation will remain a neutral nation, but I cannot ask that every American remain neutral in thought as well. Even a neutral has a right to take account of facts. Even a neutral cannot be asked to close his mind or his conscience." He concluded with a solemn promise. "As long as it remains within my power to prevent, there will be no black-out of peace in the United States."

The second Armageddon was not the unexpected shock that 1914 had been. Only the willfully blind could have ignored the ominous portents. Anti-German feelings were also very much more pronounced. Yet in September, 1939, as a quarter of a century earlier, most Americans confidently relied on their geographical separation and diplomatic detachment; the neutrality legislation, they felt, provided an additional bulwark.

With war, the arms embargo automatically went into effect. British and French orders for war matériel had to be canceled; yet to achieve victory the Allies would need all possible assistance. Again, Roosevelt sought repeal of the arms ban through a revision of the Neutrality Act which would permit the cash-and-carry provision to include the sale of armaments. He still had to proceed cautiously, for the outbreak of war had not moderated the attitude of the congressional isolationists. At the special session of Congress which he convened on September 21, Roosevelt emphasized that repeal of the embargo would safeguard America from involvement. He sincerely believed at this point that, with substantial aid, England and France could successfully withstand the Nazi onslaught. "I regret that Congress passed that Act," he said. "I regret equally that I signed that Act. . . . I give you my deep and unalterable conviction based on years of experience as a worker in the field of international peace that by repeal of the embargo, the United States will more probably remain at peace than if the law remains as it stands today" because the government would insist that American citizens and American ships stay out of the actual zones of conflict.

Although Roosevelt did not ask that the neutrality legislation be scrapped but merely that arms be made available to the democracies, the isolationists responded with their usual hue and cry. Senator Borah took to the radio to assert that European wars were caused by "the unconscionable schemes of remorseless rulers" and warned that to remove the embargo would be equivalent to taking part in a conflict in which no American interests were involved. He was echoed by other leaders in Congress. Colonel Charles A. Lindbergh, still the idol of millions, added his judgment that the United States had no stake in the outcome of the war. Public opposition ranged the full gamut from the pacifists, who insisted that the only way to avert war was to have nothing to do with the instruments of war, to the Communists, who, in view of Soviet-Nazi collaboration, were declaiming that any aid to Britain and France furthered the aims of capitalist imperialism.

In this charged atmosphere, the White House campaign was planned with care, the President skillfully exercising his influence with Congress. Friendly legislators were urged to mobilize votes; patronage complaints were satisfied; the "silver" senators were promised a higher price for domestic silver;

efforts were made to obtain the support of the titular leaders of the Republican party, Alfred Landon and Frank Knox. Pleas went out to community leaders throughout the country to apply pressure upon congressmen. The task of winning over public opinion was entrusted to private groups, notably the newly organized Nonpartisan Committee for Peace Through the Revision of the Neutrality Law, headed by the liberal Republican editor, William Allen White.

Roosevelt was cautious not to utter a word that might possibly boomerang. "I am almost literally walking on eggs," he wrote to Lord Tweedsmuir, Governor General of Canada, in asking him to postpone a visit until the neutrality fight was over. "I am at the moment saying nothing, seeing nothing and hearing nothing." He kept the legislative docket in Congress free from all other business. A constant communication link was maintained with Capitol Hill, and reports reached him almost hourly.

By mid-October, the tide was definitely in the President's favor, owing to the support of the nearly solid phalanx of southern and eastern Democrats, the business community, the majority of the metropolitan press, and a large section of the intellectual leadership of the nation. At the end of the month, the embargo provision was finally repealed by a vote that ran largely along party lines, with six Republicans in the Senate and nineteen in the House supporting the administration. Several days later, Congress approved a resolution permitting war matériel to be sold on a cash-and-carry basis. Most of the protective features of the existing neutrality law were allowed to remain in force: the ban on the sale of securities by a belligerent within the United States; the prohibition of Americans to travel on ships of a nation at war; and the President's authorization to designate war zones barred to American ships. "Cash and carry" was intended to avert involvement through loans, and also the risk of American arms carriers being torpedoed, since payment would be made in cash and the cargo transported on belligerent vessels. The President had won his first victory over the isolationists. Although the Neutrality Act remained on the books, its major provisions would be steadily whittled away one by one in the months that followed.

To make the American people understand the nature of the international situation and its implications for the nation's security presented a crucial test of leadership. During the interwar years, fear of involvement had developed into a virtual psychosis. Significantly, in a national poll published in November, 1939, on the reasons for American entry into the first war 34 per cent believed the country had been victimized by propaganda and selfish interests, while only 18 per cent attributed participation to reasons of national interest. So wary were the people of traveling the same road to war as in 1917 that when a British vessel was sunk in September with the loss of several American lives, no outcry was heard. Some Americans, suspicious of plots, even thought it a British machination to drag the country into the conflict. The task of bringing home to the public their stake in an anti-Axis victory would not be an easy one.

Franklin Delano Roosevelt

13. Arsenal of Democracy

AFTER Poland had been crushed by the Nazis, an uneasy quiet settled over Western Europe, the "phony war," which lasted for about five months. In the meantime, the Russians, motivated by strategic considerations, began to make territorial demands on Finland, which the tiny country stubbornly resisted. Roosevelt attempted without success to avert a clash. When the Red Army launched an invasion at the end of November, 1939, the President had to proceed with great caution. While he declared angrily that "all peace-loving peoples . . . will unanimously condemn this new resort to military force," he could not take any drastic steps for fear, as Hull later wrote, of doing anything "that would drive her [Russia] further into the arms of Germany." Moreover, although the heroic Finns aroused great popular sympathy—some isolationists even demanding that financial and military aid be contributed —isolationist sentiment in Congress and the country generally was still powerful enough to delay passage of a measure for non-military financial assistance until it was too late. The President went no further than to refrain from invoking the neutrality act and placing a moral embargo against Russia on certain war matériel of which she was a heavy purchaser.

Throughout the winter of 1939-40, Roosevelt attempted to prevent the anti-Comintern powers from entering into an active military coalition. With the Japanese plunging ever deeper into China, there was considerable agitation for a tight embargo against Japan, but again the President was reluctant to take a step that might solidify that country's alliance with Germany. Instead, he added a few items to the existing moral embargo and placed trade with Japan on a day-to-day basis after the Japanese-American commercial treaty expired in January, 1940. He was extremely circumspect with Mussolini in the hope that Il Duce, who was not too happy about the Soviet-Nazi pact, would remain neutral. In that connection, and to provide a listening post not available through the usual sources, he sent Myron C. Taylor, an Episcopalian business-man, as his personal representative to the Vatican.

The President was deeply disturbed by the popular attitude toward the war in Europe. Americans—and many Europeans, too—with more hope than reason thought that Hitler might have had a change of heart and would be content with his conquests. They also dangerously underestimated German strength while exaggerating that of England and France. In September, 1939, the British Navy was considered to be invin-cible and France's Maginot Line impregnable, according to a public opinion poll. Early in 1940, another poll revealed that only 23 per cent of the American public believed that the na-tion should become involved even in the extreme case of a British and French defeat. "I fear most people are merely going around saying 'Thank God for Roosevelt and Hull—no matter what happens they will keep us out of war,'" Roosevelt wrote to his old friend, William Allen White. Some way would have to be found to make Americans "think of conceivable conse-quences. . . ."

In his State of the Union address in January, 1940, Roosevelt sought to shake the public out of its detachment. He upbraided those "who wishfully insist, in innocence or ignorance or both, that the United States of America as a self-contained unit can live happily and prosperously, its future secure, inside a high wall of isolation while outside the rest of civilization and the commerce and culture of mankind are shattered." There was a tremendous difference, he argued, between staying out of war and being deluded that the war was none of our business.

Searching for any opening, however remote, that might lead to settlement, Roosevelt sent Under Secretary of State Sumner

Welles to London, Paris, Rome, and Berlin with instructions to ascertain "what the views of the four governments might be as to the present possibilities of concluding any just and permanent peace," but to make it plain that any "temporary or tentative armed truce" would not be acceptable. The motive was laudable, but diplomatically the mission was a blunder. Many Europeans were alarmed that the United States might support "peace at any price" and feared that, should the Allies refuse a settlement they considered undesirable, the American people would turn against them. American interventionists suspected the possibility of appeasement, while isolationists denounced the idea as another example of meddling. More important, the Nazi government exploited the mission for its own propaganda advantage by using it to arouse hopes for peace while planning for attack.

Nevertheless, Welles's assignment served one useful purpose. The report he brought back demolished any remaining illusion in Washington that either the British or the Germans were willing to settle for anything less than military victory. And, within a month after the Under Secretary's return, the war ceased to be "phony."

Without warning, the Nazis struck on April 9, 1940, and with terrifying speed began their engorgement of Europe. The first to go were Norway and Denmark, to be followed only a few weeks later by the Netherlands, Belgium, Luxembourg.

The appalling ease with which the Germans achieved victory stunned the American people. Although the Spanish Civil War had offered a preview of Nazi tactics, it was somehow expected that war would be waged in the traditional manner. United States military experts had doubted that the Reich would win, and from the beginning military commentators kept turning out reassuring pieces about German weakness.

Complacency vanished with the sudden realization that the conquest of Europe by the Nazis was a distinct possibility. Only 30 per cent of the American people, according to a poll taken in May, 1940, now believed that the Allies would win the war. An even more impressive indication of the reversal of opinion was the large number, about 63 per cent, who believed that Hitler would attempt to seize territory in the Western Hemisphere.

An intensive build-up of the nation's defenses now assumed top priority. In a special message to Congress on May 16, the President called for an appropriation to provide for an output of 50,000 planes a year, a staggering figure ten times the rate of current production. He cited statistics on bomber speed and radius that graphically illustrated the vulnerability of the United States to attack from the air and warned that "our defense as it was yesterday, or even as it is today, does not provide security against potential developments and dangers of the future." In this instance congressmen, internationalists, and isolationists were united in support of his program. By year's end, more than seventeen billion dollars had been appropriated for naval and military preparedness, and the first peacetime conscription measure in American history had been approved, even if only by a very narrow vote.

In a resolution initiated by the United States, the foreign ministers of the Western Hemisphere, meeting in Havana in July, 1940, declared that an attack by a non-American state upon any American nation would be considered an aggression against all. The impressive unity that was demonstrated in this multilateral approach toward aggression was a happy effect of the good neighbor policy. An Act of Havana also provided for a system of collective trusteeship for hemispheric possessions of conquered European nations, if that should be necessary.

On June 5, the Nazis launched an attack against France. The supposedly impregnable Maginot Line crumbled before the Wehrmacht like "walls of sand that a child puts up against waves on a seashore," as Premier Paul Reynaud heartbrokenly told the American ambassador. Five days later, when France was in the throes of death, Italy came in for the kill. Through April and May the President had made several appeals to Mussolini to refrain from joining forces with the Germans. But it was soon obvious that Il Duce was waiting only for the opportune moment, and finally "the hand that held the dagger . . . struck it into the back of its neighbor," as Roosevelt said with contempt. Great Britain now stood alone. In all Western Europe, only the remnants of the British army rescued from

Dunkirk remained to oppose the full might of the German juggernaut.

If the President's position in the past had been ambiguous, he now made it unequivocal. Unlike Wilson, who had struggled heroically to maintain an untenable neutrality, Roosevelt knew from the outset that aid to the foes of the Axis powers constituted America's first line of defense, that a victory by the dictators would pose an intolerable economic and military threat to the United States. To furnish that aid, however, would require the partial abandonment of neutrality. He would have to find a way to convince the American public that the nation could not remain inviolate surrounded by hostile dictatorships, that its security was linked with that of the Allies.

Addressing the graduating class of the University of Virginia on that June day when Mussolini joined his partner in iniquity, Roosevelt said bluntly that the nation could no longer risk ultimate devitalization by remaining shackled to neutrality restrictions. "Some, indeed, still hold to the now somewhat obvious delusion that we of the United States can safely permit the United States to become a lone island . . . in a world dominated by the philosophy of force." That was a dream of those who still clung to the isolationist position, but to the majority of Americans it was "a helpless nightmare of a people . . . lodged in prison, handcuffed, hungry, and fed through the bars . . . by the contemptuous unpitying masters of other continents." As victory "for the gods of force and hate would endanger the institutions of democracy in the western world . . . the whole of our sympathies lies with those nations that are giving their life blood to combat against these forces." He then announced a future American policy which, he said, combined two obvious and simultaneous courses: "We will extend to the opponents of force the material resources of this nation; and, at the same time, we will harness and speed up the use of those resources" in order to have the equipment and training "equal to the task of any emergency and every defense."

The isolationists reacted in characteristic fashion—Father Coughlin shrilled frenetically over the radio and others, like Charles A. Lindbergh, denounced the President's speech. They were still adamant in their conviction that the war in Europe

and its outcome were of no concern to the United States, that
the nation should remain scrupulously aloof. In sharp opposition was a group of Americans who had rejected neutrality and
were agitating for all-out aid to the Allies. One of the leaders in
this movement was William Allen White. In September, 1939,
he had formed the Committee to Defend America by Aiding
the Allies. Sponsored by an impressive list of outstanding citizens, the committee soon had branches in many parts of the
country. The fall of France stripped many Americans of any
remaining illusion of immunity. Senator Key Pittman, who had
initiated the neutrality legislation of the thirties, now declared
that aid to the European democracies was perfectly legal. If
Hitler was offended, he said, he would have to declare war on
us, but if our support of the Allies helped to stop him, that
would prove to have been our best defense. Nevertheless, in
attempting to implement his policy, Roosevelt would be challenged every inch of the way, his task made no easier by the
obvious predicament of defining the precise limits of "short of
war."

Some of the arms and planes which Britian desperately
needed could be supplied under an old 1917 statute which
permitted the government to sell surplus equipment to private
firms for resale to a belligerent nation. Early in June, the
President directed Chief of Staff General George C. Marshall
to locate any arms and equipment that could be spared for
the Allies. Several hundred freight cars were soon loaded with
armaments and ammunition from the days of World War I,
and two hundred overage planes made available. Presumably
the matériel was sold by the government to a private firm,
which then transferred it to England.

But this solution had limitations, for Army and Navy chiefs
were reluctant to surrender even obsolete equipment until
modern replacements could be acquired. Moreover, a rider to
the naval bill enacted on June 28 forbade disposal of any supplies unless the Chief of Staff or the Chief of Naval Operations
certified that they were not essential for the nation's defense.
And, in any case, it was at best an emergency stopgap. About
half of the British fleet had been either damaged or lost. Requiring large-scale aid, England was pleading for forty or fifty

overage destroyers. At the end of July, Winston Churchill, who had succeeded Neville Chamberlain as Prime Minister, urgently cabled the President, "If we cannot get a substantial reinforcement [of ships] the whole fate of the war may be decided by this minor and easily remediable factor."

A number of influential Americans, members of a small group concerned with having assistance provided to beleaguered Britain, sent a memorandum to the President suggesting that old destroyers be exchanged for British bases in North America. The transaction, they maintained, could be justified as a defense measure for the Western Hemisphere. At a Cabinet meeting on August 2, 1940, the problem of how best to arrange such a transfer was discussed. "It was agreed that legislation to accomplish this is necessary," Roosevelt wrote in the notes he made during the meeting, but that, "if asked for by me without any preliminaries, [it] would meet with defeat or interminable delay in reaching a vote." The matter required deft handling, especially because the country was on the eve of a presidential campaign. Success would require effective groundwork to insure support from every center of political power. It was decided, the President recorded, that "I would call up William Allen White, who has recently talked with Willkie on this subject; ask White to come to Washington at once to see Hull, Knox and Stimson and after that to see me." If the support of Wendell Willkie, the Republican candidate for President, could be obtained, White could then attempt to win over Joseph Martin, House Republican leader, and Senator Charles L. McNary, Willkie's running mate. Should this procedure prove effective, the President would at once request the legislation from Congress. Roosevelt emphasized that the measure would probably be defeated unless substantial Republican support could be mustered: "I stressed the importance of having the issue acted on without regard to party politics in any way."

When Willkie refused to make a definite commitment, the President decided to test public opinion. He arranged to have Ambassador Bullitt deliver an address before the American Philosophical Society in Philadelphia on August 18. If Britain should be defeated, stated Bullitt, this country would be next on the Nazi list. "The soothing words 'Atlantic Ocean' are being used now by the propagandists of the dictators in the hope that they may become the lullaby of death for the United States. . . . The truth is that the destruction of the British Navy would be the turning of our Atlantic Maginot Line."

Bullitt received 22,000 letters and telegrams applauding his talk, but the isolationists denounced it as "little short of treason" and called the ambassador himself a "multi-millionaire, New Deal warmonger." The *Chicago Tribune* warned that "the sale of the Navy's ships to a nation at war would be an act of war. If we want to get into war, the destroyers offer us as good a way as any of accomplishing the purpose."

The explosive nature of the issue made it apparent that the proposed legislation would be subjected to prolonged debate on Capitol Hill, and delay was dangerous. A way of bypassing Congress was suggested to the President in a letter published in the *New York Times* on August 11. Signed by four prominent attorneys, one of whom was Dean Acheson, later to become Secretary of State, it demonstrated that the sale of the destroyers could be accomplished by executive action within the framework of existing law. Roosevelt promptly asked the Attorney General for a legal opinion. The latter ruled that the Constitution bestowed on the President, as commander in chief, authority to proceed with an executive agreement where the national defense was concerned without the Senate approval required for treaties.

The President lost no time in undertaking negotiations, this time indifferent to congressional opposition such as that expressed in a radio address on August 13 by Senator David I. Walsh, chairman of the Naval Affairs Committee, who declared that "the transfer of naval destroyers from our flag to the British flag, no matter by what method or device, makes mockery of our declared policy of neutrality and non-intervention. It is an act of belligerency and of war." On September 2, the destroyer-bases deal was consummated. In a message to Congress reporting the event, Roosevelt declared that the arrangement was "not inconsistent in any sense with our status of peace. . . . It is an epochal and far-reaching act of preparation for continental defense in face of grave danger . . . probably the most important . . . since the Louisiana Purchase."

The wind had been taken out of the sails of the isolationists, for they themselves had long been campaigning for the acquisition of bases in the Western Hemisphere. But the die-hards were unreconciled. In full-page advertisements in leading newspapers throughout the country, they charged that the President had become "America's first dictator," passing down "an edict that compares with the edicts . . . by Hitler, Mussolini and Stalin." Assessing the implications of the agreement more soberly, one newspaper asserted, "It makes our official neutrality, already highly diaphanous, a well-nigh transparent cover for non-belligerent cooperation on the side of Great Britain," while one expert expressed the view that the country had now entered on a "state of limited war." The American public, for the most part, however, reacted favorably to Roosevelt's departure from neutrality.

While the desire to aid Britain was widespread, it was an act of courage and of leadership for the President to instigate a controversial transaction of such far-reaching significance just before a national election. A seasoned politician, he knew well the fickle nature of the public and the tenacious roots of isolationism. During the preparation of his message to Congress announcing the agreement, he remarked to his secretary, "Congress is going to raise hell about this, but even another day's delay may mean the end of civilization. Cries of 'warmonger' and 'dictator' will fill the air, but if Britain is to survive, we must act." The reception was not as violent as he feared, but a less skilled political campaigner might have been seriously bruised when he sought re-election.

Not until the Democratic convention met in July had Roosevelt ended the uncertainty about his candidacy for a third term. His long silence had discouraged both James Farley and John Nance Garner from exerting any real effort to seek the nomination. In a message to the delegates, Roosevelt said that he had no desire to be nominated again and they were accordingly free to vote for anyone they pleased. The effect was to invite a draft.

The Republican convention was carried away by a grass-

roots swell of enthusiasm for the dark horse, Wendell L. Willkie. Lawyer and utilities executive, Willkie had never been in
politics and, until he whirled onto the national scene just a few
weeks earlier, was relatively unknown. He had been promoted
by a group of eastern, internationally minded Republicans who
had been impressed with his comprehension of the forces that
were destroying democracy in Europe, and who were fearful
that an isolationist candidate could not win the election. Although Willkie was opposed by aspirants strongly favored by
the Old Guard, his extraordinary personal appeal and the skillful management of his supporters enabled him to carry the
convention.

Willkie launched a whirlwind campaign, delivering over five
hundred speeches. In fundamental agreement with the administration's domestic and foreign policies, he began by attacking
Roosevelt for inefficiency, criticizing his methods and inveigh-
ing against the third term. As the campaign progressed, however, his charges became increasingly reckless, and by October
he switched to denouncing the President as a warmonger. In
Kansas he charged that by meddling in international politics,
the President had "encouraged the European conflagration. . . .
And he was the godfather of that unhappy conference at
Munich. . . . I warn you . . . if because of some fine speeches
about humanity, you return this Administration to office, you
will be serving under an American totalitarian government
before the long third term is finished." He promised that if
elected President, "I will never send an American boy to fight
in any European war," ridiculing similar pledges made by
Roosevelt. "If his promises to keep our boys out of foreign
wars is not better than his promise to balance the budget
they're already almost on the transports."

Roosevelt, who stated in his acceptance speech that he
would have neither the time nor "the inclination to engage in
any purely political debates," ignored his opponent for the first
month of the campaign. Then, disturbed by the enthusiasm
which Willkie was arousing, he took to the platform. At first
he merely repeated the Democratic Party pledge to keep the
country out of war, "except in case of attack," and warned that
the only way to prevent involvement in the struggle was to

help stop aggression abroad. But his speeches did not seem to have the impact party workers hoped for. The Republican candidate had aroused apprehensions which Roosevelt, they felt, was not successfully allaying. Robert Sherwood, one of the President's speech writers, recounts that a constant stream of letters and telegrams poured into party headquarters, pleading for a more forceful response to Willkie's charges.

At the end of October, on his way to Boston to deliver an address, Roosevelt received a barrage of wires warning him that he would be defeated unless he pledged explicitly to keep the nation at peace. Sherwood, who accompanied Roosevelt, urged him to declare categorically that American troops would not be sent to fight abroad. In this atmosphere of urgency, the President made a statement that would later return to plague him. "And while I am talking to you mothers and fathers, I give you one more assurance. I have said this before, but I shall say it again and again and again. Your boys are not going to be sent into any foreign wars. They are going into training to form a force so strong that, by its very existence, it will keep the threat of war far away from our shores. The purpose of our defense is defense." The episode pointed up the difficulty of being a presidential leader and a presidential candidate at one and the same time.

Strong and bitter emotions rose to the surface during the campaign. Herbert Hoover, who had become increasingly hostile toward Roosevelt, was convinced that "the whole future of the American people hangs upon the decision of this election." Losing all sense of proportion, he wrote to Chief Justice Hughes urging him to resign so that he would be free to issue an appeal for a complete change in the administration. But the most skillful campaigner in American history scored once again, capturing the support of twenty-seven million people, or 54.7 per cent of the voters.

Back at his desk, Roosevelt turned to the critical situation abroad. From August on, swarms of the deadly Luftwaffe had been ceaselessly droning across the Channel, subjecting Britain to a merciless bombing that left large areas of her cities in smoking ruins, incinerating or crushing thousands of people. British dollar resources to purchase critically needed planes, ships, and matériel were practically exhausted. On December 9, 1940, Roosevelt was informed by Churchill that Britain could no longer pay for the military equipment needed "to shatter the foundations of German military power." Existing laws forbade the extension of credit, and the President knew that the American people would never consent to repeat the loan experiences of World War I that had left such an unhappy legacy. He finally came up with a novel solution that he revealed at a press conference on December 17 in the form of a homely analogy. "Suppose my neighbor's house catches fire and I have a length of garden hose. . . . If he can take my garden hose and connect it up with the hydrant, I may help him to put out his fire. . . . I don't say to him . . . 'Neighbor, my garden hose costs me fifteen dollars; you have to pay me fifteen dollars for it.' What is the transaction that goes on? I don't want fifteen dollars—I want my garden hose back after the fire is over." He would ask Congress when it returned in January for authority to make available to Britain arms which were to be returned in kind at the end of the war.

In a fireside chat on December 29, Roosevelt announced frankly and plainly that the nation would have to become "the great arsenal of democracy" if totalitarian aggression was to be defeated. Events had tragically demonstrated that the Nazis could not be appeased. "No man can tame a tiger into a kitten by stroking it," he said. Germany, Italy, and Japan had united into a partnership aimed at world domination, and if Britain went down they would control the continents of Europe, Asia, Africa, Australia, and the high seas. "It is no exaggeration to say that all of us in the Americas would be living at the point of a gun." Those who believed that the Axis powers would not be interested in attacking the Western Hemisphere were deluding themselves with "the same dangerous form of wishful thinking which has destroyed the powers of resistance of so many conquered peoples." The vast resources of this hemisphere "constitute the most tempting loot in the world."

In striving to make the country aware of the larger and long-range threat to the national interest, Roosevelt's task was easier than Wilson's had been to the extent that the issue in 1941 was more clear-cut than in 1917 and the danger more obvious.

World War I had been the outcome of "traditional" imperialist rivalries and nationalist ambitions, so that the onus of responsibility could not easily be placed. On the other hand, the isolationism that surged back during the inter-war years was far more acute than before, and while Americans were shaken by the impact of events, a hard and powerful core of isolationists remained to hobble the President. Of considerable influence was the America First Committee. Organized in the summer of 1940 to agitate for non-intervention, it was headed by such isolationists as Charles A. Lindbergh, Senators Burton K. Wheeler and Gerald P. Nye, General Robert E. Wood of Sears Roebuck, and other prominent industrialists. It maintained that Roosevelt's policy of aid to Britain increased the likelihood of war, that the security of the United States would not be jeopardized by a Hitler victory, and that therefore the nation had no reason to become involved in England's struggle for survival. While many of the organization's supporters were sincere, patriotic Americans, it also attracted numerous Nazi sympathizers, anti-Semites, and Fascists.

In his annual message of January 6, 1941, Roosevelt gave official expression to his "garden hose" idea, asking Congress "for authority and for funds sufficient to manufacture additional munitions and war supplies of many kinds, to be turned over to those nations which are now in actual war with aggressor nations." Payment for this assistance was to be made in goods and services at the end of the war. He concluded with the hope for "a world founded upon four essential freedoms"— freedom of speech, freedom of religion, freedom from want, and freedom from fear. Several days later, a bill "To Promote the Defense of the United States" was introduced granting the President power to sell, lease, or lend defense articles under whatever terms he thought appropriate to the government of any country deemed vital to the security of the United States. With this bill, designated H.R. 1776, the administration intended to drive another nail into the coffin of neutrality.

For the next two months Congress and the country debated the measure, the America First Committee marshaling all its strength to fight it. Senator Arthur Vandenberg wrote in his diary that he felt he was witnessing the suicide of the republic.

"We have torn up 150 years of traditional American foreign policy," he lamented. "We have tossed Washington's Farewell Address into the discard. We have thrown ourselves squarely into the power politics and the power wars of Europe, Asia and Africa. We have taken the first step upon a course from which we can never hereafter retreat."

The senator was correct; there was no turning back. But he ignored—or failed to comprehend—America's stake in the global struggle, which had long been plain to Roosevelt. Twentieth-century forces had converted the threads once loosely connecting his country with nations overseas into steel cables forever binding the continents together. In January, the President had written to Ambassador Joseph C. Grew in Tokyo that "hostilities in Europe, in Africa, and in Asia are all parts of a single world conflict. We must consequently recognize that our interests are menaced both in Europe and in the Far East." Then, replying to Grew's question as to whether American entry into a war with Japan might not so adversely affect aid to Britain as to make the difference between victory or defeat for that country, he said it was necessary to consider if England's chances of winning against Germany would not be decreased should Japan gain possession of the Netherlands East Indies and Malay Peninsula regions. To insure American security, he continued, Britain must be kept supplied by the United States and her channels of communication to various parts of the world kept open so that other important sources of supply would not be cut off. The problems, he wrote, were "so vast and so interrelated that any attempt even to state them compels one to think in terms of five continents and seven seas."

Having abandoned the status of a neutral by 1941, the Roosevelt administration moved steadily toward undeclared war against Germany. Early that year, American military and naval officers and their British counterparts met to exchange information. A common strategy for defeat of the Axis was secretly planned should the United States be compelled to resort to war.

To insure that the lend-lease supplies actually reached their destination, Roosevelt declared in April that the Red Sea and Indian Ocean were not combat zones. American ships were thereby permitted to supply the British army in Egypt, and the Air Force was instructed to patrol the Atlantic as far as Iceland so that British merchant vessels could be warned of the presence of submarines. Roosevelt informed Congress that same month, that the United States had been granted permission to fortify Greenland, and in July, again by mutual arrangement, that American forces had been sent to Iceland. The purpose in both cases, the President declared, was to prevent Germany from occupying these "strategic outposts in the Atlantic to be used as air or naval bases for eventual attack against the Western Hemisphere." He offered only a partial explanation, neglecting to mention that another reason was the strategic location of both countries on the sea lanes to Great Britain, and that later on United States warships might be used to protect British freighters between Greenland and Iceland if they joined American and Icelandic cargo carriers under escort.

The torpedoing and sinking in May of the unarmed American freighter, the *Robin Moor*, in the South Atlantic by a German submarine provided the President with an opportunity to bring home some facts and prepare the public for the eventuality of yet deeper involvements. Nazi submarines, he said, were sinking ships twice as fast as they could be replaced by both Britain and America. "We can answer this peril . . . by speeding up and increasing our great ship-building program; and second, by helping to cut down the losses on the high seas." An actual military danger to the country was "the presence in the Western Hemisphere waters of Nazi battleships of great striking power." Most of the supplies for Britain, he pointed out, were sent along the northerly route close to Greenland and Iceland, and should the Nazis occupy either of those two areas the United States would be endangered.

He had repeatedly emphasized, Roosevelt continued, that the nation was mustering men and resources "only for purposes of defense. . . . But we must be realistic when we use the word 'attack'. . . . Some people seem to think that we are not attacked until bombs actually drop on New York or San Francisco. . . . When your enemy comes at you in a tank or a bombing plane, if you hold your fire until you see the whites of his eyes, you will never know what hit you. Our Bunker Hill of tomorrow may be several thousand miles from Boston." Military necessity required that Britain be assisted in every possible way. American patrols, he informed his listeners, were now helping to insure delivery of needed supplies. "All additional measures necessary to deliver the goods will be taken." On May 27, 1941, the President proclaimed an unlimited national emergency.

While Roosevelt was accelerating aid to Great Britain, a new factor in the European war claimed his attention, and his response placed him at the center of yet another storm of controversy. In the early dawn of June 22, Hitler hurled the full force of the Wehrmacht against his Soviet "partner." The President was not greatly surprised; he had never had much faith in the viability of the Soviet-Nazi non-aggression pact. Moreover, as far back as the previous summer, the State Department had received intimations that the Fuehrer intended to scuttle his agreement with Stalin, and in January, 1941, the American Commercial Attaché in Berlin obtained a copy of a secret document, the Barbarossa Directive, which outlined definite plans for an invasion of Russia.

In the War and State Departments, the dominant view was that the Soviet Union would either capitulate immediately to German demands or collapse almost at once. Just prior to the invasion, Secretary of War Stimson recorded in his diary that "from all the dispatches, it seems nip and tuck whether Russia will fight or surrender. . . . I think the chances are she will surrender." On June 12, a State Department memorandum outlined policy in the event that Russia was attacked. No overtures were to be made to the Soviets, it declared. If aid was requested and the United States considered offering some, priority should be given to British and American needs. No advance promises or commitments should be made. "In particular, we should engage in no undertaking which might make it appear that we have not acted in good faith if later we should refuse to recognize the Soviet Ambassador in Washington as the diplomatic representative of Russia in case the Soviet government should be obliged to leave the country."

The American Ambassador in Moscow expressed greater confidence in the Soviet intent to resist the Germans, but he doubted their capacity to survive an onslaught. Roosevelt did not share this pessimism. He also agreed with Winston Churchill that Russia should be regarded as a fighting partner and assured the Kremlin that "any announcement that the Prime Minister might make welcoming Russia as an ally" would receive his support. His first steps were to seek the removal of the moral embargo against the Soviet Union and to lift the ban on export licenses. Then, almost singlehanded, against intense, even rabid opposition, he fought for a policy of substantial aid. Fulton Oursler, editor of *Liberty* magazine, expressed a common view when he editorialized that, although the Russian people were suffering, "our sympathies must not betray our reason. Communism Is Still Anti-American, Anti-Democratic, Anti-Christ. . . . So, to Mr. Stalin, and to all his friends . . . we may say again: 'To Hell with Communism.'"

Since Oursler's periodical had a nationwide circulation, the President thought a reply advisable. He wrote to Mr. Oursler on June 25 that while the Russian dictatorship was no less reprehensible than the German, "the immediate menace at this time to the security of the United States lies in the threat of Hitler's armies . . . we should not forget that fact in retaining the immediate objective of the United States, which is to prevent world domination by Hitler."

The President was completely unimpressed by the dire predictions of high Army officials and military commenators that the German armies would cut through Russia like a hot knife through butter. To Ambassador William Leahy in France he wrote that, with the Russians in the war, "the liberation of Europe from Nazi domination" was assured. In the first days following the invasion Roosevelt intervened personally to expedite shipment of supplies to the Soviets, and on July 9 he informed Sumner Welles that he wanted large-scale aid sent before October. In his judgment, if the Russians could hold out until the onset of winter, Hitler would be stopped for months, and the immobilization of his troops might contribute to his ultimate defeat. Moreover, with the Nazis thus tied down, a threatened junction with the Japanese across Eurasia would be impossible.

Joining the isolationists and America First in opposing aid to the Soviet Union were many religious groups. Soviet atheism repelled many Protestants, but the most hostile were the Roman Catholics. Roosevelt considered it important to win over the latter, not only to strengthen his hand at home but to avert a rupture in western hemispheric unity in view of the Church's dominant position in Latin America.

A number of outstanding Catholic laymen supported the administration's position, and one of these, Associate Justice Frank Murphy, was probably enlisted to buttress it with his prestige. Addressing the International Convention of the Supreme Council of the Knights of Columbus on August 19, he told the distinguished gathering that while communism was a threat to Christianity, "it is not today the greatest danger. The over-shadowing menace . . . is the philosophy of nazism [which] . . . with its . . . perverted intelligence . . . its profound belief in racial superiority and destiny, its fanatical intolerance . . . its tremendous military power" poses the greater danger to free nations and institutions.

Appeals such as these, however, had little effect on the majority of Catholics, who followed the Papal encyclical of Pius XII, *Divini Redemptoris,* which forbade any collaboration with communism. Seeking to have this injunction modified if possible, Roosevelt dispatched Myron Taylor to the Vatican to try to impress the Pope that in the present crisis the President regarded communism as the lesser of two evils, and to point out the distinction between aid to Russia and support of communism. Taylor was also to emphasize that churches in the Soviet Union had been opened for worship, and to assure His Holiness that the President would press the Soviet government to grant freedom of religion to its citizens. With Taylor, Roosevelt sent a letter to the Pope in which he said that he considered the survival of Russia less perilous to religion, to the church, and to humanity than German totalitarianism. Furthermore, he believed that "the leaders of all churches in the United States should recognize these facts clearly and should not close their eyes to these basic questions and by their present attitude . . . directly assist Germany in her present objectives."

Pope Pius complied with the President's request, forwarding

to the apostolic delegate in Washington an interpretation of the encyclical along the suggested lines. The hierarchy was now free to instruct that the United States was assisting the Russian people, which was a worthy endeavor; if communism profited thereby, the evil must be accepted along with the good. For a brief period opposition subsided.

In the meantime, to assist him in influencing public opinion, Roosevelt sought to obtain a statement on religious freedom from the Soviet government. When Ambassador Constantine Oumansky appealed for lend-lease aid on September 11, the President explained that "the prejudice or hostility to Russia . . . among large groups in this country who exercise great political power in Congress" made it extremely difficult to obtain the necessary authority from the legislative body. He suggested that a declaration on religious freedom from the Russian government "might have a very fine educational effect before the next Lend-Lease Bill comes up in Congress." Nothing came of it, but Roosevelt persisted in his efforts to mitigate religious hostility, which he was convinced was the prime stumbling block in securing aid for the Soviet Union.

Toward the end of September, the President was informed that Catholic and Jewish chaplains had been assigned to Polish army contigents which were being formed in the Soviet Union. At his request, the Polish ambassador submitted a letter containing this information, and on September 30, while the House Committee on Appropriations was holding hearings on lend-lease, he had the State Department release it to the press. That same day, Roosevelt held a news conference. In reply to a question on the subject, he said, "the letter speaks for itself," and then went on to make a comment that incensed religious elements of all persuasions. Article 124 of the Soviet Constitution, he stated, provided substantially the same religious freedom as in the United States. Anyone in Washington could get up on a street corner and talk either for or against religion, and the same was true in Russia.

As might have been expected, a shower of denunciations poured down on the President's head from pulpits throughout the country. One clergyman declared that the Stalin regime had been assaulting Christianity in a way that was unparalleled since the days of Diocletian, and "to discuss the point on the written words [in the Soviet Constitution] is to engage in sophistry." Even Roosevelt's supporters criticized him for a disingenuous effort to create an image of ideological compatibility instead of resting his case for Russian assistance purely on grounds of national interest.

Having blundered, the White House hastened to issue a "clarifying" statement: it was hoped that "an entering wedge to the practice of complete freedom of religion is definitely on its way." That same day the President cabled W. Averell Harriman in Moscow that since the question of religion was so important to public opinion, "the President earnestly hopes that from the highest authorities of the Russian government you may be able to secure some statement that can be sent to this country's press which would be confirmatory of, and responsive to, the statements contained in . . . [the remarks at the September 30 press conference]. Please make every effort to see that the Soviet authorities make some statement of this kind at the earliest moment possible."

The astonishing naïveté of the request was possibly due to the tremendous importance which Roosevelt attached to public opinion where sensitive issues were involved. Or perhaps it was the memory of the Catholic attitude during the Spanish Civil War that persuaded him to find some means of moderating the hostility of this group. Only one statement could reasonably have been expected. The Soviet government replied that freedom of religion was guaranteed to citizens of the U.S.S.R. by its constitution. Since the guarantee existed only on paper, the inevitable American reaction was disgust with Russian hypocrisy and hostility intensified rather than decreased.

Robert Sherwood later commented that many Americans felt at the time that Roosevelt was exaggerating the extent of Catholic opposition, "but it was his way to tread with extreme wariness wherever religious sensibilities were involved." As it turned out, the President was indeed too fearful, for on October 10 the House rejected by 217 to 162 the amendment forbidding lend-lease to Russia. With the Senate taking similar action two weeks later, Roosevelt had authorization for the massive aid program he had requested.

In less than a month the Nazi juggernaut had strafed, bombed, pillaged, and ravaged its way to the very gates of Moscow. Could the Soviets possibly hold out against this savage onslaught? Refusing to give way to the general despondency, Roosevelt prepared a statement for public release. "The Russian government is carrying a heavy burden in the world-wide attack against Nazism. To strengthen the hand of Russia, the President has declared that the defense of Russia is vital to the defense of the United States" and will "carry out to the limit its policy of aid." Although the Soviet capital was in danger of falling, the battle of Moscow, he said, would not decide the war, and he was convinced that the Russians would carry on. He gave "full assurance that an increasing flood of American supplies will continue to reach the Russian armies by all available routes."

Meanwhile, it seemed to Roosevelt in the summer of 1941 that the time had come for a personal discussion with Winston Churchill. He had maintained a correspondence with the British Prime Minister ever since Churchill took office, but the two men had never met. The rendezvous was arranged in complete secrecy. On August 3, Roosevelt boarded the Presidential yacht *Potomac* on what was officially described as a private cruise. Not until August 14 was a statement released that the two statesmen, accompanied by high ranking officials and Army, Navy, and Air Force Officers, had conferred off Newfoundland. Practical problems of supply under the Lend-Lease Act were discussed, but an equally significant, if less concrete, result of the conference was the issuance of a joint statement of their ideals and peace aims, since known as the Atlantic Charter. Reminiscent of the lofty aspirations of Wilson's Fourteen Points, it was, however, dissimilar in embodying general principles rather than specific proposals.

Expressing their "hopes for a better future for the world," the two leaders declared that they sought no aggrandizement, opposed any territorial changes contrary to the wishes of the people involved, and endorsed the right of self-determination for all peoples. They pledged themselves to maintain freedom of the seas, to provide equal access for all nations to world trade and raw materials, and to work for improved labor standards

and increased social security. They would endeavor to establish a peace so that "all men in all lands may live out their lives
in freedom from fear and want." The eighth and final point
stated that "all of the nations of the world . . . must come to the
abandonment of the use of force," and since no future peace
can be maintained unless nations which may threaten aggression are disarmed, therefore "pending the establishment of a
wider and permanent system of general security," it is essential
that those nations be disarmed. Moreover, all practical measures would be taken to lighten the crushing burden of armaments. As the United States was still a non-belligerent, the
Charter was especially significant in that it underscored the nation's profound commitment to both the war and the peace.

On the whole, the Charter was favorably received in the
United States. Axis newspapers, however, ridiculed the document, comparing it with Wilson's "dishonest" Fourteen Points,
but they feared its propaganda value sufficiently not to publish
the text. The immediate impact of the Atlantic Charter could
not be measured, but, as a cogent expression of peace aims, it
offered hope to a strife-torn world. It also provided the ideological foundation for the United Nations.

Ambassador Grew wrote that "it will take a long time . . .
before such a program can be carried out in effect, but its
announcement at this time seems to me to be an act of the
highest statesmanship." And Roosevelt later commented that
the document was merely a statement of objectives toward
which humanity was expected to aspire. "A great many of the
previous pronouncements that go back many centuries have
not been attained yet," but their objective was still sound, and
so he believed was the Atlantic Charter.

In the late summer of 1941, the Germans intensified their
submarine warfare. As further measures were obviously required to insure the safety of lend-lease cargo bound for Britain, Roosevelt announced at the end of August that merchant
ships in the North Atlantic would be escorted by naval vessels
as far as Iceland. The torpedoing of the destroyer *Greer* on
September 4, while radioing the position of a German submarine, brought the country to the verge of war. A week later,
in a fireside chat which was rebroadcast to the world in eight-

een languages, Roosevelt asserted that the time had come for Americans to stop deluding themselves that they could go on living peacefully in a Nazi-dominated world. They must not be deceived by the "tender whisperings of appeasers that Hitler is not interested in the Western Hemisphere," or by the "soporific lullabies that a wide ocean protects us from him." Nazi submarines and raiders were "rattlesnakes of the Atlantic," and when a rattlesnake is poised to strike, "you do not wait until he has struck before you crush him." As President, his obligation was historic, clear, inescapable. "It is no act of war on our part when we decide to protect the seas which are vital to American defense. The aggression is not ours." Ships of any flag "engaged in commerce in our defensive waters" would be protected by American patrolling vessels and planes. He concluded with a warning that "if German or Italian vessels of war enter our waters, the protection of which is necessary for American defense, they do so at their own peril. The orders which I have given as Commander-in-Chief to the United States Army and Navy are to carry out that policy—at once."

Up until then the President had been dissuaded both by supporters, including Secretary Hull, and by isolationist sentiment from pressing for the repeal of the remaining features of the Neutrality Act. In actual practice, they had been nullified by the decision to provide naval escort for belligerent and neutral merchantmen in the waters between Newfoundland and Iceland, and by the directive to shoot on sight at any Axis warships in that area. Logically, the next step was to permit merchant vessels to be armed. Roosevelt accordingly asked Congress in October to repeal those sections of the act which forbade the arming of cargo vessels engaged in foreign trade, to allow them to enter combat zones. As he thought of Britain as America's first line of defense, he sought to prevent the Nazis from controlling the Atlantic, thereby insuring safe delivery of lend-lease matériel. After six weeks of heated debate, the measure passed, by 50 to 37 in the Senate, and 212 to 194 in the House, a margin which reflected the still potent force of the anti-interventionists. But most Americans and their representatives in Congress were apparently willing to adopt any measures, short of a declaration of war, to bring about the defeat of the Germans.

While preoccupied with Europe, Roosevelt had also been compelled to give constant attention to events in the Far East, where Japan's expansionist activities, accelerated since the fall of France, increasingly threatened American security. What was feared most was a Japanese drive through Malaya and Singapore to the Dutch East Indies, which would not only paralyze the British position in the Far East, by closing Empire sea lanes, but wreak economic disaster by cutting off the supply of petroleum and most of the world's supply of rubber, tin, and quinine.

Within Japan, a struggle for power between the militarists who favored aggressive action and the civilian leaders who counseled moderation caused a continual seesaw of governments. When Premier Fumimaro Konoye returned to power in July, 1940, Roosevelt hoped that his moderation would prevail over the aggressive pro-Axis Foreign Secretary Yosuke Matsuoka and War Minister Hideki Tojo. But on September 22, the army occupied northern Indochina. The President promptly imposed an embargo on iron and scrap steel, adding these items to previous commercial restrictions. Undeterred, the Japanese that same day signed a military alliance in Berlin with Germany and Italy. Under the Tripartite Pact, Japan recognized German and Italian hegemony over Europe, and, in turn, its own supremacy in Asia was acknowledged, while each pledged military, economic, and political cooperation whenever necessary.

Still Roosevelt moved cautiously, informing Admiral Richardson, Commander of the Pacific Fleet, in October, 1940, that he would not act if Thailand, Malaya, or the East Indies were attacked. When Secretary Ickes urged a complete oil embargo the following summer, he refused to take this drastic step, explaining in a letter on July 1 that "it is terribly important for the control of the Atlantic for us to help keep peace in the Pacific. I simply have not got enough Navy to go round—and every little episode in the Pacific means fewer ships in the Atlantic."

Events, however, were moving swiftly toward a critical stage. That month, the Japanese compelled Vichy France to turn over air and naval bases in southern Indochina, a palpable augury of a drive south to the Anglo-Dutch possessions. Only severe countermeasures, Roosevelt was convinced, might possibly halt Japan. Late in July, he froze Japanese assets in the United States, subjected all commercial transactions to government control, barred Japanese vessels from the Panama Canal, and sharply curtailed the export of oil. When similar steps were taken by Great Britain, the Commonwealth countries, and the Netherlands, he followed through with a total embargo, thus depriving Japan of desperately needed oil. Some of his advisers feared that these sweeping measures might precipitate the clash it was meant to avert, but both the Congress and the people completely approved.

For Japan, it was absolutely essential that the oil embargo be lifted, and efforts were made to reach an understanding with the United States. On August 6, 1941, Ambassador Kichisaburo Nomura presented a proposal for a *modus vivendi* to which Washington could not assent. Shortly thereafter Normura sought to break the impasse by means of a face-to-face meeting between Premier Konoye and the President. While Roosevelt, with his great faith in personal diplomacy, was attracted to the idea, he was discouraged by Hull and most of his other advisers. The Secretary distrusted Nomura, whose pledges of peace and friendship were in direct contradiction to Japan's record and professed ambitions. Moreover, he doubted that Konoye was strong enough to persuade the militarists in his cabinet to agree to the terms, especially about China, on which the United States would insist. After a prolonged exchange of notes, Secretary Hull informed Nomura on October 2 that an agreement in principle on fundamental questions must first be reached before any such meeting could take place. As Tokyo refused to accede, the meeting was never held.

When the Konoye cabinet fell in mid-October and General Tojo became Prime Minister, the chances for peace diminished ever further. At the Imperial Conference on November 5, two plans with a twenty-day deadline were prepared for presentation to the United States. If neither Plan A, providing for a general settlement of differences, nor Plan B, for a more limited temporary arrangement was accepted, war was to be declared.

That the Japanese had already discounted the possibility of an agreement is apparent from the orders sent out that same day to the navy: "War with Netherlands, America, England, inevitable; general operational preparations to be completed by early December."

Having broken the Japanese diplomatic code some months earlier, the American government learned of the deadline at once, but the President was urged by his Joint Chiefs to tone down any representations he might make and to play for time. Meanwhile, the Japanese government sent over a special envoy, Saburo Kurusu, presumably to aid with negotiations and impress the public with Japan's desire for peace.

Both plans A and B were completely unacceptable to Roosevelt and Hull. There was nothing new in the first, and two of the points in the second would have obliged the United States to abandon all further aid to China and to assist Japan in obtaining the vital resources she needed. Hull was preparing a three-months *modus vivendi* as a counter offer, but an appeal from Churchill against weakening Chiang's regime, reports from Manila of Japanese troop movements, protests from Chungking, and cries of appeasement at home caused him to abandon this effort. Instead he drew up ten-point note which was presented to the Japanese envoys on November 26. Among other things, it demanded that Japan withdraw completely from Indochina, cease its campaign against China, and surrender all that had been acquired since the 1931 aggression, including the puppet Manchukuo regime. In return, the United States would remove the restrictions on Japanese trade and negotiate a new commercial agreement.

Japanese policy precluded an acceptance of those terms, and only acquiescence to Tokyo's position as set forth in plans A and B would have averted the impending clash at that point, for a task force of six aircraft carriers had already sailed from the Kuriles with orders to bomb Pearl Harbor unless recalled. The decision for war was ratified by the Imperial Conference on December 1, and instructions issued the following day to proceed with the attack on December 7. The President, Secretary Hull, and the top military planners knew from decoded messages intercepted several days before that a surprise assault was planned, but all assumed that it would be somewhere in Southeast Asia. On November 27, London had been warned about a Japanese attack on its Asiatic possessions, and American military and naval commanders in the Philippines and Hawaii were alerted for any eventuality. On December 1, the President sent a memorandum to Hull and Welles that he had received reports during the past few days of continuing Japanese troop movements in Indochina, indicating further aggression "conceivably . . . against the Philippine Islands . . . the many islands of the East Indies . . . Burma . . . Malaya, or . . . for the purpose of . . . the occupation of Thailand." Would they ascertain at once from Nomura and Kurusu the reason for these movements?

On the evening of December 6, the Japanese reply to Hull's ten-point note, a lengthy one, was partially decoded, and the entire message was in the President's hands the next morning. Hull's terms, it stated, were unacceptable and further negotiations were therefore useless. Nomura and Kurusu were scheduled to deliver the note to Hull at one o'clock, but the envoys asked for a slight delay. At 1:50 P.M., E.S.T., and just at dawn in Hawaii, the incredible news came crackling over the air waves that Pearl Harbor was being bombed from the air. Within hours, the fleet which had been concentrated there, in anticipation of its operational use in the Pacific to counter the expected aggression in southern Asia, was so seriously crippled as to be rendered almost impotent. Later that day, Washington learned that Japan was attacking simultaneously in the Philippines, Siam, Malaya, and other points.

Secretary Stimson that night recorded in his diary, "When the news first came that Japan had attacked us, my first feeling was of relief that indecision was over and that a crisis had come in a way which will unite all our people. This continued to by my dominant feeling in spite of the news of catastrophes which quickly developed. For I feel that this country united has nothing to fear, while the apathy and divisions stirred up by unpatriotic men have been hitherto very discouraging." Stimson had long considered the Roosevelt leadership too halting and too timid in preparing the American people for the military involvement which he felt was inevitable. He wanted a bolder and more forthright approach, believing that if the President had been more direct in bringing home the threat to the national interest, the nation would have followed his lead.

Yet Roosevelt did try to alert the country. His warnings about the Axis menace to the democratic way of life made it plain that a Hitler defeat was imperative if the national interest was to be safeguarded. To have stated bluntly that the United States must prepare for war would not have been courageous, but foolhardy. In the first place, American involvement was not inevitable; it was possible, if only faintly so, that by aiding the Allies the United States might escape being drawn in. Secondly, open reference to the likelihood of American military participation might have provoked an attack by either Germany or Japan much earlier, when the nation was not as well prepared. On the whole, Roosevelt's approach was a gradual program of education to awaken the American people to the grim realities of international life, and to make it plain that risking war was far preferable to chancing an Allied defeat.

Moreover, the isolationist opposition was more formidable than Stimson and others who were impatient with Roosevelt's caution were willing to acknowledge. Time and again the President found it necessary to camouflage his basic strategic objective if important measures were not to be jeopardized. With a keen sense of the popular mood and an awareness of the limitations of leadership, he refrained from proposing policies that were too far in advance of the public pace. He used every available method for testing or discerning public opinion—trial balloons, press conferences, editorials, opinion polls. If opposition to a policy appeared to be very strong, he modified the policy. Or, if he believed the stakes were crucial, as in the case of aid to Russia, he would go all out in trying to convert public opinion.

From the outset Roosevelt had no illusions about the consequences for the United States if Britain went down in defeat. The most formidable military machine in history, having digested one continent, would be ready for another, and the nation would have to face it alone. If the Nazis could be defeated with the help of massive aid, Americans would be fortunate; if not, the time to join the battle was while the British were still an effective fighting force.

The President's commitment to the defeat of the Axis, long before the attack upon American soil, later led his critics to charged that he deliberately maneuvered to bring about the day "which will live in infamy," that he provoked the Japanese assault so that the United States would be plunged into the conflict. Extremists have even accused him of cunningly plotting to bring about Pearl Harbor. To accept this indictment is to assign so sinister a motive to the President as to assume that he was willing to sacrifice the entire Pacific Fleet and thousands of American lives for the sake of "getting his war" against Hitler.

The actual fact is that while the administration was resigned to the inevitability of war with Japan, Roosevelt steadfastly resisted pressure to precipitate it. He had no desire to undertake a two-front, two-ocean military engagement. His goal was first to assist in the defeat of Germany. If the United States were drawn into a Pacific war before that was accomplished, much needed aid would be siphoned away from the Atlantic.

A passage in Stimson's diary for November 25, 1941, has been used to buttress the indictment against Roosevelt. He recorded that at a meeting of the "War Cabinet," attended by Hull, Knox, Chief of Staff Marshal, Naval Chief Stark, and himself, the President "brought up the event that we were likely to be attacked perhaps (as soon as) next Monday, for the Japanese are notorious for making an attack without warning, and the question was how we should maneuver them into the position of firing the first shot without allowing too much danger to ourselves. It was a difficult proposition." If the President had *expected* the Japanese to strike at American territory because he had been plotting it, why the necessity for a "maneuver?" Even the Phillipines were not regarded as a likely target, since that naturally would engage the United States at once, a contingency for which Japan did not appear eager. An assault on non-American soil in Asia was another matter. With the strength of isolationist sentiment, the Japanese could very likely swallow a good deal of territory before action was taken against them.

The logical assumption, therefore, was a blow against Southeast Asia, which presented the problem of convincing the American people how devastating it would be to the national interest if sources of vital raw materials were cut off while they were made available to the Axis powers. The "we" in the first sentence of Stimson's note could then only mean the Allies, so that the problem was how to equate a move against Siam or Malaya with a "first shot" against the United States.

With the advantage of hindsight, the errors made in the past appear glaring. What should have been seen and what should have been done appears so obvious now, it seems astonishing that it was not apparent then. But those involved in the events at the time had no crystal ball in which the future could be seen. The debacle at Pearl Harbor was due not to a devious plot or a treasonable conspiracy, but to the fact that neither Roosevelt nor any of his advisers were omniscient. They acted in accordance with what they thought would be to the best interest of their country, and their only guilt was in being subject to the ordinary frailties of mankind.

Franklin Delano Roosevelt

14. The Grand Coalition

PEARL HARBOR united the nation behind its commander in chief, and the President asserted his leadership so effectively that virtually every major political and military decision bore the personal mark of Franklin D. Roosevelt. He completely dominated the policy-making scene. Of all the highly competent men around him, some of whom were politically powerful, only his personal confidant, Harry Hopkins, and the Joint Chiefs of Staff shared the responsibility for determining the basic wartime strategies. Because of his tremendous prestige as a wartime leader and the confidence which he and his military advisers inspired, Roosevelt was able to infringe on the authority of high-ranking officials in their conduct of foreign affairs without jeopardizing political support. On military matters he counseled much less frequently with Secretary of War Stimson and Secretary of the Navy Knox than with the Chiefs of Staff, with whom he shared a remarkable identity of views. In only two instances, according to Robert Sherwood, did he override the opinions of the Chiefs.

Critical decisions were rarely made at Cabinet meetings, which generally provided merely a sounding board for the President. For the most part, Roosevelt consulted his intimate advisers and then reached his own conclusions. Secretary Stimson complained that, as a result of a lack of communication and coordination, Roosevelt's policies were often either unknown or unclear or contradictory, and those who had to execute them frequently worked at cross purposes. "Franklin Roosevelt as a wartime international leader proved himself as good as one man could be," he wrote, "but one man was not enough to keep track of so vast an undertaking." What he favored was the creation of a War Cabinet which would consist of the Secretaries of War, Navy, State, and Treasury, where efforts could be made to integrate diplomatic and military problems. The regularly constituted Cabinet, he complained, was little more than useless, with meetings a formality—"the same old two and sixpence, no earthly good."

Secretary Hull was also aggrieved at being shunted aside. Before the war, he wrote in his *Memoirs*, he had been a member of the war council and participated in its meetings, but after Pearl Harbor he was never invited. He had also been excluded from the conferences at Casablanca, Cairo, and Teheran, and from the President's military discussions with Prime Minister Churchill in Washington, "some of which had widespread diplomatic repercussions." When he had protested to Roosevelt that he was not looking for increased responsibilities "but I do believe the Secretary of State should attend these meetings" and referred to the British practice of having Foreign Secretary Eden participate in all the war councils, "the President's reply was that we had a different system here." Of all the numerous high-level international gatherings during the war, Hull attended only the Quebec Conference in 1943 and the Foreign Ministers' Conference in Moscow the same year. The Joint Chiefs, on the other hand, were present at all of them, with the exception of the one at Moscow and the United Nations preparatory conference. Harry Hopkins, "minister without portfolio," missed only a few, an indication of the great esteem in which he was held by Roosevelt.

Throughout the war years, no man was as close to the President as the frail Hopkins. A nearly fatal illness had purged him of all personal political ambition, and he was selflessly devoted to Roosevelt as an individual and as chief of state. Like Wilson's confidant House, Hopkins was the alter ego of a wartime President. But he was perhaps even more psychologically astute. He "never made the mistake of Colonel Edward M. House which caused the fatal breach with Wilson of assuming that he knew the President's mind better than the President did," wrote Robert Sherwood. "Roosevelt could send him on any mission . . . with absolute confidence that Hopkins would not utter one decisive word based on guesswork as to his chief's policies or purposes. Hopkins ventured on no ground that Roosevelt had not charted." At no time did he enter into any commitment for his chief which he had no authority to make.

A War Department citation bestowed upon Hopkins spoke of his "piercing understanding," and Roosevelt, fully appreciating his incisive mind, trusted him without qualification. When he dispatched him to Moscow in July, 1941, to discuss with Stalin the question of aid, he gave him a message for the Marshal which read, "I ask you to treat him with the identical confidence you would feel if you were talking directly to me," and sent along no written instructions for Hopkins himself. Not only could his judgment be relied on, but "Hopkins made it his job, he made it his religion to find out just what it was that Roosevelt really wanted and then to see to it that neither hell nor high water, nor even possible vacillations by Roosevelt himself, blocked its achievement," Sherwood wrote.

Such qualities alone would be sufficient to endear him to the man carrying the immense burden of a nation at war. But perhaps his most important function, and the one valued above all by those who have occupied the essentially lonely position of President, was that of the completely dedicated lieutenant. Roosevelt was once asked by Wendell Willkie why he kept Hopkins so close, since so many people mistrusted him and resented his influence. "Some day," he replied, "you may well be sitting here where I am now. . . . And when you are, you'll be looking at that door over there and knowing that practically everybody who walks through it wants something out of you. You'll learn what a lonely job this is, and you'll discover the need for somebody like Harry Hopkins who asks for nothing except to serve you."

Unlike Colonel House, Hopkins was not a roving statesman working on plans of large scope which he hoped to insinuate in the President's mind. He was a special agent, an intermediary, a confidential contact man between the President and strategically situated figures, both public and private. Unconcerned with the political implications of the war, Hopkins was interested only in winning it and unqualifiedly concurred that it be fought within the framework of an international coalition. As chairman of the Munitions Assignment Board, his duties brought him into close and constant contact with the leading officials in Britain and Russia. With Churchill he developed a warm friendship which was extremely useful to Roosevelt. The Prime Minister, who had a great admiration for his quick and practical mind, which enabled him to strip a problem to its core with lightning speed or pull the participants in a discussion down to earth when they were soaring off into the stratosphere, dubbed Hopkins "Lord Root of the Matter."

Alone of all the White House staff, Hopkins had unlimited access to the top-secret Map Room. Yet, despite his unique and privileged position, his unassuming manner was so completely disarming that there was rarely any friction or clash with the Secretary of State or with any of the ambassadors with whom he dealt.

It was one of Roosevelt's gifts, especially valuable to a war leader, that he knew how to make use of the human repositories of talent and skill. He surrounded himself with men of imagination and ideas and was receptive to novel proposals. A notable example of his open-mindedness was later to have a profound impact on the war's outcome and incalculable consequences for the fate of mankind.

In 1939, American scientists learned that the Germans were feverishly conducting research on a process to construct an atomic bomb and had already split the uranium atom. If the Nazis were successful, the effect on the democratic world would be catastrophic. An attempt had been made earlier that year to interest the Navy Department in research on atomic fission, but there seemed to be no prospect of any action. Increasing apprehension over the situation led a number of atomic physicists to enlist the aid of Dr. Alexander Sachs for a personal meeting with the President. An interview was finally arranged in October. Sachs presented a letter from Albert Einstein and a memorandum from Leo Szilard which described the expected destructive power of an atomic bomb and pointed out that the limited budgets of university departments were insufficient to finance the experimental work required.

Although Roosevelt knew as little about atomic energy as any layman, he quickly grasped its import and appointed an Advisory Committee on Uranium. The initial appropriation in February, 1940, for the purchase of raw materials was a piddling six thousand dollars. Later that year, when the German attack on the Low Countries threatened to cut off the supply of pitchblende from the Belgian Congo, Sachs urged the establishment of a scientific council to mobilize a national effort for an intensive program. About the same time, Dr. Vannevar Bush, president of the Carnegie Institute, representing another group of eminent scientists, presented a similar plan to the President.

Bypassing all existing channels, Roosevelt established the National Defense Committee on June 15, with Vannevar Bush as chairman, and arranged for an allocation of two billion dollars, which was later utilized by the Manhattan Project. He acted virtually on his own, for his military advisers were little impressed. Admiral Leahy remarked that he knew all about explosives, and the idea of a superbomb was "damned professors' nonsense."

To lead a nation in a global war required skill of the highest order, not only as commander in chief but as statesman. An effective coalition had to be maintained among powers whose interests often diverged and conflicted. Perspective was all important, as was the capacity to view the picture in the large without overlooking the details and to balance principle and expediency so that military victory might not be jeopardized, by an undue emphasis on the one, or national morale be permitted to suffer, by excessive reliance on the other.

At home, Roosevelt had the task of infusing the nation with purpose and confidence. During the bleak period when the Axis was achieving one victory after another and the hopes of the American people kept plummeting, he endeavored to counteract defeatism with inspiring addresses. On numerous occasions he recalled other times of trial in the history of the nation which, he emphasized, had always ended in triumph. In one of his most eloquent fireside chats, when the end of the struggle seemed remote indeed, he compared conditions with those that had prevailed at Valley Forge. Quoting the words of Thomas Paine, "These are the times that try men's souls," which had then rallied a despondent nation, he asserted that the Americans of 1776 who condemned "the summer soldier and the sunshine patriot," and who realized that "tyranny, like hell, is not easily conquered," spoke the same language as their descendants today.

Complex and impersonal issues were reduced to terms that had meaning for each individual. After the President submitted to Congress a seven-point program to check inflation, he went on the air to point out the relationship of this domestic measure to the larger struggle for survival. He discussed the global character of the conflict and the military difficulties yet to be overcome. If the war were to be won, he said, sacrifices made by the soldiers had to be accompanied by the lesser privations the government was asking from civilians.

As military strategist, President Roosevelt had to make the fateful decision as to whether the European or the Asian theater should be the point of concentration for American power. Top priority had been assigned to Europe before Pearl Harbor, but the Japanese attack created strong pressure for shifting the emphasis. In his state of the Union message in January, 1942, Roosevelt explained why the nation should adhere to its original position. The enemy, he declared, had failed in its intent to "terrify" us to such an extent that we would divert our industrial and military strength to the Pacific area or even to our continental defense." For the time being the major effort would be directed against the Reich, while a delaying action would be carried on in the Pacific until the nation was strong enough to launch an offensive there. This priority was essential, he explained, because the formidable Nazi war machine, having enslaved the peoples of so many nations to produce weapons of destruction, controlled industrial and manpower resources superior to those of Japan and therefore had to be destroyed first. Furthermore, supply lines to the Pacific presented an enormous problem, as no bases like those in England were available from which air or sea operations could be launched.

This strategy was criticized throughout the war by "Asia Firsters," many of whom had been pronounced isolationists before Pearl Harbor. But Roosevelt never doubted his judgment, with which the Chiefs of Staff completely concurred. Events were to demonstrate that he was correct.

As ideological spokesman in a war that required the use of ideas as well as bullets, Roosevelt was censured both by conservatives, who resented any attempt to use the struggle as an opportunity to reform society, and liberals, who felt this aspect was inadequately emphasized. The latter wished the President to lead a social crusade and concentrate upon humanitarian goals. Vice President Henry Wallace became the spokesman for the liberals. In an address in 1942 he declared that the world had failed to build a peace after the last conflict, because "the fundamental doctrine of the people's revolution" had been ignored. This revolution, he said, a dynamic force for more than a century and a half, had now reached the vast continents of Asia and Africa. That fact must be recognized, all forms of imperialism abandoned, and the continents assisted to industrialize. The upsurge, he warned, would continue until freedom from want had been achieved everywhere.

The Vice President accurately and perceptively diagnosed the anti-colonial ferment, but he was premature. Roosevelt, too, believed that imperialism would have to go after the war, but for the present he was allied with those who were committed to the status quo. He could not at this point sound the trumpets to blow down the walls of injustice.

Support for Wallace's ideas came from an unexpected source. Wendell Willkie, after a globe-girdling tour which took him to Africa, the Middle East, China, and the Soviet Union, returned to champion the cause of anti-colonialism. Everywhere he went, he said, he found a demand for self-government, a determination by the people to be done with imperialist rule. Though a "reservoir of good will" for the United States still existed, he feared that it was being drained by the failure of the democracies to announce war aims reflecting the aspirations of the masses. He also attacked the administration for what he regarded as an excessive use of expediency. "The peoples of the world," he declared, "must be given again the conviction that the banners Americans fight under bear bright clean colors."

Unfortunately, the immensely complicated strategy of a global struggle made a simon-pure policy untenable, even necessitating a relationship with the two unsavory regimes of Fascist Spain and collaborationist France. Since the fall of France in June, 1940, Roosevelt and Churchill were apprehensive that Francisco Franco's non-belligerency might give way to an active alliance with Hitler, a development that could seriously hamper activities in the Mediterranean and jeopardize the chances for offensive action in North Africa. If the Spaniards used their shore batteries in the Straits of Gibraltar to protect German troops pouring in from the North, Allied forces could be cut off and the operation turn into a disaster. Moreover, 100,000 troops stationed across the Straits in Spanish Morocco along the contemplated invasion route could also deal decisive blows, especially if supported by the Nazis.

As one step in safeguarding the interests of the Allies, Roosevelt permitted "preclusive" buying—the purchase from Spain at high prices of strategic materials such as mercury, cork, and wolfram, to prevent them from going to Germany. Then, in an endeavor to keep Spain neutral, he sent a prominent Catholic, Columbia University historian Carlton J. H. Hayes, as ambassador and offered the dictator carefully rationed quantities of food, cotton, and oil. When Spain was threatened by famine in the winter of 1940-41, Roosevelt, fearful that it might force Franco into the arms of Germany unless he received adequate help, authorized additional shipments of food.

While the President was strongly criticized by many Americans for "appeasement," his policy was vindicated by documents captured after the war revealing that Franco had been negotiating with Hitler. The Spanish dictator had been willing to enter the conflict, but the price he demanded for participation in the Axis effort was much too high for the Fuehrer. Then, in February, 1941, when Hitler wanted to get to North Africa via Spain and Gibraltar, Franco turned down a request to join forces just about the time a relief shipment arrived from the United States. Whether Roosevelt's courting of Franco actually influenced his decision to retain non-belligerent status cannot be known. But it was a gamble the war leader had to take.

Infinitely more complicated was the problem of the French. Considerations of expediency motivated Roosevelt in establishing diplomatic relations with the authoritarian and collaborationist French government of Marshal Henri Pétain at Vichy, while Great Britain supported what was, in effect, a French government in exile headed by General Charles de Gaulle, who had escaped to England. The President hoped to encourage the aged and feeble Pétain to restrain his Vice Premier, Pierre Laval, and his commander in chief of the armed forces, Admiral Jean François Darlan, from complete collaboration with the Nazis, to prevent the French from surrendering their fleet and their North African bases to the Germans, and to use unoccupied France as a source of information on Axis activities. Coolness to de Gaulle was a natural corollary of the Vichy policy. In any case, both Roosevelt and Hull were antipathetic to the imperious and difficult general, and they were not convinced of his claim that he had the allegiance of all Frenchmen.

In February, 1942, relations with Vichy became strained when Pétain ignored a request by the United States for assurance that he would not give the Axis any military assistance or turn over any French vessels to them. Ambassador William Leahy wrote to the President that America would lose prestige unless the threat to recall him, which accompanied the request, was carried out. Roosevelt's reply indicates the extent to which military consideration dictated the adherence to certain policies. The Joint Staff missions, he wrote, have "very definitely urged that we postpone as long as possible any evidence of change in our relations with France, and they consider that to hold the fort as far as you are concerned is as important a military task as any other in these days." The presence of the United States in France and North Africa was not only the last bridgehead to Europe, he continued, but helped to hold the Iberian peninsula in line. Military developments within the next few weeks would be vital, and "we cannot afford to risk any possibility that an abrupt action on our part would lose ground anywhere."

The Anglo-American invasion of North Africa required an even greater compromise of principle. Preparations for this undertaking at first involved an arrangement with General Henri

H. Giraud, a distinguished French army officer and war hero, to land with the troops. It was hoped that he could persuade the French forces to support the invaders, but his cease-fire order was not recognized and the Allies met with resistance everywhere, especially in French Morocco. By coincidence, or more likely by design, Darlan suddenly appeared in Algiers. Since his legal authority would be respected by the French troops, the two generals in command, Dwight D. Eisenhower and Mark Clark, made a "deal" with him, though his reputation as a pro-Nazi and arch-collaborationist was notorious. In return for his cease-fire, Darlan would be recognized as the political head in North Africa. Several days later, French resistance ended.

The President's decision not to break with the Pétain regime, coupled with the Darlan arrangement, subjected him to the most acrimonious attack that he was to experience during the entire war. Years later, opinion remained divided as to the merit of his policy, but on the whole the President seems to have been justified. Roosevelt's primary objective was to achieve a military victory at the least possible cost. To accomplish this he believed it was sometimes necessary to walk with the devil to cross the bridge. Moreover, he dared not hesitate in making his decision.

Probably the President's most demanding role was that of international leader. The problems of waging a coalition war on a global scale were far different from those of 1917. The far-flung fronts, the conflicting strategies, the mutual suspicions greatly complicated the task of leadership. As one observer put it, "There are some patriotic citizens who sincerely hope that America will win the war—but they also hope Russia will lose it; and there are some who hope that America will win the war, but that England will lose it; and there are some who hope that America will win the war but that Roosevelt will lose it."

Two weeks after Pearl Harbor, Prime Minister Churchill and his staff arrived in Washington for diplomatic and military discussions. Agreements were reached on war strategy, and it was decided to establish immediately a combined Chiefs of Staff in Washington as well as a joint British, American, and Dutch command in the Pacific. Then, on New Year's Day, the United States, Great Britain, the Soviet Union, China, and twenty-two other nations at war with the Axis powers signed a declaration in Washington endorsing the principles of the Atlantic Charter, pledging to prosecute the war with all available resources, and under no circumstances to make a separate peace. Thus was formally organized the Grand Alliance, which Roosevelt denominated the United Nations. To keep it from disintegrating would require his consummate skill.

Most challenging of all the problems of coalition warfare was maintaining amity with the Soviet Union. Russian cooperation, the President believed, was indispensable to win the war in Europe as quickly and as cheaply as possible and to defeat Japan. He feared that divisive discussions with Stalin of political questions such as eastern European boundaries and insistence on the independent status of countries in that area would only delay or even impede victory. Accordingly, when an Anglo-Soviet alliance was being negotiated in the spring of 1942, he intervened, opposing both Stalin's demands that the treaty include turning the Baltic states and parts of Rumania, Poland, and Finland over to Russia and Eden's equally stubborn insistence that these areas be specifically denied to the Soviets. He succeeded in having the treaty omit any reference to this issue. Churchill was gratified at the outcome, declaring, "This was a great relief to me and a far better solution than I had dared to hope."

Also influencing Roosevelt's approach was his confidence that an international security organization, which would most certainly be created when the fighting ceased, would provide the machinery to settle any disputes among the Big Three. In any case, his reluctance to force the issue was hardly responsible for the postwar difficulties, as his critics subsequently charged. Even if Stalin had been persuaded to make pledges about Eastern Europe that were agreeable to the West, he would probably have broken them later on. Yet Roosevelt might have used the Soviet's dire need for assistance as leverage to insist on political settlements. If he had succeeded and they were later violated, at least he would have escaped censure.

Looking beyond the war, Roosevelt was convinced that lasting peace was possible only if the United States and the Soviet

Union could live in harmony. While he was wary of the Marshal—"In all our dealings with Stalin we must keep our fingers crossed," he once told Poland's Prime Minister, Stanislaw Mikolajczyk—he was sanguine about future Soviet behavior. Writing to a friend he recalled that when he initiated negotiations to recognize the Soviet Union, he and Maxim Litvinov "had a four or five day drag down and knock out fight in regard to a number of things." Litvinov kept objecting, and Roosevelt finally threw up his hands, saying, "What is the use of all this anyway? Your people and my people are as far apart as the poles." The Soviet envoy replied, "I hope you will not feel that way, Mr. President, because I do not. In 1920, we were as far apart as you say. At that time you were one hundred per cent capitalistic and we were at the other extreme—zero. In these thirteen years we have risen in the scale to, let us say, a position of twenty. You Americans, especially since last March, have gone to a position of eighty. It is my real belief that in the next twenty years we will go to forty and you will come down to sixty . . . while it is difficult for nations to confer with and understand each other with a difference of twenty and eighty, it is wholly possible for them to do so if the difference is only between forty and sixty."

Russian conduct in recent years, Roosevelt thought, justified some optimism. Since the Soviets had joined the League of Nations in 1934, they had given every evidence of peaceful intentions. The invasion of Finland had been undertaken, he asserted, not to add additional territory but to bolster Russia's western defenses. At Cairo, the President told General Stilwell that he did not believe the Soviet Union would seek to obtain control of Manchuria. "Stalin doesn't want any more ground. He's got enough. He could even put another hundred million people into Siberia." And publicly he stated, "They have got a large enough 'hunk of bread' right in Russia to keep them busy for a great many years to come without taking on any more headaches."

While regarding the Soviet Union as a ruthless dictatorship, he believed that no society was static, and that in time Russia could evolve into a democratic commonwealth. He saw a hopeful sign in the dissolution of the Comintern in 1943, which indicated that efforts to foment world revolution were diminishing. With the expected rise in the standard of living and increase in foreign trade, he trusted that the wall of political and economic isolation would come down. Once Soviet society was opened up, he thought, the Russian people would become informed about the nature of the western world and a general liberalization would follow.

Coalition diplomacy was an essential element of Roosevelt's wartime leadership in planning military strategy and laying the foundations for peace. Throughout the war he traveled thousands of miles to conferences with one or both of the Allied leaders. On January 14, 1943, during the North African campaign to clear the Mediterranean as a prelude to a landing on the continent, Roosevelt and Churchill met at Casablanca to discuss procedure. Also under consideration was policy toward France, for which both Generals de Gaulle and Giraud claimed to speak. Both men were invited to attend. De Gaulle came only after Churchill threatened to give his support to Giraud if he did not appear. Despite all efforts by the Allied leaders, only a surface accord between the two generals could be reached.

The Casablanca conference is particularly significant for the statement on "unconditional surrender" issued by the President. Later Roosevelt was severely censured for having made it, partly because he gave the impression that an announcement of such consequence was delivered on the spur of the moment. "We had so much trouble getting those two French generals together," Roosevelt had said, "that I thought to myself that this was as difficult as arranging the meeting of Grant and Lee—and then suddenly the press conference was on, and Winston and I had had no time to prepare for it, and the thought popped into my mind that they had called Grant 'Old Unconditional Surrender' and the next thing I knew, I had said it."

Actually, the phrase was used a year earlier, according to Elliott Roosevelt, at a luncheon on January 23, 1942, attended by Churchill, the President, Hopkins, and himself. "For what it is worth, it can be reported that it was Father's phrase," Elliott writes, "that Harry took an immediate and strong liking to it, and that Churchill, while he slowly munched a mouthful of food, thought, frowned, thought, finally grinned, and at length announced 'Perfect!' " That spring, a State Department study committee recommended unconditional surrender, rejecting an armistice as a means for ending the war. The Joint Chiefs of Staff approved, and when the President left for Casablanca he informed them that he intended to propose it as a basic Allied war aim. After he and Churchill discussed the policy at great length, it was approved by Churchill's war cabinet, to whom the Prime Minister cabled for a reaction. What impelled Roosevelt to make his casual remarks to the reporters will probably never be known. Robert Sherwood tries to explain it by saying that the President "often liked to picture himself as a rather frivolous fellow who did not give sufficient attention to the consequences of chance remarks," but that is too light a comment about so vital a matter.

Roosevelt was motivated by several considerations in demanding unconditional surrender. Primarily he wished to avoid the consequences of 1918 which later enabled Hitler to claim that Germany had never really been defeated. This time not a shred of doubt should remain as to why the enemy had capitulated, so that no basis would exist for mythmaking. Furthermore, he sought to reassure the Russians of the good faith of the Western powers. At that point the Soviets were bearing the brunt of the Nazi assault, and the North African landings were not sufficient evidence to them that the British and Americans were doing everything in their power to relieve some of the pressure from the eastern front. As it would be some time before landings on French soil could be undertaken, "unconditional surrender" would provide an earnest of Allied intentions. Another motive was probably to allay the fears of the liberals at home that the traffic with Darlan would not set a pattern for future dealings with the Axis powers.

At the joint press conference, Roosevelt declared, "Peace can come to the world only by the total elimination of German and Japanese war power . . . [which] means unconditional surrender by Germany, Italy, and Japan. That means a reasonable assurance of future world peace. It does not mean the destruction of the population of Germany, Italy, or Japan, but . . . the destruction of the philosophies in those countries which are based on conquest and the subjugation of other people."

Critics charged that unconditional surrender was an open invitation to unconditional resistance, that it discouraged opposition to Hitler within Germany, stiffened Axis resistance generally, and lengthened the war. But as Prime Minister Churchill later contended, "It is false to suggest that it prolonged the war. Negotiation with Hitler was impossible. He was a maniac with supreme power to play his hand out to the end, which he did; and so did we." Moreover, unconditional surrender did not compel the Germans to fight until the end; as soon as they agreed to capitulate, the war would have been over.

During the next two years the President was strongly urged to modify the surrender policy, but he was adamant in refusal. In 1944 he wrote to a senator, "It is amazing how many people are beginning to get soft on the future terms of the Germans and the Japs." At about the same time he communicated with the exiled Queen of Holland, telling her that he had no sympathy with those who are hoping "by loving kindness to make them [the Germans] Christians again. I want the Germans to know that this time at least they have definitely lost the war."

At the same time he continually drew a distinction between the leaders and the people, affirming that while the former would be punished, the latter would not be harmed. As he stated in a public address, "The United Nations have no intention to enslave the German people. We wish them to have a normal chance to develop in peace as respectable and useful members of the European family. But . . . we intend to rid them once and for all of Nazism, and Prussian militarism, and the fanatic, disastrous notion that they constitute the 'Master Race.'"

By 1943, with the tide of war turning in favor of the anti-Axis coalition, Roosevelt and his advisers could begin to direct their attention to the mammoth problems of the postwar world. In March, the President, Secretary Hull, and Harry Hopkins engaged in exploratory conversations with Foreign Minister Eden. Germany, they agreed, should be completely disarmed and divided into a number of states. They talked in general terms about the need for a postwar security organization. To avoid repeating the tragedy of Woodrow Wilson, Roosevelt and Hull were already thinking about how to enlist congressional support behind such a project.

Allied conferences were held with increasing frequency. In May, Prime Minister Churchill and his staff came to Washington for a comprehensive discussion on war strategy. Plans were approved for a huge increase in the strategic air bombardment of Germany. General Eisenhower was authorized to plan for an invasion of the Italian mainland, and a tentative date was set for the cross-channel invasion of the continent.

After the conquest of Sicily in July and the overthrow of Mussolini, a rift developed between Churchill and Roosevelt over the new government established by King Victor Emmanuel and headed by Marshal Pietro Badoglio, a Fascist and "hero" of the Ethiopian campaign. Churchill was unconcerned about the nature of the Italian government, writing to Roosevelt, "I don't think myself that we should be too particular in dealing with any non-Fascist government, even if it is not all we should like. Now Mussolini is gone, I would deal with any non-Fascist government which can deliver the goods." Roosevelt was opposed to negotiating with Badoglio on any basis but unconditional surrender. As he declared in a broadcast on July 28, the terms for Italy would be the same as for Germany and Japan. "We will have no truck with Fascism in any way, shape or manner. We will not permit any vestige of Fascism to remain."

To resolve their differences and also consult on further military plans, the two leaders met at Quebec in August, 1943. They agreed to demand unconditional surrender from Badoglio, and on September 3 an armistice was signed. A major cross-channel invasion was scheduled for May of the following year. Measures were also formulated for offensive operations in the Pacific.

For some time Roosevelt had felt that a meeting with Stalin would be desirable. Both he and Churchill had urged the Soviet leader to join them at Casablanca, but he had replied that he could not leave the front where he was personally directing military operations. In the late spring of 1943, a conference seemed particularly important, since Russian relations with the Western Allies had taken a downward turn. The full fury of the

Wehrmacht was still being hurled against the Soviet Union, and Stalin was resentful at the failure to open a second front in Western Europe. He had also indicated displeasure with the manner in which the British and Americans were handling North Africa and Italy. Never absent from Roosevelt's mind was the fear that Russia might sign a separate peace with Germany.

The President wrote Stalin that they could confer either on the American or Russian side of the Bering Strait, and he would come only with Hopkins, an interpreter, and a stenographer. "I want to get away from the difficulties of large Staff conferences or the red tape of diplomatic conversations. Therefore, the simplest and most practical method that I can think of would be an informal and completely simple visit for a few days between you and me." Stalin proposed instead a conference of foreign ministers to pave the way for an early gathering of the Big Three.

In October, Cordell Hull and Anthony Eden journeyed to Moscow to meet with V. M. Molotov. Favorable reports from all the battle fronts had relaxed tensions, and they found the Foreign Commissar cordial and hospitable. Agreement on a number of matters was achieved, including joint action on the surrender and disarming of the Axis powers, and a pledge to bring to trial those responsible for German atrocities. A European Advisory Commission was to be established in London for investigating all problems resulting from the war and to recommend policy. One declaration, which was signed by the Chinese ambassador to Moscow, called for the establishment "at the earliest practicable date a general international organization," open to all sovereign states for the maintenance of "peace and security." On the last night of the conference, Stalin, without solicitation, informed Hull "clearly and unequivocally" that the Soviet Union would join the war against Japan as soon as Hitler was defeated.

The atmosphere of good will, which led Roosevelt to call the conference "a tremendous success" and even the more cautious Churchill to declare that the West "had every reason to be content with these results," was also to prevail at the meeting of the Big Three at Teheran the following month. On his way to the rendezvous, the President stopped off at Cairo for prior consultations with Churchill and for discussions with General-issimo Chiang Kai-shek. The Chinese leader was promised increased assistance and assured that the offensive in Burma would be intensified.

At Teheran, the three leaders, meeting in almost continual session from November 28 to December 2, held wide-ranging discussions on war strategy and postwar planning. Stalin was assured that a second front would be opened in May or shortly thereafter, and the Marshal again promised that he would join the Allies against Japan when Germany surrendered. Russia, Stalin said, intended to retain control over all the areas acquired during the period of collaboration with the Germans; he also wanted the portion of East Prussia situated on the Baltic Sea, and the area of Finland adjacent to Leningrad. As these demands violated the principles of the Atlantic Charter, Roosevelt, ever conscious of his military goals, preferred to postpone their disposition until after the war. Churchill acknowledged that the needs of security made the Soviet case for Eastern Europe reasonable.

On the question of Germany, Stalin recounted the unimaginable suffering being endured by the Russian people. Unless the German nation was fragmented so that its power was completely destroyed, he declared, it would rise again to inflict new horrors on humanity. Churchill was sympathetic, but concerned that a vacuum in Central Europe would give free rein to Soviet ambitions. Roosevelt had less compunction about imposing a harsh peace upon Germany and more faith in mutual agreements to restrain the Russians. He advanced a tentative proposal to divide Germany into seven parts, five of which would be self-governing while the other two would be administered by an outside agent, perhaps the United Nations. Churchill opposed so radical a step, arguing that the truncated parts, lacking viability, would be bound sooner or later to reunite and challenge their erstwhile enemies. He suggested, instead, that Prussia be separated from the rest of the country, and that such southern sections as Bavaria and Saxony also be detached to become part of a confederation of other states on the Danube. As no final decision was reached, the matter was referred to the European Advisory Commission for further consideration. On the strategy for destroying Hitler's empire the Allies were in complete accord.

The Teheran Conference was the high point of the Grand Coalition. "We came here with hope and determination," stated the official communiqué. "We leave here friends in fact, in spirit, and in purpose." Reflecting Roosevelt's great hope for future collaboration, it continued, "We express our determination that our nations shall work together in war and in the peace that will follow." The military staffs' plans for the destruction of the German forces have been solidified, and "we are sure that our concord will win an enduring Peace." In resounding terms the three leaders summoned all mankind to join them in their righteous cause: "We shall seek the cooperation and active participation of all nations, large and small, whose peoples in heart and mind are dedicated . . . to the elimination of tyranny and slavery, oppression and intolerance."

One American participant in the conference did not share the spirit of optimism which the official pronouncement exuded. Summing up what he regarded as the full implications of the Stalin proposals with respect to Europe, he observed that the Soviet Union would be left as the only important military and political force on the continent, with the rest of Europe reduced to impotence. Roosevelt did not subscribe to this Cassandra-like prediction. After the meeting, he remarked about Stalin, "He is a man who combines a tremendous, relentless determination with a stalwart good humor. I believe he is truly representative of the heart and soul of Russia; and I believe that we are going to get along very well with him and the Russian people—very well indeed." He was encouraged, he said, by the decision at Moscow to proceed with plans for an international security organization. Not only did this imply that the wartime coalition created in the crucible of conflict would survive, but that the Soviet Union was abandoning isolation to enter the family of nations as a willing partner. Troublesome issues, he was confident, would be amicably resolved by the future international organization.

Roosevelt had supreme confidence in his ability to iron out problems through personal negotiation, to apply the political

craftsmanship to the Russian dictator that served him so effectively at home. ". . . I tell you that I think I can handle Stalin
personally better than either your Foreign Office or my State
Department," he wrote to Churchill on one occasion. With
characteristic optimism, he was not unduly disturbed by disa-
greements arising out of the Soviet position on territorial and
boundary questions. Time, he felt, would prove the great
healer. Recalling his conversations with Stalin at Teheran on
the Polish situation, he said, "I formed the conviction that
sitting around the table and talking it over would do nobody
any harm, that there can be a meeting of the minds, leaving out
the smaller details, such as certain portions of what we call
boundaries, deferring them until a somewhat later time." War
did not provide the most suitable atmosphere, he explained, for
the settlement of delicate and complex political problems.
People were in a state of "shell shock" and "some things must
await the return of a word . . . which a former President
used—'normalcy'—when we can think rather more quietly and
think in the larger, in the longer, terms of what is going to
happen not next year, or the year after or even ten years hence,
but fifty years and a hundred years hence." Yet perhaps something might have been gained if an attempt had been made to
resolve some of the troublesome issues while the Russians, fighting for survival, were so dependent on Western good will.

The constitutional processes of a democratic nation permitted no suspension, even in wartime, of the national referendum represented by a presidential election. The country had
become sharply divided on domestic policy. In the mid-year
elections of 1942, Republicans had scored gains in both Houses
of Congress, and a conservative coalition of southern Democrats and northern Republicans had succeeded in wresting
control of legislative policies from the President. As the 1944
national convention approached, Democratic Party leaders
found themselves helpless to determine the choice of the presidential candidate. They were eager to avoid a fourth-term
nomination, but once again Roosevelt foreclosed the possibility
of a pre-convention race by delaying the announcement of his
intentions. Many of the politicians, and especially the southern

conservatives, were antagonistic to Roosevelt's liberalism, preferring someone more "dependable" in the White House.

Not until July 11, a week before the scheduled opening of the convention, did the President write to the chairman of the Democratic National Committee that he would accept, but "would not run in the usual partisan political sense." If the people wanted him to continue in office, then "I have as little right to withdraw as the soldier has to leave his post in the line." At the same time, he wanted to make it clear that, "For myself, I do not want to run. . . . After many years of public service . . . my personal thoughts have turned to the day when I could return to civil life. All that is within me cries out to go back to my home on the Hudson River, to avoid public responsibilities, and . . . the publicity which . . . follows every step of the Nation's Chief Executive." But, he continued, he was of the generation which had felt the impact of attack upon the United States. His country's future existence and its chosen method of government were at stake. "Therefore, reluctantly, but as a good soldier, I repeat that I will accept and serve in this office, if I am so ordered . . . by the United States."

While these were the words of a skilled politician, they also contained a ring of sincerity, even of poignancy. Roosevelt must have been greatly ambivalent about the prospect of a fourth term. Enjoying to the hilt his role as world leader, he had nevertheless been drained by his years in office during the most harrowing period in the nation's history, and he was weary. As he wrote to his friend, Hamilton Holt, "as far as individual preference goes I would, quite honestly, have retired to Hyde Park with infinite pleasure in 1941."

On the Republican side, the war did not inhibit the usual campaign oratory, but Thomas Dewey was battling against a seasoned politician. Moreover, circumstances did not favor his prospects. The successful military operations in Europe and Asia, the economic stabilization at home, the natural reluctance to change leadership in time of crisis all worked against him. The only thing he could try to capitalize on was the seemingly failing health of the President.

Roosevelt had decided to refrain from an active campaign. As war leader, he did not feel justified in making the traditional "swing around the circle," and his attitude appeared to be that if the people wanted him they would re-elect him. Not until the closing weeks, when the public opinion polls indicated a rise in Dewey's stock, was he persuaded to enter the lists in the usual partisan manner. And then, after twelve grueling years, the unrivaled campaigner exceeded even his own past performances. One of his addresses stands out as a masterpiece of political strategy, especially remembered for a paragraph which he himself had written. "The Republican leaders," he said, "have not been content to make personal attacks upon me, or my wife, or my sons—they now include my little dog, Fala. Unlike the members of my family, Fala resents this. When he learned that the Republican fiction writers had concocted a story that I had left him behind on an Aleutian Island and had sent a destroyer back to find him—at a cost to the taxpayers of two or three or twenty million dollars—his Scotch soul was furious. He has not been the same dog since. I am accustomed to hearing malicious falsehoods about myself but I think I have a right to object to libelous statements about my dog." Americans roared with delight. As one commentator put it, "From now on the . . . people will consider this a contest of Dewey versus Fala." Dewey lost. Roosevelt was returned to office with a popular vote of 27,244,160 as against his opponent's 22,305,-198, and an electoral vote of 449 to 82.

Even as the campaign was in progress, the President had to give serious thought to the problem of a defeated Germany. With the Nazis reeling under a mammoth Allied assault, their capitulation was only a matter of time. Roosevelt's own views had not yet entirely crystallized, and members of his administration had differed sharply for some time on what the American position ought to be. At a Cabinet meeting, Secretary of the Treasury Henry Morgenthau submitted a plan prepared by a subcommittee in his department which was designed to keep Germany from ever again becoming an industrial and military power: parts of the country were distributed among Poland, Russia, Denmark, and France, and the remainder divested of all industrial potential. Opposed vehemently by Secretaries Hull and Stimson, who believed that the plan was motivated more by a spirit of vengeance than by a desire to achieve a stabilized Europe, it was nevertheless approved by the President.

When Roosevelt met with Churchill for the second time in Quebec in mid-September of 1944 to discuss postwar Germany, he was accompanied not by his Secretary of State but significantly by his Secretary of the Treasury. The President was convinced that it was imperative not only to prevent a resurgence of German military might, but that Europe be freed of dependence on the German economy. The British, however, thinking in terms of a postwar market in the defeated nation, argued against a Draconian solution. Finally, Churchill agreed to support the plan, possibly persuaded by the tentative assurance of a substantial postwar loan by the United States.

The Prime Minister drew up a memorandum for release to the press which he and the President initialed, stating that the world knew from bitter experience how easily German industries could be converted from peacetime to wartime use. Countries devastated by the Nazis were justified in removing from Germany whatever equipment might compensate for their losses. The Ruhr and the Saar should be stripped of industry and to "make sure that they were not started up again by some subterfuge," the dismantling should be supervised by the projected world organization. "This programme for eliminating the war-making industries . . . is looking forward to converting Germany into a country primarily agricultural and pastoral in its character."

In the United States, reaction against the Morgenthau Plan was vehement. Roosevelt's approach to Germany was attacked not only as vindictive but absurd—the European economy, critics argued, could never recuperate and thrive without a prosperous Germany. Henry Stimson was convinced that eradicating German industry would envenom the German people and produce future wars. Others believed the greater danger in the postwar world would be the Soviet Union, against which a strong, revitalized Germany was essential as a buffer.

Roosevelt's endorsement of the Morgenthau Plan stemmed from his profound conviction that unless the evil of Axis militarism was extirpated for all time, any hope for a tranquil world would be vain. Twice in one generation the Germans had endangered the American national interest, and thousands of American youth had given their lives in its defense. If an impotent Germany resulted in a power vacuum on the Russian flank, then the solution lay in abandoning traditional power politics. In his view, lasting peace was possible only if the two major powers, the United States and the Soviet Union, cooperated within the framework of an international security organization.

The extent and the intensity of the opposition compelled the President to abandon the Morganthau Plan, but he never altered his views on the hazard of a rearmed Germany. In one of his last addresses he stated that the Allies were agreed that not "a shred of control, open or secret, of the instruments of government" should be left to the Nazis. "We shall not leave them a single element of military power or of potential military power. . . . We bring no charge against the German race as such for we cannot believe that God has eternally condemned any race of humanity. . . . But it will be necessary for them to earn their way back into the fellowship of peace-loving and law-abiding Nations. And in their climb up that steep road, we shall certainly see to it that they are not encumbered by having to carry guns. We hope they will be relieved of that burden forever."

Franklin Delano Roosevelt

15. Expectations and Realities

THE ring of steel that the coalition had been battling to draw around Germany began to close and throttle the Nazis by the beginning of 1945. An offensive in the West had liberated France, Brussels, and Antwerp, and Allied troops were approaching the Rhine. At the same time on the Eastern front, Soviet troops had crashed out of Russian territory to occupy a line extending all the way from the Baltic to the Balkans; by February, they were only forty-five miles from Berlin. With victory in sight, such matters as the coordination of final military operations, the nature of the German occupation, and a common strategy for the war against Japan required an early settlement. Moreover, the differences that the Allies had submerged for the sake of military unity were mounting to the surface to threaten the Grand Alliance.

At Roosevelt's request, another Big Three conference was arranged to meet at Yalta in the Russian Crimea, at which he hoped they could resolve their differences. For eight days, from February 4 to February 11, 1945, the three heads of state grappled with momentous issues. Their decisions would affect the politics of the world for generations to come. Major items on the agenda were the future of Germany, the governments of Poland and other East European countries, the Far East settlement, and the United Nations organization.

This was the last meeting of the Big Three; two months later, Roosevelt would be gone, struck down by a cerebral hemorrhage which took his life. The great hopes he had encouraged for a future of peace and justice already had begun to wither. Disillusionment with the diplomacy of Yalta was evident even before he passed from the scene. In the years that followed, critics laid at the door of the President, because of his negotiations at that conference, almost all the problems which have afflicted the world since the defeat of the Axis.

It has been charged that Roosevelt was already a dying man and no longer alert when he participated in the deliberations. While he was worn and exhausted—the nation was shocked by his gaunt and frail appearance when he returned from the Crimea—the records of the conference show conclusively that his mental acuteness was unimpaired. Nor were the famed buoyancy, charm, and humor absent. The President's deteriorating health was entirely inconsequential as a factor influencing the decisions. Settlements hammered out at Yalta reflected not only Roosevelt's judgments but those of his diplomatic and military advisers, high-ranking officers in the State Department, as well as of Prime Minister Churchill and his staff.

Another unfounded accusation is that the President went to the conference unprepared. On the contrary, Roosevelt and his new Secretary of State, Edward R. Stettinius, Jr., devoted considerable time and thought in advance of the meeting to formulating a program and achieving a harmony of views with the British. Stettinius conducted an extensive briefing session in French Morocco with his staff, then went on to Malta, where he was joined by the President for detailed discussions with Churchill and Eden before they all left for Yalta. A comparison of the pre-conference briefing papers prepared by the State Department with the minutes of the Yalta proceedings reveals that Roosevelt was thoroughly familiar with the major policy statements contained in those documents.

Rarely in recent times has the leader of a democratic state been blamed for so much. Roosevelt has been charged with surrendering Eastern Europe and its peoples to Soviet hegemony and with perpetrating a monstrous sell-out of the Far East. Much of the indictment, however, has been made with the omniscience of hindsight and without taking into account the

situation as it existed in 1945. With regard to Europe, the conference was held at a time when circumstances militated
against advantageous territorial and political decisions for the
West. The Allies had not yet bridged the Rhine, the advance in
Italy had bogged down in the Apennines, and the troops were
still staggering from blows they had received in the Battle of
the Bulge. Soviet troops, on the other hand, were triumphantly
hurling back the Nazis. They had just swept through almost all
of Poland and East Prussia, had at some points reached the
Oder River in Germany, and had captured most of Hungary
while the Yugoslav Partisans had retaken Belgrade. Except for
Czechoslovakia, all of Eastern Europe was thus in the hands of
the Red Army. It was, therefore, not a question of what
Churchill and Roosevelt would permit Stalin to do, but what
they could persuade him to accept. George F. Kennan, veteran
diplomat and historian, later commented, "The establishment of
Soviet military power in Eastern Europe . . . was not the
result of [Yalta]" but of military operations. "There was nothing the western democracies could have done to prevent the
Russians from entering those areas except to get there first, and
this they were not in a position to do."

In connection with the Far East, one of Roosevelt's major
objectives at Yalta was committing the Russians to an early
date for entering the war against Japan. The bloody campaign
in the Pacific to eject the Japanese island by island was still in
progress, and plans had been projected for a major invasion of
the country in the fall of 1945. Secretary Stimson recorded
that, in the War Department's judgment, Japan would probably
resist to the end in all the areas under her control. "In such an
event," he wrote, "the Allies would be faced with the enormous
task of destroying an armed force of five million men and five
thousand suicide aircraft belonging to a race which had . . .
demonstrated its ability to fight literally to the death. . . . I was
informed that such operations might be expected to cost over a
million casualties to American forces alone." With the help of
the Soviet Union countless American lives would be saved, and
all the President's advisers were agreed that the United States
dare not go it alone against Japan. The atom bomb had not yet

been tested. Not for another five months would word come from Los Alamos that the experiment had succeeded.

Still another consideration motivated the President throughout the involved discussions. He was convinced that peace could not endure in the postwar world without Soviet cooperation, which he believed could be obtained by making some concessions where American vital interests were not directly affected. Moreover, he felt that when the sound and the fury had subsided, many problems could be resolved through calm discussion in a United Nations organization.

The divergent views of East and West were clearly revealed in the debate over the Polish issue, which was more controversial than any other at Yalta. Both the United States and Great Britain felt bound by the Atlantic Charter's pledge of self-determination. For their part, the Russians were influenced by considerations of national security. Twice within one generation, Stalin emphasized, Poland had been used as an invasion route to the Soviet Union, and the Poles themselves had attempted to seize the Ukraine in 1920. He was unwilling to risk an unfriendly government at his back door. Also, boundaries must be drawn in such a way as to offer protection for his country. In general, as Ambassador Averell Harriman had noted earlier, "The overriding consideration in Soviet foreign policy is the preoccupation with 'security.' The Soviet Union seeks a period of freedom from danger during which it can recover from the wounds of war and complete its industrial revolution." And in pursuing its objective it was not prepared to consider "the similar needs or rights of other countries."

The suggestion made by Roosevelt and Churchill that Poland's eastern boundary, known as the Curzon Line, be extended to permit Lwów and some of the oil fields to be included within Polish territory was categorically rejected by Stalin. That demarcation, he said, had been made in 1919 by Clemenceau and the Americans at Versailles, a conference to which the Russians had not been invited. Then he added passionately, "Now some people want that we should be less Russian than Curzon . . . and Clemenceau. . . . You would drive us into shame. . . . I could not take such a position and return to Moscow with an open face." It was finally agreed that the eastern boundary of Poland should follow the Curzon Line and the western boundary extend into German territory, the precise lines to be determined at the future peace conference.

The proposed composition of the Polish government provoked further controversy. There were currently two governments, the one in exile at London and the Soviet-sponsored one in Lublin, two armies, and two constitutions. To Roosevelt, the most practical course was to scrap both, establish a provisional body composed of representatives from London, from the Lublin group, and from among representative elements within Poland, and then schedule a free election as soon as possible. Churchill and Stalin both objected. The former contended that the London group should provide the leadership for the provisional government. The latter claimed that the London group was highly unpopular in Poland and out of touch with sentiment and conditions at home. Russia must have a neighbor, he said, which would be strong enough to "shut the door of this corridor [Poland] by her own force," as this was "not only a question of honor but of life and death for the Soviet state."

Both Roosevelt and Churchill remained firm in their opposition to the Lublin group, despite Molotov's claim that it enjoyed the enthusiastic support of the Polish people. The suggestion that it be enlarged to include some members of the exiled government proved equally unacceptable to the Russians. At last, Stalin agreed to Roosevelt's original recommendation that the provisional government remain in power only until free elections were held. When Roosevelt asked how soon this would be, Stalin replied within a month, barring the unlikely possibility of a catastrophe at the front. He refused to agree, however, to the President's proposal for international supervision of the elections. Instead, the British and American ambassadors would be permitted to investigate the situation to ascertain whether the pledge for bona fide elections had been fulfilled.

When the discussion was over, Roosevelt commented privately that he knew the agreement could be stretched by the Soviets to fit their purposes, but "it's the best I can do for Poland at this time." With the Red Army already in occupation of the country, the Western powers had little choice. If Roosevelt had left Yalta without reaching an accord, what possibly could have prevented the Communist-led Lublin group from seizing control with Soviet assistance? And would the absence of any agreement have produced the desired free elections? At least a solemn promise was made, and responsibility for its breach could clearly be fixed.

Stalin also pledged free elections for the Balkan countries as soon as the occupying Nazis were ejected. In the Declaration on Liberated Europe, the Big Three agreed to "jointly assist the people in any European liberated state or former Axis satellite state" to establish peace and provide emergency relief, "to form interim governmental authorities broadly representative of all democratic elements in the population," and as soon as possible to establish through free elections "governments responsive to the will of the people." This statement promised a great deal but contained no machinery to establish such provisional governments or supervise early elections. The harsh fact was that implementation could be effected only by the power in military occupation, which, in this case, was the Soviet Union.

About Germany there was no prolonged argument. Stalin, desiring to neutralize the country permanently, asked that plans for dismemberment be formulated. Churchill stated that the issue was too complex to be settled in a few days, and Roosevelt's suggestion was accepted that the principle be endorsed but details worked out at a future conference of the foreign secretaries. Meanwhile, the northern part of East Prussia, including Königsberg, was to be turned over to the Soviets, the southern half to Poland, and the remainder of the country divided temporarily into four zones of occupation. Stalin had been strongly opposed to assigning a zone to the French, who "had opened the gates to the enemy," but finally yielded when Roosevelt informed him that the British would require help in the occupation as he did not believe the American people would consent to keep an army in Europe for more than two years. The city of Berlin, one hundred and ten miles within the Soviet zone, was also divided among the four occupying powers, with overall administration to be exercised by an inter-Allied governing authority.

The matter of reparations was thorny. All agreed that Germany should be expected to indemnify the Allies, but with about one-third of Soviet territory scorched and devastated and millions of Russians slaughtered, Stalin demanded huge reimbursements. He suggested a figure of twenty billion dollars to be obtained from foreign assets and industrial equipment. Churchill demurred that this would hopelessly impoverish the country, reducing the Germans to virtual starvation, and then "will we be required to keep them alive? If so, who is going to pay for that?" Roosevelt added that after the last war the United States poured billions of dollars into Germany, but "We cannot let that happen again." As with other issues, Roosevelt once again mediated, achieving a decision to turn the matter over to a reparations commission. During the conversations, the President's statement that the commission "should take [the sum of twenty billion dollars] in its initial studies as a basis for discussion," was later to be seized upon by the Russians as an indication that he had endorsed their position. But Roosevelt at no time committed himself to any specific figure.

For his consent to participate in the Pacific conflict, Stalin presented a number of demands designed to restore Russia as a major power in the Far East. He asked for and was granted the return of the territories and rights which Russia held before "the treacherous attack of Japan in 1904": the southern part of Sakhalin and adjacent islands, the lease of Port Arthur as a naval base, recognition of Russia's "preeminent interests" in the ice-free port of Dairen (which was to be internationalized), and re-establishment of joint operation with China of the Chinese-Eastern Railroad and the South Manchurian Railroad. In addition, the Kurile Islands were to be turned over to the Soviet Union, and the status quo in Outer Mongolia (the Mongolian People's Republic) was to be preserved.

In return for surrendering China's claims in Manchuria and Outer Mongolia, Roosevelt exacted a promise from Stalin that he would recognize Chinese sovereignty over Manchuria and support the Chinese Nationalist government in its struggle against Japan. In view of Russia's neutrality, the Far Eastern agreement was classified top secret and not made part of the Yalta protocol. Chiang Kai-shek was not consulted in advance, since it was feared that secrets could not be kept in Chungking, notorious for corruption and security leaks. It is doubtful whether the Generalissimo could have exacted better terms had he been present. Later, when the details of the agreement reached him, he approved them, welcoming a treaty of friendship and alliance with Russia which Stalin at Yalta told Roosevelt he would be willing to conclude. On August 14, 1945, a Sino-Soviet treaty was signed in Moscow containing the arrangements made with Stalin and officially establishing the postwar relations of the two nations.

Churchill, who did not participate in the Far Eastern negotiations, found the accord completely acceptable, declaring that he was "in favour of Russia's losses in the Russo-Japanese War being made good." Nevertheless, when the agreement was made public about a year later, it was more bitterly denounced than any other measure in Roosevelt's entire wartime diplomacy. Critics branded it as an appalling act of appeasement, claiming that the President had tossed away the gains achieved by military victory and that the balance of power in Asia had been altered in Russia's favor. In this instance, too, they ignored the limitations on Roosevelt's choices imposed by existing military realities.

A memorandum prepared by the War Department in April, 1945, analyzed the circumstances then prevailing. The concessions, it stated, "are within the military power of Russia to obtain regardless of U.S. military action short of war." The Soviet Union "was militarily capable of defeating the Japanese army deployed on the Chinese mainland and occupying Karafuto, Manchuria, Korea and Northern China" before American troops could reach those areas. Only in the Kuriles could the United States circumvent the Russians, but this would have to be "at the direct expense of the campaign to defeat Japan, and would involve an unacceptable cost in American lives." Furthermore, "the Russians can, if they choose, await the time when the United States' effort will have practically completed the destruction of Japanese military power and can then seize the objectives they desire at a cost to them relatively much less than would be occasioned by their entry into the war at an early date." In view of all this, the War Department concluded, "it appears we can bring little if any military leverage to bear on the Russians insofar as the Far East is concerned unless we choose to use force."

In consenting to the agreement, Roosevelt did not abandon the Chinese government but, on the contrary, was instrumental in having it accorded a position of high prestige in the international community. Through his efforts, China was included as one of the five permanent members in the United Nations Security Council when such recognition could be justified only by a sentimental regard for her fight against the Japanese, and not in terms of any objective standards of power. Though fully aware of the many limitations of Chiang Kai-shek's government, Roosevelt was determined to assist in its revitalization. In 1944, the President had sent General Patrick Hurley to China for conferences with Chiang and the Communists, hoping to achieve unity in the war against Japan. Hurley had succeeded in opening negotiations, but his efforts foundered on the refusal of both factions to agree on the nature and extent of government authority over the Communist troops. Moreover, he could not persuade Chiang to undertake a broadly based coalition government and a program of social and economic reform.

Fearing that civil war might again flare up after the defeat of Japan, with the Soviets assisting the Communists, Roosevelt desired to obtain Soviet endorsement and support for the Nationalist government. This he achieved at Yalta in the form of the promised pact of friendship and alliance, which he felt would also facilitate Chinese unification. If China's strength developed, it would act as a countervailing force checking Soviet ambitions in the Far East. Roosevelt never wavered in his loyalty to Nationalist China.

It is not likely that anything Roosevelt chose to do or not to do could have prevented the re-emergence of the Soviet Union as a Pacific power—Russia had formerly been one for more than a centrury and would naturally take advantage of the war situation to claim the territories taken from her by Japan. Roosevelt feared that an open break with the Soviet Union might destroy any possibility of bringing her into the United Nations and thus sacrifice the chance for a stable, peaceful world; nor would it thereby have prevented the extension of Soviet influence in the Far East.

The President operated within the framework of realistic alternatives as presented to him by his military advisers, including General Marshall, who was a brilliant strategist, and on the basis of advantages which he hoped would accrue to China through an agreement with the Soviets. Every statesman is frequently obliged to take a calculated risk. Roosevelt's actions were predicated on the assumption that China would become a viable state in the postwar period.

Each of the Big Three made and received concessions at the Crimea conference, but Roosevelt does appear to have been more conciliatory than the others. Exaggerating Allied dependence on the Soviets, he was apprehensive about jeopardizing the alliance. Though the situations in Eastern Europe and Asia were beyond his control, he could have attempted a more resolute stand, at least for the record. Perhaps Stalin, who mistook friendliness for weakness, might even have yielded to firmness on one point or another.

Two days before the conference ended, Stalin was host at a large dinner. The usual lengthy toasts exchanged by the three heads of state are highly revealing of their personalities and outlooks. The President declared that the dinner had a family atmosphere, which was how he liked to characterize relations among the three countries. Great changes had occurred in the world, he said, and greater changes were yet to come. It was their united purpose to give every human being the possibility of security and well-being. The Prime Minister toasted the President for his incalculable accomplishment in making possible an effective war against Hitler, though the United States had not been directly imperiled. Stalin struck a somber note. In toasting the alliance he declared that it was not difficult to maintain unity in wartime, while the desire to defeat the enemy provided a common bond; it was afterward that unity became strained by divergent and conflicting interests. He was confident, however, that this test would be met and peacetime relations would continue on a friendly basis.

Churchill and Roosevelt left Yalta in a mood of high hope. Addressing the House of Commons, the realistic Prime Minister, who had always been hostile to the Soviet regime, was now sanguine about the future. "The impression I brought back from the Crimea, and from all my other contacts, is that Marshal Stalin and the Soviet leaders wish to live in honorable friendship and equality with the Western democracies. I feel also that their word is their bond. I know of no Government which stands to its obligations, even in its own despite, more solidly than the Russian Soviet Government," he declared.

The President was exultant that Yalta had laid down a solid foundation for winning the war and the peace. In his address to Congress on March 1, he asserted, "I may say we achieved a unity of thought and a way of getting along together. . . . Never before have the major Allies been more closely united—not only in their war aims but also in their peace aims." With his characteristic optimism and confidence in his ability to deal personally with any situation, Roosevelt was convinced that any future problems could be settled by sitting down around a conference table with Churchill and Stalin. Believing also that it would take years before the Soviet Union could recover from the appalling devastation the country had suffered, he had an exaggerated confidence in the Russians' eagerness to cooperate in the postwar period.

Yalta, then, was compounded of wartime exigencies and the fears and hopes that prevailed on the eve of victory. As the President saw it, the new world organization would provide both the atmosphere in which defects of wartime agreements could be remedied, and the framework within which American-Soviet cooperation could maintain the peace.

Sumner Welles wrote, "One man and one man alone made it possible for us to have a working United Nations organization before the end of the Second World War. That man was Franklin Roosevelt." Resentment of Hull may have caused Welles to ignore the Secretary's significant contribution, but undeniably Roosevelt was the prime mover. The President had considered it essential for the Big Three to lay the foundations for an international body while military necessities kept the coalition intact.

The bombs which fell on Pearl Harbor also demolished America's historic isolationism, and Roosevelt gave it the *coup de grâce* when he told the nation on December 9, 1941, "We must begin the great task that is before us by abandoning once and for all the illusion that we can ever again isolate ourselves from the rest of humanity." The United States, he declared, must assume a position of leadership in a postwar collective security system. That some kind of international organization would have to be established, Roosevelt never had any doubt, but for a time he was not sure what form it should take. Remembering Wilson's tragic failure, he was resolved to avoid Wilson's errors. Concrete steps must be taken before the end of the war dissipated national and congressional unity. The covenant should not be linked with the peace treaty. The nation should be prepared by careful and constant publicity. And, probaby most important, utmost caution must be taken to insure congressional approval at every step of the way.

Not until a bipartisan group of senators introduced a resolution on March 16, 1943, urging that the United States take the initiative in forming a United Nations organization with machinery to settle disputes and enforce compliance, did Roosevelt go on record officially in behalf of American affiliation with a world body. At the Moscow Foreign Ministers' Conference in November, 1943, the first official statement calling for an international organization was issued. Later that month at Teheran, Roosevelt and Stalin exchanged views on the nature of the proposed world organization. Informally, the President expressed some tentative thoughts that the world body should be composed of three elements: first, a group of forty or more countries empowered to discuss freely any international dispute but not to take action; second, an executive committee, empowered only to make recommendations, consisting of the four nations which had signed the Moscow Declaration and six other selected countries representing the various geographical areas of the globe; and, finally, the "four policemen"—the United States, the Soviet Union, Great Britain, and China—authorized to deal with any threat to the peace. Responsibility for maintaining peace, he thought, should on the whole devolve on those powers which possessed the might to take the requisite action.

At home, carefully planned machinery was set up for cooperation between the executive and legislative branches to implement the Moscow Declaration. One highly effective group was the Advisory Committee on Postwar Foreign Policy, ultimately composed of key Cabinet officers, Senate and House leaders, technical experts in the Executive Department, and leading public citizens. In addition, special committees were created consisting of members of both Houses which met regularly with the Secretary of State, and a high-ranking department official was assigned the task of working with Congress on policy questions. Roosevelt and Hull took the initiative in suggesting procedures, submitting proposals, organizing conferences.

A political agenda group in the State Department worked on a draft charter, and by March, 1944, it had reached a point where Secretary Hull believed that congressional advice should be solicited. With Roosevelt's approval, he invited some members of both parties in the Senate Foreign Relations Committee to review the plan. Four meetings of this bipartisan group were held. During the quiet, informal discussions, Hull made no attempt to press for any commitment to a specific position or for an endorsement of the administration's views. He merely sought a frank exchange of ideas.

Early in June, shortly before the party conventions, Roosevelt issued a statement, outlining in broad terms the American position and plans for a postwar organization, and emphasized the bipartisan nature of the discussions that had taken place. "We are not thinking of a superstate with its own police forces and other paraphernalia of coercive power," he said. "We are seeking effective agreement and arrangements through which the nations could maintain, according to their capacities, adequate forces to meet the need of preventing war and of making impossible deliberate preparation for war and to have such forces available for joint action when necessary."

Painstaking preparations by Roosevelt and Hull insured the support of Congress for a collective security system, eventuating in the first successful experience in bipartisanship on a highly significant issue. The next step was to submit the draft charter for detailed discussion and mutual planning to representatives of the other two powers. At Dumbarton Oaks in

Washington, D. C., Britain, Russia, and the United States, meeting from August 21 to October 7, 1944, reached agreement on the general structure for an international organization to be called the United Nations.

The President's cherished goal was coming into sight. As he had subordinated certain considerations to the overriding objective of military victory, he now minimized differences with the Soviet Union for the sake of achieving his world body. In the opinion of George Kennan, counselor of the embassy at Moscow, this was an unwise, even dangerous approach. "An international organization for the preservation of peace and security cannot take the place of a well-conceived and realistic foreign policy . . . and we are being . . . negligent of the interests of our people if we allow plans for an international organization to be an excuse for failing to occupy ourselves seriously and minutely with the sheer power relationships of the European peoples." Intent, however, on avoiding a repetition of 1919, when the United States abdicated its responsibilities as a world power by failing to enter the League, Roosevelt considered the United Nations issue incalculably significant.

Although a number of knots still remained to be tied, the proposed charter embodied Roosevelt's major conceptions. Membership would ultimately be universal. But responsibility for maintaining peace would remain with Britain, Russia, China, and the United States, who would be obligated to prevent or stop aggression, intervening with force if necessary.

At Yalta, discussions on the United Nations were continued in a generally amicable spirit. Stalin acceded to a number of points on which the Americans had insisted at Dumbarton Oaks, including the controversial formula for voting. He had advocated that a permanent member of the Security Council be permitted to veto consideration of a dispute in which it was involved, but he yielded to Roosevelt's objection. Both leaders agreed, however, that when the Security Council was ready to take action in a dispute, then the permanent member, though itself a party, should have the right to employ the veto. Secretary of State Stettinius stated that both the American military chiefs and the Congress were insistent that "the United States should not join any world organization in which its forces could be used without its consent." The Soviet Union wished to make certain that the organization could not be used against it, as had occurred during the Finnish war, when it was isolated and expelled from the League.

Other stumbling blocks were removed. Stalin withdrew his demand for sixteen votes in the General Assembly, one for each of the Soviet Republics, but insisted on seats for the Ukraine and White Russia. He consented to Roosevelt's proposal that membership should be open to all nations at war with the Axis on or before March 1, 1945. Since some of the Latin-American countries had entered just shortly before that deadline, the position of the United States would be strengthened by having a full complement of support south of the border. Another minor triumph for Roosevelt was the decision to have the organizational meeting of all the participating nations take place in the United States.

The enthusiasm which greeted the President's report to Congress on the United Nations and other achievements at Yalta was short-lived. News soon leaked out that Roosevelt had failed to disclose the agreement on Soviet representation in the General Assembly. The President blundered in withholding information about the two extra seats granted the Soviet Union, especially since this was bound to come out at the San Francisco conference. Suspicion was aroused that other "secret" deals might have been arranged. Robert Sherwood observed, "It can only be said that this time he made a mistake which was thoroughly uncharacteristic of him—he underrated the intelligence of the American people." Yet, it is interesting that when Stalin at Yalta had proposed that reference to Russia's three votes in the General Assembly be included in the official communiqué, it was Churchill who requested that it be omitted. The flurry over this episode passed, but misgivings about Yalta had taken root and were to sprout like rank weeds when reports of the Far Eastern agreement were later made public.

Meanwhile, relations with the Soviet Union had begun to suggest the unhappy shape of things to come. The first sign of the fissure that was to widen into a chasm between East and West appeared shortly after the end of the Crimea

conference. It started with a series of relatively minor irritations: refusal by the Soviets to permit entry of teams into
Poland to assist in evacuating American prisoners of war; rejection of the American request to send a mission to Moscow to
arrange for the use of airfields in Budapest; refusal to permit
American naval officers to oversee the unloading of relief supplies from American ships in Constanta harbor. Repeated requests to improve courier, freight, and mail services to the
American Embassy in Moscow were ignored.

The situation became serious when the Soviet Union, in violation of its pledge with respect to liberated areas, imposed a
Communist regime on Rumania. Ambassador Harriman advised Washington that Soviet intransigence should be met
with firmness, even retaliation. "Up until recently," he wrote,
"the issues we have had with the Soviets have been relatively
small compared with their contribution to the war, but now we
should begin to establish a new relationship. I am, as you
know, a most earnest advocate of the closest possible understanding with the Soviet Union, so that what I am saying relates only to how best to attain such understanding."

Distressing also was the situation in Poland, where the Russians refused to honor their promise to reorganize the puppet
Lublin government. Their delaying tactics and transparent
devices for circumventing the agreement disturbed the President, who wrote to Stalin, "Any such solution which would
result in a thinly disguised continuation of the present government would be entirely unacceptable and would cause our
people to regard the Yalta agreement as a failure."

On his side, Stalin, whose suspicion of the Western powers
always lurked just beneath the surface, became enraged by
Anglo-American negotiations with a German officer for the surrender of German troops in Italy. In a letter to Roosevelt, the
Soviet leader virtually accused the President and Churchill of
excluding the Soviets from negotiations for the capitulation of
all German forces in the West in order to enable the British
and American armies to occupy Berlin before the Russians.
Ignoring the intemperate tone of Stalin's letter, Roosevelt explained the circumstances involved and concluded, "It would
be one of the greatest tragedies of history if at the very mo-

ment of the victory now within our grasp, such distrust, such lack of faith, should prejudice the entire undertaking after the colossal losses of life, material, and treasure involved."

To the end of his life, Roosevelt hoped to achieve an amicable relationship with the Soviet Union. In March, when Donald Nelson suggested sending an Allied relief mission to devastated Greece, he consulted Churchill by cable on the advisability of including Russia in this undertaking. The Prime Minister questioned the wisdom of bringing in the Soviets, as they could offer no economic assistance and could not be counted on to "behave correctly." He also thought it unwise to invite them at a time when the Western powers were being firmly excluded from Rumanian affairs. Roosevelt replied that he was not yet prepared to admit that relations had deteriorated to the point where they could not be improved by diplomacy, that he still believed the Yalta agreements might prove a viable basis for a *modus vivendi*. He conceded that the creation of a tripartite commission might be inadvisable at present, but he also felt that a purely Anglo-American effort would create an unfortunate precedent. "This would look as though we, for our part, were disregarding the Yalta decision for tripartite action in the liberated areas and might easily be interpreted as indicating that we consider the Yalta decisions as no longer valid. . . . We must be careful not to do anything that would weaken the effectiveness of our efforts to get the Russians to honor those decisions on their side."

In his last message to Winston Churchill on April 12, 1945, the day of his death, Roosevelt offered some advice regarding East-West relations. "I would minimize the general Soviet problem as much as possible because these problems, in one form or another, seem to arise every day, and most of them straighten out . . . we must be firm, however, and our course thus far is correct."

Roosevelt's experience in practical politics buttressed his philosophical conviction that with time problems would "straighten out." Moreover, he had great faith in the United Nations, which he regarded as structurally a tremendous improvement over the old League. The Security Council sitting in continuous session could act at a moment's notice to preserve the peace and, if necessary, employ the international police force toward which member states were expected to contribute. Highly beneficial, too, were the specialized agencies concerned with social and economic problems which would abate some of the causes of war by working to alleviate distress throughout the world.

At the same time, Roosevelt did not regard an international organization as a magic talisman to insure peace but rather as an instrument which would provide the opportunity to moderate the dangerous struggle for power among nations. To a Europe maimed, mutilated, and almost bloodless; to an America which for the second time in a generation had been required to send her sons into slaughter on foreign soils; indeed, to all mankind the United Nations would be a beacon of hope.

As he was not a visionary but a hardheaded realist planning for the age and not for the ages, he thought of the world body not as a completed edifice but rather as a protean structure which time and circumstances would shape and change. He cautioned against expecting too much too soon, tempering his enthusiasm with sober restraint. Only with the elimination of social and economic distress would lasting peace be achieved. Ultimately, he hoped, a world federation would evolve. Then national armies would be eliminated, big power vetoes abandoned, and government conducted by democratic methods with public opinion as the main guiding force. Meantime, it would be necessary to operate within the limits of the possible.

To his friend, William Allen White, he wrote shortly after World War II began, "I do not entertain the thought of some of the statesmen of 1918 that the world can make, or we can help the world to achieve, a permanently lasting peace—that is a peace which we would visualize as enduring for a century or more. On the other hand, I do not want this country to take part in a patched-up, temporizing peace which would blow up in our faces in a year or two."

With the experience of an earlier generation in mind, he implored Congress in his last annual message in January, 1945, not to expect "perfectionism" in the postwar world. An insistence on absolutes, he declared, had kept the country from joining the League, with the result that it had failed to cooperate in preventing a second major disaster. A perfectionist approach to international relations could be as perilous as adherence to isolationism or imperialism. On another occasion, he declared that the postwar peace would undoubtedly be far from perfect. "The world will be mighty lucky if it gets fifty per cent of what it seeks out of the war as a permanent success. That might be a high average."

Fully comprehending the revolutionary nature of the age, the aspiration for a better life that spurred men everywhere to seek change, he considered it vital that the social and economic plight of underprivileged people everywhere be ameliorated. Addressing the conference of the International Labor Organization during the war, the President warned that unless governments actively concerned themselves with the well-being of the masses, the goals for which men were fighting would not be attained. For some countries he believed a degree of socialism might be necessary and, according to Mrs. Roosevelt, he thought the world generally would be a good deal more socialistic after the war, a prospect which did not seem to disturb him.

At the same time, he recognized that many nations were limited in what they could accomplish alone. International collaboration offered the only solution, and the "have" nations, for considerations of self-interest, he suggested, should assist those less fortunate. All during the war years he kept emphasizing the economic and social interdependence of the world. In his annual message of 1943, he pointed out that the stability of the American economy hinged on the stability of the world economy.

If cooperation to provide more food, clothing, shelter, higher labor standards, and social security were to be effective, thorough scientific planning would be required. Not temporary, stopgap measures, but a permanent cure should be the objective. Toward the end of the conflict he asked Dr. Vannevar Bush of the Office of Scientific Research and Development to investigate whether the methods employed to mobilize science during the war could be applied in peacetime to combat disease and the privations that afflicted people in so many parts of the globe.

In 1943, Roosevelt was contemplating the advisability of a series of conferences to be held after the war in different parts of the world. One on oil resources might take place in Moscow, one on the distribution of raw materials in Rio de Janeiro, one on finance in London, and so on. That year he personally initiated a conference on food and agriculture in Hot Springs, Virginia. Others dealing with economic problems followed, and these laid the basis for the United Nations specialized agencies.

At Teheran, Roosevelt anticipated President Truman's Point Four Program when he suggested that Iran be used as a pilot project to demonstrate that raising living standards in destitute areas was feasible. Mingled with his altruism was a solid core of business practicality. After his return, he wrote to his old Groton mentor, the Reverend Endicott Peabody, about the appalling poverty and disease in the Middle East, observing that "we can help those countries in the days to come, and with the proper management, get our money back, if only we do not revert to the ostrich policy of 1920." He also felt that technical assistance should be extended to the countries that had suffered devastation, to restore their highways, bridges, and communications. According to Henry Morgenthau, the President intended to request a continuation of lend-lease to help the shattered European continent achieve economic recovery and rehabilitation.

Roosevelt foresaw that in the postwar world traditional patterns of colonialism would be greatly altered, that Asians and Africans would no longer be willing to submit to subjugation. He was more prescient than Winston Churchill, who said defiantly on one occasion that he had not been selected the King's First Minister in order to preside over the liquidation of the British Empire. Elliott Roosevelt relates that after a lively exchange on colonialism between the President and the Prime Minister during their first meeting, he suggested to his father that he and Churchill might get along very well as long as they kept off the topic of India. The President replied that more talk about India would be necessary before they were through. Then he added, "And Burma. And Java. And Indo-China. And Indonesia. And all the African colonies. And Egypt and Palestine. We'll talk about all of them."

At the Quebec meeting in 1943, Roosevelt submitted a draft memorandum containing recommendations for the disposition of dependent territories. Among other things he proposed that the colonial powers plan to give their possessions independence at the earliest practical date. Pending final liberation, they should provide their subject peoples with material assistance, promote their educational and social advancement, offer training in government administration, and grant increasing measures of self-government. The suggestions were received with distinct coolness by the British. Nevertheless, Secretary Hull was instructed to bring the matter up again at the Foreign Ministers' Conference in Moscow, and before his departure the President added a few points. For dependencies of the Axis powers, he suggested, international trusteeships should be created wherever the people were not yet prepared for autonomy, and a chain of bases girdling the globe, including Hong Kong and Dakar, should be put under a similar arrangement.

According to foreign correspondent Edgar Snow, the President told him in an interview during the war, "We are going to have to tell our friends, the European allies, that they must have faith in the ability of Orientals to govern themselves." That included not only India, Burma, and Indochina, but also Java, Malaya, and even New Guinea. The Dutch claimed that they would give the colonial peoples real power when they recovered their possessions, he continued, but what they and the British and the French meant was the kind of "self-government" that would see them "still sitting in the saddle a century from now. . . . It almost seems that the Japs were a necessary evil in order to break down that old colonial system, to force the reforms that have to be made."

At Yalta, when Roosevelt proposed that the trusteeship provisions of the United Nations Charter apply to the British possessions as well as to those of Japan, Churchill protested sharply. He objected to having any outside agency govern or administer territory under the British flag. Admiral Leahy relates that the Prime Minister declared hotly, "While there is life in my body, no transfer of British sovereignty will be permitted!"

Colonialism in Africa was another problem that Roosevelt

predicted would agitate the postwar world. At a press conference with members of the Negro Newspaper Publishers' Association, he said that at home suffrage for the Negro people was an essential prerequisite for their obtaining the benefits of American society, but the people of the African colonies required assistance by the Western powers to secure education and better living standards. And, in a half-humorous manner which thinly veiled his serious intent, he told his audience that he was planning to discuss with Prime Minister Churchill the idea of having the United Nations send an inspection committee to all those colonies which were "way, way down the line" as a result of deprivations by the governing power. If Churchill should counter by asking that a committee be sent to the American South, he would reply, "Winston, that's all right with me. Go ahead and do it. Tell the world. You can right a lot of wrongs with 'pitiless publicity.' . . . I wouldn't mind if we had a committee of the United Nations come here and make a report on us. . . . We have got some things to be ashamed of and other things that are not as bad as they are painted. . . . Bring it all out."

Franklin D. Roosevelt died before his leadership could be tested in coping with upheavals that altered continents. The ferment of nationalism in Asia and Africa, the accelerated trend toward independence by the colonial peoples, the Negro movement in the United States toward equality all testify to his insight. His genius, however, was not as a theorist or a prophet but as a practical politician, adept at influencing men individually and in multitudes. His skill in handling people was extraordinary. It could almost be said of Franklin D. Roosevelt as Nathaniel Hawthorne wrote of another President, "Surely he was a great man, and his native strength, as well of intellect as of character compelled every man to be his tool that came within his reach; and the more cunning the individual might be, it served only to make him the sharper tool." This great gift, however, generated one of Roosevelt's most serious shortcomings—an overconfidence in his powers of persuasion when dealing with other heads of state which, in turn, blinded him to the limitations of his personal diplomacy.

A variety of elements contributed to the character of Roose-

velt's leadership: a deeply rooted belief in democratic and constitutional values; social compassion and a sense of moral duty
deriving from his religious faith and encouraged by Eleanor
Roosevelt; sensitive awareness of historical forces developed by
his education and experience; courage in the face of adversity
that was reinforced by the ordeal of illness; a pragmatic and
instrumentalist approach; and an intuitive grasp of politics.

Temperament and personality disposed him, and experience
taught him, to deal with complicated and emotionally charged
problems by seeking expedient and short-range solutions. He
was philosophical about crises, for he knew that they occurred
in every age in one form or another. His obligation would
be fulfilled if he coped with immediate and specific issues as
they arose, applying the test of workability to the solutions he
attempted. He presented his basic outlook in one inaugural
address when he told his audience that there would always be
peaks and valleys, but the important thing to keep in mind was
that "the trend of civilization itself was forever upward, that a
line drawn through the middle of the peaks and the valleys of
the centuries always has been an upward trend."

He possessed the unique talent, unsurpassed by any previous
President, to make comprehensible the economic, social, and
political issues of the time. His fireside chats introduced an
entirely new relationship between the White House and the
people, drawing the citizens of the country into an intimate
association with their leader in the adventure of government.
To countless Europeans, he far surpassed Woodrow Wilson's
achievement in becoming the symbol of hope for a better
world.

Few could remain indifferent to him. Even his enemies, and
they were legion, for he had the capacity to arouse bitter passions as well as impassioned admiration, were constrained to
acknowledge his fascination. As William Allen White put it,
"Biting nails, good, hard, Republican nails, we are compelled
to admit that Franklin Roosevelt is the most unaccountable
President that this United States has ever seen. He has added a
vast, impudent courage to a vivid but constructive imagination,
and he has displayed his capacity for statesmanship in the large

and simple billboard language that the common people can understand. . . . We, who hate your gaudy guts, salute you."

Informing Roosevelt's leadership at home and abroad was his penetrating grasp of the nature of the presidency. In the tradition of other strong chief executives, he was a superb practitioner of the theory of executive ascendancy in times of national crisis. As commander in chief during the war, he allowed his Chiefs of Staff great latitude and freedom of action, but Admiral Leahy, his personal Chief of Staff, later commented, "There were two men at the top who really fought out and finally agreed on the major moves that led to victory. They were Franklin Roosevelt and Winston Churchill. They really ran the war. Of course, they had to have people like us to help them, but we were just artisans building patterns of strategy from the blueprint handed us by our respective commanders in chief."

The presidency had been taken to the center of the international arena by the other wartime leader, but Wilson's experience with world leadership was brief and tentative. Roosevelt's proclivities, together with the international situation, restored the office of President to a pivotal position from which it would never again retreat. Moreover, by his consummate and vigorous exercise of leadership, he added substantially and irrevocably to its dimensions.

Harry S. Truman

16. Thrust into Power

MANY liberal Democrats were outraged that the nomination for the vice-presidency in 1944 went to Harry S. Truman rather than to the incumbent, Henry A. Wallace. Although the latter had been Roosevelt's personal choice, strong opposition which threatened to divide the convention led him to endorse the senator from Missouri as a "harmony" candidate, acceptable to such disparate elements as the southern Democrats, northern political bosses, and organized labor. Astonished at this totally unexpected honor, Truman told the party chieftains in the unceremonious manner with which the country was soon to become familiar that yes, he would run, "but why the hell didn't he tell me in the first place?"

Less than a year later, without any preparation and ignorant of the inside aspects of administrative policies, Harry Truman was abruptly thrust into the most influential position in the world at a critical juncture in history. Added to the shock at the sudden death of the President whose leadership he had faithfully followed for ten years was the awesome thought of having to step into his shoes. Truman had accepted the vice-presidential candidacy like a loyal party man, but his ambitions had gone no further, and the nation had not expected to see the apparently nondescript senator in the White House. Many Americans, including those in high government places, were extremely dubious of his ability to conclude successfully the most terrible war in American history, launch an international organization, and direct the transition to peace, all of which would have taxed the skill and resourcefulness of the highly experienced former President.

During his first day as chief executive, Truman paid a last visit to the Senate Chamber and looked around wistfully, for "here I had experienced the most exciting adventure I had ever expected to have." Greeting the reporters, he said, "Boys, if you ever pray, pray for me now. I don't know whether you fellows ever had a load of hay fall on you, but when they told me yesterday what had happened, I felt like the moon, the stars, and all the planets had fallen on me."

Superficially, Harry Truman appeared to have none of the attributes of background, training, or personality essential for guiding the destiny of a twentieth-century world power. The oldest son of a farmer and livestock merchant of moderate means, he attended public schools, turned to bank clerking and farming after high school graduation, and saw service overseas in the first war. Returning to civilian life, he opened a men's apparel shop in Kansas City, but was soon forced out by the severe depression of 1921-22. His first elective office, a position equivalent to a county commissioner, was secured with the help of the Pendergast machine. He held it for two years, during which time he studied law. Defeated for re-election, he took a minor job for a while. In 1926, he was elected presiding judge of Jackson County Court, remaining in that post until he entered the United States Senate eight years later. He faithfully supported New Deal legislation, but his career as a freshman senator was undistinguished. Re-elected in 1940, he won prominence during the war as chairman of the Committee to Investigate the Defense Program, which brought him to the attention of Roosevelt and the party leaders.

His unspectacular achievements and his unassuming manner and appearance made President Truman an ideal target for caustic wit. One journalist suggested that if the Republican Party had hoped to capitalize in 1948 on the traditional desire of the American people to return to "normalcy" after an era of crisis leadership, Truman had taken the wind out of its sails. "Normalcy" had already arrived, but with a Democrat in the White House. "Truman," wrote this commentator, "not only looks like a haberdasher: he was one. His whole personality, in fact, is practically an infringement of the Republican copyright; nobody since Coolidge has ever seemed quite so much like a sedative in a double-breasted suit."

Truman's greatest initial handicap was the comparison with his predecessor. Any man except one of a similar caliber who followed the towering, dazzling figure of Roosevelt could not but appear less than life-size. In the succeeding months and years, however, Americans on the whole learned to appreciate and value the solid if undramatic qualities of their chief executive: his simplicity, integrity, and frankness; his directness of manner; the tenacity with which he held to his purpose even under great pressure. Many developed a genuine affection for "Harry," even if they were sometimes embarrassed by tactless remarks or public displays of temper. His critics, on the other hand, were never reconciled to having in the White House a man who epitomized the small-town, middle-class citizen, completely lacking polish and sophistication. They magnified his mistakes, deplored his outspokenness, and denounced his policies. But they could not deny, indeed were compelled to pay grudging admiration to, the strength he exhibited as executive leader.

A plain, uncomplicated personality, with a clear, uncomplicated philosophy, Truman possessed the self-confidence that stems from this combination. He knew he was not brilliant, but he did not underestimate his sound intelligence, his common sense. When a decision had to be made, he collected all the facts, evaluated them, and proceeded to act. "All my life," he once said, "whenever it came time to make a decision, I made it and forgot about it." Not inclined to introspection, he was also free from inner doubts.

Few men came to the White House with a greater respect for the office or with a deeper appreciation of its potentialities for the effective exercise of power in a democratic society. From the outset he made it plain that he would be President in his own right and completely accountable for all policy matters. While fully aware of his crushing responsibilities, of how much he had to learn, he was completely sanguine about his ability to master his job. Unremitting effort and persistence had served him in the past; they would do so again.

That all his resources would be called on was apparent within minutes after he repeated the oath of office in the Cabinet Room of the White House. He was now not only President of the United States but a global leader. As soon as the news photographers were finished, he met with his Cabinet and made his first decision. With the United Nations conference scheduled to meet in less than a fortnight, should it not be postponed to give the President time for adjustment? Unhesitatingly Truman replied that it would be held as scheduled by President Roosevelt.

Immediately thereafter, he was caught up in the complexities of international affairs, about which he had only an outsider's knowledge. Before he could take a step he had to be briefed on the inner details of the entire world scene; to be informed, for instance, that scientists were planning to explode an atomic bomb.

A two-page memorandum containing a summary of the important diplomatic developments, prepared daily at President Roosevelt's request by the State Department, was now turned over to Truman. With the war in Europe almost won, every corner of the continent demanded attention from the White House. Most serious was the problem of the Soviet Union, which, as the memorandum informed Truman, "has taken a firm and uncompromising position on nearly every major question that has arisen in our relations." Of immediate concern was Poland, where Russia steadily refused to implement the decisions of the Crimea conference. A cable from Churchill that he wished to present the matter to the House of Commons required a prompt reply. Truman believed that Roosevelt's reason for not publicizing the Polish issue was still valid. He suggested a joint British-American message to Stalin, concluding, "I feel very strongly that we should have another go at him."

Next to be considered was Stalin's refusal to send Foreign Minister Molotov to San Francisco, an action which might prevent the conference from succeeding. A message from Ambassador Harriman that had just arrived sounded hopeful. He had talked with Stalin that day and had been told that if the President granted Molotov an interview the Soviet leader would consent to his attendance. Truman was happy to acquiesce, authorizing Stettinius to draft a reply.

The United Nations Conference on International Organization with fifty nations present convened on April 25, 1945, as the Allies were crashing through to victory in Europe. The Third Reich, which Hitler had boasted would last for centuries, lay in smouldering ruins. Within two weeks it would surrender unconditionally. Roosevelt's plan was to be fulfilled. A collective security system would be organized before the war's end, its covenant kept out of the treaty and cooperation from Congress assured.

Slowly the complex body was being assembled when an obstruction developed on the same point of the voting formula that supposedly had been agreed upon at Yalta. As Harry Hopkins was then in Moscow, Truman cabled that he and Ambassador Harriman put the matter directly to Stalin. Four days later, Hopkins replied that "Stalin had not understood the issues . . . [now] overruled Molotov and agreed that the American position was acceptable to him."

By the end of June, the United Nations Charter was completed, and on July 2, 1945, the President presented it to the Senate for ratification. The choice, he said, "is not between this Charter and something else. It is between this Charter and no Charter at all." Senate approval was a foregone conclusion, for the ground had been well laid. There was virtually no opposition, and no amendments or reservations were suggested. Debate lasted six days instead of eight months, as in 1919, and when it was over the Senate endorsed the Charter by a vote of 89 to 2.

Even before the San Francisco meeting was called to find a means of binding the nations of the world together, the Soviet Union had begun to pull away and travel its own path. Despite their pledges, the Russians obviously had no intention of cooperating with the Western powers in the countries they had liberated. Churchill, more mindful of political considerations in military strategy than the Americans, kept urging that United States troops retain their position on the farthest advanced lines they had reached. Four days after VE Day, he cabled the President, "Surely it is vital now to come to an understanding with Russia or see where we are with her before we weaken our armies mortally or return to the zones of occupation." He also pleaded for retention of large-scale military forces in Europe to counteract the influence of the Russian armies.

On the first point, President Truman felt bound by the Yalta agreements; the second his advisers considered impractical and inexpedient. Some troops had to be deployed to the Pacific while the others had to be sent home as rapidly as possible in response to strong public demand. General Marshall and Secretary Stimson agreed with Truman that the Roosevelt policy to achieve a working relationship with the Soviets should continue. Moreover, since the task of defeating the Japanese still lay ahead and since the Soviets had thus far honored their military commitments, they opposed any approach which might jeopardize cooperation.

Under Secretary of State Joseph Grew, on the other hand, pessimistically warned the President, "A future war with Soviet Russia is as certain as anything in this world can be certain." The Russians were demonstrating in Eastern Europe their future world pattern, he wrote, and control of that area would enable them "through successive stages" to spread throughout Europe "and eventually the Near and Far East." He urged that no confidence be placed in Russian professions of good faith but that the United States rely upon the control of strategic naval and air bases.

The American people's animosity to the Soviet Union, repressed during the struggle against a common foe, revived as the coalition began to show signs of discord. Fearing that a flare-up of public rancor might exacerbate the mounting diplomatic tension, Truman endeavored to prevent it. At a press conference in June, 1945, with the Directors of the American Society of Newspaper Editors, he offered some "off the record" views which reporters could use as background material. When asked what the Western nations could do about Russia's policy in Eastern Europe and the Balkans, he replied, "Be as patient with them as you possibly can. . . . I don't blame them for wanting to have these states around them, just as we want

Mexico and Canada to be friendly to us." Was it not true, someone else inquired, that the Russians had made more concessions at San Francisco than any other nation? The President agreed and went on to explain that a misunderstanding about the original agreement had caused difficulty at the conference among all the powers. Furthermore, "We had damned near as many differences with the British and not so much publicity about it," but it was easier to discuss things with them because of the absence of a language barrier. "But I can't talk to Stalin. You have to talk through three men."

When another questioner mentioned that the Russians were suspicious of everyone, Truman replied, "They have got a right to be suspicious. They are not a bit more suspicious of us than we are of them. . . . Half the editorials in this country are suspicious of Russia." He pointed out that it had taken quite a while for the Americans and the British to develop a harmonious relationship, and the Russians had come out of the "dark ages" only twenty-five years ago.

Several days later, meeting privately with members of the Association of News Analysts, he returned to the subject of Russia when a member asked how the group could aid in furthering the national interest: "Help me keep a clear and peaceable approach and understanding. . . . I really think the Russians want to get along with us. . . . They have always been our friends, and it is to their best interest." Some Americans, he continued, appeared to have a "phobia" about the Russian form of government. For his part, the kind of government the Russians had was of no concern to him. They seemed to be satisfied with it "or some twenty million of them wouldn't die for it."

After Truman took office, he felt he should meet with Churchill and Stalin as soon as possible to become acquainted with the other leaders of the coalition and also to discuss personally whatever further planning was required. Urgent matters, however, prevented him from leaving the country until the middle of July, 1945, at which a time a meeting was arranged at Potsdam. To lay the groundwork, he dispatched the ailing Harry Hopkins to Moscow "to tell Stalin that I was anxious to have a fair understanding with the Russian government, that we never made commitments which we did not expect to carry out to the letter, and that we expected Stalin to carry out his agreements."

Hopkins later reported that during his conversations with the Russian leader, Stalin had brought up the abrupt termination of lend-lease supplies to the Soviet Union which, he claimed, had aroused wide-spread resentment and suspicion of the West among his people. An unfortunate blunder had been responsible for stopping the shipments. On May 8, Truman had been handed an agency directive for an immediate cutback of lend-lease and, thinking it a routine document, had signed it. So literally was the order executed that even ships on the high seas were called back. Although the Soviet Union was not the only country affected, the Russians interpreted the move as having been directed against them. Truman rescinded the order, but the matter continued to rankle.

From Ambassador Harriman, who was present at the discussions with Stalin, the President gained an insight into Soviet thinking which helped to explain the cleavage between the Americans and the Russians. "I am afraid," Harriman wrote, "that Stalin does not and never will fully understand our interest in a free Poland as a matter of principle. The Russian Premier is a realist in all of his actions, and it is hard for him to appreciate our faith in abstract principles . . . why we should want to interfere with Soviet policy in a country like Poland which he considers so important to Russia's security unless we have some ulterior motive."

At Potsdam, for two weeks from July 17 through August 2, the three heads of state wrestled with a staggering number of highly complex problems. Requiring settlement were the administration for occupying Germany, machinery and procedures for writing the peace treaties, methods to implement the Yalta Declaration on Liberated Europe, German reparations, and Russian participation in the Pacific war.

Unaccustomed to diplomatic palaver, Truman frequently became impatient. At one session, an exchange between Churchill and Stalin on the subject of Franco "ranged ahead in seesaw fashion, with both the Premier and the Prime Minister restating their earlier arguments," he recalled. With no agreement in sight, he persuaded them to pass on to another matter. The next point about Yugoslavia became equally congealed. "I felt that I had heard enough of this. I told Churchill and Stalin that I had come . . . to discuss world affairs . . . not . . . to hold a police court hearing on something . . . which would eventually be settled by the United Nations. If we started that . . . we would become involved in trying to settle every political difficulty. . . . I did not wish to waste time listening to grievances but . . . to deal with the problems which the three heads of government had come to settle . . . if they did not get to the main issues I was going to pack up and go home."

Recognizing that the problems were too numerous and too involved to be settled at one time, Secretary of State Byrnes proposed that a Council of Foreign Ministers be established to draft peace treaties which would then be submitted to the United Nations for discussion. In the meantime, Germany was to be occupied according to previous plans, completely disarmed, and its war potential destroyed. The Nazi Party and every Nazi influence was to be thoroughly rooted out and educational and judicial systems reformed so that German political life could eventually be reconstructed on a democratic basis. Nazi war criminals were to be brought to trial promptly.

On the matter of reparations, the American position had altered considerably since Yalta. Soviet penetration into Central Europe and difficulties with the Kremlin led to second thoughts about Germany, the conviction that a reconstituted Reich was essential to create a balance of power in Europe. Truman and Byrnes accordingly resisted Russian efforts to impose a crushing debt on Germany. Stalin was finally persuaded to relinquish the twenty-billion-dollar figure that Roosevelt had agreed would be only a "basis for discussion." No amount was fixed. The four powers were to collect their claims from their own spheres of occupation, but Russia was to receive some additional compensation from the Western zones.

The issue over Poland's western boundary remained unsettled, with the Russians insisting that it be extended westward to the Oder-Neisse line and the Western powers as firmly opposed. Finally, after prolonged wrangling, it was decided to postpone final determination until a peace settlement. In the meantime, however, the Poles were permitted to occupy the disputed territory which the Russians had earlier turned over to them for administration, and a *de facto* situation was created.

Potsdam was the last of the wartime conferences. Of the original triumvirate, Stalin alone survived as head of state. The man who had cemented the coalition was dead, and while the conference was still in progress Britain's great wartime leader was replaced as Prime Minister when his party lost the election. To the divisive forces between East and West which victory had brought to the fore was added a new factor. On the day President Truman arrived in Germany, he was informed that an atomic bomb had been successfully detonated at Los Alamos. Not only was this event to influence relations with the Soviet Union, but it would drastically alter the entire world scene. On August 6, while Truman was on the way home, the bomb was dropped with his approval over the Japanese city of Hiroshima and three days later over Nagasaki.

Probably the most crucial decision that the President was ever called upon to make was whether the atomic bomb should be used against Japan. That the Japanese were prepared to resist to the bitter end as long as the war was fought with traditional weapons seems apparent from their rejection of the ultimatum issued from Potsdam on July 26 warning of "prompt and utter destruction." They did not capitulate even after the bomb had obliterated Hiroshima. Not until the Emperor himself pressed for surrender after the second atomic cataclysm were the Allies notified that Japan would accept the Potsdam conditions. Possibly another consideration, never publicly stated, motivated some policy makers in Washington. Secretary of the Navy James Forrestal in a diary entry of July 28, 1945, wrote, "Byrnes said he was most anxious to get the Japanese affair over with before the Russians got in." In any event, the Japanese government should have been informed of the nature of the weapon to be employed against their country. Then, if they had refused to yield, the American position would have been somewhat more defensible.

A high-level presidential committee, composed of top administration officials, heads of the bomb project, and outstanding scientists directed to assess the implications of the bomb, had recommended that it be used as soon as it was available. In opposition was a report made to the War Department on June 11, 1945, by seven scientists who had worked on the bomb and felt impelled to speak out because "the development of nuclear power is fraught with infinitely greater dangers than were all the inventions of the past." It might be difficult to persuade the world, they argued, that a nation "capable of secretly preparing and suddenly releasing a new weapon" of such unparalleled destructive power "is to be trusted later in any agreement. . . . Thus . . . the military advantages and the saving of American lives . . . may be outweighed by the ensuing loss of confidence and by a wave of horror and repulsion sweeping over the rest of the world."

Truman issued the order seemingly free from any doubt. When the Federal Council of Churches of Christ wired him of the anxiety and deep distress of many Christians over the indiscriminate destruction and the dangerous precedent that had been established, he replied that he, too, was greatly disturbed over the use of the bomb, but equally disturbed by the unwarranted attack on Pearl Harbor and the murder of American prisoners of war by the Japanese. "The only language they seem to understand is the one we have been using. . . . When you have to deal with a beast you have to treat him as a beast." In later years, he continued to justify the use of the atom bombs. Once, replying to an inquiry, he said that the decision to bomb Hiroshima and Nagasaki was not as hard to make as some others in his career because "I came to the conclusion that we were saving lives both on our side and on the Japanese side by bringing the war to an end." He "hated very much to make that decision," he said at another time, but he did not doubt then or since that it was necessary.

The effect of a weapon which until then had existed only in the fertile imagination of science-fiction writers shocked and terrified the world. "There is widespread anxiety as to whether the new power will be used to serve or to destroy civilization," Prime Minister Clement Attlee wrote to the President on August 8, 1945. He urged an immediate declaration by the two nations of their intentions to utilize it "not for our own ends, but as trustees for humanity in the interests of all peoples in order to promote peace and justice to the world."

No longer merely another weapon for ending a war, the bomb was now the most vital adjunct of American foreign policy. Some way must be found, Truman felt, to control this horrendous force. For the time being, the United States had the advantage of possessing the secret of harnessing atomic energy, but this would probably not last long. In a memorandum, the Joint Chiefs of Staff urged that steps of a "political nature should be promptly and vigorously pressed during the probably limited period of American monopoly" for international control to restrict or outlaw the use of atomic weapons.

The immediate problem was to enlist Russian cooperation. Secretary Stimson was persuaded that Soviet-American relations "may be perhaps irretrievably embittered" by the manner in which the United States handled the matter. "For if we fail to approach them now and merely continue to negotiate with them . . . having this weapon rather ostentatiously on our hip, their distrust of our purposes and motives will increase." He expressed these thoughts in a memorandum to the President on September 11, 1945, and went on to propose a method of procedure. After discussions with the British, a direct proposal should be made to the Russians for an arrangement to control and limit the use of the atomic bomb as an instrument of war and encourage development of atomic power for "peaceful and humanitarian purposes." Manufacture of the bomb as a military weapon would be halted if both the Russians and the British agreed to do likewise, and furthermore, if both nations agreed that in no event would it be used as an instrument of war without the consent of all three, America was prepared to impound all bombs in her possession. A covenant might also be considered for an arrangement to provide that all three nations exchange the benefits of future developments for commercial or humanitarian purposes. "I emphasize perhaps beyond all other considerations," Stimson wrote, "the importance of taking this action with Russia as a proposal of the United States— backed by Great Britain, but peculiarly the proposal of the United States."

Stimson repeated these opinions at a Cabinet meeting ten days later, the day of his retirement from office. Most of the members expressed general agreement, but some were concerned that the Soviet Union would profit from an exchange of scientific information. Secretary of Agriculture Clinton Anderson, for one, said that he did not trust the Russians or their willingness to reciprocate. But Dr. Vannevar Bush, Director of the Office of Scientific Research and Development, pointed out in a memorandum to the President that while a closed society like that of the Soviet Union, which practiced scientific espionage, "would benefit to a considerable degree by our scientific progress, and we would benefit little by hers . . . we cannot keep scientific secrets from Russia without also keeping them from the major portion of American scientists." He therefore advocated a proposal to Russia for exchange of scientific information, which, he felt, would lead to international collaboration and eventually to effective control. It would also enable the United States to find out whether it was possible to work with and trust Russia. "But the general advantage is that this move, when it became known, would announce to the world that we wish to proceed down the path of international good will and understanding." The alternative, he warned, was an atomic arms race.

Truman decided against bilateral negotiations with the Soviet Union, preferring to seek a control agreement within the United Nations. On November 15, 1945, the British and Canadian Prime Ministers and the President issued a joint statement proposing that the United Nations create a commission to submit recommendations for control of atomic energy for peaceful purposes, the elimination of atomic weapons, and the establishment of effective international inspection. They also declared their intention to make the benefits of atomic energy for peaceful development available to all nations "just as soon as effective enforceable safe-guards against its use for destructive purposes can be devised." The following month at the Moscow Foreign Ministers' Conference the proposal was endorsed by the Soviets, and in January, 1946, a commission was established by the U. N. Assembly.

In the meantime, it was necessary for Congress to pass legislation governing the manufacture and use of atomic energy. On October 3, 1945, Truman sent a message to Congress requesting the creation of an Atomic Energy Commission and recommended that all aspects of research, development, and exploitation in the field of atomic energy be placed under the jurisdiction of this body. "The disadvantages of Government monopoly are small," he said, "compared to the danger of permitting anyone other than the Government to own or produce these crucial substances, the use of which affects the safety of the entire nation." He also suggested that the commission be empowered to carry out any agreement that provided for international action on inspection, dissemination of information, or other relevant functions.

Shortly thereafter the May-Johnson Bill was introduced into Congress, but as it left control of atomic energy in the hands of the military, many groups throughout the country who favored a civilian authority protested vociferously. In December, a bill sponsored by Senator Brien McMahan and approved by the President provided for a commission composed exclusively of civilians. This being unacceptable to the military partisans, the controversy raged for more than half a year. A compromise amendment offered by Senator Arthur Vandenberg that would require the President to appoint a military liaison committee to "advise and consult" with the civilian commission satisfied neither side. The altercation was finally resolved. On August 1, 1946, the Atomic Energy Act was passed, providing for government monopoly of fissionable materials, and complete control of research and production vested in the commission, a civilian body.

During this period, at President Truman's request, a group of consultants headed by David E. Lilienthal and J. Robert Oppenheimer was preparing a plan for the international control of atomic energy under United Nations auspices. On June 14, 1946, Bernard Baruch presented to the U.N. Atomic Energy Commission a sweeping proposal based on the Lilienthal report for the creation of an International Atomic Development Authority which would have exclusive jurisdiction over every aspect of atomic production and appropriate powers of inspection and enforcement. The United States was thus offering to

turn over to an international body an incredibly valuable secret, capital assets worth at least four billion dollars, and its
stockpile of atomic weapons, if agreement could be reached on
its proposals for effective inspection, control, and enforcement.

Suspicious that the authority would be dominated by the
United States and her Allies, the Russians charged that this
was a plot for "a sort of international trust . . . in which American financial and industrial monopolies would exercise command as they saw fit." They countered with a proposal to outlaw the manufacture and use of the atomic bomb, destroy all
existing stockpiles within three months, and vest enforcement
in the Security Council, where they possessed the veto. As this
would have required the United States to eliminate atomic
weapons preliminary to the establishment of a control arrangement, no agreement could be reached.

The impasse over atomic weapons was but another symptom
of the growing estrangement between the United States and
the Soviet Union. In Truman's first comprehensive foreign policy address in October, 1945, he had plainly reaffirmed the
principles to which Franklin D. Roosevelt had been committed
but which Soviet practices now threatened to erode. The
United States, he declared, would continue to uphold and
promote the objectives of the Atlantic Charter. All peoples
which were prepared for autonomy should be permitted to
choose their own form of rule, and the United States would
refuse to recognize any government imposed by foreign force.
Truman pledged to promote the Four Freedoms proclaimed
by the former President, and to support the United Nations as
an essential instrument for peace.

When in the spring of 1946 the fledgling United Nations
organization was confronted with its first major challenge in
the Soviet refusal to evacuate Iran, Truman was asked whether
its future would not be imperiled if Russia insisted upon going
down a one-way street. "We are not going to let it collapse," he
replied firmly. And on another occasion, he said, "If it doesn't
work, and then you simply drop back to the old power politics
and spheres of influence, you will have exactly the same
trouble that we have had all the time."

Divergent approaches to the future of Germany, representing a fundamental conflict of national interests, contained the seeds of potential trouble. Russia was still intent on neutralizing the country to prevent a resurgence of militarism, and in this was joined by the French, who were apprehensive that America and Britain would abandon the program of heavy reparations. To reassure the Soviets, to demonstrate the good faith of the United States and thus possibly prevail on Russia to relieve her pressure in the Balkans, Germany, and Western Europe, Secretary of State James Byrnes proposed a four-power pact. Encouraged by tentative indications of support by the British and French as well as by Stalin, and with President Truman's strong endorsement, Byrnes proceeded to draft a treaty under which the victors would cooperate to keep Germany demilitarized for twenty-five years or more and would take common action in the event of any violations.

Molotov curtly repudiated the plan, calling it "completely inadequate." After trying to meet Soviet objections, Byrnes finally realized that the Russians wanted to keep America out of Europe for the next several decades. "The pressure of American power," he later wrote, "would restrict the freedom of action which the Soviet Union, as the predominant military power in Europe, might otherwise enjoy."

Rejection of the treaty, coinciding with the decision of the United States on May 3, 1946, to suspend the delivery of reparations to the Soviet zone, marked the end of efforts at a common policy for Germany. Mutual distrust, with each nation regarding the other as a threat to its security, was creating an apparently unbridgeable gap. With wartime unity now completely gone, the United States appeared to have no alternative but to proceed on its own course wherever a clash of interests with the Soviet Union occurred. Truman's attitude had begun to stiffen early in 1946. He told Byrnes that "unless Russia is faced with an iron fist and strong language, another war is in the making."

Nevertheless, not yet prepared to announce his private beliefs publicly, the President probably was inwardly pleased at Winston Churchill's "iron curtain" speech at Fulton, Missouri, in March, 1946. As a private citizen, the ex-Prime Minister could loose thunderbolts injudicious for a head of state. Denouncing the Soviet Union for ringing down an "iron curtain" on half of Europe, he called for a vigorous, united response by the Anglo-American partners.

Truman insisted that he had not been informed in advance of Churchill's speech, but he was responsible for the invitation to make the address at Westminster College and, knowing the Englishman's attitude toward the Soviet Union, must have anticipated his tack. In any case, since endorsement of Churchill's rousing statement was considered imprudent, the President replied with a "no comment" when reporters asked him for his reaction. Shortly thereafter, a correspondent who queried Truman about the current state of relations with Russia was informed that they were "as cordial as they have always been. When two horse-traders get to bargaining, they sometimes get pretty rough with each other, but they hardly ever wind up in a fist fight. They usually make a trade. That is what we propose to do with Russia. I have no feeling but of the friendliest sort for Russia."

To some Americans, these homely comments of good will smacked of hypocrisy. Among those highly critical of Truman's policies as largely contributing to the rift was Secretary of Commerce Henry Wallace. One of the last Roosevelt men to remain in high office, and regarding himself as the true heir of the New Deal, Wallace felt best qualified to explain and elaborate those policies which he was convinced were being jettisoned. In March, 1946, when Truman appointed General Walter Bedell Smith as ambassador to Moscow, Wallace sent the President a memorandum in which he suggested that, in order to improve relations, the United States should "discuss with the Russians in a friendly way their long range economic problems and the future of our cooperation in matters of trade. We know that much of the recent Soviet behavior . . . has been the result of their dire economic needs and of their disturbed sense of security." Truman in his *Memoirs* says that he ignored the memorandum. "I had expressed my policy to Bedell Smith and had suggested the approach he should take to the Kremlin. I could see little to be gained from the Wallace proposal."

Increasingly troubled by what he concluded was a drift toward war, Wallace addressed a mass meeting at Madison

Square Garden in New York on September 12, 1946. "The real peace treaty we now need is between the United States and Russia," he declared. "On our part we should recognize that we have no more business in the *political* affairs of Eastern Europe than Russia has in the *political* affairs of Latin America, Western Europe, and the United States." As the Balkans were closer to Russia than to the United States, the Soviet Union could not permit the Western powers "to dominate the politics of that area."

Reaction to the address was mixed both at home and abroad. But more serious than the plaudits or brickbats was the sentence in Wallace's speech, "When President Truman read these words he said that they represented the policy of this Administration," and the President's confirmation at a press conference that he had been quoted accurately. Still worse, when Truman was questioned further if his approval extended to that sentence or the entire address, he said, "I approved the whole speech."

What, then, was the foreign policy of the administration?

Caught in the web spun by his carelessness, Truman tried to disentangle himself. He informed the press, "It was my intention to express the thought that I approved the right of the Secretary of Commerce to deliver the speech. I did not intend to indicate that I approved the speech as constituting a statement of the foreign policy of this country."

Then, several days later, to Truman's dismay, Wallace released to the press the text of a letter he had sent the President several months before in which he charged, among other things, that in trying to create bipartisanship the Democrats had given in too much to "isolationism masquerading as tough realism in international affairs. . . . Unity [at home] on the basis of building up conflict abroad would prove to be not only unsound but disastrous." This criticism was generally interpreted as a slap at Senator Arthur Vandenberg, Republican foreign policy spokesman, and reports spread that "Wallace had told Democrats they had been 'sucked in' on an anti-Russian Republican policy through Vandenberg's influence."

Vandenberg and Byrnes, who were in Paris at a meeting of the Council of Foreign Ministers, were incensed, protesting

that Wallace had made their position untenable. Byrnes told
the President in a teletype conference that he would resign
immediately if Wallace could not be kept quiet on foreign
policy. At this point there was only one thing Truman could
do: within a week he issued a press release in which he declared that while individuals may naturally disagree on foreign
policy, "the government of the United States must stand as a
unit in its relations with the rest of the world. I have today
asked Mr. Wallace to resign from the Cabinet." It had become
clear, he concluded, that the views of the Secretary of Commerce on foreign policy differed fundamentally from those of
the administration. The impression of divided council and of
ineptitude in the White House could have been averted if
Truman had been more alert, but the damage was done.

Of even greater significance that year was Secretary of State
Byrnes's resignation from the Cabinet. The break was symp-
tomatic of Truman's increasingly firm attitude towards the Soviet Union, and also reflected his determination not to permit
any infringement of his leadership in foreign affairs. The rift
began, according to Truman, when at the Moscow Foreign
Ministers' Conference in December, 1945, Byrnes went counter
to the President's policy at Potsdam that free governments
must be established in Rumania, Bulgaria, and other satellite
states before recognition would be accorded. "Byrnes lost his
nerve in Moscow," the President said, conceding too much to
the Russians in relation to those countries. Later, Truman was
infuriated when Byrnes released a report of the conference
without first consulting him.

The Secretary's version differed. He relates that he was
summoned by Truman to the presidential yacht moored off
Quantico for a report on the Conference. "The fact is," he
wrote, "the President did not . . . express to me disapproval of
any position I took at the meetings. . . . Nor did he ever express
to me disapproval of any statement I made on our foreign policy. In the President's letter to Stalin written before the Moscow Conference, the President approved most of the proposals
agreed to at Moscow."

Truman relates that he sent for his Secretary, and "Byrnes
got the real riot act after Moscow. I told him our policy was

not appeasement and not a one-way street." He summoned Byrnes again on January 5 as he wanted "to make things perfectly clear between the Secretary of State and myself . . . without delay, without publicity, and in writing." Then he read him a lengthy letter which he had written out in longhand. In it he stated that although he believed in delegating authority to Cabinet members in carrying out policy, "I do not intend to turn over the complete authority of the President nor to forego the President's prerogative to make the final decision." A review of American-Soviet relations followed, ending with, "I'm tired of babying the Soviets." In April, 1946, the Secretary of State submitted his resignation "for health reasons" but was persuaded to remain at his post until the peace treaties for the liberated countries were concluded.

As in foreign affairs, where the Soviets made it impossible to maintain the spirit of cooperation fostered by Roosevelt, at home a recalcitrant Congress blocked Truman's efforts to honor his predecessor's promise to revive the New Deal when the war ended. The problems resulting from reconversion of the economy from a war to a peacetime basis were prodigious: demands by labor for higher wages which exploded into strikes, fear of runaway inflation, prospects of large-scale unemployment produced by rapid demobilization, premature pressure for the repeal of price and other controls. When on September 6, 1945, Truman submitted to Congress a list of twenty-one legislative proposals, including expansion of social security, slum clearance and public housing, a full-employment law, and a rise in the minimum wage, only two were even given serious consideration.

Before he took office, Truman was confident that he would have no problem in getting along with the legislative body; after all, he had been a senator and had served with distinction. He soon found, however, that the distance between the Capitol and the White House was far longer than it had seemed. After an initial period of timidity in his relations with Congress, during which he sought vainly to placate the legislators, he realized that appeasement was futile. Increasingly he asserted his independence, even defiance, as he kept pressing for his social legislation, but the currents were against him.

Truman became the target for all the accumulated resentment of diverse segments, each with its special grievances, with the result that in the mid-year elections of 1946, the Republicans won control of Congress for the first time since 1928.

This victory and the general lack of confidence in Truman prompted Senator J. William Fulbright, a Democrat, to propose that the President appoint a Republican Secretary of State and then resign. Under the terms of the Presidential Succession Act, the Secretary of State was next in line, which would put a Republican in the White House. Fulbright, a former student at Oxford, may have been impressed with the British Parliamentary system. Though completely impractical, the proposal was seriously debated for a few days. Truman was reported to have said that a little more land-grant college education (Fulbright had served as president of the University of Arkansas) on the Constitution and what it meant would do Fulbright a lot of good. From another quarter came a suggestion that the Cabinet be transformed into a coalition, with the implication that key posts be awarded to Republicans. Equally unrealistic, such an arrangement would have resulted in the surrender of the President's executive power.

Truman acknowledged the election results with a dignified message to the nation that he respected the verdict of the people, and with a plea for cooperation from Congress. In foreign policy the administration's program had been developed and executed on a bipartisan basis, he said, and he was proud "to have done his best to strengthen and extend this practice. . . . It has been a national and not a party program. It will continue to be a national program so far as the Secretary of State and I are concerned." He hoped that the Republican members would continue to work as "intelligently and cooperatively" as in the past.

With regard to foreign policy, bipartisanship on the whole was maintained, but on the domestic program Truman battered vainly against the stone wall of Republican intransigence. The Eightieth Congress ignored or blocked every piece of social legislation he presented. For his part, Truman set a record for executive vetos, rejecting measures which in his judgment favored the affluent sections of society and those which were injurious to the interests of labor. Later, in reflecting on his successful 1948 campaign, he concluded that the "Eightieth Congress was the luckiest thing that ever happened to me." It enabled him to persuade the American people that the "do-nothing" legislature, by refusing to enact his program, had been indifferent to their welfare.

Every effort was made by political leaders to dissuade Truman from seeking the candidacy in 1948. "Even some of my closest friends and advisers were counseling me to change my mind about going after the nomination in July," he wrote. With the polls showing that the President's popularity had reached the nadir, Democratic Party leaders were completely disheartened, but having failed to persuade the popular General Eisenhower to accept the candidacy, they were "stuck with Harry." The Republican candidate, Governor Thomas E. Dewey, a proven vote-getter, and the vice-presidential nominee, California's popular Governor Earl Warren, presented formidable opposition. To add to the gloom, the Democratic Party was split three ways, with Dixiecrats on the right and Wallace progressives on the left. Truman knew that the division would cut into his voting strength, but this did not deter his resolution to continue with "the program that had taken the nation from the depths of the depression to prosperity and world leadership." Moreover, he was convinced the American people would support him if they had the facts, "and these I was determined to give them."

In his acceptance speech at the convention, Truman announced that he would call Congress back into session and request the enactment of all the social legislation the Republicans were claiming to support in their party platform. "Of course I knew that the special session would produce no results in the way of legislation," he wrote later. This astute political strategem boosted morale among the Democrats, but more important it was to serve him well during the campaign.

With little help, either moral or financial, from the party whose funds had dwindled sadly, Truman on his own initiative engaged in one of the most strenuous campaigns in the annals of American politics. He traveled more than 30,000 miles delivering 356 speeches, many of them at "whistle stops." On one day he spoke sixteen times. With the exception of five major addresses, his delivery was extemporaneous in his habitual, plain, unvarnished language. "I talked to them as human beings with real needs and feelings and fears," he later related. "I talked to them about their jobs, their homes, and the cost of living. I treated them not like crowds of people but like businessmen, tenant farmers, housewives, married veterans, laboring men, teachers—individuals with interests for whom I, as President, had a genuine concern."

Despite his valiant and energetic campaign, a Dewey victory seemed inevitable. Indicative was an advertisement in a national weekly by the *Kiplinger Magazine:* "What Will Dewey Do? Find out in the November issue just off the press. . . . Accurate . . . analysis and forecast of what to expect from the new administration. . . ." Apparently the only man in the country who had confidence in his success was the President himself. He attached no importance to the polls "because in my judgment they did not represent a true cross-section of American opinion," they "did not represent facts but mere speculation, and I have always placed my faith in the known facts." Confounding seasoned observers and trained political analysts, Truman carried the country by a two-million majority and received 303 electoral votes. It was the most astounding upset in United States political history. In view of the great value he placed on presidential leadership, this was an especially significant victory for Truman, for no longer would he be President "by accident." He could now exercise power in his own right.

During the campaign, Truman had ignored the journalistic prophets of doom. But throughout his White House career he always kept himself informed of the temper of the nation by reading the major newspapers regularly and carefully. In the early morning hours he scanned the leading Washington and New York dailies, and the *Baltimore Sun, Philadelphia Bulletin, St. Louis Post-Dispatch, Kansas City Star,* and the editorial comments in numerous other papers.

"I find lots of things about myself that I never heard of," he once told reporters. He claimed to be indifferent to the attacks hurled against him by the press, shrugging off such "morons as Bertie McCormick and his minions." He was being treated rather kindly, he thought, compared to Jefferson, Jackson, Lincoln, Cleveland, and Wilson, who had been targets for journalistic vituperation. "I've stood quite a bit of abuse myself but it doesn't bother me like it seemed to have bothered those gentlemen. I have always been of the opinion that lies will answer themselves and that turned out to be true with all the Presidents." He was disturbed, however, by the effects of press attacks on his subordinates, men like James Forrestal and Lewis Johnson, whose services he valued. Because of it, he complained, able persons, many of whom were "thin skinned" and sensitive to criticism, were reluctant to remain in Washington.

He deplored the bias of what he termed a "one-party press." Newspapers had become big business "and big business traditionally has always been Republican," he said at a conference with newsmen. "I suggest that Americans bear this in mind and add a dash of salt to every Republican helping of news." At the same time, he continued, "it is a rather pitiful situation the small amount of political influence that the great free press of the United States has." His own experience, he said, was testimony to that lack of influence, when as a candidate for the United States Senate he was elected despite the strong opposition of Missouri newspapers.

Nevertheless, he found the press conference the most effective channel through which to reach the American people and the rest of the world. During his almost eight years in office, Truman met with the reporters on an average of once a week. His "style" was typical of the man. The atmosphere was informal, and the President was completely at ease. He was unpredictable, sometimes inconsistent, often lightly bantering, sprinkling his comments with salty humor, always cocky and self-assured. At the beginning his temper was inclined to be short, but with experience he learned to hold it in check. On the whole, the White House press corps were friendly and on some of its members he bestowed special favors. One veteran newsman was granted the unprecedented privilege of exclusive access to Truman's personal diaries and papers in preparation for publication of his memoirs. During the last weeks of his administration, he took the equally unusual step of granting personal interviews to a small number of favored correspondents.

As a seasoned politician, Truman was sensitive to public opinion, always conscious of its role in shaping government policy, but genuinely unconcerned about volatile attitudes that were admiring one day, hostile the next. Like Theodore Roosevelt, he was neither troubled by the bricks nor seduced by the bouquets. Moreover, he was convinced that critics were more apt to make themselves heard than those who were satisfied with an established policy, since the latter had no reason to make any noise. In his opinion, the President must not be influenced by the deceptive appearance of public opinion. "A man who is . . . afraid to make decisions which may make him unpopular is not a man to represent the welfare of the country," he said. "A President cannot always be popular. He has to be able to say yes and no, and more often no" to partisan and special-interest groups constantly pleading for one thing or another.

He was quick to say "no" also to any attempted encroachment by Congress on the executive prerogative, as when he refused to permit the Commerce Department to turn over to the House Un-American Activities Committee the file on the scientist, Dr. Edward Condon, considering the material privileged. And when the Senate proposed an amendment to the Atomic Energy Act of 1946 empowering the legislative body to direct the Federal Bureau of Investigation to check on the loyalty of presidential appointments to the commission, Truman responded with a sharply worded veto. The bill, he declared, "is objectionable in that it would permit an unwarranted encroachment of the Legislative upon the Executive branch," permitting senators to authorize a bureau of the Department of Justice to conduct investigations for them. "The complete independence of the Executive branch renders it imperative that the Executive have sole authority over the officers whom he appoints." Informed by the Budget Director that a bill had been introduced which would authorize a joint congressional committee to participate in the budget-making process, he declared that this appeared to be another attempt by Congress to take over the Executive branch. "I hope it will get no further than other such attempts have."

Nowhere is his view of presidential prerogative more clearly stated than in his defense some years later of his seizure of the steel mills during the 1952 strike: "I believe that the power of the President should be used in the interest of the people; and in order to do that, the President must use whatever power the Constitution does not expressly deny him. When there is danger that a vital portion of the economy will be crippled at a time that is critical to the nation's security, then, in my opinion, the President has a clear duty to take steps to protect the nation."

His firm executive authority was also evident in his relations with his Cabinet. Truman introduced the device of prepared agenda for Cabinet meetings. All general policies were discussed with his advisers. He made a point of evaluating their collective judgment, but made it clear at the same time that they must follow his direction. He would not brook public insubordination. As he put it, "When a Cabinet member speaks publicly, he usually speaks on authorization of the President, in which case he speaks for the President. If he takes it upon himself to announce a policy that is contrary to the policy the President wants carried out, he can cause a great deal of trouble."

From the outset, Truman took the reins firmly in his hands. A memorandum he sent to his Secretary of State six months after entering the White House illustrates his immersion in the details of the office. Meticulously outlined were steps he regarded as necessary to achieve his legislative program. He was making specific assignments to each of the agencies directly concerned with a particular portion of his proposals and expected vigorous, responsible action. The Secretary himself was to handle three matters: appropriations for the United Nations Relief and Rehabilitation Administration and additional interim lending for a rapid transition to peacetime world trade, sale of surplus ships in the Merchant Marine, repeal of the Johnson Debt Default Act. He suggested the branches of government with which his Secretary should consult and stated that he was requesting both the Office of War Mobilization and the Budget Bureau to lend assistance when necessary in resolving "differences which may arise where several agencies are interested in the legislation." He ended by asking for a prompt report on the status of the legislation and a memo on the first and fifteenth of each month showing current developments.

Truman never relaxed his hold or his pace. "Within the first few months I discovered that being a President is like riding a tiger," he later wrote. "A man has to keep on riding or be swallowed. The fantastically crowded nine months of 1945 taught me that a President either is constantly on top of events or, if he hesitates, events will soon be on top of him. I never felt that I could let up for a single moment."

Harry S. Truman

17. Cold War Statesmanship

IN the spring of 1947, the situation in the Middle East was responsible for a decision by President Truman that was to revolutionize American foreign policy: henceforth the power of the United States would be engaged in peacetime to *prevent* a threat to the peace overseas. The springboard was Britain's notice to Washington that, with her own financial resources in a precarious state, she would be compelled to withdraw her armed forces from Greece no later than April 1, and that assistance to Turkey would also be impossible.

Critically important to the United States for its oil and strategic location, the Middle East was equally vital to the Russians, who for two centuries had endeavored to penetrate it to obtain an outlet to the sea. With only the weak states of Iran, Turkey, and Greece to block them, the Soviets now sought to obtain a dominating influence over all three countries. Frustrated on Iran by the joint efforts of Truman and the United Nations, the Russians turned to Greece, impoverished by years of war and ravaged by civil strife. From 1944 on, the rightist Greek government had been supported by British troops in a desperate and savage attempt to suppress the Communist-led EAM which was struggling to seize power. Britain's withdrawal would mean certain victory for the EAM unless other aid was forthcoming. Turkey by herself would be unable to resist the internal and external Communist pressure.

Informed unofficially of England's intention on February 21

while Secretary of State George C. Marshall was away from Washington, Truman acted promptly. He instructed the State-War-Navy Coordinating Committee to prepare a detailed policy memorandum. During the rest of the week the departments involved fully explored the matter, as did the members of the Cabinet on March 7. Truman conferred twice with congressional leaders of both parties, all of whom agreed that a dangerous vacuum would be created in the Middle East which must be filled by the United States.

The State Department planned a comprehensive program to prepare the American public for the unprecedented step of furnishing economic and military assistance to foreign countries in peacetime. Francis Russell, Director of the Office of Public Affairs, enlisted the cooperation of newspapers, radio, journalists, public officials, teachers, publicists, and other opinion molders. To further emphasize the gravity of the situation, Senator Vandenberg suggested to the President that he "make a personal appearance before Congress and scare hell out of the country."

On March 12, addressing a joint session of Congress, Truman asked for four hundred million dollars for emergency assistance to Greece and Turkey. "I believe," he said gravely, "that it must be the foreign policy of the United States to support free peoples who are resisting attempted subjugation by armed minorities or by outside pressures. . . . The free peoples of the world look to us for support in maintaining their freedoms. If we falter in our leadership, we may endanger the peace of the world—and we shall surely endanger the welfare of our own Nation."

The Truman Doctrine, as it came to be known, aroused widespread and stormy controversy. Those who supported it agreed with the *New York Times* that "The epoch of isolation and occasional intervention is ended. It is being replaced by an epoch of American responsibility." Critics denounced it as economic imperialism, interference in the domestic affairs of other nations, assistance to anti-democratic governments. Senator Joseph O'Mahoney cautioned the President, "The United States should be very slow to embark upon a foreign policy so likely to lead to war." Others felt that the country should enlist the United Nations and not undertake unilateral action.

Senator Vandenberg, who also disapproved of bypassing the world organization, added an amendment which stated that the program was of an emergency and temporary nature to be terminated as soon as the United Nations declared it no longer necessary. Nevertheless, he admitted that "Greece could collapse fifty times before the U.N. itself could ever hope to handle a situation of this nature." After nearly nine weeks of heated debate, Congress voted the appropriation requested by the President.

A century and a quarter earlier, the Monroe Doctrine had been proclaimed to defend the Western Hemisphere against the encroachments of European ideologies and power. With the Truman Doctrine, the President was bringing the American ideology and power to bear upon the European continent. Under Theodore Roosevelt, Woodrow Wilson, and Franklin D. Roosevelt, America became involved in Europe only in special circumstances or because of a specific danger. Now the nation was undertaking a comprehensive commitment in anticipation of danger. Henceforth, involvement in world crises, however remote, would be a permanent feature of the country's international relations. Truman added a new dimension to the world leadership of the United States. While the Greek-Turkish aid bill was designed to meet an urgent problem in a concrete manner, its implications extended far beyond the immediate purposes of the measure.

The Truman Doctrine initiated the American response to the "cold war," a phrase, first used by Walter Lippmann to describe the political conflict produced by clashing philosophies and systems of government—the Soviet Union and its satellites on one side, the United States and the democracies on the other. George F. Kennan, chief of the newly created State Department policy planning staff, proposed a diplomatic strategy for survival which, as the policy of "containment," he presented anonymously in the July, 1947, issue of *Foreign Affairs*. The United States, he wrote, must in the future follow "a policy of firm containment, designed to confront the Russians with unalterable counter-force at every point where they show signs of encroaching upon the interests of a peaceful and stable world . . . at a series of constantly shifting geographical and political points, corresponding to the shifts and maneuvers of Soviet policy." This did not mean "outward histrionics," "blustering," or gestures of "toughness" but called for firmness, patience, and long-range planning. The security of the American people depends "on their pulling themselves together and accepting the responsibilities of moral and political leadership that history plainly intended them to bear."

Aid to Greece and Turkey was paltry compared to what would be required for Western Europe, which Winston Churchill characterized in May, 1947, as "a rubble-heap, a charnel house, a breeding ground of pestilence and hate." The enormous sums which the United States had already poured into Europe since VJ Day merely sufficed to prevent starvation and chaos. Millions of people in Great Britain, France, Italy, and Germany, stalked by cold, hunger, and disease, had reached the nadir of hopelessness. Unless the drift toward collapse was arrested, violent social upheavals were inevitable, with disastrous consequences for America's defense position in Western Europe.

A column by Walter Lippmann on April 5, 1947, served to crystallize the thinking of the State Department's policy planning staff. What he had to say might seem sensational, Lippmann began, but it was "only what responsible men say when they do not have to keep up appearances in public. . . . The truth is that political and economic measures on a scale which no responsible statesman has yet ventured to hint at will be needed in the next year or so." To prevent disaster, he went on, "the measures will have to be very large—in Europe no less than an economic union, and over here no less than the equivalent to a revival of Lend-Lease." He suggested that for purposes of making aid more effective, the European continent be considered as a unit. The countries concerned should confer as to their needs, assess their requirements for the recovery program, and present their common findings to the United States.

The President planned to make use of Lippmann's suggestions in a talk he was scheduled to give in the South, but unable to leave Washington, he sent Under Secretary of State

Dean Acheson. On May 8, at Cleveland, Mississippi, Acheson related the grim facts of the European situation, suggested the scope of the economic tasks involved, and pointed out that "European recovery cannot be complete until the various parts of Europe's economy are working together in a harmonious whole. And the achievement of a coordinated European economy," he emphasized, "remains a fundamental objective of our foreign policy."

Acheson's talk created little stir, but an opportunity to bring the issue forcefully to the American public was presented by Harvard University's invitation to Secretary of State George Marshall to deliver the commencement address the following month. Marshall prepared his talk with great care, using the policy memorandum drawn up by George Kennan's staff which stressed the Lippmann idea. Unless normal economic health was restored to the world, he said, "there can be no political stability and no assured peace." The United States was willing to help in this endeavor. "Our policy is directed not against any country or doctrine but against hunger, poverty, desperation, and chaos," to revive a working economy so as to permit "the emergence of political and social conditions in which free institutions can exist." The initative, however, must come from Europe. "The role of this country should consist of friendly aid in the drafting of a European program and of later support. . . . Any government that is willing to assist in the task of recovery," he promised, "will find full cooperation . . . on the part of the United States Government."

Britain's Foreign Minister Ernest Bevin responded with alacrity. As soon as he received the text of the speech, he summoned a conference of senior Foreign Office officials. When one of the group inquired if Washington should not be asked whether the commencement address represented official policy, Bevin replied, "No. I don't want to take any chances that it wasn't meant. I want to go on the assumption that it was fully meant, and give an answer myself." He proceeded immediately to galvanize the European nations into action. Although Marshall's invitation did not exclude the Soviet Union, and at a press conference he specifically stated that his offer was open to all European countries, the Russians denounced the program as a weapon of economic imperialism, a device for controlling the continent through dollar aid. Molotov did join Bevin and French Foreign Minister Georges Bidault at Paris on June 27 for consultations, but his hostile attitude resulted in failure to reach any agreement.

Undeterred, Britain and France issued invitations for a planning conference to all European countries except Germany and Spain. Fourteen responded. While the satellite countries had been included, Stalin decided not to cooperate, and none of them participated in the meeting held at Paris in July. A committee of European Economic Cooperation was promptly formed and after detailed study submitted a report to Secretary Marshall in September requesting $22.4 billion in aid over a four-year period.

To determine the extent of assistance which could be furnished, the President authorized three groups to investigate the nation's economic capabilities and dispatched a nine-man committee to Europe for an on-the-spot survey. During the next three months, careful preparations were made to win acceptance of the proposed Marshall Plan by Congress and the public. Among other measures, Truman exchanged views with congressional leaders, delivered a radio talk, and addressed Congress on the European nations' dire need for aid. In the meantime, the steady deterioration of economic conditions abroad made immediate assistance urgent. A special session of Congress, which Truman called on November 17, responded to his request for stopgap emergency aid to Italy, France, and Austria by appropriating $432 million. In December, when the regular session convened, the President requested an appropriation of $17 billion, part of which was to be spent before the end of June, 1949, and the balance during the next three years to assist in bringing about permanent recovery. The program, Truman said, would prove "that free men can effectively join together to defend their free institutions against totalitarian pressures."

Opponents of the measure made a strange combination: the economy-minded Republicans, who were planning to campaign the following year on a platform of a balanced budget and reduced spending, and the followers of Henry Wallace, who criticized Truman for having "betrayed" the Roosevelt heritage of cooperation with a wartime ally. The latter denounced the Marshall plan as an instrument of cold war diplomacy, convinced that the United States was embarking on a dangerous course which would only widen the rift between the two great powers and result in armed conflict.

Leading the fight for the measure in the Senate was the Republican from Michigan, Arthur H. Vandenberg. He was unexpectedly aided when a Communist *coup* in February, 1948 obliterated democracy in Czechoslovakia, a country for which many Americans had a sentimental regard. He swept all doubts aside and brought senators and spectators to their feet in a resounding ovation when he declared, "The greatest nation on earth either justifies or surrenders its leadership. We must choose. . . . The iron curtain must not come to the rims of the Atlantic either by aggression or by default." The following month, the bill was approved in the Upper Chamber by an overwhelming majority. When the House delayed, the President warned that if action were not taken before the Italian elections which were soon to be held, the Communists very likely would win. The House quickly gave its assent and the bill became law on April 3.

As originally conceived, the program was meant to combat starvation, regardless of the political situation in the country to receive aid, but communism soon became the target. In requesting funds to restore Western Europe's economy, the administration left no doubt that the motive was to help create viable states capable of withstanding the force of communism. Humanitarianism was thus combined with considerations of security to produce a policy based on enlightened self-interest.

Congressional approval of the Marshall Plan was a tribute to President Truman's vigorous leadership, especially since he was a "caretaker" President whom almost everyone expected to be out of office in less than a year. Moreover, his unpopularity with the Republicans was equaled only by the low esteem in which he was held by large numbers of Democrats. Even the President's official family had been dubious about the plan. The Treasury Department, striving for a balanced budget, was cool toward the idea of huge financial commitments which the

European Recovery Program would require. The defense establishment, resentful of reduced appropriations and sustained cutbacks, was hostile toward any "giveaway" program when funds could be used to strengthen the nation's security at home. Domestic agencies, which were pressing for support from Congress for various welfare programs, did not welcome the competition for funds.

Yet, within ten months after Marshall's speech at Harvard, the European Recovery Act had been passed, an administration organized, and the machinery for implementing the program created. A policy so unparalleled, launched in so short a time, and in the absence of any direct and visible threat to the country, would have been an extraordinary accomplishment for any President. Truman's success was due in no small part to the highly competent men who consituted his "first team"— Secretary Marshall, Dean Acheson, Robert Lovett, Will Clayton, and Senator Vandenberg, chairman of the Committee on Foreign Relations. He worked extremely well with all of them, gave them his unstinted backing, and they in turn reposed great confidence in him.

The Marshall Plan was another nail in the coffin of East-West unity. Even as it was being debated, a crisis was brewing over the fate of Germany. Secretary Byrnes, in a speech at Stuttgart in September, 1946, had declared that the United States was opposed to a "prolonged alien dictatorship" over Germany. In effect he served notice that, in view of American-Soviet relations, the United States intended to resist Russian plans for permanent neutralization of Germany, and that a policy based on the revitalization of that country could be expected. Three months later, the British and Americans merged their zones for administrative and economic purposes after a London meeting to work out plans for the creation of a new West German state, and they were joined in February, 1948, by France and the Benelux countries.

Soviet resentment of Western policy came to a head in mid-June of that year when a new Deutsche mark was introduced to replace the unstable currency. Retaliating first by interfering with traffic into the city of Berlin, the Russians on June 24 established a complete blockade, which gave them a great psychological and strategic advantage in the struggle for Germany.

With two million people in Berlin's western sector requiring food and fuel, a policy decision had to be made promptly. On June 28, officials of the State, War, and Navy Departments met with the President. When the question was raised whether or not the United States should stay in Berlin, Truman immediately replied that there was "no discussion on that point. We are going to stay, period." And when it was pointed out that it might be necessary to "fight our way" into Berlin to provision the city, he said, "We will have to deal with the situation as it develops," but the main consideration was that "we were in Berlin by terms of an agreement and . . . the Russians had no right to get us out by either direct or indirect pressure."

General Lucius Clay promptly instituted an airlift. On July 22, he returned home to report on the situation to the President and the National Security Council. Discussion centered on whether the airlift should be continued or armed convoys employed. Truman asked what the risks would be if convoys were used. General Clay thought the Russians might meet them with armed force, but he felt they would not attack planes unless they were prepared to risk war. The Air Chief protested that the deployment of aircraft which such an operation required would reduce American air strength elsewhere, so that an emergency might find the United States unduly exposed. The President concluded, however, that the airlift involved less risk of triggering off a conflagration, and directed an all-out effort to provision Berlin.

For almost a year, as the diplomatic haggling to resolve the situation went on, British and American pilots carried about four thousand tons of food and other necessities into the city each day. Some impatient Americans urged a convoy operation, with military action if necessary, to move trains and trucks into the beleaguered outpost; others demanded a break with the Russians. But, as Truman later said, "These people did not understand that our choice was only between negotiations and war. There was no third way. As long as the Russians were willing to continue talks—however futile—there would be no shooting." In the meantime, the Soviets were suffering a loss of prestige. The blockade intensified anti-Communist feeling among the Germans, who were impressed with the determination of the Western powers to resist the Russians. Finally realizing that their stock was continuing to plummet, the Soviets capitulated, ending the blockade on May 12, 1949.

While the Berlin crisis was at its height in October, 1948, a conference of Foreign Ministers meeting at Paris to negotiate several matters was running into the kind of difficulties with the Russians that had become chronic. Truman relates that "our normal diplomatic channels . . . being stifled and frustrated by Russian truculence," he pondered over "every precedent I could recall in an effort to arrive at some new and more promising approach." Recollecting that during the first World War an English Chief Justice had quietly and informally helped to smooth troubled Anglo-American relations, it occurred to him that Chief Justice Fred M. Vinson might perform a similar service for Soviet-American relations. That, according to Truman, was the origin of what turned out to be the abortive Vinson mission to Moscow.

Other sources claim that the idea for the mission originated with members of the White House staff who were gravely concerned about Truman's chances in the November election and were casting about for some device that might turn the tide. The tense international situation, they thought, provided an opportunity for a dramatic peace gesture by the President and a display of leadership that would enhance his popularity. Possibly the President also had the election in mind, and perhaps even a third consideration. By engaging in personal diplomacy, he would disprove the prevailing impression that the nation's foreign policy was being determined by the State Department, demonstrating that he held the reins of power firmly in his hands.

In any case, Truman committed a blunder by proceeding with arrangements before he consulted with Secretary Marshall, who was in Paris at the conference. He conducted the affair with great secrecy, informing no one in the State Department, and personally calling Vinson to the White House to persuade him to accept the assignment. Stalin must be impressed, he told the Chief Justice, "that the folly and tragedy of another war would amount to an act of national suicide," that the United States was "prepared to go to any practical lengths to insure the future survival of the world."

Vinson was extremely reluctant to accept the assignment, but finally yielded. Truman then instructed Press Secretary Charles Ross to ask the networks that they allocate a half hour for a public statement of major importance and went off to the Map Room to discuss the matter with Marshall on the teletype. When the Secretary expressed apprehension that the mission might be misconstrued by Britain and France as unilateral action on subjects then under negotiation, Truman decided to hold it in abeyance until they could discuss it personally, and requested Marshall to return home.

Unfortunately, in the meantime the plan for the proposed mission leaked to the press, which carried stories containing considerable misinformation. Among other things it was alleged that the President's purpose was to have Vinson discuss with Stalin the lifting of the Berlin blockade. By the time Marshall arrived, Truman had abandoned all thought of the mission.

The President was attacked both by Republicans, who accused him of renouncing bipartisanship for a political stratagem, and by the liberals, for not carrying out his plan. Generally, it was felt that he had been inordinately inept. Some of his closest advisers who had been concerned about his chances for re-election before the incident now thought his defeat at the polls inevitable. Truman shut his ears to the din and continued imperturbably with his campaign. He proved to be the better prophet.

With the cold war being waged on a global scale between two opposing powers and ideologies for the allegiance of peoples and governments, unprecedented demands were made on the President's leadership. The revolution in technology that had brought industrialization and higher living standards to Western Europe and North America in the nineteenth century now began to agitate the underdeveloped areas of Asia, Africa, the Middle East, and Latin America. Also spreading to politically backward areas were the contagious ideas of nationalism, the rights of man, freedom from the tyranny of overlords.

Whole continents were in ferment. Whether their peoples chose liberal, constitutional government or were lured by the false promises of communism would depend in large measure on the United States, the only democratic nation in a position to provide the kind of help that would enable them to emerge from the morass in which they had been engulfed by centuries of deprivation and exploitation.

Recognizing these factors of international life, President Truman in his inaugural address of January, 1949, proposed a "bold new program" to make "the benefits of our scientific advances and industrial progress available for the improvement and growth of underdeveloped areas . . . to help them realize their aspirations for a better life." More than half the world, he said, was living in misery, suffering from hunger and disease, their poverty "a handicap and a threat both to them and to more prosperous areas. For the first time in history humanity possesses the knowledge and the skill to relieve the suffering of these people." The Point Four Program, as it came to be called —it was the fourth in a series of recommendations—was designed to help the nations to help themselves in developing their own resources by providing technical and scientific assistance.

To dramatize and implement a humanitarian plan of this kind, to personalize and make vivid what was for most Americans a remote abstraction, required the imaginative skill of a Franklin Roosevelt. This, unfortunately, Truman did not possess. After weeks of preparatory work, the State Department drafted a bill which, as one White House aide commented, "is a very small beginning for a 'bold new program'. Of course, we have to start somewhere, but a bill of this essentially bureaucratic nature will not generate the degree of public support from business, liberals and others that a broader program could be expected to command."

Americans generally were sympathetic to Point Four, but they were not aroused to any great enthusiasm. Truman later said that he "utilized every opportunity to point out the possibilities of the plan," citing a businessmen's dinner forum as an example. He also urged adoption of the legislation in his State of the Union message in January, 1950, but it all added up to a relatively feeble effort. None of the tools of bipartisanship were employed, and the lack of coordination with the legislative branch in general left even the Democrats apathetic. When the Senate took action late in 1950, it cut $10.5 million from the President's modest request for $45 million.

Truman was incensed at what he considered the short-sightedness of the legislature. He wrote to Speaker Sam Rayburn that if the reduction was not restored by the Lower House the effectiveness of the program would be largely de-stroyed. More important, "it will be regarded throughout the world as evidence that this country cannot be depended upon the help the millions of people in the underdeveloped areas" to better their lot. The small economy resulting from the cut, he went on, would be of more service to "the Communists in their attack on the free world than hundreds of millions of dollars of their own propaganda. . . . I can conceive of no more tragic blunder than to throw away this opportunity of doing so much to strengthen the cause of freedom at such little cost."

In the meantime, Truman directed the State Department to enlist the service of outstanding officials and national groups in an effort to put pressure upon Congress. Generals Marshall and Eisenhower were asked to make public statements; the Ambas-sador to the United Nations was requested to address the U.N.; Assistant Secretary of State Barrett's assignment was the press and other public relations media; farm groups and labor organ-izations were urged to exert their influence. But Congress could not be persuaded. The bill for technical assistance which the President signed was for the amount the Senate originally stipulated.

By the end of 1951, thirty-three countries were receiving the benefits of the Point Four program. In the President's State of the Union message in January, 1952, he summarized some of its achievements and asked for more funds, stating that "there is nothing of greater importance in all our foreign policy." Con-gress responded by appropriating a substantial sum, $147.9 million that year, and $155.6 million in 1953, but the program was never considered a major undertaking deserving high pri-ority.

The immediate problem had been, and still remained, a military one. With the world increasingly a divided camp, the nations of Western Europe began to take countermeasures against the Soviet threat. On March 17, 1948, Britain, France, Belgium, the Netherlands, and Luxembourg signed the Brussels Pact, a fifty-year treaty of alliance. Truman welcomed it as "a notable step in the direction of unity in Europe" and promised that "the determination of the free countries of Europe to protect themselves will be matched by an equal determination on our part to help them to protect themselves." Without America's active participation the Brussels Pact was a paper deterrent, but how was this to be achieved in view of the nation's traditional aversion to any sort of alliance with Europe?

Senator Vandenberg threw the great weight of his prestige behind the move for a military partnership, proposing a formula designed to resolve any doubts concerning its feasability. He introduced a resolution based on the "regional and other collective arrangements for individual and collective self-defense" as provided by Article 51 of the United Nations Charter and the Treaty of Rio de Janeiro for Western Hemispheric defense. Negotiations were undertaken with the European nations to form a North Atlantic Treaty Organization, which culminated in a pact formally signed in Washington on April 4, 1949. An attack against any signatory was to be considered "an attack against them all," it declared, and each country would assist the victim of aggression with "such action it deems necessary, including the use of armed force." The absence, however, of any provision pledging automatic action in case of attack left with Congress its constitutional power to declare war.

In the Senate, the treaty was subjected to sixteen days of public hearings by the Committee on Foreign Relations, followed by vigorous debate on the floor of the Chamber. Opponents challenged its constitutionality, questioned its strategic necessity, and argued that it was more likely to incite war than to prevent it. Nevertheless, on July 21, 1949, the Senate voted approval by a margin of 82 to 13. Not since the military alliance with France during the American Revolution had the nation "entangled" itself with Europe in the kind of arrangement that had been commonplace on that continent.

This major achievement of the Truman administration was in part a logical outgrowth of the sobering experiences of the postwar years, but mainly it was due to the careful ground-work laid in obtaining support from Congress. Policy preparation within the executive branch had been thorough and well coordinated. Consultations between the State Department and Senate had been held long before the treaty was consummated, and leaders of both parties had been invited to make whatever suggestions they deemed advisable. As implementation of the treaty would require an expenditure of funds, the White House made it a point to confer with House Foreign Affairs, Armed Services, and Appropriations Committees, thereby bringing both branches of Congress into active collaboration.

In general, the success of Truman's foreign policy can be attributed largely to bipartisan cooperation. An astute politician, he was keenly aware of his role as party leader, but he was also conscious of the strategic value of inter-party cooperation. Moreover, unlike Wilson, he was not hampered in achieving a working relationship with the opposition by harboring any prime ministerial approach to the presidency. Contrasted with Wilson in 1918 when he appealed for a Democratic legislature was Truman's reaction to the Republican congressional victory in 1946. "I do not claim for myself and my associates greater devotion to the welfare of our nation than I ascribe to others of another party," he said. "We take the same oath of office. We have at one time or another been equally willing to offer our lives in the defense of our country. . . . The change in the majority in the Congress does not alter our domestic or foreign interests or problems." Members of both parties had joined in the formulation and execution of the government's foreign policies. "It has been a national and not a party program," and so far as he and the Secretary of State were concerned, it would continue to be.

At the beginning, since he lacked a popular mandate, Truman was especially eager to court the opposition. Later, concerned about the danger of a resurgent isolationism, he assiduously cultivated bipartisan support. Nevertheless, he had no intention of evading his executive obligations in the conduct of foreign policy. He made it clear that the role of the minority party must be limited to consultation and cooperation. Responsibility must remain where the Constitution placed it, with the President of the United States, and not with either or both parties in Congress.

Success in forging an effective bipartisan coalition was as much due to the fortuitous circumstance that the leading Republican was Senator Arthur Vandenberg, chairman of the Foreign Relations Committee, as it was to Truman's own leadership. The war had transformed Vandenberg from an inveterate isolationist to an ardent internationalist. In March, 1941, he led the senatorial fight against lend-lease, but in 1943 he was committed to the principle of collective security and was one of the eight senators whom Cordell Hull consulted about the proposed United Nations organization.

Vandenberg's speech on the Senate floor on January 10, 1945, advocating a "hard and fast treaty" among the victorious Allies to prevent any resurgence of fascism, marked his emergence as a leader of statesmanlike stature. Courageous, imaginative, incisive, he was also moderate and prudent. During the period of the Republican-dominated Eightieth Congress, when support for the administration's foreign policy was imperative, Vandenberg provided the small phalanx of internationalists in his party with direction and leadership. He enjoyed a warm relationship with the President, and the two men deeply respected each other. Wilson had been afflicted with his Lodge; Truman was blessed with his Vandenberg.

Unfortunately, early in 1950, Vandenberg, already suffering from the illness that caused his death the following year, was compelled to curtail his activities. In March, the President wrote him with deep feeling:

You just don't realize what a vacuum there has been in the Senate and in the operation of our foreign policy since you left. . . . I mentioned you yesterday in a press conference as one . . . who could appreciate exactly what the country needs in its foreign relations. Personally, I am not confining that need to foreign relations alone. It is very seldom that men really become statesmen while they are yet alive in the minds of the people and their associates. As you well know, I have always held you in that category.

Take good care of yourself, and if there is anything I can do to
contribute to your welfare and recovery, all you need do is name
it.

On every possible occasion the President emphasized the
high value he placed on bipartisanship and the efforts he was
continually making to preserve it. At one press conference he
made it a point to mention that he had just discussed some
important foreign relations matters with Senator Styles
Bridges, ranking Republican in Vandenberg's absence, and
other members of the Senate from both parties, and that he
had instructed Secretary Dean Acheson, who had succeeded
the ailing Marshall in January, 1949, to consult with certain
congressmen. "It will be my purpose as well as that of Secretary Acheson," he said, "not only to keep the members of the
minority currently informed, but to solicit their views and take
them into serious account in both the formulation and implementation of our foreign policy."

Yet the record on bipartisanship was not consistent. During
Truman's first years in office, Latin-American policy was not
characterized by any inter-party consultations, but the important inter-American security arrangement, the Treaty of Rio de
Janeiro signed in September, 1947, was a collaborative effort.
Bipartisanship was not employed in the development of the
military and political policy toward Germany, but it was
promptly utilized at the time of the Berlin blockade. It was a
decisive factor in securing aid to Greece and Turkey, but not in
the administration's Palestine policy; in the evolution of the
Marshall Plan, but not the China policy; in the formation of
NATO, but not in the creation of the Point Four Program. On
the whole, however, the "loyal opposition" maintained its fe-
alty until the fall of 1950.

Bipartisanship shattered that year over the issue of sending
troops to Europe in connection with the nation's responsibility
to NATO. During the hearings on treaty ratification, Secretary
Acheson had assured Congress that under no circumstances
would American troops be sent abroad, but if such action were
contemplated, congressional consent would be requested.
When the Senate approved the document, it stipulated that

troops could be furnished only with the consent of Congress. However, after the foreign ministers of the NATO powers agreed to establish an integrated military force "adequate for the defense of the freedom of Europe," the President agreed to participate, informing Congress only after he had conveyed his intentions to NATO. The struggle in Korea, where the Western powers were caught unprepared, had impressed Truman with the necessity of bolstering the European defenses.

Censure of this executive action, sharp and loud, came first from isolationists outside the government. Disapprobation of Truman's foreign policy was at its height. It had begun to mount when China fell to the Communists in 1949, was intensified when Red China's intervention in the Korean war threatened military defeat of the United Nations forces, most of which were American, and rose still higher as the casualty lists lengthened and the military budget soared. Out of a sense of frustration and bitterness, "Asia Firsters"—those who felt that American interests in the Far East had been jeopardized by an unjustified priority to Europe—now unleashed a full-scale attack.

In an address on December 12, Joseph P. Kennedy, former ambassador to Great Britain, declared that American foreign policy, both politically and morally, was bankrupt and suicidal, that America's defense line should be limited to the Western Hemisphere. But it was Herbert Hoover's nationwide radio address eight days later that initiated "the great debate" in which the Senate was soon to be involved: should troops be sent to Europe, and did the chief executive have the authority to dispatch them across the ocean in peacetime? Hoover, echoing Kennedy, declared that a revamping of strategy was essential to make the Western Hemisphere the Gibraltar of western civilization. The defense of Europe, he insisted, should be the obligation of the nations of that continent, and assistance should be withheld until such time as they demonstrated an intention to defend themselves. American policy should be one of "watchful waiting." Even if Europe succumbed to communism, the American people would have no reason to become hysterical or lose confidence in their own security and future. "In American security rests the future security of all mankind."

Two days after Hoover's address, Secretary Acheson, just returned from Brussels where he had conferred with the NATO representatives, announced that General Dwight D. Eisenhower had been chosen supreme commander of all NATO forces. The isolationist Senator Robert A. Taft, who had replaced Vandenberg as chairman of the Senate Foreign Relations Committee, proposed a re-examination of foreign and military policy. "We had better commit no American troops to the European continent at this time . . . ," he said. "There is no legal obligation to send American land soldiers to Europe." If the President or his advisers planned such a move they were "usurping the authority given them by law and their program should be submitted to Congress for consideration before we became obligated." He also denounced the administration's appeal to bipartisanship as a stratagem for concealing the errors in national policies and the secrecy that had surrounded them since the days of Franklin D. Roosevelt.

With the nation and the leadership of both parties in a furious wrangle, Truman devoted the major part of his State of the Union message on January 8, 1951, to a discussion of American defense strategy. "Our own national security," he stated, "is deeply involved with that of the other free nations. . . . Our national safety would be gravely prejudiced if the Soviet Union were to succeed in harnessing to its war machine the resources and the manpower of the free nations on the borders of its empire. . . . The Soviet Union does not have to attack the United States to secure domination of the world. It can achieve its ends by isolating us and swallowing up all our allies." That same day Senator Wherry introduced a resolution that no forces be assigned to Europe under the North Atlantic Treaty "pending the adoption of a policy with respect thereto by Congress."

Neo-isolationists, who now wished to withdraw the nation's commitment to European defense, cloaked their purpose by harping on the legal and constitutional issue. If NATO troops which included those of the United States should be employed to resist an aggression, the power of Congress to declare war would be nullified, they contended. The authority given the President to commit troops to the common defense would represent a clear infringement of the powers of the legislative branch. This was a hair-splitting argument. The President's prerogatives in foreign policy were in no way augmented by the NATO treaty, and his authority to dispatch troops gave him no additional power to meet his obligations as guardian of the nation's defense. Apart from authority sanctioned by the Constitution, chief executives on numerous occasions have exercised broad and bold leadership to meet a threat to the republic's safety. Congress then generally followed with a formal consent to the action, a procedure likely to occur even more frequently in the future.

The "troops to Europe" question was eventually settled. A compromise to satisfy the White House and the opposition on Capitol Hill was proposed by Senator Tom Connally, administration spokesman in the Senate, that "before any considerable number of troops is sent to Europe, the Congress will be advised about it." General Eisenhower also lent his assistance, addressing Congress on the necessity of furnishing ground troops for the defense of Europe, and later, in executive session, pleaded for a flexible American commitment unhampered by congressionally imposed ceilings or rationing of military forces. Finally, a resolution, introduced by Senator John L. McClellan, endorsing both the administration's plan to defend Europe with American ground troops and the Republican demand that Congress share in the decision to assign military units abroad, was passed by 69 to 21.

The "great debate" was over, but the rancor continued. For the remainder of Truman's term in office he was harassed by bitter partisan feuding. The China policy, the Korean war, the policies of Secretary of State Acheson provided the grounds for a concerted effort to repudiate a decade's foreign policy and the men who were its major architects. Apparently bipartisanship, no matter how carefully and assiduously cultivated, could not long survive the cold blasts of controversial international issues, or the exploitation of those issues for political purposes by some partisan spokesmen.

Harry S. Truman

18. Countering Aggression

OF all the international events since the war, none shocked the American people more profoundly than the China debacle, contained more grist for the Republican political mill, or produced such bitter and enduring recriminations against the Truman administration. Roosevelt had struggled with the problem of China, and Truman inherited the colossal task of trying to rehabilitate a land ravaged by war, torn by civil strife, desperately poor, with a population ninety-five per cent illiterate, and exploited by a small, corrupt ruling class. Moreover, at the end of the conflict, China, as Truman expressed it, was "only a geographical expression," with Chiang Kai-shek governing the southwest corner, South and East China still occupied by the Japanese, North China controlled by Mao Tse-tung's Communists, and Manchuria by the Russians.

While the Nationalist or Kuomintang government, riddled with venality, was steadily losing ground among the people by failing to undertake even a modicum of desperately needed reform, the Chinese Communists were winning the support of the peasantry, the small merchants, and the professional groups by instituting moderate relief measures wherever they gained power. General Albert C. Wedemeyer, Chief of Staff to Chiang Kai-shek, reported pessimistically to the President shortly before the end of the war that neither the Communists nor the Kuomintang were democratic in spirit or intentions. The people wanted peace and were little interested in ideologies. "Conditions here," he went on, "could best be handled by a benevolent despot or a military dictator," and it made no difference from which side, as "practically all Chinese officials are interested in their selfish aggrandizement." Nevertheless, he thought that the Generalissimo's leadership might offer the best opportunity for stability.

Truman and the State Department were most concerned that civil war might break out again. Sporadic clashes which kept flaring up portended a major eruption. Convinced that such a development could only lead to Chiang's defeat, the President decided to send General George C. Marshall to China in December, 1945, to "endeavor to persuade the Chinese government to call a national conference of representatives of the major political elements to bring about the unification of China and, concurrently, to effect a cesation of hostilities, particularly in North China." Marshall was instructed to tell Chiang frankly that "a China disunited and torn by civil strife could not be considered realistically as a proper place" for the credits and technical, economic, and military assistance that he requested. If, however, the country showed signs that it was progressing toward peace and unity, then the American government would be willing to extend every possible assistance.

For a year Marshall labored at his Herculean assignment. At one point a cease-fire was actually arranged, only to be violated several months later first by one side and then by the other. Chiang, making no real effort to clean house and blaming the Communists for whatever ailed China, refused to agree to a military truce until the Reds acquiesced to the political settlement he desired. The Communists, for their part, displayed no real interest in arriving at a compromise, pursuing instead a "rule or ruin" approach to unification. Marshall returned home in December, 1946, blaming the "dominant reactionary group" in the Kuomintang and the "irreconcilable Communists" for the failure of his efforts.

Almost immediately thereafter the civil war was renewed in earnest, and soon the Communist drive gathered dangerous momentum. To assess the situation, the President in July, 1947, sent General Wedemeyer to China, where he remained for about two months. His report was completely discouraging.

Although he believed that Chiang would like to create a demo-cratic government, "I am not certain that he has sufficient de-termination to do so if this requires absolute overruling of the political and military cliques surrounding him." The Kuo-mintang, he noted, was corrupt and riddled with nepotism, and force was increasingly used to maintain its position. "Secret police operate widely, very much as they do in Russia and as they did in Germany. People disappear. . . . No trials and no sentences. . . . Everyone lives with a feeling of fear and loses confidence in the government." The present trend, he con-tinued, "points toward a gradual disintegration of the National Government's control, with the ultimate possibility of a Com-munist-dominated China." Yet, should the United States at-tempt to stop Communist expansion while ignoring "an un-popular repressive government," then, warned Wedemeyer, American prestige in the Far East would be gravely impaired and "wavering elements" might turn away from the Kuo-mintang to the Reds. Fighting must cease immediately, he con-tinued, and recommended that the matter be turned over to the United Nations. He favored a broad five-year program of eco-nomic and military support by the United States, but not until Chiang promised to undertake sweeping social and political reforms.

All factors considered, the State Department concluded that defeat of the Communists could be accomplished only if the United States would "underwrite permanently" the Chiang regime with a financial commitment of billions of dollars, command of the Nationalist armies by American officers, and employment of large-scale land, air, and sea forces. Even if funds could be made available, as was highly questionable in view of Western Europe's critical economic situation, it was extremely unlikely that the American people would consent to assume the massive burden necessitated by such an effort. Moreover, not only was the prospect of being bogged down interminably in the vast reaches of China a distinct possibility, but aiding the Kuomintang might provoke Stalin to help Mao Tse-tung, and the conflict could escalate into World War III.

The administration, therefore, decided to continue limited emergency assistance, President Truman recommending in a special message to Congress in February, 1948, that $570 million be appropriated for one year, and an additional $60 million "for a few selected reconstruction projects." He explained that the deterioration of the Chinese economy was of deep concern, and that the problem had been under continuous study since the return of General Marshall. "Conditions have not developed as we had hoped," he went on, "and we can only do what is feasible under circumstances as they exist." It was now up to the Chinese government to take the requisite measures which would lead to economic recovery.

Although numerous Republican members were criticizing the administration policy on China, the Republican-dominated Congress slashed $167 million from the amount requested by the President. In general, Congress displayed little anxiety about the Chinese situation until the Nationalist government was on the verge of collapse. Senator McMahon, a Democrat, was later to observe, after having examined the record of the Senate Foreign Relations Committee, "In the years between '47 and '49 there was not a single, solitary suggestion made for the formation of policy, change of policy, or disagreement with policy [on China] by any member of this committee in its executive sessons."

The victory of the Communists precipitated one of the lengthiest and most divisive political controversies the United States had ever experienced. Truman and his administration were vitriolically attacked for a policy about which only a tiny minority in either Congress or the nation had been concerned. Perhaps Truman might have been spared some of the fire if he had attempted to enlighten the public on the realistic alternatives for American policy. Late in November, 1948, the China section of the State Department had recommended "going to the American public now to explain the inadequacies of the Chiang Kai-shek government," but Secretary Marshall dissuaded the President from authorizing this, believing that to do so would administer the final *coup de grâce* to the Nationalists. Truman himself was reluctant to open a discussion on the discordant China question, fearing to risk loss of support for his European programs, but any advantage he gained was probably more than offset by the consequences of silence. He should

have outlined, clearly and concisely, all the grim aspects of the
situation in China, allowing the people to decide, first, whether
they wished to commit their lives and their fortunes in a possibly hopeless attempt to save that country from communism,
and, secondly, whether they preferred attempting to salvage
China instead of Europe, where a positive contribution could
be made, as resources were not available for both.

A White Paper, released by the State Department on August
6, 1949, documented the background and reasons for the disaster. It pointed out that although some two billion dollars had
been poured into China from 1945 to 1949, a very substantial
part of the assistance had been dissipated by inefficiency and
corruption. Suggestions for reform had gone unheeded, expert
military advice was ignored. That the problem was of staggering proportions and incapable of ready solution was later
made abundantly clear by Gerneral Wedemeyer in his testimony before a joint session of the Senate Foreign Relations and
Armed Services Committees. "The [Chinese] people were tired
of war," he said. "All they wanted . . . was food, shelter, and
peace. And the Communists exploited these basic . . . desires
. . . and they exploited the corruption and the maladministra-
tion . . . to such a degree that Chiang Kai-shek . . . was repudiated as a leader. The troops were dispirited and they didn't
fight."

Many Americans, however, regarded such explanations as a
whitewash and condemned the President, Dean Acheson, and
the State Department's Far East experts for Chiang's defeat. A
number of influential Republican leaders in Congress, cloaking
their neo-isolationism in an "Asia first" policy, advocated all-
out aid to China in preference to European commitments.
Some joined with the "China lobby," a vague but apparently
well-financed pressure group, in advocating that men and
matériel be sent to Chiang on Formosa, where he had established the Nationalist government headquarters.

Great Britain promptly accorded Communist China diplomatic recognition, but sentiment in the United States against
such a move was so strong that Truman could not follow suit,
even had he wished to do so. Voluble demands in Congress
that the nation guarantee the defense of Formosa against a

possible assault by the Communists presented Truman with the necessity for an immediate decision. Months earlier, in anticipation of the debacle, the Joint Chiefs had concluded that military action to prevent possible Communist domination of Formosa would not be justified. Their position was upheld by the National Security Council. Shortly thereafter, in January, 1950, the President issued a policy statement declaring that the United States does not intend to utilize armed forces "to interfere in the present situation" or "pursue a course which will lead to involvement in the civil conflict."

For a while Truman and Acheson seemed to be nurturing hopes of a "Titoist" development in China. A week after the President's statement, Secretary Acheson in an address asserted that the basic interest of China and the Soviet Union conflicted; therefore, "We must not undertake to deflect from the Russians to ourselves the righteous anger and the wrath and the hatred of the Chinese people which must develop."

Truman's position of "watchful waiting" was endorsed by most Democrats in Congress as well as by many other Americans, but in May, thirty-five senators signed a round robin asking for a positive statement by the President that Mao's regime would not be recognized and that the government would oppose any efforts to seat the Communists in the United Nations in place of the Kuomintang. Nevertheless, the administration might possibly have accorded diplomatic recognition if the Korean war had not erupted.

Later, in looking back over the action-filled years of his presidency, Truman said that the most difficult decision he ever had to make was to commit the nation to the defense of South Korea against the attack by the North Koreans on the night of June 25, 1950. It did indeed take courage to send American troops into combat five years after a devastating war, to a remote area that was merely a spot on the map to most citizens, especially as this represented the very first action by the nation in fulfilling its collective security obligations.

By one of the accidents of history, the obscure, rugged peninsula, a Japanese possession since 1910, became a pawn in the conflict between East and West. Korea's postwar status was first discussed at Cairo when Roosevelt, Churchill, and Chiang

Kai-shek declared that "in due course" the country should achieve independence. The commitment was reaffirmed at Potsdam, and on entering the war against Japan, the Soviets publicly pledged themselves to the principle of independence for Korea by announcing their adherence to the Potsdam Declaration. When Japanese resistance suddenly collapsed, a purely military expedient was responsible for the creation of two Koreas. As the Russians were in a position to occupy the entire country, the Joint Chiefs suggested that the enemy's troops surrender to the Americans south of the thirty-eighth parallel and to the Soviets north of that line. That temporary demarcation became frozen into a permanent split, with the Americans ruling one zone through a military government and the Russians the other through so-called Korean "people's" committees.

Repeated attempts at unification over the years failed. Finally, in 1947, the United Nations, asked to break the diplomatic stalemate, recommended a general election supervised by a special commission. The Soviets refused to permit the commission to enter its zone, but elections were held in the south. The Republic of Korea was established with Syngman Rhee as president, and American troops, except for a small police force, were withdrawn by the end of June, 1949. The Russians also evacuated their zone, leaving behind a satellite regime known as the "Democratic People's Republic." Thus two hostile governments remained, backed by rival powers, each claiming sovereignty over the peninsula.

Border clashes began to occur at once, and signs increasingly pointed to the outbreak of civil war. Yet, although the State and Defense Departments were aware that North Korea was being heavily supplied with arms by the Soviets, Secretary of State Acheson told the National Press Club on January 12, 1950, that Korea did not fall within the American "defense perimeter," which in the Far East extended from the Philippines through the Ryukyus, Japan, and the Aleutians to Alaska. Should aggression occur outside that arc, "the initial reliance must be on the people attacked to resist it and then upon the commitments of the entire civilized world under the Charter of the United Nations." While Acheson's statement was consistent with the President's declared policy of non-embroilment in Asia and may have been intended to temper Syngman Rhee, who kept threatening to invade North Korea, it could have been interpreted by the Communists as a green light.

Notified of the invasion while visiting with his family at Independence, Truman responded immediately, instructing Secretary Acheson to request a meeting of the United Nations Security Council in order to charge the People's Republic with aggression. At the same time, expecting that the North Koreans would ignore the United Nations, he began to think ahead about other steps. On the flight home to Washington, the President decided that this violation of the peace could not go unchallenged. He recalled other occasions "when the strong had attacked the weak . . . Manchuria, Ethiopia, Austria . . . how each time that the democracies failed to act it had encouraged the aggressors to keep going ahead." Furthermore, "the principles of the United Nations were at stake."

As Truman anticipated, the North Koreans disregarded the Security Council's order for the immediate cessation of hostilities and within forty-eight hours had smashed their way to Seoul, capital of the South Korean government. The President immediately directed General Douglas MacArthur to use air and naval forces to support the Republic south of the thirty-eighth parallel. To keep the conflict from spreading, he dispatched the Seventh Fleet to the Formosa Straits, thereby neutralizing both the Chinese Communists and the Nationalists. "The attack on Korea," Truman said in a press release on June 27, "makes it plain beyond all doubt that Communism has passed beyond the use of subversion to conquer independent nations and will now use armed invasion and war."

While the American people and Congress in general supported Truman's decision, Senator Taft raised a constitutional question. Did the President have the right to send forces into combat without legislative authorization? Truman insisted, however, that the United States was engaged in "a police action under the United Nations." Even when ground troops were required, enlarging the conflict beyond a "police action," Truman empowered General MacArthur to utilize all those under his command without the customary joint resolution from Congress. As swift action was essential, the President wished to avoid a possibly prolonged discussion by the legislature, but it is not clear why he never requested its approval in the ensuing weeks. His measures undoubtedly would have been confirmed and his political position thereby strengthened.

Familiar with the terrain, thoroughly trained and seasoned, the North Korean troops hurled the defenders back until by August they over-ran almost the entire peninsula. In September, however, a brilliant counterattack by General MacArthur reversed the tide, driving the invaders completely out of South Korea. With the Army poised at the thirty-eighth parallel, should it be permitted to cross, crush the enemy, and thereby unify Korea? Secretary Acheson had stated in June that American intervention was "solely for the purpose of restoring . . . the peace broken by that aggression." MacArthur's victory led to a reconsideration. On September 15, the Joint Chiefs authorized operations north of the dividing line provided that no large concentrations of Russians or Chinese Communists were encountered. Three weeks later, the United Nations General Assembly in a resolution declared its aim to be the establishment of "a unified, independent and democratic government" and that "all appropriate steps . . . to insure conditions of stability throughout Korea" be adopted.

Truman flew to Wake Island in mid-October for a discussion with MacArthur, who had his own ideas on the nature of the conflict. Of great concern in Washington was possible intervention by the Chinese Communists, who were threatening to come to the defense of North Korea. Foreign Minister Chou En-lai denounced the United States as "the most dangerous enemy of the People's Republic of China," warning that his countrymen would not "supinely tolerate seeing their neighbors being savagely invaded by the imperialists." But MacArthur assured the President that the Chinese Reds were unlikely to intervene, "that the victory was won in Korea," and that "all resistance would end . . . by Thanksgiving." His intelligence was tragically defective.

Launching a full-scale offensive to the Yalu River on November 24, MacArthur's troops advanced to within fifty miles of the Chinese frontier when they were overwhelmed by a massive concentration of Chinese "volunteers." Compelled to retreat, the U.N. troops were steadily forced back until, on January 4, 1951, Seoul was retaken by the Reds. MacArthur now began to urge that he be permitted to blockade China, bomb Chinese targets, and use Nationalist troops stationed on Formosa for diversionary assaults on the mainland. Only these measures, he declared, could insure victory, but in the judgment of Truman, Acheson, and the Joint Chiefs, they could result only in enlarging the conflict, possibly even setting off World War III. "If we began to attack Communist China," Truman later wrote, "we had to anticipate Russian intervention." Moreover, General Omar N. Bradley, chairman of the Joint Chiefs, feared that a large-scale commitment of American strength in Asia, leaving Europe exposed to Soviet armies, might even encourage an attack on that continent. Nothing would please the Kremlin more, he said, than "the enlargement of the war in Korea to include Red China . . . it would necessarily tie down additional forces, especially our sea . . . . and air power, while the Soviet Union would not be obliged to put a single man into the conflict." The United States would be involved in waging "the wrong war, at the wrong place, at the wrong time, and with the wrong enemy."

Truman recorded that he never permitted himself to forget that Russia was the principal enemy, that the United States could not afford to squander its power while the Soviets remained intact, pulling the strings. The most critical points, he wrote, were Berlin, Western Germany, Indochina, Yugoslavia, and Iran. "In each of these areas a minor incident could easily be created which would give the Russians an excuse for open intervention." The Kremlin's bluster about a new world war might not be bluff, and plans had to include the possibility that "the time was in fact ripe for a general war with the United States."

Britain and France concurred in the President's views. Both nations understandably were terrified by even the remotest possibility of another global conflict. When Truman replied to a question at a press conference in November, 1950, concerning the use of the atom bomb in the Korean conflict, that "there has been consideration of this subject . . . just as there is . . .

of the use of all military weapons," his words created a near panic in Britain. Prime Minister Attlee immediately flew to Washington for assurances that no such action was planned, and also to inform the President that if the measures Mac-Arthur advocated were followed the United States would have to fight the war alone. At stake was not the outcome in Korea, where the United States was contributing ninety per cent of the armed forces, but the future of the western alliance system.

In a personal message to MacArthur on January 13, 1951, the President tried once again to impress on him that the Korean war must be prosecuted in accordance with policy objectives considered necessary by the United States and the United Nations. "Our course of action at this time," he wrote, "should be such as to consolidate the great majority of the United Nations. This majority is not merely part of the organization but is also the nations whom we would desperately need to count on as allies in the event the Soviet Union moves against us."

The war in Korea was unlike any other engagement in which the United States had ever participated. In the past, when the object was simply to defeat the enemy as quickly and as cheaply as possible, military strategy could be entrusted to the military, with the civilian commander taking a secondary role; but in Korea, military considerations were subordinate. The course of events in that small, remote peninsula could have world-wide repercussions. Decisions on strategy, therefore, could be made only within the framework of American foreign policy.

Complicating the problem for President Truman was General MacArthur's view of war as a political instrument, in contrast to the belief of most American military leaders that victory on the battlefield was the only consideration. Moreover, his political objectives were diametrically opposed to those of the administration. Although he talked of "victory" seemingly in military terms, his strategy was based on the contention that Asia, not Europe, should be given priority, that the Far East was not a peripheral area but the very center of the global struggle, where Russian power would rise or fall. In his view, the Korean war was the right war with the right enemy, and if China, an integral part of the Communist coalition, were de-

feated, Soviet fortunes and the world balance of power would
be vitally altered. Conversely, if the United States behaved
timidly, American prestige in the Far East would sink, while
that of Red China would soar, thereby demonstrating to the
neutral nations that their policy was correct. The destruction
of Chinese military depots and industrial power, he maintained, would undermine Sino-Russian capacity for aggression
in the Far East. Korea, therefore, was Europe's front line, the
real testing ground for NATO.

Since the United States enjoyed atomic superiority, the
bombing and blockade of China, in his estimation, involved no
risk. The Strategic Air Force would serve as an effective deterrent to the Soviets, confining the action to the Chinese-Korean
theater. Tactically, superior American air power could provide
the necessary protection for ground action. It was ridiculous to
permit the Soviet Union, with inferior strategic capability, to
immobilize an adversary of far greater strength. American policy makers, he charged, were simply psychologically incapable
of exploiting the nation's advantage in atomic striking power.
If the Soviet Union considered itself capable of launching a
total war, an excuse was hardly needed; what restrained the
Russians, what would continue to deter them, he was certain,
was America's superior atomic power. To try to hold together
an alliance which refused to recognize the locus of the real
threat was not only pointless but could well be injurious to the
national interest. In any event, the United States, with its powerful resources, was less dependent than the European members on the western alliance. To avoid a frustrating Korean
stalemate, he would urge unilateral action if cooperation could
not be obtained.

The conflict between the general and the President began in
August, 1950, when MacArthur sent a message to the Veterans
of Foreign Wars urging the incorporation of Formosa into the
American security system. "Nothing could be more fallacious,"
he said, "than the threadbare argument by those who advocate
appeasement and defeatism in the Pacific that if we defend
Formosa we alienate continental Asia." As this statement flatly
contradicted the announced stand by the President, MacArthur
was asked to withdraw it. He complied promptly, but the

damage had been done, as it was already circulating in a national weekly magazine.

Through press interviews and communiqués, MacArthur continued to challenge the policies of the United States and its commander in chief, creating confusion at home and abroad as to who really spoke for the nation. Finally, on December 5, 1950, the President issued a directive to all government agencies that "no speech, press release, or other public statement concerning foreign policy should be released until it has received clearance from the Department of State." For a time MacArthur was silent. Meanwhile, General Matthew Ridgway, advancing slowly and inflicting major casualties, recaptured Seoul on March 7, 1951, thus belying MacArthur's prediction in December that American troops might have to evacuate Korea unless his policy on blockade and bombardment of China was carried out.

MacArthur was informed by the Joint Chiefs that the President was planning shortly to announce terms for a cease-fire, but he decided to present his own terms. On March 24, he issued a communiqué which combined an offer to meet the enemy commander on the battlefield and arrange a truce with a threat to expand military operations and inflict utter defeat upon the Chinese should they turn down his offer—virtually a demand for unconditional surrender. By submitting an ultimatum, MacArthur could be certain of achieving what he sought, a continuation of the war on his terms, since no great power is willing to accept defeat unless it is *in extremis*.

As the administration had already circulated to the allied nations the President's proposed statement for a cessation of hostilities, this sudden apparent reversal came as a shock, and the wires of the State Department were clogged with alarmed inquiries. Even Acheson's explanation that MacArthur's proposal was unauthorized failed to allay apprehension. The British feared that the "irresponsible statements" which came out at "frequent intervals from highly placed quarters" might provoke such powerful popular support that the American government would be compelled to adopt the policy sponsored by its critics. "By this act," Truman later wrote, "MacArthur left me no choice—I could no longer tolerate his insubordination."

It not only defied his authority, but "also flouted the policy of the United Nations." If he permitted the general to spurn the civil authorities, "I myself would be violating my oath to uphold and defend the Constitution."

A cable immediately sent to MacArthur reminding him of the President's directive on policy statements apparently left him unmoved, for he made no effort to request Republican House Leader Joseph Martin, Jr., to keep private a letter he had sent him several days before, in which he expressed his opinion on foreign policy. MacArthur wrote that Chiang's troops on Formosa should be used to open "a second Asiatic front to relieve the pressure on our forces in Korea," concluding, "It seems strangely difficult for some to realize that here in Asia is where the Communist conspirators have elected to make their play for global conquest . . . that here we fight Europe's war with arms while the diplomats there still fight it with words; that if we lose this war to Communism in Asia the fall of Europe is inevitable, win it and Europe most probably would avoid war and yet preserve freedom." On April 5, Martin read the letter on the floor of the House.

By then the President had already concluded that "the time had come to draw the line." The letter reinforced his decision, substantiating that "the general was not only in disagreement with the policy of the government, but was challenging this policy in open insubordination to his Commander in Chief." For two days Truman discussed the MacArthur problem with Secretaries Acheson and Harriman and Generals Marshall and Bradley, carefully concealing the action he had already decided upon, so as not to influence anyone's judgment. At the last meeting, General Bradley reported the unanimous recommendation of the Joint Chiefs of Staff that General MacArthur be relieved of his command. All the others concurred. On the previous day General Marshall had told the President that, after reviewing the record, he believed the general should have been dismissed two years earlier.

Nevertheless, political courage was required to remove a war hero of General MacArthur's stature, since the cause was not a military disaster but a constitutional issue, the implication of which would not readily be apparent to most Americans. The uproar that followed shook the country. Congress and the White House were deluged with telegrams hysterically denouncing the President's decision. In one city Truman was burned in effigy; in others, automobiles were plastered with signs: "Oust President Truman." State legislatures approved resolutions condemning "the irresponsible and capricious action of the President." On the Senate floor, William Jenner charged that a "cancerous conspiracy" directed by "agents of the Soviet Union" was in control of the government, and that "our only choice is to impeach President Truman" in order to expose it. Senator Richard Nixon of California declared that MacArthur's dismissal was tantamount to appeasement of world communism and called for censure of the President. The Wisconsin Senator Joseph McCarthy's attack on the President was obscene.

When the general arrived home, he was wildly acclaimed as he triumphantly toured one city after another. New York "roared and shrilled itself into near exhaustion" for six hours and twenty-five minutes, showering the general with 2,850 tons of ticker tape and confetti. An estimated seven and a half million people turned out to greet him, nearly twice the record crowd that welcomed General Eisenhower on his return from Europe in 1945. In MacArthur's address to Congress, which was televised, the General gave a memorable performance as he dramatically and eloquently defended his policies, concluding with the emotion-charged, "Old soldiers never die; they just fade away. . . . Good-by."

The Truman-MacArthur controversy kept boiling while the Senate Armed Forces and Foreign Relations Committees investigated the case against the entire background of the administration's Far Eastern policy. When the diverse positions of Truman and MacArthur were thoroughly chewed over, no change in the Korean policy was effected. The conclusion of the Joint Chiefs was that "the operation in Korea has been a success," with Communist aggression checked, its imperialist aims severely set back, and collective security strengthened. The American people, for their part, were not prepared to endorse a solution which might invite catastrophe. Whatever enthusiasm remained for MacArthur's prescription for victory drained away as General Ridgway, now in command, continued to drive the Chinese Communists from South Korea.

Unsuccessful in their efforts to absorb South Korea, the Communists finally decided to accept the stalemate, and on June 23, 1951, the Russian delegate to the United Nations, Jacob A. Malik, indicated that his country was prepared to discuss a cease-fire. Negotiations for a truce began on July 10 but for the next two years were hopelessly mired on the matter of repatriation of prisoners. In the end, Truman's successor accepted a settlement for which the Democratic President would have been pilloried. As Walter Lippmann put it, "President Eisenhower signed an armistice which accepted the partition of Korea and a peace without victory because, being himself the victorious commander in World War II and a Republican, he could not be attacked as an appeaser. . . . The Democrats were too vulnerable to attack from the political followers of General MacArthur and of the then powerful Senator McCarthy, and indeed to attack from the whole right wing of the Republican Party."

The partisan assault against President Truman, precipitated by the Communist victory in China, gathered momentum during the following months. Leadership in the Senate had shifted to a group of conservative Republicans who completely rejected the philosophy of bipartisanship in foreign policy. They were persuaded that at election time a successful foreign policy benefited only the party in power, since it bore the administration's label, whereas the opposition would suffer from failure because it had collaborated. Moreover, many Republicans were convinced that the country was being undermined by the New Deal philosophy, and that a change of leadership in the White House was essential to halt and reverse the invidious trend.

Augmenting the opposition of such Republican senators as Taft, Bridges, Wherry, and Knowland was the aberration of McCarthyism, which went beyond criticism of specific measures to impugn the loyalty and patriotism of the major architects of the Truman policies, who were charged with responsibility for any and all successes achieved by international communism. On February 8, 1950, the senator from Wisconsin, using the China debacle as a lead, initiated a fantastic witch hunt with his accusation that the State Department was infested with Communists. "How can we account for our present situation," he thundered, "unless we believe that men high in the government are concerting to deliver us to disaster? This must be the product of a great conspiracy on a scale so immense as to dwarf any previous venture in the history of man."

During the next four years an "anti-red" hysteria swept the country as McCarthy, in language that exceeded all bounds of propriety, continued to malign government officials, sparing not even Presidents Truman and Eisenhower. A smothering blanket of fear enveloped the country. Lives and reputations were ruined as canons of Anglo-Saxon due process gave way to guilt by association. To Europeans, it seemed that the United States had incomprehensibly been infected by a dangerous lunacy. The *New York Times* reflected the attitude of many thoughtful Americans when it asserted, "If a major objective of Russian foreign policy is to undermine the faith of democratic peoples in their governments, then the Kremlin must rejoice every time that Joseph R. McCarthy opens his mouth in the Senate of the United States." One of the most degrading periods in the nation's history was made more shameful by the fact that intelligent and honorable men like Senator Taft either endorsed or tacitly acquiesced in McCarthy's tactics.

President Truman lost little time in striking back. Asked at a press conference on March 30, 1950, whether McCarthy's charges of disloyalty in the State Department had any basis in fact, he replied, "I think the greatest asset that the Kremlin has is Senator McCarthy." He went on to cite statistics about the loyalty program which he had instituted three years before. Out of more than two million civil servants, he said, only about two hundred resigned or were dismissed as a result of investigations. The Republicans, he continued scathingly, having failed with their charges of statism, the welfare state, and socialism in attempting to achieve control of Congress, were now making a political issue of loyalty. In order to do that, they were willing to "sabotage" the bipartisan foreign policy. "And this fiasco which has been going on in the Senate is the very best asset that the Kremlin could have in the operation of the cold war." He was fed up, he said, with such antics.

The alacrity with which a large segment of the American people swallowed the "devil" and "conspiracy" thesis of McCarthy and his supporters was a measure of their frustration, bewilderment, and fear. The world, and the role of the United States in it, had become unintelligible. In the past, problems with foreign nations had yielded to quick and clear solutions. A few shiploads of Marines had been adequate to handle any difficulties in Central America. Twice the nation had mobilized and crushed an arrogant Germany, and Japan had learned what it meant to challenge American might. The country had always been capable of controlling events and shaping its own future. Now, when the United States was at the height of its strength, with superiority in the mightiest instrument of destruction ever created by man, the government was powerless to annihilate the Soviet threat. Instead it pursued methods of "containment," hoping to find means of coexistence with a regime obnoxious in every respect. The success of the Communists in China, which turned an old friend into an implacable enemy, was a deep blow. And frightening in its implications for the national security was the fact that the Soviet Union was now also an atomic power.

As the Korean war dragged on and casualties mounted without any end in sight, frustration became almost unendurable. One woman expressed this feeling when she wrote to the White House, "I am only one of the many mothers who is nearly out of my mind with grief, at the horror and awful bloodshed. . . . Why does this war in Korea have to be prolonged? Is it a 'stop and go War' at Mr. Truman's dictation? . . . Why don't we use the wonderful weapons which we have perfected? If the 'Reds' are building up air bases, why can't we bring them to their knees as we did the Japanese? It was a quick decision after the atom bomb was dropped. . . . In the name of 'Common Decency' let's get this Korean war over. It is the worst thing that has ever happened to our dear country."

Many Americans found the truce negotiations equally baffling. To have so much blood spilled for the limited objective of restoring the *status quo* appeared the height of folly and

futility. They ignored the achievements of the President's Korean policy: that his prompt response had averted possible disaster for the United Nations by serving notice that aggression
would not be tolerated, that the American armed forces had
been strengthened, the North Atlantic coalition solidified,
American prestige immeasurably enhanced in Asia, and the
nation in a much better position to defend Europe. Americans
desperately clung to the illusion that the security they had
known in the past was still obtainable. Finding it impossible to
bridge the gap between their longings and what was actually
possible, they were led to grasp at the scapegoats being offered
them.

Most vulnerable in the administration was the Secretary of
State. In appointing George C. Marshall and later Dean Acheson, the President demonstrated that he possessed a vital in-
gredient of leadership: the ability to select competent advisers.
Acheson was regarded by both American and foreign observers
as an extraordinarily brilliant and accomplished diplomat. The
British commentator Alistair Cooke, writing in the *Manchester
Guardian,* praised the new Secretary of State as one of the most
creative political minds of the time and predicted that "he
must become the most impressive Secretary of State since
Elihu Root," and the Republican senator from Iowa, Bourke
Hickenlooper, in approving the nomination, said, "He . . .
brings to the office personal integrity, high ability, and unusual
experience. . . . I am convinced that he is completely devoted
to . . . the principles by which our Government lives, and that
he will defend these principles for us and for the world."

President and Secretary quickly developed a relationship of
mutual esteem and warm affection, despite their dissimilarity
in background and interests. Truman relied completely on
Acheson's judgment. Regarding him as his principal adviser on
foreign affairs, he conferred with him almost daily. On matters
of policy, both men were in firm agreement.

The vicious attacks on Acheson which began in 1950 infuriated Truman, not only because of his high regard for his Secretary but because the bitter partisan assaults prevented him
from carrying out policies he considered essential. The President spared no effort to counter them. While on a brief vaca-

tion at Key West in March, he wrote to Senator Styles Bridges, "I noticed a statement in the press this morning that you were joining the wolfhounds in the attack on Dean Acheson. I am really sorry to hear this, and I don't believe you would do it if you fully understood all the implications involved in this unwarranted attack on the bipartisan foreign policy." The approach recently taken by several senators has been very pleasing to the Politburo, he continued bluntly. The Kremlin never had as much help from the so-called loyalty risks as they have been receiving from the indefensible attacks on the Secretary. He cited Acheson's record of unselfish and distinguished public service, and continued, "I have no objection to your attacking me and the policies of the Administration on any subject you choose," but Bridges should confine himself to domestic affairs and not "under any circumstances at this critical time, upset the solid front here at home for our approach to the world situation. . . . I am appealing to you as your old-time personal friend and Senate colleague to weigh this situation carefully, to discuss it objectively with your colleagues, and then if you desire a further discussion of it with me personally, I will be glad to go into every detail with you, and anyone else you want to bring with you."

Indicative of how impassioned and extreme was the assault on Secretary Acheson was the refusal by critics to acknowledge the indisputable fact that he had worked consistently and firmly to check Soviet aggression, for which the Russians resented him more than any other Western diplomat. No Secretary of State had ever been so vilified at home and so honored abroad. In playing for partisan advantage, the Republicans persuaded millions of Americans that if only the villains were removed from office, if only the devils were exorcised, then the nation's fortunes would change.

Many Americans could not comprehend the fantastically complex nature of the international situation. The Truman administration had inherited a Europe stripped of countervailing forces against the Soviet Union, the only military power which the war had left on the continent. Not even possession of the atom bomb could mitigate the danger to the United States arising out of the European vacuum. With the

balance of power weighted in favor of Russia, it was vital that
America maintain the allegiance of key areas in Western
Europe, and win in the contest for such areas as Greece,
Turkey, Iran, and China. As in a chess game, each move had to
be calculated with the utmost finesse.

Against constant, relentless Russian pressure to expand its
power, Truman raised one bulwark after another. Each time
Russia was thwarted, it represented the loss of a goal to the
Soviets in an area where the West's position was tenuous. By
the time he left office, Truman had succeeded in achieving a
partial readjustment of the power balance, the first peacetime
President to actively engage the nation's moral and material
resources for that end. With the redress of the balance of
power came a hardening of international lines. By 1953, few
nations were still uncommitted, and those mainly in the Arab-
Asian bloc. In Southeast Asia, where the situation was still
fluid, neither protagonist saw much prospect of making any
appreciable gains at the expense of the other.

Truman's extraordinary achievements as a world leader
during the critical period in which he held office were ob-
scured for the majority of Americans, partly as a result of the
virulent Republican attacks on his administration, to some
degree because he did not possess a commanding presence, and
also because he lacked the genius for the President's schoolmaster role. When he had to deal with concrete situations, with
tangible crises, he was effective in rallying the nation behind
him. But he was unable to convey adequately a sense of the
new dimensions of the age. Preoccupied with the danger of
Communist imperialism, he failed to enlighten the people
about the problems created by economic, demographic, psychological, and technological upheavals, which were producing fundamental changes throughout the world. Probably no
President could have completely reached a public whose past
experience made them resistant to an acceptance of the revolutionary aspects of the current scene, but possibly a more
dynamic leader, with an awareness of the subtleties of international life, might have made some inroads.

In character with his concept of the presidency and of his
own sense of presidential responsibility, Truman set about to
make the transition to the new administration as orderly as

possible before retiring from office. A vacuum in power at the White House during a period when one crisis trod on the heels of the previous one could be calamitous, especially when a "lame duck" President is to be succeeded by one of another party. Even before the 1952 conventions, "I had made up my mind to keep both candidates informed about the important developments of our foreign policy," Truman wrote. "I had a double purpose in mind. First, I wanted to keep foreign policy out of partisan politics. Second, I wanted to make sure that because of our responsibility of world leadership whoever was elected would be fully informed and prepared to conduct foreign affairs."

At the same time, he would not make Hoover's error by expecting the President-elect to share in the responsibilities before he assumed the powers of the office. He would be President until January 20 and make all necessary decisions, but his successor would be advised on all important developments. No one was better aware of how greatly handicapped a new President could be when without adequate briefing he was required to cope with a whole series of critical problems, each requiring early decisions. Truman supplied both candidates with weekly reports by the Central Intelligence Agency, accepting Eisenhower's reservation that these would not limit his "freedom to discuss or analyze foreign programs as my judgment dictates."

On the day following the election Truman sent a message to his successor, inviting him to send a representative to the Budget Bureau. He also informed his staff of his desire to effect a continuity of policy in foreign affairs and requested them to assist General Eisenhower in every way possible. The President-elect responded promptly that he would have his man meet with the Director of the Budget. Truman then sent another message asking him "to meet with me in the White House at your early convenience to discuss the problem of this transition period, so that it may be clear to all the world that this nation is united in its struggle for freedom and peace."

Before the formal conference between the two men and their staffs which took place on November 18, they had a private conversation during which Truman said he understood Eisenhower's natural and proper reluctance to assume responsibility until he was in office. However, as the success of certain issues in foreign policy depended upon their continuity, "We will tell you about these issues and would welcome concurrence if you want to give it. . . . But we will not press for it. This is a matter on which you will have to make up your own mind on the basis of what is best for America."

The two men then joined W. Averell Harriman, Dean Acheson, Robert Lovett, John Snyder, and the incoming President's aides, Joseph Dodge and Henry Cabot Lodge, after which the Eisenhower party went to the Pentagon for a military briefing by General Bradley and the Joint Chiefs of Staff. Truman noted that Eisenhower had been "rather appalled at all that the President needs to know," and one columnist noted, "The President-elect seemed to observers to be a different and changed man when he came from the conference. . . . His face wore a grim and startled look as he confronted the horde of newspapermen."

Truman presented Eisenhower with three large volumes, prepared by the National Security Council, containing country-by-country summaries of United States policies abroad, an estimate of critical trouble spots, and plans for dealing with Communist attacks in potentially explosive areas. This was later followed by another book which dealt with the status of the various national security programs. Almost every agency had been requested to prepare similar projects and had been instructed by Truman that they were to be brief and "essentially informational," explaining but not urging adherence to existing policies. Finally, he arranged for his key assistant, John R. Steelman, to stay on until the new administration had settled in.

When a reporter inquired at a press conference in December whether Truman would ride to the Capitol with Eisenhower on inauguration day, the President promptly corrected him. On the way to the ceremony, the *President-elect* would ride with the *President*. Later, the *President* would return to the White House and a particular private citizen would take care of himself.

After twenty years of rule, the Democratic Party acquired a new elder statesman and the Republicans a national hero in the White House.

Dwight David Eisenhower

19. Hero in Politics

IN awarding the highest office in the land to Dwight David Eisenhower, the American people responded once again, as they had several times in the past, to the glamour of a military hero. Commander of a great fighting coalition which he led to stunning victory, Eisenhower achieved a popularity and prestige that brought to his door as early as 1947 politicians of both parties seeking a winning presidential candidate. Refusing all pleas, he explained that "politics is a profession; a serious, complicated and, in its true sense, a noble one. . . . I see no dearth of men fitted by training, talent and integrity for national leadership. On the other hand, nothing in the international or domestic situation especially qualifies for the most important office in the world a man whose adult years have been spent in the country's military forces. At least this is true in my case." Five years later, he yielded to Republican leaders who succeeded in persuading him that a military career was no handicap for presidential leadership.

Entering his country's armed forces, like so many other steps in Eisenhower's life, was unpremeditated. One summer when he was twenty and working in an Abilene, Kansas, creamery, a chance acquaintance who was preparing for Annapolis influenced him to apply also. Informed that he was overage, Eisenhower sent an application to West Point and was admitted. After graduation, he moved up steadily in the Army ranks, performing a variety of duties. During the first World War,

although eager to be sent overseas, he was assigned as commander of the Tank Training Center at Camp Colt. In succeeding years he studied at the General Staff School in Kansas,
the new Army War College in Washington, D.C., and served in
a number of posts, including the office of the Assistant Secretary of War. In 1933 he was assigned to the staff of General
Douglas MacArthur, who took him to the Philippines two
years later when he was sent there as military adviser. After
serving in the islands for four years, Eisenhower returned to
the states. He was a full colonel, chief of staff for the commander of the Third Army, when Pearl Harbor rocked the
nation.

Summoned to Washington as assistant chief of the War
Plans Division, Eisenhower worked under Chief of Staff General George C. Marshall. From that point his rise was spectacular. Marshall chose him to head the Allied Command, and then
the President appointed him Supreme Commander for the
cross-channel invasion. Actually, at Quebec, Roosevelt and
Churchill had decided on Marshall for the latter post, with
Eisenhower to replace him in Washington. But then the President came to feel that Marshall's services at home were indispensable and was persuaded that it was best "not to monkey
with a winning team."

When victory was won in Europe, Eisenhower was accorded
a popular acclaim experienced by few men. In Britain, in
France, in the United States, he was swept from one triumphal
procession to another, showered with tributes and accolades
from grateful governments and people. On his return home in
1945 he reached the apex of a professional Army career when
he was made Chief of Staff.

The pattern of Eisenhower's life had been an unbroken upward spiral. Some men passionately court fame; to some, a tiny
minority, it comes unbidden. Ike, born of an undistinguished
family on literally the wrong side of the tracks, was one of the
fortunate few. He never struggled or maneuvered for advancement. Each major step in his career was taken at someone's
suggestion or because he happened to be in the right place at
the right time. Although he possessed uncommon ability, his
own ambitions had always been modest. When he achieved the

rank of colonel at the age of fifty, he regarded it as the pinnacle of his expectations.

Eisenhower's most valuable characteristic was his great personal attractiveness. Self-confident but without arrogance, his manner genial and relaxed, he effortlessly drew individuals to him. The sincerity, assurance, and good will that he projected, the wide, infectious grin, drew the multitudes. Americans saw in him a leader who could carry on his broad shoulders the burdens of the nation. At the same time, he was "one of us," quickly becoming "Ike," an affectionate appellation that implied no diminution of respect.

Probably the greatest factor in molding Eisenhower's personality was the influence of his mother. An apparently indomitable woman who refused to be broken by financial disaster, she impressed for all time on her sons that inner despondency or distress must never be exposed to the world. The façade should always be optimistic and cheerful. Only Eisenhower's intimates were aware that he often suffered from serious tension, that the famed equanimity was at times more a studied pose than a true indication of his state of mind.

In 1948, Eisenhower retired from active duty to assume his first civilian post as president of Columbia University. His campus office quickly became the Mecca to which both Democrats and Republicans periodically made pilgrimages, beseeching him to be their party's candidate, to subordinate personal considerations to the higher duty. A Roper poll in June indicated that he was by far the preferred choice of voters of both parties.

He resisted all Republican efforts that summer, but, undeterred, some Democratic politicians, at their party gathering, started a "draft Eisenhower" movement which rapidly gained momentum. With virtually no clue to the general's position on domestic questions, a motley combination of Democrats toiled to dump Truman, who they were convinced would be defeated, and obtain Eisenhower's nomination. Included were the New Deal senator from Florida, Claude Pepper, the conservative Governor Tuck of Virginia, and "I am the law" Hague, machine boss of Jersey City. It took two strongly worded, unequivocal statements by Eisenhower to quash the drive to recruit him.

Four years later, the Republicans made another effort to draw Eisenhower into the race. In January, 1952, Senator Henry Cabot Lodge, returning from SHAPE headquarters in Paris where Eisenhower now served as commander of NATO forces, told reporters that the general's name would be entered in the New Hampshire primary. The following day, Eisenhower issued a formal statement which implied that he was at last succumbing to the persistent pressures. He confirmed Lodge's statement to the press that his political convictions were compatible with Republican Party views and pointed to his "Republican voting record."

While declaring that "under no circumstances" would he ask to be relieved of his NATO assignment to run for office, he went on to say that "there is no question of the right of American citizens to organize in pursuit of their common convictions." Senator Lodge and his associates, he continued, were exercising this right in endeavoring "to place before me next July a duty that would transcend my present responsibility." In the absence of any "clear-cut call to political duty," however, he would continue to devote all his time and energy to his assigned task. Two months later, he asked to be relieved of his command so that he could return home and enter the election campaign. An important factor in his decision was his concern that the Republican Party might retreat into isolationism.

A bitter primary battle ensued with the isolationist Senator Taft, dubbed "Mr. Republican" because of his pre-eminent leadership of the party. At the convention, however, Eisenhower won on the first ballot, though not without a prior struggle among the delegates. His triumph over Taft was clearly a victory for the internationalist wing of the party, and for all those who were confident that with a national hero as standard-bearer success at the polls was assured.

As the campaign progressed, some of Eisenhower's most fervent supporters became increasingly disillusioned with their candidate. To their dismay, the disinterested patriot summoned to save the nation was campaigning like any other politician bent on victory. Internationalists were disconcerted by the pact he made with Senator Taft resolving their differences, and by some of the isolationist overtones in his speeches obviously designed to appease the right-wingers in the party. Others were repelled by the way he played to different galleries. He told an audience in Michigan that he was a Vandenberg Republican, but the next day he declared in Illinois that if there must be war in the Far East, "let it be Asians against Asians." He implied that sounder policies might have prevented the United States from involvement in World Wars I and II as well as the Korean war.

Perhaps most disheartening was Eisenhower's capitulation to political expediency by tacitly endorsing Senators McCarthy and Jenner and failing to defend his admired friend, General George C. Marshall, from their coarse and malicious attacks. Privately he cordially detested both men, telling an aide after Jenner embraced him on the platform in Indianapolis, "I felt dirty from the touch of the man." He allowed himself to be persuaded by Wisconsin Republican leaders to delete a defense of Marshall from a major address he was to deliver in Milwaukee, although he himself had suggested its inclusion when the speech was being prepared. The omission became public knowledge, since it was made at the last moment after the prepared talk had been turned over to the press. With reference to McCarthy, he said that he differed from the senator only in the methods of eliminating Communists from government. Eisenhower's shining armor was tarnishing before the very eyes of some of his supporters, but to most of the nation its luster remained undimmed.

President Truman was completely disgusted with Eisenhower's political tactics, and the cordial relationship between the two men which originated when they first met at Potsdam began to disintegrate. Long after the smoke of political battle cleared away, the former President in characteristic fashion told the National Press Club, "I gave him hell when he didn't knock Jenner off the platform when he called General Marshall a traitor, and he's been mad at me ever since, and I don't give a damn." Truman was referring to a campaign rally when Eisenhower stood silently by while Jenner referred to Marshall as "a front man for traitors."

Although Adlai Stevenson was the Democratic standard-bearer, the campaign resolved into a debate between the Republican contender and Truman. Eisenhower hammered away at the vulnerable Korean issue, suggesting at one point that Koreans be trained to defend their front lines so that United Nations troops could be withdrawn. Truman replied that the general should know better, since in his military capacity he had been given confidential information by the Defense Department that without aid the Koreans were incapable of resisting the Communists, and if they were placed in the front lines, the Far East defense would be seriously weakened. Eisenhower attacked the Truman record, denouncing "trickery in government" and "the complete indifference apparently to dishonesty in government." Not only was it time to clean the Communists out of office, he declared, but the people who put them there. Truman charged that the Republican candidate was trying "to win votes by playing upon the casualties and sacrifices in Korea."

At the polls, Eisenhower won a spectacular victory, with all but nine states in the Republican column, a testimony to his personal appeal, for the Republicans barely squeaked through to gain the narrowest of majorities in Congress.

Shortly after the election Eisenhower fulfilled a dramatic campaign pledge, which had aroused wild enthusiasm, to go to Korea and personally investigate the stalemate. Once there, he stated at a press conference that unfortunately he had no magic formula or panacea for ending the war. That same day, at a meeting of the National Association of Manufacturers in New York, General MacArthur hinted that he had a solution. He refused to give details, intimating that basic decisions were involved which could not properly be mentioned in public discussion.

On his way home from Korea, Eisenhower invited MacArthur for a conference so that "my associates and I may obtain the full benefit of your thinking and experience." MacArthur responded with extreme cordiality. "You know, without my saying, that my service is, as it has always been, entirely at the disposal of our country. My best to you, Ike." Both messages were made public by Eisenhower's press secretary.

President Truman was naturally indignant. If anyone, he said, had a plan for terminating the war in Korea, it was his duty to present it at once to the properly constituted authorities, that is, to the chief executive. At his press conference the next day he expressed doubt that MacArthur had any kind of constructive proposal, recalling that he had once made a fourteen-thousand-mile journey to confer with the general and had only been given misinformation. The trip to Korea by the President-elect he characterized as a piece of demagoguery. Eisenhower made no public comment, but the friendship between the two men was shattered, not to be repaired until they met again at President Kennedy's funeral.

The new occupant of the White House, by his own evaluation, had no real preparation for the office. The professional soldier's career in the narrow and circumscribed world of the Army had excluded any concern with partisan politics and civilian government. Moreover, lacking intellectual interests— his recreational reading was confined to "westerns"—he possessed only a minimal knowledge of the presidency or of the theories of presidential leadership. The chief executives he most admired were Washington and Lincoln, whose singleness of purpose he considered their outstanding quality. Unlike Truman, also basically unidealogical and unintellectual but engrossed by every aspect of government, Eisenhower was to find the operational side of administration dull and tedious and be glad to delegate it to others.

Army training and experience had conditioned Eisenhower to the use of a staff system. While President Truman had institutionalized the presidency to some extent, he never achieved the administrative orderliness that characterized the Eisenhower administration. The White House staff and the executive office were enlarged to a combined personnel of about 2700. Under the Administrative Reform Act of 1939, six assistants were provided for the President; on Eisenhower's staff, in addition to his special assistant, were fifteen other assistants, two secretaries, three counsels, several special advisers, and an assorted number of people bearing such designations as assistant to the deputy assistant to the President. In addition, each assistant headed a staff of about ten. There were also the secretariats of the Cabinet and of the National Security Council and countless agency coordinators.

Responsibility was methodically delegated so that the proper individual could present to the chief the appropriate information or execute the appropriate action. At SHAEF and SHAPE Eisenhower's job had been to handle the major problems, make the big decisions, and leave the details to his subordinates, and he continued this procedure in the presidential office. As one White House aide described the system, "Nowhere did the lack of civilian experience so betray itself as in this system's cheerful assumption that, once the Chief Executive had pointed in a certain political direction, the full force of government would move in that direction, in concert as precise and as massive as battalions and divisions wheeling through field maneuvers." The President conducted his affairs systematically and efficiently. Weekly sessions were scheduled with Republican congressional leaders, with the National Security Council, and with the Cabinet.

Under Eisenhower's leadership, the Cabinet was elevated to a position of unique influence and importance. Here, too, his experience with the staff system was apparent, as well as his confidence in experts and specialists. At a meeting before his inauguration, the President-elect informed the newly appointed members, "No one of you, whether a Cabinet member or one who functions as such, is relieved of his part of the responsibility for making governmental policy. No major decision will be made by the National Security Council but what will be reviewed by the Cabinet and brought back to the NSC." Briefed regularly by Secretary of State John Foster Dulles on all major foreign policy problems, each member was expected to discuss any matter under consideration at the moment.

Cabinet meetings were as formal and organized as sessions of a large corporation's board of directors. One of Eisenhower's innovations was the post of Cabinet Secretary, whose responsibility was coordination. The Secretary worked with the Cabinet assistant in each department to prepare an agenda for the meetings. Items submitted to him for consideration were carefully sifted. A detailed agenda was then prepared which was transmitted to all Cabinet members together with a memorandum signed by the President describing the nature of the problems, proposing alternative courses of action, and suggesting the personnel to be assigned for further study of the matter.

For each item elaborate policy papers, often running to fifty or more pages, were prepared by the department concerned and circulated in advance. The views of each Cabinet member were recorded. On the day before the meeting, booklets containing information on each item slated for discussion were distributed to all Cabinet officers. The member scheduled to make the "presentation" was carefully rehearsed by the Secretary, sometimes going over the statement three or more times until he achieved perfect timing. After the meeting, the Secretary reviewed the decisions for the departmental assistants, who were then expected to make daily checks on implementation within their respective departments.

Undoubtedly this elaborate system was advantageous to Eisenhower by reducing the demands on his time. The public was also treated to an outward display of interdepartmental harmony and efficiency. While Cabinet officials had no cause to complain, as some did under other Presidents, that they were ignored on policy recommendations, they found the chief executive less accessible for private consultation, and the free exchange of views was inhibited.

A similar rigid formality was maintained at meetings of the National Security Council, created by Congress in 1947 at the recommendation of Secretary Forrestal to assist the President on foreign policy problems. Alternative policies were rarely discussed, since diverse views had already been carefully reconciled by the Council's planning board. The plenary sessions, though held regularly, were for the most part *pro forma*.

President Eisenhower generally leaned heavily on staff counsel and collective judgment, withholding authorization for a policy directive until differences of opinion had been resolved. If a conflict of views persisted, his solution was to appoint a presidential commission to study the problem and make further recommendations.

As a military leader, Eisenhower had been accustomed to the services of a chief of staff; when he became President, he appointed Sherman Adams, former governor of New Hampshire, to this position. Technically the Assistant to the President, Adams exercised more authority and influence than any previous presidential aide. As he later said, the President "never specifically defined my responsibilities or outlined their limits. He never gave me, nor did I ever seek, a delegation of presidential power and authority . . . [he] simply expected me to manage a staff that would boil down, simplify and expedite the urgent business that had to be brought to his personal attention and to keep as much work of secondary importance as possible off his desk." Nevertheless, Adams's zeal in relieving Eisenhower of all but the most consequential problems, and his chief's willingness to be so relieved, accomplished, as one competent observer put it, "one of the most thoroughgoing withdrawals from the duties of the presidency in the history of the office." Adams "made decisions and performed acts which Presidents, since the establishment of the Republic, have been given to doing themselves. Indeed, it is demonstrable that his power and impact upon the national destiny have exceeded that of not a few Presidents."

One of Adams's major functions, as buffer for the President, was performed with such efficiency that frequently even congressmen on important business were unable to get past the barrier of the reserved and taciturn New Englander. While the arrangement was a time-conserver for the President, it also insulated him from many sources of information that would have enabled him to gauge more accurately the temper of public opinion.

From the point of view of the Republican Party, Adams was probably most valuable as a convenient whipping boy for Eisenhower. His tremendous authority and his vulnerable position made him and not the President the target for hostile critics, enabling Eisenhower to maintain the image of a benign and magisterial figure "above the battle." This exalted state was a rare phenomenon for a chief executive.

Eisenhower never found the presidency the "splendid misery," as Thomas Jefferson characterized it, nor did he suffer from the depressing isolation that Wilson frequently experienced. He surrounded himself with a large coterie of unofficial advisers and a great many companions with whom he could relax at golf, fishing, or bridge. Closest to him was his younger brother, Milton, president of Pennsylvania State College when Eisenhower took office and later of the Johns Hopkins University. An Army plane took him nearly every week end to Washington, where he occupied an office suite in the old State Department building. His wide-ranging functions included such diverse tasks as polishing a draft for a presidential talk, preparing recommendations for the reorganization of an executive bureau, conducting a fact-finding or good-will mission to Latin America. In some ways he was more influential than Colonel House or Harry Hopkins had been. Other close advisers were Generals Alfred M. Gruenther and Walter Bedell Smith. The latter enjoyed a special status beyond his official post as Under Secretary of State. Even after he retired from public service, he could, through the ivory telephone in his business office, be put in instant communication with the President.

For recreational companions, the chief executive chose a group of men from big business and corporate finance with whom he became acquainted after he embarked on his political career. These included presidents or officers of corporations such as Chase Manhattan Bank, Coca-Cola, Continental Can, General Electric, Standard Oil, U.S. Steel. Representing powerful elements in the internationalist wing of the Republican Party, they had all backed Eisenhower's candidacy.

In his new career, the man who had spent forty years in the military service often gave the impression that he was irked by his heavy duties. Shortly after he took office, he remarked to a visiting French general that he found the presidency much more trying than his post as commander of the European defense forces. Perhaps because he lacked real zest for his job, he sometimes appeared to be totally unaware of an event that dominated the news of the day.

Background, temperament, and inclination combined to preclude that Eisenhower view the presidency as the center of political activity or relish the practical pursuits of the active political leader. His attitude that he was above politics led critics sarcastically to denominate him "a constitutional monarch." In the fall of 1953, a reporter asked whether Eisenhower

planned to participate in the congressional campaign the following year. He was deeply interested, he replied, in the make-
up of the Senate and House, but "I do not intend to make of
the presidency an agency to use in partisan elections . . .
anybody occupying this office is President of all the people"
and must develop a program of benefit to everyone. "What I
am trying to do with the party of which I am a part is to
establish a record that so nearly as possible a great overwhelming majority of Americans approve of it." And, he concluded, "I
have no intention of going out and getting into partisan strug-
gles in any district or in any State because I know that I, for
one, in such a State would resent that kind of intrusion from
the President of the United States."

In theory, the occupant of the White House is, of course,
"President of all the people," but the party is a vehicle through
which he can hope to exercise power. Moreover, he abdicates
national and moral leadership by excessive efforts not to offend
any section or group, as Eisenhower did on the issue of school
desegregation. When the Supreme Court directed in May, 1954,
that segregation in the nation's public schools must end, the
President carefully refrained from commenting on the merits of
the decision. Two years later, at a press conference, a reporter
asked whether he would amplify an earlier statement that his
endorsement of the Supreme Court's decision was not important, that the significant thing was its enforcement. "Look, I
put that in this way," Eisenhower replied. "We start out with
Article I of the Constitution, and we go on right down to the
end, including its amendments, and the Constitution as it is
interpreted by the Supreme Court. I am sworn to uphold it. I
don't ask myself whether every single phrase of that Constitution, with all its amendments, are exactly what I agree with or
not. I am sworn to uphold it, and that is what I intend to do."
He firmly refused to discuss the moral issues involved in desegregation.

During the crisis at Little Rock, Arkansas, in the late summer of 1957, the President was asked by reporters for his opinion on Governor Faubus's action in ordering state troops to
prevent Negro children from entering a public school. That
was a "broad subject that you are giving me," he replied. The

incident had come to his attention only that morning, and he had communicated with the Attorney General's office, which was "taking a look at it." He could not comment further because he knew nothing else about the matter, but he did add that "time and again a number of people—I, among them—have argued that you cannot change people's hearts merely by laws. Laws presumably express the conscience of a nation and its determination or will to do something. But the laws here are to be executed gradually, according to the dictum of the Supreme Court." He understood that a ten-year plan had been worked out by the school board of Little Rock and approved by the district judge. "Now there seems to have been a roadblock thrown in the way of that plan and the next decision will have to be by the lawyers and jurists."

Another correspondent inquired whether he planned to intervene personally by making an address or communicating with Faubus. "My speaking will be always on this subject, as I have always done," he answered, "urging Americans to recognize what America is, the concepts on which it is based, and to do their part so far as they possibly can, to bring about the kind of America that was visualized by our forebears." It was a slow process, he continued, and there were "very strong emotions on the other side, people that see a picture of mongrelization of the race as they call it."

These vague, flaccid generalizations were scarcely calculated to deter a Faubus, particularly when the President had stated firmly at a press conference in July that he could not imagine "any set of circumstances that would ever induce me to send federal troops . . . into any area to enforce the orders of a federal court," that he would "never believe that it would be a wise thing to do." After a federal court, on September 10, was petitioned to enjoin the governor, Faubus requested and was granted a conference with the President, who was vacationing at Newport, Rhode Island. No accord was reached, and with Faubus encouraging mob action by his stand, the federal law was defied. The President now had no alternative but to exercise his executive authority, federalize the Arkansas National Guard, and send troops into the city.

Early and decisive action by Eisenhower might have prevented the situation from getting out of hand. If his personal feelings on desegregation prevented him from discussing the moral issue, it still was his constitutional obligation to compel obedience to the law. Instead he talked blandly and ineffectually about the difficulties arising from the ancient conflict between law and custom. Moreover, he was derelict in his obligation as an international leader, for the affair at Little Rock provided the Soviets with an ideal subject for exploitation. They trumpeted across Asia and Africa the debasing details of how the nation that proclaimed its devotion to equality treated its Negro citizens.

In another area, that of chief legislator, Eisenhower's leadership lacked force, and again, because of his outlook. Influenced by the Republican Party's views on governmental aggrandizement during the twenty years of Democratic incumbency, Eisenhower exemplified a "Whig" concept of executive-legislative relations. Roosevelt and Truman, he believed, had upset the proper equilibrium between the two branches of government which he would restore by diminishing the authority of the White House. "I am not one of the desk-pounding types that likes to stick out his jaw and look like he is bossing the show," he once commented. Ignoring the factor of inherent conflict between President and Congress, he felt that personal relationships could overcome institutional barriers. As one of his friends summed up his attitude, "Mr. Eisenhower holds firmly to his constitutional concept that the Chief Executive should not dominate the legislative branch. He believes in separation of powers. He would not bludgeon Congress even if he could because he thinks it important to preserve a balance of powers."

Although the President met regularly with congressional party leaders, he pressed for his own legislative program only sporadically. By failing to exert himself at critical moments, he frustrated the moderate Republicans who looked to the White House for support. His employment of patronage was so inadequate that it was of little value as a White House weapon. Some months after he had left office, he was asked if he had ever put pressure on Congress by threatening to withhold patronage. "No, never," he replied. "I took very seriously the mat-

ter of appointments and qualifications. . . . Possibly I was not as
shrewd and as clever in this matter as some of the others, but I
never thought that any of these appointments should be used
for bringing pressure upon the Congress." While this sounds
laudable, in the American governmental system it represents a
renunciation of power resulting in the failure of the President
to realize his legislative objectives.

Eisenhower regarded himself as a moderate who would use
his talent for conciliation and compromise that had served him
so effectively at SHAEF and NATO, to bring order and harmony to a country torn by the partisan strife of previous administrations. Reasonable men, he was confident, were able to
compromise, and he would be willing to meet anyone half way.
"I, as you know, never employ threats," he said at a press conference after four years in office. "I never try to hold up clubs
of any kind. I just say, 'This is what I believe to be best for the
United States,' and I try to convince people by the logic of
my position. If that is wrong politically, well then, I suppose
you will just have to say I am wrong." Domestically, his intention was to steer a middle course and accomodate all views
within his party. In his opinion, the federal government should
step in only when the states, local communities, or individuals
proved completely inadequate to handle any particular situation. With regard to foreign affairs, his purpose was to keep to
the established course of internationalism and collective security, avoiding the extremes of reckless adventures or timid
withdrawals.

The President's passive approach toward Congress was reflected in his press conferences. Unlike other chief executives,
he failed to use them to influence the legislative body. Characteristically, the weekly interview was preceded by elaborate
preparations and painstaking care to make it as efficient as a
Cabinet session. Several hours before the reporters arrived,
Sherman Adams assembled key members of the White House
staff who were presented by press secretary James Hagerty
with a list of possible questions to which they were expected to
supply the most effective answers. When the President arrived
at his office about a half hour before the scheduled conference,
he found on his desk reports from the State Department, the

CIA, and Military Intelligence. A dress rehearsal was then conducted by Hagerty, who threw out a number of questions likely to be put to the President to which a knowledgeable staff member supplied an answer.

Televising meetings with the press originated during the Eisenhower administration, but the conferences were filmed and edited before being released. A relatively free exchange of questions and answers was thereby possible, as any injudicious statements could be deleted. "The White House must have control over the spoken word of the President," Hagerty said. "There are too many unpredictable consequences that can flow from the slightest off-hand remark."

Eisenhower enjoyed a friendly relationship with the press for a longer period than any of his predecessors. With memories of his cordiality and helpfulness during the war, and almost in awe of the sacrosanct image that had developed, reporters treated him with silk gloves even on "hot" questions like the McCarthy issue or the internal security policy of the federal government. This honeymoon with members of the fourth estate lasted until about the fall of 1957, when the country's mood began to change as a result of Sputnik. The Russian achievement was a shattering blow to national pride, jolting American complacency about economic growth, power, and prestige. Reflecting this atmosphere, the reporters' questions became sharper and more critical. In turn, Eisenhower showed less patience, and at times was unable to conceal his annoyance or irritation.

Toward the end of his second administration, press interviews became sporadic. To a newsman who asked the President on what basis he decided to hold one, he replied, "I suppose that there is some little bit of whim that comes in there once in a while. But, in fact, I don't try to be talking all the time. . . . One week I make a speech on Monday, I said about all on the subject then that seemed to be engaging the headlines that I could think of, and there seemed to be very little reason for a press conference. . . . Whenever the day seems to be free and I can do it, well, frankly, I enjoy many of them, you know. And so it is not any running out on the thing; it's just, as I say, how it happens to strike me, I guess." On the whole, the

President had little cause for complaint about his treatment by the press. The barbs were directed at members of the Cabinet or White House staff, while he remained inviolate.

The nation, apparently content that their President merely touch the helm lightly, nevertheless required the assurance that he was at the helm. In recognition of this need, and to convey an image of their chief actively in charge of the command post, elaborate arrangements were made to reassure the public that Eisenhower was still capable of handling routine matters of state when he suffered a heart attack in the fall of 1955. Profiting from the lesson of history, his staff did not make the disastrous mistake of keeping the country in the dark as had occurred during President Wilson's incapacity. Every twinge the President experienced was reported to the press. Hagerty issued bulletins three times a day, meticulously detailing his progress—when he first sat up in bed, his first steps, et cetera, et cetera. Throughout his first and subsequent illnesses, Eisenhower lived in a constant white glare of publicity.

Not a single moving part creaked in the well-oiled White House machine during the period that Eisenhower was incapable of performing his duties. After he received news of the President's attack, Vice President Nixon promptly called a Cabinet meeting, addressing the members on the subject of running the government in the chief executive's absence. Routine business, he said, should not be permitted to accumulate. Departments and agencies would carry on as usual, with important matters channeled through the Cabinet or the National Security Council, which would continue to meet and review policies. Cabinet members were admonished to thrash out any interdepartmental issues among themselves and avoid giving the public even the slightest impression of discord. Aware that the President's illness might have political repercussions, he instructed that questions likely to be raised regarding the possible effect on Republican Party prospects should be dismissed as unworthy when the entire nation was concerned about the recovery of its chief.

A statement was released to the press that, following a full discussion by the Cabinet, "it was concluded that there are no obstacles to the orderly and uninterrupted conduct of the foreign and domestic affairs of the nation during the period of rest ordered by the President's physicians." Sherman Adams would present any essential matters to the President. As the policies and programs of Mr. Eisenhower were well known, they could be continued by the governmental departments "within the framework of these policies" so that "the functions of the government will be carried forward in an effective manner" during the President's absence.

The emphasis was on business as usual. As soon as Eisenhower was convalescent, a steady stream of officials began to pour into his hospital room, each visit carefully reported in the newspapers. Statements were issued from the bedside about instructions by the President to specific individuals or about government business discussed with his visitor. By this careful staging, an impression was created for the public that the head of state was in complete control. Actually, of course, Eisenhower was taking only a minimal part in the conduct of domestic and foreign policies. For a time, in fact, he was not even permitted to read the newspapers.

When Eisenhower resumed his duties, the appeals to declare his availability for a second term, which had begun before his illness, multiplied. While the Republicans were divided on foreign affairs, they were united in the conviction that only Ike could insure victory at the polls. At a Cabinet meeting on February 13, 1956, Eisenhower, Sherman Adams relates, "complained that he was finding himself in a position that he had hoped would never occur," that people seemed to think "he was the only man who could do the job as President." Eisenhower recalled that in 1953, he had wanted to insert in his inaugural address a statement of intention to serve for only one term, and regretted having been dissuaded by his advisers from doing so. According to Adams, the President went on to say that his administration had achieved a good record, "implying that he had done his share of work." Reluctantly, however, he yielded to the insistent pressure of party leaders that he continue in office.

On February 29, in a radio and television address, President Eisenhower announced his candidacy for a second term. While he assured his listeners that "there is not the slightest doubt that

I can now perform as well as I ever have all of the important duties of the presidency," he reminded them that as a recovered heart patient he would be obliged to eliminate many of the ceremonial and social duties.

On basic issues, little distinguished one party platform from the other in 1956, but Eisenhower and his opponent, Adlai Stevenson, presented a striking contrast in personality and philosophy. With the country prosperous and at peace, the electorate was little interested in the issues raised by the campaign orators. As in the previous election, the dominant note was President Eisenhower's tremendous popularity, against which the Democratic contender vainly pitted his eloquently phrased, often brilliant speeches. Once again, Eisenhower won an overwhelming victory, and again it was entirely personal. He ran seven million votes ahead of his party, and the Republicans were still unable to gain control of either House of Congress. The fact remained, as the newspaper columnist Joseph Alsop observed after the 1952 election, that "while Stevenson was appealing and appealing strongly to the people's minds, Eisenhower, as a man and as a figure, was appealing far more strongly to far more peoples' emotions." Eisenhower's image as a wise and judicious leader on whom both the nation and the rest of the world could rely was enduring.

Dwight David Eisenhower

---

20. Policy by Slogans

FEW Presidents have faced as grave and complex an international situation as Dwight D. Eisenhower when he took office in 1953. The balance in the deadly world-wide rivalry with the Soviet Union was precarious, and, with both powers in possession of unprecedented means of destruction, a clash was too terrifying to contemplate. At the same time, if fear were allowed to paralyze action, the Russians would take full advantage, creating an intolerable situation for the United States. In Korea a war of attrition was dragging on with apparently no prospect for a decisive and satisfactory settlement.

During the election campaign, the Republicans had charged that the Democrats' "appeasement" of the Russians encouraged the expansion of communism throughout the world, that their "tragic blunders" in diplomacy had undermined national security. With a new party in power, with new faces in Washington, and above all, with a President and his advisers untarnished by any association with the foreign policies of the previous two decades, the past would be repudiated, errors corrected, and new measures undertaken. The policy of containment, which Secretary of State John Foster Dulles characterized as "negative, futile and immoral," must be replaced by a positive course of action. It was not enough merely to hold the tide in check; dynamic policies were required to roll it back. A psychological and political offensive must be waged, a policy of "liberation" that would encourage the captive countries behind the iron curtain. Merely by making it "publicly known" that the United States "wants and expects liberation to occur," the mood of the subjugated peoples would change "in an electrifying way."

While Dulles believed that at Yalta the United States had surrendered the "great moral principles" upon which the nation was founded, neither he nor Eisenhower shared the obsession of those extreme conservative and nationalist Republicans who were convinced that all the world's ills were due to Democratic sell-outs at the wartime conferences. Resolved, however, not to expose himself to the kind of attacks leveled at Secretary of State Acheson, Dulles set out to mollify the right-wing contingent with the statements they were yearning to hear.

The foreign policy plank of the Republican platform which Dulles drew up pledged repudiation of "secret understandings such as those of Yalta." President Eisenhower, in his first State of the Union message, also referred to the subject. "We shall never acquiesce in the enslavement of any people," he promised. "I shall ask the Congress . . . to join in an appropriate resolution making clear that this government recognizes no kind of commitment contained in secret understandings of the past . . . which would permit this kind of enslavement." But when the President and his Secretary were preparing the resolution, they realized that concessions to the right wing of their party could not be made without taking into account vital national and international considerations. For one thing, repudiation of wartime agreements was a two-edged sword that could be turned against American interests. Secondly, the Democrats made it plain that they would not support any direct or implied denunciation of Franklin D. Roosevelt, and without comprehensive bipartisan endorsement the statement would have little effect abroad.

The resolution presented to the Senate therefore omitted specific reference to Yalta. It denounced "any interpretations or applications" of agreements that had been "perverted to bring about the subjugation of free peoples" by Soviet depotism, thus making Stalin, not Roosevelt, the villain. The resolution also modified a strong declaration made by Dulles in a telecast on January 3 that the subjugated peoples "could depend on United States' assistance" to regain their freedom, Eisenhower having inserted a statement precluding the use of force. Bitterly disappointed at the moderate tone of the resolution when a sweeping indictment of Roosevelt's and Truman's agreements had been expected, the Republicans refused to accept it. Senator Robert Taft, through an amendment which had the approval of the Foreign Relations Committee, stipulated that the resolution did not reflect the judgment of Congress as to the "validity or invalidity" of the wartime agreement. As this was an obvious slap at Roosevelt, the Democratic Policy Committee voted it down. A partisan fight began to brew, but Stalin's death on March 5 led the President to ask the Republican leaders to drop the whole matter, and the resolution was quietly entombed.

Eisenhower had been quickly disabused of his hope that he would be able to keep the conservatives in his party under control. As time went on they became more, not less, recalcitrant. The first challenge he faced was over his nomination of Charles E. Bohlen as ambassador to the Soviet Union. An acknowledged expert on Soviet affairs, present at most of the war and postwar conferences with the Russians, Bohlen was endorsed by a group of distinguished Foreign Service officers. But to Senator McCarthy and his supporters, who were incessantly snarling that the Democratic era represented "twenty years of treason," Bohlen's loyal service to Roosevelt and Truman made him a "security risk," and he was denounced as "Acheson's architect of disaster." When Bohlen appeared before the Senate Foreign Relations Committee on March 2, he was closely questioned especially about the Yalta Conference. He firmly denied that the agreements represented a sell-out or that the American delegation had been influenced by Alger Hiss. But as several senators still opposed his appointment, the vote was postponed.

Secretary Dulles informed the committee, when it reconvened on March 18, that he personally had examined the FBI report on Bohlen and had not found anything in it that was incriminating. The committee unanimously recommended confirmation, but on the Senate floor, two days later, Senators McCarthy and McCarran loosed a barrage of accusations. They charged that Scott McLeod, State Department security chief, had urged Bohlen's rejection but was overruled by Dulles. When the Secretary denied this, McCarthy accused him of lying, demanding that he be brought before the Senate Foreign Relations Committee to testify under oath. Furthermore, blustered the senator, *he* knew what was in the FBI file, and calling Bohlen a security risk was "putting it too weak."

The country was then treated to the unseemly spectacle of a President apparently cowed by the absurd and malicious rantings of two senators, for Eisenhower uttered not a word in defense of his candidate. Senator Taft, who had not participated in the controversy, now stepped in. Although Bohlen would not have been his choice, he said, the President was entitled to his own selection in the absence of any valid reason for opposing it. Furthermore, the senators—with their irresponsible charges, their demands for lie detector tests—were bringing the Republican administration into disrepute. As a compromise solution, he arranged for himself and Senator Sparkman to inspect the FBI files. The charges proved to be complete fabrications, but only after Taft confirmed this did Eisenhower issue a statement to the press supporting Bohlen.

Fear of alienating a segment of his party in Congress had kept the President silent, permitting a gross affront to the dignity of his office and an unwarranted challenge to the executive's prerogative in the conduct of foreign policy. It also moved him and Dulles to shut their eyes to the ill-concealed collusion between the Secretary's subordinate, Security Chief Scott McLeod, and the Wisconsin senator. Bohlen's nomination was overwhelmingly approved on March 27, but for the President it was a pyrrhic victory. Taft warned him that there must be "no more Bohlens," and it was plain that, having been rescued by the senator from Ohio, Eisenhower would have to be especially careful in the future about appointments that might antagonize the right-wing Republicans.

McCarthy was soon back on his charger riding full tilt against executive authority. The day following Senate confirmation of Bohlen, he smugly announced that in an area where the administration had dismally failed he had struck a telling blow by negotiating an agreement with the Greek owners of several hundred vessels to cease trading with Red China. Since the outbreak of the Korean conflict, the State Department had been trying to persuade some nations, receiving American aid and supporting the United Nations effort, to forbid shipments to Communist China. The trade, of no military value, was steadily declining and neither the Truman nor the Eisenhower administration considered it significant enough to risk alienating friends by applying undue pressure.

This time Harold Stassen, head of the Mutual Security Agency, intervened. He promptly issued a statement to the press charging that McCarthy's methods were "irregular" and his claims "phony." Called before the senator's Committee on Government Operations, he repeated his accusations, adding that McCarthy was undermining American foreign policy. A feud began to brew but once again was averted by appeasement. McCarthy's ruffled feathers were smoothed down by Vice President Nixon's mediation. After a conference between the senator and Secretary Dulles, the two men issued a joint statement. The latter expressed his thanks for the senator's assistance, which, he said, was in the best interests of the government; the former, disavowing any intent to interfere with matters that lay within the executive's jurisdiction, promised that in the future he would take information on this subject to the appropriate authorities.

The President carefully remained uninvolved. At his press conference shortly thereafter, he refused to be drawn into criticism of the Wisconsin senator and entangled the issue in a skein of dense ambiguities. When a reporter asked him if he considered it in the national interest for a congressional committee to conduct negotiations with foreign ship owners to obtain an embargo on trading with Communist countries, he said, "Personally, I don't believe they can possibly have the facts that would make such negotiations really profitable . . . [unless] they might have some personal contact that might work out for the good of the United States. You know, there is an aphorism: 'There is no never.' Well, I am not going to say there never could be any good come out of such things. I should say, on the average, now, I would doubt it."

To another reporter who inquired whether an earlier comment by the President implied disagreement with Harold Stassen's accusation that Senator McCarthy's actions undermined the prestige of the government, he replied that he thought Stassen had intended to use the word infringe rather than undermine since "to undermine required a lot more doing than merely making an error, no matter how badly [sic] I might consider the error to be." According to Senator McCarthy's own statements, the President explained, he had no idea he was engaged in negotiating anything, and as long as he was not negotiating he was probably within proper bounds. "He can discuss, suggest, advise—and that's all right; but negotiating is something else."

Many Americans were shocked at the blatant attempt by a senator to usurp executive power, but even more so by the irresolute response of the head of state. It was incomprehensible that the President should not censure the man whose outrageous behavior was lowering the nation's moral tone, making the government appear ludicrous in the eyes of the world, and debasing the prestige of the chief executive in his conduct of foreign policy. McCarthy, unchastened by any authoritative voice, attempted during the following weeks, although unsuccessfully, to conclude an agreement with Greek ship owners in London. Blaming Stassen for his failure, he demanded that the administration put pressure on England, writing directly to the President for a statement of his position. Once more Nixon hastily intervened, persuading McCarthy to retrieve the offensive letter, which lay at the White House for two days officially "unreceived."

The President's distaste for the unsavory McCarthy, his refusal to "get into the gutter with that guy," as he is reported to have said, might be commendable in a private citizen. In the case of the head of state to whom the nation looked for guidance, remaining aloof under the circumstances was a dereliction of duty. He not only left the people floundering in a morass of lies and half truths that created a miasma of suspicion and fear, but his silence encouraged the senator to become increasingly abusive and meddlesome to the serious detriment of United States prestige abroad.

In February, 1953, McCarthy dug his claws into the International Information Administration, accusing the agency of circulating Communist propaganda. What followed during the next few months was painfully farcical and shocking in a democratic state. The agency was thrown into a turmoil, with a plethora of policy directives raining down on intimidated employees, resignations, suspensions, mass firings. McCarthy, who was conducting the investigation, made himself unavailable to Robert L. Johnson, head of the administration, while allowing his arrogant, intemperate aides to run rampant. It required weeks of delicate negotiations and the assistance of the columnist, George Sokolsky, for Johnson finally to obtain a meeting with the senator.

Meanwhile, an abject State Department issued a directive concerning books that were to be eliminated from overseas libraries and information centers. When security officers and then McCarthy added their own lists, the bewildered librarians, to play it safe, practically emptied their shelves. Europeans were aghast, and many courageous Americans denounced this "book burning" so shamefully reminiscent of Nazi tactics. The President was at last moved to break his silence. At the Dartmouth College commencement address on June 14, 1953, he urged his listeners not to "join the book burners. . . . Don't be afraid to go in your library and read every book, as long as that document does not offend our own ideas of decency. That should be the only censorship." At a press conference three days later, however, he retreated, at the same time revealing his own confused thinking. Asked whether he had directed his remarks against Senator McCarthy, he replied, "I never talk personalities," and went on to assert that when he discussed free access to knowledge, he did not refer to "any document . . . that attempts to persuade or propagandize America into communism." But a little later on, he said, "I just do not believe in suppressing ideas. I believe in dragging them out in the open and taking a look at them." Most unseemly were his concluding remarks: "And let no one try to think that I am attempting to propagate Communist beliefs by using governmental money to do it." The President of the United States found it necessary to reassure his nation that he was not supporting communism!

During this period, and for an entire year, the President had to cope with a serious challenge to executive authority from his own congressional leadership. This time he met it with force and determination. An amendment to the Constitution was proposed which would restrict the chief executive in the conduct of foreign affairs by tightening congressional control over treaties and limit his authority to make executive agreements with other nations. First introduced by Senator John W. Bricker of Ohio in September, 1951, it was an expression of intense disapprobation of Roosevelt's and Truman's personal diplomacy, of the conviction that agreements made at the various wartime conferences were responsible for the cold war.

Presented again on January 7, 1953, the Bricker Amendment was promptly endorsed by sixty-two senators of both parties. Despite the elimination of some curbs, Dulles informed the President that it would seriously attenuate the executive's authority and reduce the flexibility he required in diplomatic relations. This version provided that a treaty conflicting with the Constitution would be invalid, that it could become law only after passage of federal or state enabling legislation "which would be valid in the absence of a treaty," and that Congress would have power to "regulate" executive agreements. The "which clause," as it came to be called, would have had the effect of turning the clock back to the days of the Articles of Confederation, when the states could frustrate the central government.

For months the President and his advisers struggled to reach a compromise. At one point, Eisenhower completely lost patience. He was reported to have burst out at a Cabinet meeting, "I'm so sick of this I could scream. The whole damn thing is senseless and plain damaging to the prestige of the United States. We talk about the French not being able to govern themselves—and *we* sit here wrestling with a *Bricker* Amendment." Nevertheless, several months later the President informed a press conference that he would support the amendment if it were modified to provide that a treaty or agreement conflicting with the Constitution would be void. Senate Majority Leader William Knowland came up with a compromise proposal that was acceptable to the administration. Bricker, however, found it unacceptable.

The altercation went on and on while proponents of the amendment were abetted by the unreconstructed isolationist *Chicago Tribune,* the Daughters of the American Revolution, and the American Medical Association. One group, the Vigilant Women for the Bricker Amendment, describing itself as "a volunteer organization of housewives and mothers of boys overseas," bombarded Congress with petitions containing an estimated half million signatures.

Eisenhower refused to be swayed. The basic issue as he saw it was the nation's willingness to accept world leadership, with the Bricker Amendment being used by its supporters as a cloak for their reluctance to assume this responsibility. On January 25, 1954, he wrote to Senator Knowland that he was "unalterably opposed" to the suggested law as it would so restrict the conduct of foreign affairs that the country "could not negotiate the agreements necessary for the handling of our business with the rest of the world." Moreover, the President "must not be deprived of his historic position as the spokesman for the nation in its relations with other countries." And, he warned, the amendment "would be notice to our friends as well as our enemies abroad that our country intends to withdraw from its leadership in world affairs. . . . It would impair our hopes and plans for peace."

Advocates of the proposal were not deterred, and the extremists among them abandoned rationality while they hunted bogeys. Senator Jenner, for example, linked the opposition to the Communist conspiracy.

In February the President, meeting with congressional leaders, reaffirmed his opposition to any plan which would destroy the traditional balance between the executive and legislative branches. It was ironical, he told them, that while the Republicans for two decades had been accusing the Democrats of unconstitutional actions, now that they controlled the government they were attempting to alter the traditional constitutional pattern in foreign policy. Did they not recognize the profound implications of the proposed legislation?

The Senate defeated the proposal, but the following day another amendment, sponsored by Democratic Senator Walter George of Georgia, was submitted. While more moderate than Bricker's, it was equally unacceptable to the White House. It failed of adoption by only one vote short of the requisite two-thirds, although Knowland deserted the administration, arguing that he could not ignore "a dangerous tendency towards executive encroachment on legislative powers." By standing firm, Eisenhower won this battle, but only by the narrowest possible margin. His supporters, who hoped he would continue to resist the conservatives in his party, were to be disappointed. Setting Republican unity above bipartisanship in foreign policy, Eisenhower ignored the efforts of the extremists to stigmatize the Democrats as having been the party of treason. To appease the Knowlands and the Bridgeses, he cooperated with Congressional investigations that undermined morale in the State Department and supported Dulles in eliminating many able diplomats. The investigations demoralized the country and scandalized the world.

In an area where the President's military background gave him an undisputed competence, he was less wary of treading on sensitive party toes, although his approach was always judicious, even deferential. Early termination of the Korean war, to which he had committed himself while campaigning, occupied top priority on his agenda. Thousands of American soldiers had been killed and wounded, thousands were moldering in enemy prison camps, and additional thousands remained exiled on that distant peninsula while the truce negotiations hobbled painfully on. Exasperation was turning to anger among large segments of the American public.

The "Asia first" contingent in Congress, which included not only McCarthy and Jenner but Taft and Knowland, were still demanding that the United States cease "coddling" China. The President considered their approach completely unfeasible. It would, he said, not only mean total mobilization, which was seldom mentioned by those eager for total war against Red China, but would leave the United States fighting by itself. He disagreed with Senator Taft, who said that if the stalemate in negotiations continued the nation should "go it alone," declaring emphatically that he had no intention of abandoning the system of collective security to which the country was committed. "If you are going to go it alone one place," he said, "you . . . have to go it alone everywhere. . . . No single free nation can live alone in the world. We have got to have friends. Those friends have got to be tied to you, in some form or another."

A truce would be sought along the same lines President Truman had tried to obtain: to settle for approximately the pre-1950 boundary dividing North and South Korea. The problem was to exert enough pressure to impel Red China to negotiate but not so much as to inflame her into an all-out battle. Psychological tactics were employed first. Eisenhower announced in his State of the Union message on February 2, 1953, that the Seventh Fleet would no longer "be employed to shield Communist China." While "unleashing Chiang" appeared to have little practical significance, as the forces on Formosa were not likely to launch an offensive against the mainland without American support, the Communist flank was exposed to potential attack. A series of military movements followed, which might indicate the likelihood of a renewed offensive in Korea. Heavy bombers presumably carrying atomic bombs were sent up to Okinawa, improved jets were dispatched to Air Force units in Korea, and weapons, supplies, and manpower were poured in.

In yet another effort to force the issue, Secretary Dulles while visiting India in May informed Prime Minister Nehru that the United States was determined to end the war quickly, by negotiation if possible, by a resumption of the fighting if necessary, with the possible use of tactical atomic weapons. As Nehru had been acting as a middleman, Dulles knew the warning would reach Peiping promptly. Then a final offer backed by a strong public statement from Eisenhower was made on May 25. Shortly thereafter, the Communists agreed to resume truce talks.

The United States had pulled itself out of one bog only to plunge almost immediately into another. President Syngman Rhee, adamant against any peace that would leave Korea divided, announced that he would continue fighting the Communists regardless of any negotiated peace. He seemed unable to comprehend that his major ally and protector would not hazard a possible world war for the unification of his country. "We do not intend to employ war as an instrument to accomplish the world-wide political settlements which we believe to be just," Eisenhower wrote to him, adding that a falling out between their two countries "at this critical hour would be a tragedy."

Negotiations with the Communists continued, and agreement was at last reached on the major stumbling block, repatriation of prisoners. Eisenhower, like Truman before him, insisted that no prisoner be compelled against his will to go back to his native land. Only a few minor matters remained to be settled when Syngman Rhee, in a desperate attempt to stop the truce talks, released 27,000 prisoners of war who allegedly did not want to return home. For a while it appeared that the armistice was off, with the Chinese and North Koreans accusing the United Nations of bad faith. Eisenhower, however, firmly repudiated Rhee's action, and the talks were resumed. Assistant Secretary of State Walter Robertson flew to Korea, where he managed to reassure Rhee that his country would not be left without support when a truce was concluded.

Finally, on July 27, 1953, more than three years after the beginning of the "police action," the armistice was signed. Later on, a "political conference of a higher level" presumably would settle such basic questions as withdrawal of troops and unification of the country, but it never met, as agreement could not be reached on its composition. From the other participants in the United Nations operation, Secretary Dulles secured a pledge to resist at once any violation of the armistice, and he warned the Communists that "in all probability a resumption of hostilities could not be limited to the confines of Korea." Eisenhower had fulfilled his campaign pledge and ended the war, for which the majority of Americans were devoutly grateful. Only the political right denounced it as a peace without honor.

While a settlement was being achieved in Korea, an eruption occurred in Europe which demonstrated to many Americans and to even a greater number of Europeans that Secretary Dulles's bold new policy of liberation was more a slogan than a policy, "a case of excessive salesmanship," in the words of Walter Lippmann. In June, 1953, the workers of East Berlin and East Germany rose in revolt against their Communist government, battling fiercely for days until they were ruthlessly quelled. Neither the administration nor the American people were prepared to risk war by sending in troops to help the embattled Germans attain their freedom. Barring military aid, little could be done in a practical way beyond the offer of food. Congress issued the helpful declaration that the courage displayed would inspire and assist the cause of freedom elsewhere in Eastern Europe. The United States was equally ineffectual three years later when the Hungarians attempted liberation from Russian control. While Budapest burned and Hungarians were being crushed beneath Soviet tanks, America stood by helplessly offering expressions of sympathy. Congress voted an appropriation for relief to refugees.

At a press conference shortly thereafter, a reporter asked Eisenhower to comment on a statement by Vice President Nixon that the uprisings proved the correctness of the "liberation position." His reply underscored the hollowness of the policy. We never asked, said he, "for a people to rise against a ruthless military force. . . . What I do say is the policy is correct in that we simply insist upon the right of all peoples to be free to live under governments of their own choosing." While Europeans had never been urged to revolt, the official Voice of America with its ceaseless talk of liberation and freedom undoubtedly encouraged the peoples behind the iron curtain to believe they would be supported in an uprising.

Like the meaningless policy of liberation, the doctrine and slogan of "massive retaliation" was announced by the Eisenhower administration as part of a "new look" in foreign policy. In his State of the Union message in January, 1954, the President mentioned the need for "a massive capability to strike back," but it was Dulles's address before the Council on Foreign Relations several days later that outlined the policy. Local defenses in many areas, he said, were inadequate against aggressors who could strike without warning, and therefore these defenses "must be reinforced by the further deterrent of massive retaliatory power." America's shield would be its "capacity

to retaliate, instantly, by means and at places of our choosing."
Under this new strategy, according to the Secretary, the
United States would no longer risk exhaustion in wars of attrition fought in peripheral areas, nor would the size of conventional forces be permitted to dangerously drain the treasury.
By threatening nuclear annihilation, the United States would
prevent trouble at its source. Designed to intimidate Moscow
and Peiping, the policy caused scarcely a ripple in either capital. Communist officials were certain that the United States
would not launch a nuclear war except in defense of its most
vital interests, and many in the West were equally skeptical.
The *Manchester Guardian* commented that the "new look" was
"mainly old merchandise in a new package," that there was
nothing new about it "except the sales campaign by which the
Administration is trying to persuade the American people that
some small changes make the strategy of 1954 fundamentally
sounder than the strategy of 1953."

That "massive retaliation" represented no fundamental
change in behavior became apparent during the war in Indochina, which reached a critical stage in 1954 after seven years
of bitter fighting. The stubborn refusal of the French to grant
independence to Vietnam, Laos, and Cambodia had fanned the
smoldering embers of nationalism into a fierce blaze. The situation encouraged the exploitation of legitimate discontent by
native Communists assisted by Red China. Recognizing the
threat to American strategic interests in Southeast Asia, the
Truman administration had assisted France so generously that
by 1952 the United States was bearing more than a third of the
cost of the struggle. Eisenhower and Dulles increased the aid
substantially, but the Communists continued to advance.

In March, 1954, the Vietminh troops surrounded the French
forces in the strategic fortress of Dienbienphu, presenting
Eisenhower with the choice of permitting a Communist victory, or direct intervention. That day at a news conference, the
President declared that the defense of Indochina was of tran-
scendent importance," comparing it to the first in a row of
dominoes whose fall would bring down all the others. Four
days later, Dulles stated that "the imposition on Southeast Asia
of the political system of Communist Russia and its Chinese

Communist ally, by whatever means, would be a grave threat to the whole free community. The United States feels that that possibility should not be passively accepted, but should be met by united action." Serious risks might be involved, he went on, but they would be "far less than would face us a few years from now if we dare not be resolute today."

Yet, when the French pleaded that the United States send planes from aircraft carriers to strike against the Communist besiegers as the only way to avert catastrophe, the President understandably backed away. Although Admiral Arthur W. Radford, chairman of the Joint Chiefs of Staff, and Secretary Dulles favored this aid, would Congress and the American people consent to another Korea? The answer came in the uproar that followed the Vice President's remarks, on April 16, that it would be necessary to send American troops to Indochina if the French withdrew. In Congress, Nixon was denounced for "whooping it up for war."

As the situation kept deteriorating, however, Dulles met with a bipartisan group of congressmen to urge that the President be authorized to employ naval and air power in Indochina. Informed that they would not consent to such aid without the cooperation of some of the Western powers, Eisenhower sent Dulles to confer with the British and French. The meetings proved futile. Eisenhower informed congressional leaders on April 26 that the failure of Britain and France to join in a unified endeavor meant the fall of Dienbienphu, but he did not intend to "carry the rest of the world on our back." Moreover, he continued, "we are not going to be involved alone in a power move against the Russians."

Dienbienphu surrendered on May 7. With the French unable or unwilling to continue the war alone, diplomatic efforts were made to end the fighting. In July, at the Geneva Conference on Far Eastern Affairs, an armistice was signed dividing the country at the 17th parallel with a Communist government in the north and a pro-Western regime in the south. Thus Vietnam was added to Korea and Germany as an area in which the protagonists in the cold war confronted each other at a boundary line. Free elections in the future, it was hoped, would bring about unification. Laos and Cambodia, given independent status, were prohibited from joining any regional alliance or maintaining foreign bases.

Eisenhower regarded much of the accord as unsatisfactory and stated so publicly, while Senator Knowland denounced it as "one of the greatest victories for Communism in a decade." Dulles avoided a direct endorsement of the terms by withholding his signature to the agreement, declaring that the United States would not permit Southeast Asia to be swallowed by the Communists. The London *Economist* commented on the Dulles policy that this "spectacle of vociferous inaction" had led to the "worst diplomatic disaster in recent American history." While the statement was an exaggeration, Dulles's reversal of Theodore Roosevelt's admonition to speak softly and carry a big stick was not calculated to score any successes.

Within only a few weeks, the United States was involved in another crisis, this time directly with Red China. To the Eisenhower administration, the existence of the two Chinas was a hairshirt which could not be shed. The defeated Nationalist government, "exiled" on Formosa, a symbol both of a discredited past and of a future hope, was acknowledged by Washington as the legitimate government of the Chinese people. Most Americans were implacably opposed to diplomatic recognition of Red China or to having her seated in the United Nations. Shortly after the Korean armistice, Senator Taft declared that, should Red China be admitted to the United Nations, he would resign from Congress and devote all his time to getting her expelled.

On the other hand, Eisenhower privately expressed regret that the prevailing Wilsonian approach, based on moral approval of the regime, prevented the United States from according *de facto* recognition pursuant to common international practice. He also deplored, but made no attempt to dispel, the hysteria engendered by McCarthy on the subject of communism which made calm and rational public debate on foreign policy alternatives a virtual impossibility. Privately, too, he was skeptical that the national interest was promoted by ostracizing Red China. Doubting that the Chinese and the Russians were natural allies, he believed it might be advantageous to encourage a breach.

The President resisted efforts by Republican congressional leaders to fashion a national policy so rigid that it could never be bent. He rejected Senator Jenner's demand that the administration go on record never to recognize Red China or consent to her admission to the United Nations. At a meeting with Senate leaders in June, 1953, he argued forcefully against a rider to an appropriation bill sponsored by Senator Everett Dirksen, which provided that American contributions to the United Nations be automatically terminated should membership be granted the Communist Chinese government. Not only was the international situation fluid and liable to sudden and unpredictable change, the President said, but such a step would also adversely affect world opinion of the United States. Congress had the prerogative to express its viewpoint, but it should not be linked with a threat of financial reprisal to the United Nations, man's last hope for ultimate peace. Any member state could expect to be outvoted occasionally on an issue, he suggested; the important consideration was to maintain the integrity and viability of the international organization. The rider was excised.

With his own party leaders in Congress constantly demanding more strenuous action on behalf of Nationalist China, the President's predicament was compounded by the provocative attitude of the Peiping regime, which heightened public hostility by continually jabbing at the United States. Free to start a new adventure now that Korea and Indochina were settled, Foreign Minister Chou En-lai in August, 1954, proclaimed Formosa to be his prime target. President Eisenhower's prompt reply that "any invasion of Formosa would have to run over the Seventh Fleet" did not deter Peiping from bombarding the Nationalist-held offshore islands of Quemoy and Matsu three weeks later. Eisenhower, like his predecessor, was prepared to involve the United States only in the event of a direct attack on Formosa. In December, he concluded a defensive pact with Chiang Kai-shek, whereby Formosa and the nearby Pescadores were defined as Nationalist territory under American protection. The President had returned to the Truman-Acheson policy of "leashing" Chiang, of refusing to join in any undertaking to recapture the mainland.

When the Communists captured one of the Tachen Islands a month later, Eisenhower asked Congress for authorization to employ armed force to protect Formosa and the Pescadores and, if necessary, other "closely related localities." He made it clear that he was not abdicating his constitutional right to use the armed forces on his own responsibility, but that joint action by executive and legislature would have a greater impact on Peiping. Moreover, according to Sherman Adams, "Eisenhower did not want to repeat the mistake he believed that Truman had made in 1950 in sending air and naval forces to South Korea without consulting Congress." The legislators responded promptly, voting the authorization by a large majority.

Tension kept mounting during the following weeks as the Communists refused to accede to the United Nations' request for a cease-fire. The President was criticized by congressmen for his reluctance to announce that the offshore islands, as well as Formosa, would be protected by the United States. Eisenhower remained noncommittal: by reserving the right to decide whether an attack on Quemoy and Matsu constituted a preliminary step in a larger Formosa offensive, he kept the Communists guessing, retaining the advantage of flexibility. At a discussion with House and Senate leaders at the White House late in March, 1955, Eisenhower told Sam Rayburn that he and Dulles were "living twenty-four hours a day with the question of what to do if something happens in Quemoy and Matsu. That is the most difficult problem I have had to face since I took office."

Shortly thereafter, Chou En-lai offered to negotiate, and fireworks ceased. For the next three years the area was quiet until, on August 23, 1958, the Communists for no discernible reason began to shell Quemoy once again. Several days later Dulles warned that an invasion of the offshore islands would not be a "limited operation"; that the resolution of January, 1955, could apply to Quemoy and Matsu, which "have increasingly become related" to the defense of Formosa. Eisenhower, charging that the Communists were attempting to "liquidate all the free-world positions in the Western Pacific," called on the Chinese to support the principle that military force may not be used to effect political change. At the same time he ordered the

Seventh Fleet to convoy Nationalist ships supplying the islands, and ordered other warships to the area. Khrushchev now
stomped onto the scene, bluntly serving notice that if the
United States engaged in hostilities with the People's Republic,
he would not stand idly by. America, he warned, had better
cease intervening in China's internal affairs.

Public apprehension over the prospects of another "Korea,"
coupled with European consternation at Eisenhower's apparent decision to make Quemoy, like Berlin, a test for halting
Communist aggression, brought about a modification of American policy. Although Dulles denied that he was making any
change in policy, he stated on September 30, 1958, that the
United States was not pledged to protect the offshore islands or
provide assistance for an invasion of the mainland. Furthermore, he conceded that Quemoy was garrisoned by an excessive number of troops which he would urge Chiang to reduce
if a dependable cease-fire were arranged. On October 1, President Eisenhower echoed an earlier statement by Under Secretary Herter that the offshore islands were "not strategically
defensible in the defense of Formosa."

While Chiang was outraged at this shift in emphasis, the
Chinese Reds apparently decided to retreat, saving face by
stating that they would shell Quemoy on odd-numbered days.
During the next years, the islands continued to remain a source
of potential danger. When Eisenhower left office, the problem
of China was perhaps even more complicated. The Chiang
government was steadily losing prestige as the Peiping regime
became more firmly entrenched, building a feeble colossus into
a major power. Sentiment for admitting the People's Republic
to the United Nations General Assembly kept spreading among
member states. For America the dilemma remained. Continued
support to Chiang appeared fruitless as a long-range prospect;
abandoning him, even if it appeared to be in the national interest, would be extremely difficult in view of the temper of
Congress and the public.

Over and above the world-wide tensions caused by "incidents" that, like evil genii, kept bursting out in different parts
of the globe, remained the terrifying threat to world peace of
the nuclear arms race. In August, 1953, American thermonu-

clear monopoly was ended when the Soviet Union exploded a hydrogen bomb. How could the President dramatize the magnitude of the danger that now confronted all mankind? Eisenhower thought of delivering an address to rouse world opinion against the use of the horrendous new weapons. A writing project, "Operation Candor," was organized, but seemed unable to get under way. Then an idea occurred to Eisenhower that evolved into the Atoms-For-Peace proposal. Presented by the President to the United Nations on December 8, 1953, it was a plea for the peaceful uses of atomic energy by establishing an international stockpile of fissionable material under United Nations supervision. America, he said, would be willing to share her nuclear knowledge with other nations for that purpose. Implied was the belief that an undertaking of this nature might dissipate secrecy and eventually pave the way for disarmament. Widely acclaimed—even the Russians refrained from attacking it—the proposal nevertheless had no immediate results. However, some years later it led to the formation of the International Atomic Energy Agency, composed of twelve nations, including the Soviet Union, to plan for the exchange of nuclear information under United Nations sponsorship.

On the crucial matter of nuclear disarmament, discussions in the United Nations subcommittee remained deadlocked. The Soviet Union rejected any formula involving inspection or aerial photography, insisting on the immediate abolition of all nuclear weapons without inspection or controls, plus a sharp reduction in conventional forces and a moratorium on nuclear testing. The United States was equally determined on the matter of inspection. As Eisenhower explained to reporters in the summer of 1957, America had offered to cease testing, but only under an agreement to halt the production of arms, "and, of course, the necessary inspectional system to make certain that the whole scheme was being carried out faithfully on both sides."

Finally, in March, 1958, the Soviet Union announced that it would unilaterally suspend nuclear tests, reserving the right to resume them if others did not follow suit. After a panel of distinguished scientists ascertained that many varieties of tests could be detected without inspection, the American and British governments agreed conditionally to halt tests. Meanwhile, the three powers undertook to negotiate a permanent test-ban treaty. After 273 sessions, the delegates, unable to agree on such vexatious questions as on-site inspection and the technical facilities to determine violations, decided to recess in anticipation of a new President in the White House, who might possibly bring a new approach.

In the quest for security, the phrase "summit diplomacy" was added to the vocabulary of statesmanship. The death of Stalin in the spring of 1953, and a new administration in Washington, raised hopes on both sides of the Atlantic that perhaps the new leaders could resolve the issues dividing East and West by a face-to-face meeting. Though eager to explore any possibility that might lead to peace, President Eisenhower was skeptical that a conference would be productive, and Dulles had no faith at all in such encounters, preferring the more traditional methods of diplomacy. But finally they yielded to public pressure at home and abroad for a summit conference, and the first gathering in a decade of the heads of state opened at Geneva on July 5, 1955. At Premier Bulganin's side was Nikita S. Khrushchev, already looming as the real force in Soviet policy.

That little would be resolved was apparent almost immediately. On the first day, Bulganin presented the old Soviet disarmament proposal for a ban on nuclear weapons without any machinery for control. Eisenhower countered with an open-skies inspection plan that in a somewhat different version had been rejected earlier by the Russians. The cleavage over German reunification remained, the West insisting on free elections as a condition for unification, while the Russians demanded that elections follow after a unified Germany was linked to a security arrangement outside the NATO system.

Nevertheless, the conference ended on a hopeful note. The Kremlin leaders had been affable, in contrast to their past blustering behavior, appearing to accept Eisenhower's assurance of pacific intentions. In his concluding address, the President said that in his judgment "the prospects of a lasting peace with justice, well-being and broader freedom are brighter. The dangers of the overwhelming tragedy of modern war are less."

French Premier Edgar Faure declared that "something had changed in the world in the handling of this question of disarmament." And Prime Minister Nehru wrote a warmly congratulatory letter to Eisenhower, expressing faith in his efforts to achieve peace. He invited him to visit India where, he said, the people would give him an exuberant welcome.

The "spirit of Geneva" lasted for about a year until the optimism it had generated was snuffed out by a crisis in another tinderbox, the oil-rich Middle East, where incendiary nationalism, crushing poverty, and the galling memories of colonialism made the area fertile ground for exploitation by the Kremlin. In an attempt to win the friendship of the Egyptian leader, Gamal Abdel Nasser, rapidly becoming a force in the Arab nationalist movement, the United States persuaded the British in 1954 to remove their troops from the Suez Canal zone. The following year Nasser was offered funds by both nations for a dam at Aswan, which he was eager to build; but dissatisfied with the terms of the proposed loan, he delayed negotiations. In the ensuing months, Nasser engaged in a series of actions which seemed deliberately intended to antagonize the West. He purchased arms from Czechoslovakia in defiance of an agreement that arms be kept out of the Middle East, stepped up the commando raids against Israel, aided the Algerian rebels against France, and used his controlled press and radio to laud the Soviets while excoriating the democracies. Finally, when Dulles heard inspired rumors that Nasser had been offered a twenty-year loan by the Soviet Union, he withdrew the offer of assistance. Britain followed suit.

In prompt retaliation, Nasser seized the properties of the Suez Canal Company, announcing that he would operate the canal and use the tolls to finance the dam. Alarmed at the possibility of having his nation's vital oil supply cut off, Prime Minister Anthony Eden cabled President Eisenhower that he and his Cabinet were convinced they "must be ready in the last resort to use force" to wrest the canal out of Nasser's hands. Dulles informed him that the United States would not support a military action. After several months of futile negotiations with an obdurate Nasser, the British and French decided to act on their own without informing their ally.

On October 29, 1956, Israeli troops, retaliating against Egyptian depredations and probably in collusion with England and France, invaded the Sinai Peninsula, quickly piercing Egyptian defenses to within twenty-five miles of the Suez Canal. The following day, the Western powers, under the terms of the Tripartite Declaration of 1950 by which they and the United States were empowered to intervene if Israel or Egypt broke their peace pact, called for a cease-fire. Israel was ready to comply. When Nasser refused, the British and French proceeded to bomb Egyptian airfields and land troops at Port Said.

The timing of the attack caught President Eisenhower by surprise and placed him in a painful dilemma. For one thing, it was just days before the American people were to go to the polls after an election campaign during which the Republicans had stressed the President's contributions to international peace. Secondly, the United States was just then denouncing the Soviet invasion of Hungary. For Eisenhower to support his partners would violate the principles of the United Nations Charter, yet to desert them would jeopardize the Western alliance. His decision was announced in a nationwide radio address on October 31, when he declared that "we do not accept the use of force as a wise and proper instrument for the settlement of international disputes. . . . There can be no peace without law." Standing on high moral ground, he insisted that one standard could not be used for the nation's friends and another for its rivals.

Within a week, England and France, deserted by their major ally, opposed by the Soviet Union, and condemned by world opinion, capitulated. The net result was a triumph for Nasser, whose prestige was greatly enhanced in the eyes of Arab nationalists, and for the Soviet Union which trumpeted to the Arab world that it had brought "the colonialist aggressors" to heel. For England the episode was a major disaster, revealing her loss of influence in the Middle East and her dependence on the United States. At the same time Afro-Asian fears of colonialism were revived. Equally serious was the breach in the Western alliance which Suez left in its wake.

If Eisenhower and Dulles had been more sensitive to the

vital interests of Britain and France, they might have taken a different approach and possibly the debacle could have been averted. Cancellation of the financial offer to Nasser, which was made abruptly, might have been handled more diplomatically. Careful groundwork in the summer of 1956 by all three nations might have mustered the requisite force to seize the canal and protect it against damage until Nasser could be brought to terms. An exploration might have been made of the possibility of subsidizing the canal, of exerting economic pressure upon Egypt, or of constructing large oil storage facilities.

Nasser's strengthened position provided the Soviet Union with a sharp entering wedge to the strategic Middle East at the same time that the elimination of Anglo-French influence created a power vacuum. The wedge would have to be blunted, the vacuum filled, and only America as leader of the Western alliance now had the power to do so. The United States, Eisenhower told Congress on January 5, 1957, could not afford "to leave a vacuum in the Middle East and prayerfully hope that Russia will stay out." He requested two hundred million dollars in economic and military assistance and also asked Congress for authority to use armed force "to secure and protect the territorial integrity and political independence of such nations requesting such aid against overt armed aggression from any nation controlled by International Communism." Later to be known as the Eisenhower Doctrine, this statement of American policy was aimed specifically at the Middle East, unlike the Truman Doctrine, which was directed against the spread of communism everywhere.

Congressmen of both parties contended that in seeking a resolution from the legislature the President was shirking his responsibility by attempting to make it share a decision that constitutionally belonged to him. Eisenhower explained his motive in a statement to the press: "What we want now is an expression of the convictions of the vast portion of the American people without regard to party. . . . We are trying to prevent war, not fight one. . . . I would like the nation to know that America is largely one in our readiness to assume burdens and, where necessary, to assume risks to preserve the peace, because this peace is not going to be obtained in any cheap way."

After two months of wrangling the plan was approved, but without reference to congressional authorization as requested by the President. Its effect was limited, however, principally because the major threat to peace in the area was from local conditions rather than from external communism—the Israeli-Arab conflict, rivalries among the Arab states, incendiary situations within the states that might explode at any time into civil war. Nasser ignored it, continuing his inflammatory agitation of Middle Eastern politics and his flirtation with the Soviet Union.

The first test of the Eisenhower Doctrine came on July 14, 1958, when two messages were received from the Middle East. One was that the pro-Western King Faisal of Iraq, the Crown Prince, and the Premier had been brutally murdered by insurgents. The other was a request for aid by President Camille Chamoun of Lebanon, where a revolt, inspired and abetted by Egypt, had been in progress since May. Should Iraq, the only member of the regional security organization commonly known as the Bagdad Pact, come under control of either Nasser or the Soviet Union, it might pull surrounding nations into the anti-Western orbit. With neighboring Lebanon infiltrated by pro-Nasser and pro-Communist elements, Chamoun became panic-stricken, cabling Eisenhower that his government's survival depended on the immediate dispatch of American troops.

President Eisenhower had to decide quickly whether to risk the antagonism of the Arab world and possible Soviet reprisals if he complied with Chamoun's plea. Resolving to take action, he met first with the National Security Council and then with congressional leaders. While the latter were unenthusiastic, they did not oppose the President. By the following morning, the Sixth Fleet was on its way and seventeen hundred Marines were in Beirut. Eventually, more than fourteen thousand Marines were deployed. In a nationwide broadcast, Eisenhower explained that the troops were sent to protect Americans in Lebanon and "assist the government . . . to preserve [the] . . . territorial integrity and political independence" of a country "vital to the national interest and world peace."

Enraged, Nasser flew to Moscow while Khrushchev denounced the "aggression," sending letters to Eisenhower, Mac-

millan, de Gaulle, and Nehru warning that the world tottered
on "the brink of disaster" and proposing a summit meeting at
Geneva. Eisenhower calmly replied that he was not aware "of
any factual basis for your extravagantly expressed fear," that
there would be real danger of war "if one small nation after
another were to be engulfed by expansionist and aggressive
forces supported by the Soviet Union."

For the next few weeks the issue was debated in the Security
Council until at last agreement was reached to remove troops,
the Arab League having pledged to "abstain from an action
calculated to change established systems of government." The
felicitous outcome was short-lived. The pro-Western Chamoun
became a neutralist, and the military action, by reviving memories of colonialism, provided fuel for the Kremlin's propaganda fires in the region. Those factors which made for instability in the Middle East remained as a source of continual
concern to the West.

Awareness of the crucial stakes in the vast African continent,
a potentially far more explosive area, came slowly and belat-
edly to the United States. Not until 1958 was a separate Bureau of African Affairs created in the Department of State.
American policy makers, accustomed to regarding the continent as an extension of Europe and primarily its concern, had
largely ignored it. Nor did they consider the effects upon the
national image of racial discrimination at home. When the
United States finally saw the sparks of the nationalist fuse
racing wildly across Africa, igniting the fires of independence
on every side, efforts were made to slow it down. Be patient,
the Africans were told, avoid violence and extremism, emulate
the pattern of American political and economic development.
To a people whose rising expectations made them impatient
with delay, this kind of exhortation was meaningless. As
Kwame Nkrumah of Ghana said in 1958, "Others may feel they
have evolved the very best way of life, but we are not bound,
like slavish imitators, to accept it as our mold."

In 1955, Africa had five newly independent nations; within
five years there were twenty-seven. For the United States, the
magnitude and complexity of coping with innumerable tribes
and peoples, each with its own customs and languages, was

compounded by the necessity to retain its loyalties and commitments to the colonial NATO partners. The dexterity of a highly skilled juggler was required to balance the aspirations of the nationalists and the interests of the European powers. In the Algerian struggle for independence, for example, United States support of the Moslems would antagonize an ally, while treating the revolt as a domestic matter would incur the charge of condoning imperialism. The Eisenhower administration tried to straddle the issue by seeking to avert a debate on the question in the United Nations, thereby insuring the resentment of both sides.

Another factor was the Soviet Union. During the nineteenth century, Africa had been the object of European imperialist rivalries; in the twentieth, the emergence of new nations made it a pawn in the cold war, with Russia seeking to exploit the anti-colonial sentiment by linking the West with imperialism and white supremacy. When France granted Guinea independence in 1958, the United States delayed diplomatic recognition and an offer of economic assistance for about a month on the theory that the French might be affronted by prompt action. The Soviet bloc had no such scruples, and by immediately volunteering military aid and substantial credit earned Guinea's gratitude and allegiance. Congolese independence in 1960 brought about chaos and violence that threatened world peace, a situation with which President Eisenhower's successor would have to cope.

The "balance of terror," coupled with American success in creating positions of military strength, prompted the Russian leaders to engage the West in areas and enterprises where propaganda and economic pressure could be utilized most effectively. To meet the Soviet challenge in the cold war, to respond effectively to the new strategy and diplomacy of the Russians, would require a shifting of gears. Soviet diplomacy became more polished, more adroit and flexible, in contrast to the crudeness of the Stalin era. The frontal attack was discarded for a more subtle policy designed to undermine the Western position wherever it was vulnerable. Overtures were made to the neutralist nations. Assistance on the order of Truman's Point Four Program was undertaken in the so-called backward areas. More difficult in many ways to contend with than a direct military threat, this new Kremlin approach would require the utmost in ingenuity on the part of the democratic leaders. Accustomed to quick solutions, Americans would have to adjust to a world in which these were no longer feasible. Like Truman before him, Eisenhower was obliged to lead in an era of perpetual crises. In a very real sense, the distinction between a wartime and a peacetime head of state had vanished.

Dwight David Eisenhower

---

21. Summit Diplomacy Bedeviled

O N an ordinary fall day in 1957, the area of presidential
concern was abruptly and irrevocably enlarged by the
spectacular Soviet achievement of launching a satellite into
orbit. To the problems wracking the planet Earth with which
the chief executive had to deal were now added those involving
the exploration of outer space.

The Russian feat was a traumatic shock to most Americans
complacent about what they thought was their country's unrivaled position. For years the public had been assured by
Washington that the military striking power of the United
States far surpassed that of the Soviets. But, indisputably, the
booster capacity essential for the rocket thrust which hurled
Sputnik into the heavens revealed a terrifying advance in military technology, specifically the missile field. Apprehension
intensified as one month later Sputnik II, containing a live dog,
began to circle the earth. Almost as painful was the blow to
national pride. Soviet prestige soared while the United States
was now considered to be lagging behind, not only in scientific
development but, some feared, in other areas as well.

In response to the public outburst of dismay, the Eisenhower
administration declared that the nation was not attempting a
space race with the Soviet Union. The President maintained an
"official air of serenity," as Sherman Adams later recorded, but
he was "privately as concerned as everybody else . . . by the
jump ahead that the Russians had made in scientific enter-
prise."

Space science had fallen behind for two principal reasons: money and a general disdain of basic research. As to the former, Congress was reluctant to spend the requisite large sums for scientific projects, regarding defense systems, also highly costly, as more vital to the nation's security. Regarding the latter, the spirit that permeated the administration was expressed in Postmaster General Arthur Summerfield's boast that the government was "rooting out the eggheads" from office, in Eisenhower's definition of an intellectual as "a man who takes more words than necessary to tell us more than he knows," in Secretary of Defense Charles E. Wilson's ridicule of the effort to find out "why grass is green." The program of science attachés started under Truman to help the nation keep abreast of scientific developments abroad was abolished, and funds for scientific research and expansion were cut almost in half by Wilson. Other factors retarding progress were rivalry among the armed services, and the failure, for administrative and other reasons, to integrate missile and rocket research.

Addressing the nation on November 8, the President said his scientific friends had informed him that "one of our greatest and most glaring deficiencies is the failure . . . in this country to give enough priority to scientific education . . . that a second critical need is . . . priority, both public and private, to basic research." He announced a new position on his own staff, Special Assistant to the President for Science and Technology, to which he had appointed Dr. James R. Killian, Jr., president of the Massachusetts Institute of Technology. Dr. Killian would be responsible for supervising the nation's missile and space research. Also established was the President's Science Advisory Committee. It was clear that in the future scientists would occupy a significant place in the President's decision-making process.

Competition among the Army, the Navy, and the Air Force became acute, each attempting to gain a leading position in the missile and space field. The Army won the race, sending up a tiny satellite in January, 1958, which weighed only a little over eighteen pounds as compared to the 1,120 pounds of Sputnik II. The difficulty in bringing about cooperation among the three services and concern for the nation's security led Eisenhower to inform Republican leaders in February that under the jurisdiction of the Defense Department, rocket projects rather than the conquest of outer space would be the area of concentration. When objections were raised, the President replied that, while rockets to the moon were glamorous, nuclear-armed missiles were far more important since the country had no enemies in outer space, and he was "not at all interested in volunteering to be the first man to land on the moon." Nevertheless, as prestige is an important psychological dimension of national power, a race to the moon was virtually inevitable. At the President's request, Congress, on July 17, 1958, created the National Aeronautics and Space Administration, an independent agency empowered to conduct research and develop space vehicles.

The Russians continued to launch sputniks of increasing size and proficiency. In January, 1959, their cosmic rocket Lunik came within about forty-five hundred miles of hitting the moon. Mounting anxiety in the United States prompted a reporter to ask the President at his press conference in February, 1960, whether "a dangerous state of mind" was not being created that the United States was being "forced into a position to accept a posture of second best in everything or anything" because of Soviet superiority in space projects and a higher rate of economic growth. Eisenhower replied that a totalitarian government could commandeer human or material resources for any undertaking to which it desired to assign priority. As achievements in outer space were dramatic, a government of this kind was willing to subordinate other considerations. "We place above all other values our own individual freedoms and rights. If you take our country and make it an armed camp and regiment it . . . you might do things . . . in greater tempo." Unless space activities could be justified by a discernible scientific rationale, he did not believe they should be undertaken.

A more immediate and direct challenge came from Latin America after Fidel Castro overthrew the brutal, corrupt dictator of Cuba, Fulgencio Batista, on January 1, 1959, terminating a bitter, six-year struggle. Hemispheric relations had been deteriorating for some years, but the American people were not aware how seriously until Vice President and Mrs. Nixon were physically endangered by a hostile, uncontrollable mob in Caracas, Venezuela, during a good-will tour. The Latin Americans, long mistrustful of "big brother" to the north, had become increasingly resentful at his indifference to their economic and political problems. Concern with the Red menace, they believed, led the United States to support any government, no matter how evil, which resisted communism, and to oppose popular movements that were responding to the imperative need for reform. Throughout the Cuban struggle, the savagely repressive Batista regime had been steadily supplied with arms by the United States, a factor not calculated to endear America to Castro and his followers.

Although recognition of the new Cuban regime was prompt, relations were soon strained, and within two years they deteriorated to implacable hostility. In promoting land reform as an element of his extensive social revolution, Castro expropriated all the holdings of American investors, amounting to over a billion dollars. Far more serious was his orientation to Moscow. In February, 1960, Castro signed a five-year trade agreement with the Russians, and there were intimations of a defensive alliance that could provide the Soviets with a beachhead in the Caribbean. Just weeks earlier the White House, responding to allegations by Castro, declared, "The United States government adheres strictly to the policy of non-intervention in the domestic affairs of other countries, including Cuba. This policy is incorporated in our treaty commitments as a member of the Organization of American States." The statement further emphasized that the nation had done everything possible to prevent illegal acts in the territories under its jurisdiction "directed against other governments."

In June, 1960, Eisenhower imposed an embargo against Cuban sugar. Castro promptly retaliated by accusing the United States of economic aggression before the Security Council. The atmosphere became electric when Khrushchev announced at this point that his government would support Cuba with "rocket fire" if any military intervention occurred. He went even further, striking at the core of American foreign policy in the Western Hemisphere, by declaring that the Monroe Doctrine had outlived its usefulness. The State Department immediately replied that the doctrine was still valid, warning that any attempt by the Soviet Union to extend its system to this hemisphere would be regarded as inimical to the security of the United States.

At a press conference two months later, a reporter recalled a previous statement by the President that we could not permit a Communist-dominated regime to come into this hemisphere. Did not such a regime already exist, and what did the President propose to do about it? Eisenhower's reply, that definite action was called for if a nation became a satellite of international communism, but "I am not going to propose specific plans of what we might do," intimated that the government was moving away from its declared policy of non-intervention.

Diplomatic relations were severed with Cuba in January, 1961, when Castro demanded that the staff of the American Embassy in Havana be reduced within forty-eight hours from a normal complement of about a hundred to eleven, alleging that some of the personnel were espionage agents. Six days afterward, the *New York Times* revealed that Americans were training anti-Castro exiles in a secret camp in Guatemala. Some time later it became known that the Eisenhower administration secretly had decided to come to grips with the problem by having the Central Intelligence Agency assist anti-Castro refugees in a military assault on Cuba.

Direct military intervention, which was a common practice in the past, could not be considered by the President. Not only had Soviet power introduced a new element limiting his freedom of action, but the attitude of the Latin-American nations had become an important factor. Insistence on juridical equality and national sensitivities required that hemispheric policies be arrived at by common consent rather than by the dictates of American might. While leaders in South America deplored Castro's alliance with the Soviets, popular approval of his social objectives was widespread.

The Cuban problem was the first major crisis that Eisenhower had to handle without the assistance of John Foster Dulles, who had died in the sping of 1959. From the beginning of his administration, the President permitted Dulles virtually to dominate foreign relations. His confidence in Dulles's judgment and ability was unqualified. Yet in personality and approach no two men could have been more different. Eisenhower was optimistic and conciliatory, Dulles skeptical and inflexible. Only on one important occasion, with regard to military intervention in Indochina, did the President refuse to accept his Secretary's advice.

On the anniversary commemorating fifty years of Dulles's service to public affairs, Eisenhower wrote him a personal letter in which he said, "Your accomplishments will establish you as one of the greatest of our Secretaries of State." Before Dulles retired because of the illness that was to claim his life, the President told reporters, "I personally believe he has filled his office with greater distinction than any other man our country has known . . . a man of tremendous character and courage, intelligence and wisdom."

John Foster Dulles's training and distinguished diplomatic background made him a logical candidate for a top position in public service. He himself seemed to have felt that it had been preordained for him to become Secretary of State—a grandfather and an uncle had each held that illustrious post. His impressive background coupled with a supreme self-confidence in his ability to shoulder the manifold tasks of his office probably awed Eisenhower. Dulles is said to have remarked to him at the beginning of their association, "With my understanding of the intricate relationships between the peoples of the world and your sensitiveness to the political considerations involved, we will make the most successful team in history."

The examples of his uncle, Robert Lansing, who had been completely overshadowed by Colonel House, and of Cordell Hull and Edward Stettinius, who had been frequently superseded by Harry Hopkins, caused Dulles to resolve at the outset that he would prevent anyone from coming between him and the President. Throughout his tenure no one ever did. When a clash over basic policy occurred, as with Harold Stassen, it was Stassen who was compelled to give way and forced to resign.

The authority of the Secretary of State derived not only from his unique relationship with the President but also from his extraordinary forensic skill, his forceful personality, and his familiarity with the details of diplomacy. To all intents and purposes he *was* the Department of State, devising foreign policies and relegating to his staff the task of implementing them. His tight and secretive hold on all the reins gave currency to the oft-repeated quip that Dulles carried American foreign policy under his hat. As communication between the man at the top and his subordinates in the department was often non-existent, the latter would frequently discover to their dismay that careful preparations for a project were wasted because of a peremptory decision by the Secretary.

To a considerable extent, Dulles also assumed personal responsibility for implementing and carrying out policies. During his tenure he traveled over half a million miles, visiting forty-seven nations. "He regarded too much time spent in Washington as neglect of the U.S. task of free world leadership," wrote an informed observer. "He undertook personal direction of the country's foreign affairs, assigning himself the role of No. 1 diplomat of the U.S."

With a tendency to concentrate on only one question at a time, he also lacked the wide-angled vision of Acheson that would enable him to see the interrelationship of scattered problems. He would plough directly ahead to reach his objective, completely oblivious of the effect on the area to his right or left. An inclination toward viewing things in black or white made his attitude to the world community rigid. Having decided that neutralism was immoral, he demanded a firm commitment to the United States, regarding those who withheld it as having forfeited their claim to respectability.

The widespread impression that the foreign policies of Eisenhower and Dulles were substantially different from those of the previous administration was largely due to the latter's posturing and style of diplomacy. Politically advantageous at home, abroad his bluster and threats, which were not backed up by action, confused Europe and eventually resulted in a deep mistrust of the Secretary. Dulles, gibed Senator Henry M. Jackson, Democrat, of Washington, was "the original misguided missile, traveling fast, making lots of noise and never hitting the target." Contributing to the bewilderment was the apparent discrepancy between his fiery slogans and the President's frequent pronouncements that war in the nuclear age was unthinkable, that it could no longer be regarded as an instrument of national policy.

Even when Eisenhower may have disagreed with the Secretary's approach or with his version of events, he came loyally to his defense, as when Dulles expounded on how skillfully he had employed the art of what came to be called "brinkmanship." In a widely publicized interview in 1956, which set off a storm of controversy, the Secretary of State declared that aggression is not likely to occur if the potential foe is unequivocally informed that he will be resisted with "massive retaliatory power." If Moscow, for example, had known that the United States would not equivocate in the defense of South Korea, the aggression would not have occurred. Brinkmanship, with which the President fully concurred, said Dulles, was effective in bringing peace to Korea, Indochina, and the Formosa Straits. "Of course, we were brought to the verge of war. The ability to get to the verge without getting into the war is the necessary art. . . . We walked to the brink and we looked it in the face." The President, he continued, "never flinched for a minute in any of these situations."

When Eisenhower was asked at his next press conference whether he agreed with Dulles's conclusions, he replied evasively that the tactics used to stop Communist aggression in the Far East involved decisions of the National Security Council that could not properly be discussed in public. Sherman Adams comments, "Eisenhower was very careful about what he said. . . . But he did make one remark that revealed what he felt under the surface." The President said he did not know whether certain unfortunate expressions were used by Dulles or by the author of the article, implying "in his carefully guarded way of speaking," according to Adams, that he was questioning the propriety of statements attributed to the Secretary of State.

As one of Dulles's fixed convictions was that foreign policy was best conducted through normal diplomatic channels, he apparently persuaded the President to turn down Khrushchev's request in 1958 for a second summit meeting on Berlin. The temperature had been rising to the boiling point following

Khrushchev's declaration that, unless a new arrangement on Berlin was negotiated within six months, he would sign a peace treaty with East Germany, implying that it would then have sovereign authority to deal with Berlin and control access to the city. After Dulles's death the following year, when the Foreign Ministers' Conference at Geneva reached the usual deadlock, the President concluded that if the Soviet Premier would negotiate only at the top, then the top it would have to be.

An official exchange of visits by the President and the Premier was first arranged. In September, 1959, the Soviet leader flew to the United States. After a cross-country tour, during which the Premier engaged in sight-seeing and in talks with spokesmen for American labor, management, and the entertainment industry, the statesmen conferred for two days in the solitude of Eisenhower's retreat at Camp David. The exchange of views was markedly affable, and Khrushchev dropped the time limit for a Berlin settlement. A return visit by the President to Russia was slated for the following summer after a summit conference which was to be held at Paris on May 16, 1960. The following seven months were like the placid lull before the storm, which broke with a clap of thunder just two weeks before the scheduled meeting.

On May 5, the Soviet Union announced that an American U-2 espionage plane had been shot down more than twelve hundred miles inside the country. The administration's response during the next few days was an astonishing combination of ineptitude and bad judgment. Washington denied any "attempt to violate . . . Soviet air space," claiming that the plane, on a weather reconnaissance, had been blown off course. This theme was elaborated on for two days until Khrushchev exposed it as a fabrication by announcing that the pilot was not only alive but had confessed to being on a Central Intelligence Agency espionage mission to photograph Soviet defense installations. Compelled to make a response, the State Department entangled the situation further. First a statement was issued that "there was no authorization for any such flights" from "authorities" in Washington. Later, in a complete reversal, Secretary of State Christian Herter announced that American planes had been flying over Russia for several years and implied that they would continue to do so. Then, on May 11, the world was astounded when the President acknowledged personal responsibility for the flight, adding that such activities were "a distasteful but vital necessity" to penetrate Soviet military secrecy.

Probably the man most amazed at Eisenhower's statement was Khrushchev, who only four days previously had said that he was prepared to "fully admit that the President did not know" about the flight. Traditionally, heads of state have disavowed any complicity in or knowledge of espionage acts, and the Soviet Premier seems to have hoped that Eisenhower would go along with this. While a dictator, he was not entirely a free agent; moreover, he was the center of a deadly power struggle in the Kremlin. A major issue was coexistence with the West, which he supported, fighting strong opposition by powerful Stalinist forces at home and their counterparts in Peiping. The U-2 incident provided fuel for his enemies, who were accusing him of "naïveté" toward Eisenhower, leaving him no alternative but to denounce the President. "The Russian people would say I was mad to welcome a man who sends spy planes over here," he declared on May 12.

As though determined to provide yet an additional irritant, on the eve of Eisenhower's departure for the summit conference in Paris, Press Secretary Hagerty firmly denied newspaper reports that the U-2 flights had been suspended. The picture of administrative chaos was complete when three days later the President assured the Soviet Premier that "these flights were suspended after the recent incident and are not to be resumed."

The summit meeting that had been planned in an aura of good will was an inevitable fiasco, with the Soviet Premier storming that he could not negotiate with "a thief caught red-handed" until he received an adequate apology. If, as seems possible, Khrushchev wished to sabotage the conference because he was convinced that the West would not yield on Berlin and seized on the U-2 incident as a pretext, the fact remains that he was handed the perfect tool. But even if he had still desired to negotiate, the manner in which Washington handled the affair made that impossible. To understand his position, it is only necessary to reverse the situation. What would Eisenhower's response have been if a Soviet spy plane had been shot down over American defense installations at Omaha, Nebraska, and Khrushchev had publicly acknowledged responsibility?

After returning from Paris, Eisenhower sought to justify the flight in a radio and television address. It was continually necessary, he said, to ferret out information to guard against being caught unprepared. Vigilance could never be relaxed. "Incidentally, from Pearl Harbor we learned that even negotiation itself can be used to conceal preparations for a surprise attack." But the urgency for the flight at that particular time was disproved at a congressional investigation of the U-2 incident. General Thomas D. White, Air Force Chief of Staff, testified that the national security would in no way have been endangered if this particular flight had been cancelled, and had he been consulted he would have counseled against sending out the plane. The advisability of taking precautionary measures to suspend the flight before the summit conference had never even been discussed, although there was a precedent for the possibility of disaster. A U-2 had crash-landed near Tokyo the previous December, and the editor of a Japanese magazine published a detailed report on the nature and purpose of the plane.

Sherman Adams records that in a discussion of the incident several months later, Eisenhower said, "I made the decision just as I have known about and personally approved every one of those flights. . . . I had no thought of it having any possible bearing upon the summit meeting or on my forthcoming trip to Moscow. Except for unforeseen circumstances, it would not have had any." Then he added cryptically, "Even so, the whole story of that U-2 flight as we have it at the present time may not be all that it appears." Adams does not relate whether he asked for or was offered any additional explanation.

If the President had authorized the flight, he was extremely injudicious. More likely, the White House suddenly realized that the State Department's declaration that no authority in Washington was responsible might leave Eisenhower open to a charge by the Democrats of inexcusable negligence. If, then, the President assumed responsibility to reassure the American public that he was never asleep at the switch, he chose the wrong time and the wrong occasion.

In any event, Eisenhower suffered little of the onus for the whole unfortunate affair. Instead, he was lauded for his honesty by his admirers. His immunity from the criticism to which occupants of the office traditionally have been subjected was unique. His popularity generally remained high, untouched by political reverses and unaffected by the usual ebb and flow of presidential prestige. In part, this was due to his reputation as a national hero when he entered the White House. Another factor was his appeal as the stalwart, dependable big brother, possessing the characteristics and virtues prized by Americans who basically were still distrustful of intellect. He was the embodiment of the American myth which exalted the simple virtues: self-reliance, democratic simplicity, personal morality. Partly the phenomenon was a consequence of his approach to the presidency. In keeping with his constitutional view of the office, Eisenhower remained "above the battle," and by not presenting himself as a target kept his image unblemished. The net result, as one observer put it, was that "the man who took office mistrusting politics and politicians will leave office having proved himself one of the most successful politicians ever to occupy the presidency . . . more popular than when he moved in."

In the closing years of his administration, with the loss of the two men on whom he had leaned most heavily, Dulles by death and Sherman Adams by resignation, Eisenhower became markedly independent. Exhibiting a new vitality, he tossed overboard some of his earlier concepts. Whereas in 1953 he had stated categorically that he would not extend himself in the congressional elections, in 1958 he covered almost six thousand miles in a campaign tour, vigorously championing even those party members who most frustrated him. In striking contrast to his early declarations about a hands-off policy toward the legislature, he now asserted, "There are a number of things I have recommended to the Congress, and when my conscience tells me they are right, I'm going to use every single influence I can from the executive department to get Congress to see the light. If that's lobbying, I'm guilty." Eisenhower demonstrated that the Twenty-second Amendment need not reduce a President in his second term to the status of a "lame duck."

Unfortunately, however, on domestic matters his deeply ingrained belief in the restricted role of government and the use of presidential power accounted for an absence of creative innovation. His leadership, accordingly, was exercised largely in a negative sense. Obsessed with the danger of a governmental deficit and passionately committed to a balanced budget, he used his influence to inhibit and prevent measures rather than to evolve new programs designed to meet the nation's staggering problems. During the last session of Congress he used his veto power one hundred and fifty times.

In foreign policy, he began to engage in the kind of personal diplomacy of which Dulles most vehemently would have disapproved. After inviting Nikita Khrushchev to visit the United States, he undertook good-will tours to Europe, Asia, and Latin America, where he was acclaimed by enthusiastic multitudes. As one commentator remarked, "We have a great national asset in Ike's smile and personality." If diplomatic success were measured by the size and plaudits of the crowds, the United States easily would have been the victor in the cold war. By the time Eisenhower left office, he had visited almost thirty countries, making him the most traveled President in the history of the nation. Following his return from the Orient in the summer of 1960, he declared, "No consideration of personal fatigue or inconvenience, no threat or argument would deter me from once again setting out on a course that has meant much for our country, for her friends, and for the cause of freedom—and peace with justice in the world."

The great importance which Eisenhower attached to his tours was indicative of a tendency to avoid coming to grips with basic issues. His optimistic, reassuring manner encouraged a national spirit of complacency, blunting the edge of concern at a time when it should have been honed. President Eisenhower's last annual message to Congress in January, 1961, characteristically was a rose-colored review of his administration's major accomplishments in foreign policy: peace in Korea, termination of hostilities in Egypt, Quemoy and Matsu saved from Communist seizure, the Southeast Asia Treaty Organization established, the NATO alliance militarily strengthened. Yet world conditions were no more stable in 1961 than they had been eight years earlier. Inflammatory spots in Asia, Europe, or the Middle East might ignite at any moment. Neutral Laos was being infiltrated by the Chinese Communists. Intermittent outbreaks in Korea and Indochina threatened to shatter the truce agreements. Red China was moving toward great power status and could not be wished away by being ignored diplomatically. The Berlin situation remained precarious. Penetration by the Communists in Africa and Latin America presaged increasing turmoil in those troubled continents.

With the free world's future at stake, it was vital for Americans to be fully alert, to comprehend the complex nature of the forces that were causing turbulence throughout the globe, and to be aware of their own responsibilities. Eisenhower understood the new dimensions of leadership in the White House and recognized their implications. Towards the end of his administration he was asked by a reporter what he regarded as the major problems with which his successor would have to cope. "America," he replied, "has become a leader in the world . . . almost a decisive leader. This means that the problems that come to the presidential desk, whether it's a small farm in . . . Kansas . . . or difficulty in the Middle East or with the Russians . . . have to be viewed in a broad, world context, and . . . studied earnestly both on their short-term and their long-term effects." It was essential for people to understand the basic issues in order to form intelligent judgments. "Our great danger is that we are sometimes led down blind alleys by demagogues, . . . or we just say that some popular figure will solve [our problems] for us." Yet he failed to educate and to arouse the people to the challenge that confronted them.

Apprehension that Eisenhower's military background would incline him toward bellicosity was dispelled by his words and actions from the very beginning. While his staff system was organized along military lines, his own behavior was markedly unmilitary. It almost seemed as though he made a deliberate

effort to erase from the minds of those who surrounded him
that he had spent a lifetime in the armed forces. One of his
aides records, "While the force of his presence and personality
assured his authority in Cabinet or conference, he actually presided over all such meetings with a laxness hardly conceivable
in an army command post." Perhaps this desire to abjure military habits would partly account for the restraint which characterized his leadership, for his ceaseless attempts to conciliate
factions and ideas that he should have fought, for his propen-
sity to allow himself to be persuaded against his better judgment.

He often softened the words and tempered the martial posture of Secretary Dulles, but had he been more forceful he
might have avoided the scrizophrenic appearance of his foreign policy. He did succeed in tempering his own party, a
powerful section of which was constantly agitating either for
greater militancy or for withdrawal from the international
scene. If the nationalist sentiment of the Republicans had prevailed, the nation might have reverted to some pernicious form
of isolationism.

No one was more dedicated than Eisenhower to the pursuit
of peace or more convinced that in the nuclear age no nation
could be victorious in war. At a Cabinet meeting in March,
1953, a discussion about some matter before the Atomic Energy Commission prompted the President to comment sharply
on those who believed that American atomic power could resolve the world's problems. "Any notion that 'the bomb' is a
cheap way to solve things," he said vehemently, "is awfully
wrong. It ignores all facts of world politics—and the basic realities for our allies. It is cold comfort for any citizen of Western
Europe to be assured that—after his country is overrun and he
is pushing up daisies—someone still alive will drop a bomb on
the Kremlin."

Following the death of Stalin, Eisenhower worked for several
weeks on a statement of what the United States was prepared
to offer for improving the chances of peace. The address he
delivered in Washington on April 16, 1953, was one of his most
memorable statements. Every gun, every warship, every rocket

signifies, he declared, "a *theft* from those who hunger and are not fed, those who are cold and are not clothed. . . . The cost of one modern bomber is . . . a modern brick school in more than thirty cities. . . . We pay for a single fighter plane with a half million bushels of wheat. We pay for a single destroyer with new homes that could have housed more than eight thousand people." Only trust among nations could bring enduring peace. He called for "total war, not upon any human enemy, but upon the brute forces of poverty and need." The United States, he said, was prepared to join with all nations *"in devoting a substantial percentage of the savings achieved by disarmament to a fund for world aid and reconstruction.* . . . We are ready, in short, to dedicate our strength to serving the *needs* rather than the *fears* of the world."

After eight years in office, Eisenhower regretfully acknowledged the necessity for remaining armed to the hilt. At the same time, he was gravely concerned about the danger of this factor. In his notable farewell address, a fitting climax to a career distinguished for singular service to his nation, he warned of the threat to the democratic state of a large-scale military establishment combined with a huge arms industry. The United States, he said, was annually spending on military security more than the net income of all the country's corporations. This was a new element in the American experience which could have grave implications for the future of American society. "In the councils of government we must guard against the acquisition of unwarranted influence . . . by the military-industrial complex. The potential for the disastrous rise of misplaced power exists and will persist. We must never let the weight of this combination endanger our liberties or our democratic processes." He further cautioned that public policy might become the captive of a new technological-scientific elite upon whose specialized knowledge the country's welfare depends. "It is the task of statesmanship," he concluded, "to mold, to balance, and to integrate these and other forces, new and old, within the principles of our democratic system, ever aiming toward the supreme goals of our free society."

Eisenhower was by inclination a moderate who distrusted and discounted power, who sought to cherish old values and heal old wounds, and whose leadership was characterized by restraint in both domestic and foreign affairs. With his successor, the style of leadership in the United States would change profoundly. A "political" chief executive rather than a "constitutional" one now would be presiding over the nation.

John Fitzgerald Kennedy

22. Unfinished Achievement

THAT John Fitzgerald Kennedy, the dynamic forty-three-year-old President and the youngest to be elected to the office in the nation's history, would hold the reins firmly in his hands seemed apparent during the grueling primary battles and the long, bitterly contested election campaign of 1960. This was a man who sought power; many, however—and this included even those who were impressed with his superb vitality, his quick and trenchant mind, his grasp of global problems—questioned whether he craved it for its own sake or would have the wisdom and maturity to use it to the nation's best advantage. After his election victory by the wafer-thin margin of little more than a hundred thousand votes, the big question was whether he would have the skill to enlarge this tenuous mandate in order to carry out his program.

From the outset, Kennedy set the tone for his administration and for his role in office. Other Presidents had grappled with the obligations of world leadership which they had inherited, but not until Kennedy's inaugural address did a chief executive proclaim it as a dominant fact of American life. Speaking exclusively about the global tasks and challenges facing the United States, he declared in forceful, measured tones on that January day in 1961, "Let every nation know, whether it wishes us well or ill, that we shall pay any price, bear any burden, meet any hardship, support any friend, oppose any foe to assure the survival and the success of liberty." To the new states which had freed themselves from colonial control, he pledged that they would not be subjected to any new tyranny; to those peoples struggling "to break the bonds of mass misery," that they would receive every help not because their support was desired but because it was right. To the Latin-American nations, he promised every assistance to cast off "the chains of poverty" and cooperation to oppose aggression or subversion. The United Nations would receive all possible assistance to strengthen it and enlarge its scope.

Equally novel was the fact that he made no attempt to gloss over the complex and arduous nature of the American commitment. After expressing the hope that the nation's adversaries would join in the quest for peace and use the wonders of science to enlarge the horizons of mankind, he informed his countrymen that they must not expect quick solutions to the manifold problems besetting the world. Nothing would be completed during his administration, nor even perhaps during their lifetime. Calling on them to join in the struggle against "the enemies of man: tyranny, poverty, disease, and war itself," he warned bluntly that they must expect "a long, twilight struggle, year in and year out."

Later that month in his State of the Union message, the President repeated his admonition. This was a time of national peril and national opportunity, he declared, and before his term ended Americans again would have to face the test whether a nation organized and governed like their own could endure. The outcome was by no means certain; the news would be worse before it was better. While hoping and working for the best, "we should prepare ourselves for the worst. We cannot escape our dangers; neither must we let them drive us into panic or narrow isolation." People everywhere were involved in the struggle for freedom, but the hope of the world rested most on "the pride and perseverance" of the people of the United States. This stark realism was designed to jar the American public out of the complacency into which it had sunk and to place both the national and international situation in proper perspective.

Kennedy was in a direct line of those Presidents who immersed themselves in every phase of the executive process. In an address to the National Press Club a year before his election he outlined his theory of executive leadership. The President, he said, must "place himself in the very thick of the fight" and be prepared to exercise not only the powers explicitly provided by the Constitution, but also those which tradition and forceful men have bequeathed to the office. As legislative leader he must initiate new programs for the national welfare and be prepared to fight for them, even if he thereby arouses congressional enmity. He must not disdain politics, for by neglecting to use the party machinery in the exercise of power, he not only weakens the party as an instrument of the democratic process but undermines the democratic process itself. He must also be a moral leader, for he represents the national interest, and upon him converge the needs and hopes of all Americans. It is not enough for him merely to reflect prevailing opinion; he is required to alert the people to their dangers and to their opportunities, and to demand of them whatever sacrifices may be necessary.

Some of Kennedy's theories were not always translated into practice. At times he did not fight for his legislative program or use the party machinery to maximum advantage. He also found that leading public opinion was more difficult than he had imagined. But his commitment to the principle of the vigorous exercise of executive prerogative made the White House a vital fulcrum of power.

As he believed that the President should operate at the very center of the political process, with all lines extending directly from him, Kennedy was opposed to excessive institutionalization of the presidency. For example, he met with the Cabinet infrequently and only when matters of concern to all members required discussion. Cabinet members, in his view, were primarily administrative heads of departments. He preferred to deal with them individually and accorded them wide latitude and ready access whenever they wished to consult him.

Kennedy's approach to the presidency not only was based on convictions developed from long study but also stemmed from personal qualities and characteristics which he had in common with another President who entered the White House at about the same young age, that ebullient Victorian, Theodore Roosevelt. Both men possessed unquenchable vitality, insatiable hunger for knowledge and experience, avidity for leadership, dauntless personal courage, aristocracy of taste; but Kennedy had a far subtler mind, greater sensitivity and sophistication. Both men had a world view and a vision of America; nothing could better illustrate the problems of leadership in the mid–twentieth century than the difference in their vision and the means by which they hoped to achieve it. Kennedy's ideas and attitudes completely reflected the experiences, problems, and aspirations peculiar to the America of his era.

Almost as soon as Kennedy took office he had to decide whether or not to continue with the plans initiated by the previous administration for the unofficial support of an invasion of Cuba in order to overthrow the Castro regime. The "experts," whose advice he took, assured him of a mass uprising of the Cubans to back up the invaders, although the press of Europe, South America, and Asia, which had reporters in Havana, maintained that the population was fully supporting Castro. Also, a few knowledgeable political leaders, among them William J. Fulbright, Chairman of the Senate Foreign Relations Committee, strongly advised against the undertaking.

The invasion was a complete fiasco. The liberators were met not by a grateful people but by Castro's well-armed forces. Without air or sea coverage, which had been ruled out, and with no popular support, their position was hopeless and they were quickly overwhelmed. American prestige throughout the world, and especially in Latin America, plummeted sharply. It had been public knowledge since January that the United States was secretly training and equipping the refugee invasion force in Florida and Guatemala and that the entire operation was being directed by the Central Intelligence Agency. The mighty colossus was beaten by a scrubby little dictatorship! Moreover, indignation was widespread at United States interference in the internal affairs of another country. The Soviets cackled with glee and had a propaganda ball.

To the President, whose popularity also suffered, the affair was a salutary lesson. He had not assumed personal command of the situation, relying on the advice of technicians, who operate within a narrow framework. Never again would he make a major decision until he had first conducted a personal investigation and weighed all the evidence. During the next major crisis over Cuba, he was to display the fullest and most effective use of presidential power as well as his mastery of the art of statecraft.

Throughout the summer and early fall of 1962, repeated rumors were reaching the United States that the Russians were arming Cuba with nuclear missiles. Americans were alarmed by the physical threat, but the White House was equally concerned with the serious political implications. If Cuba became a Soviet nuclear satellite, the balance of power would tip disastrously to the detriment of the United States, gravely impair the nation's influence, and undermine its bargaining position with respect to Berlin. Until the President had unimpeachable information, however, his hands were tied. He had to resist pressure from Americans of both parties who were urging a blockade of Cuba or even more drastic action. The aroused citizens were either ignorant of, or blithely ignored, the crucial fact that any encounter would be not with Cuba but with the Soviet Union.

With the Russians flatly stating that the armaments and military equipment being sent to Cuba were exclusively for defensive purposes, Kennedy could only use the diplomatic device of indirectly addressing Khrushchev while ostensibly speaking solely to the American people. On September 4, he told the nation that so far all Russian installations were of a defensive nature, but "were it otherwise, grave issues would arise." Again, on September 13, he declared that if national security was endangered by the Communist build-up in Cuba, "we intend to do everything in our power to prevent such a threat from coming into existence."

Four weeks later, on October 16, the President was shown aerial reconnaissance photographs which substantiated that the Soviets were building missile bases and supplying weapons. Within an hour a group of advisers whom he selected—later formally styled the Executive Committee of the National Security Council—assembled. For the next six days Kennedy and the group carefully and thoroughly considered every possible means of dealing with the situation. What was required was maximum effect and minimum risk, a display of American power without engaging it, a way to force Khrushchev to retreat without humiliation. In the meantime, not the vaguest hint of what was happening at the White House was permitted to leak out. Kennedy continued to travel about the country delivering campaign speeches for congressional candidates as though all was as usual.

When a decision was reached, the President on October 22 bluntly informed the world in a radio and television broadcast of Russia's reckless behavior and duplicity and of his proposed course of action. He proclaimed "a strict quarantine on all offensive military equipment under shipment to Cuba"; any ships found to contain such cargo would be turned back. At the same time he warned that a nuclear attack from Cuba against any nation in the Western Hemisphere would be regarded as an attack by Russia on the United States to which a full retaliatory response upon the Soviet Union would be made.

For six nightmarish days the world appeared to teeter on the edge of unspeakable catastrophe. Kennedy stood firm on the stand he had taken in his address that it was the nation's "unswerving objective" to secure the withdrawal or elimination of the missiles from the Western Hemisphere, a stand which he reiterated to Acting Secretary General of the United Nations U Thant in a letter on October 25: "As we made clear in the Security Council, the existing threat was created by the secret introduction of offensive weapons into Cuba, and the answer lies in their removal of such weapons."

Confronted with an unexpectedly stony determination, Khrushchev backed down. The first sign of surrender was a telegram from the Premier which reached Kennedy at 9 P.M. Friday evening, October 26, which was Saturday, four o'clock in the morning Moscow time. This document has never been made public. Kennedy had it filed among the most secret state papers because, it was later suggested, it revealed an embarrassing desperation and the President withheld it from the public out of deference for another head of state. A second communication received the next day was extremely conciliatory in tone, proposing the removal of the missile bases from Cuba in exchange for the removal of United States bases in Turkey. Although the latter were now obsolete, Kennedy flatly refused to barter. To abandon the bases meant abandoning an ally; moreover, such a step must inevitably invite new Soviet offensives.

The next morning Khrushchev capitulated. In a note to Kennedy, he declared that he trusted the President to fulfill his pledge given in his letter of October 27 that Cuba would not be attacked or invaded by the United States or any other nation in the Western Hemisphere, and he had accordingly ordered work on the missile sites stopped. The offensive weapons would be shipped back to the Soviet Union and, as Kennedy had stipulated, United Nations observers would be permitted to verify the dismantling of the sites.

President Kennedy's reply was immediate and magnanimous: he welcomed Khrushchev's "statesmanlike decision," which was "an important and constructive contribution to peace." His own behavior had been in the best tradition of statesmanship—determined but cautious, bold but without bravado or arrogance. During the harrowing days of the crisis, he had employed the minimum of military power required to make his intentions unmistakable to the Kremlin. He had also availed himself of every possible diplomatic channel: personal communication, the United Nations, and the Organization of American States. Once the Soviet leader yielded, he allowed him to save face. As he later commented, "Above all, while defending our own vital interests, nuclear powers must avert those confrontations which bring an adversary to a choice of either a humiliating retreat or a nuclear war."

The Cuban missile crisis was a turning point in the cold war. Khrushchev, taking the measure of his adversary, found that the abyss had actually yawned open. Kennedy found that his adversary's bluster was hollow, that it masked a genuine terror of nuclear conflict. Since neither leader was eager to commit national suicide, an accommodation must be sought that would remove the threat of war despite the conflict of divergent interests and goals. As the President once put it, he would never negotiate out of fear, but he would never fear to negotiate. While he would strive to close off any possible opening through which the Soviets could hope to penetrate at the expense of the security of other nations, he would strive equally to keep open at all times the channels through which reconciliation on points of mutual interest could be reached.

A major objective, and one with which Kennedy was passionately concerned, was to end the arms race before it resulted in ending the human race. "Today, every inhabitant of this planet must contemplate the day when this planet may no longer be habitable," he declared in an address to the United Nations General Assembly in September, 1961. "Every man, woman, and child is under a nuclear sword of Damocles hanging by the slenderest of threads, capable of being cut at any moment by accident or by miscalculation or by madness." The quest for disarmament could not be considered a sign of weakness, he said, for in a spiraling arms race a nation's security was diminished even as its weapons increased. The first step was a nuclear test ban agreement, which, he hoped, would ultimately lead to an accord to halt the production of fissionable materials for use in weapons, and even to the destruction of all nuclear weapons.

Throughout 1962, Kennedy tirelessly sought to achieve such an agreement, but though he made a number of adjustments in the American position, the Kremlin remained unresponsive. At last, the following June, the President struck a chord in his commencement address at the American University which elicited the first sign of genuine cooperation in eighteen years. Probably Kennedy's most memorable talk, it was directed both to the Soviet Union and to his own citizens, a plea for peace and an attempt to drive home to Americans some of the immutable facts of international existence and dispel some popular myths. Critical situations must be dealt with on a day-by-day pragmatic basis, but at the same time the nation's future could be protected only by fashioning policies that looked ahead to future administrations. Kennedy sought to make clear that the cold war would neither be won nor lost, that unless the United States found a means of resolving its problems with the Soviet Union, it would lose influence in those areas of the world where the cold war was not regarded as particularly relevant.

The most urgent task, the President said, was to assure peace for mankind, "not merely peace in our time but peace in all time." To that end it was incumbent upon every thoughtful citizen to look inward and examine his own attitude toward the cold war and toward peace. The dangerous and defeatist view that war was inevitable must be discarded. Problems which were man-made could be solved by man. "No problem of human destiny is beyond human beings. Man's reason and spirit have often solved the unsolvable—and we believe they can do it again." He was not referring, he said, to absolute concepts of universal peace and good will, but to a more practical, more attainable peace, to a series of concrete acts and effective agreements. No magic formula existed that could be adopted by one or two powers. A genuine peace would come about from the cooperation of many nations and the results of many acts, and each generation would have to meet the challenge. As with families, quarrels and conflicting interests would never disappear among nations. World peace, however, did not require that each man love his neighbor, but only that they live together with mutual tolerance, submitting their disputes for a peaceful settlement. History also taught that enmities between nations, as between individuals, did not last forever; time often brought surprising changes in the relations between countries, as between neighbors.

Secondly, it was essential that Americans re-examine their attitude toward the Soviet Union. While they naturally found communism profoundly repugnant, they could appreciate the achievements of the Russian people in science, in economic growth, in culture, "in acts of courage." Both nations were caught up in a vicious cycle. Suspicion on one side bred suspicion on the other, and new weapons produced counterweapons. Yet both, and their allies, had a mutual interest in preserving the peace and halting the arms race. Agreements were therefore in the interests of all, and even the most hostile of nations could be relied upon to adhere to treaty obligations that were in their own interest. "So, let us not be blind to our differences," he continued, "but let us also direct our attention to our common interests and the means by which those differences can be resolved. And if we cannot end now our differences, at least we can help make the world safe for diversity. For in the final analysis, our most basic common link is that we all inhabit this small planet. We all breathe the same air. We all cherish our children's future. And we are all mortal."

For breadth of view, for insight and perception, this address would be difficult to surpass. Kennedy recognized the significance of the mutation of political power which had occurred since World War II and was producing a growing diversity throughout the world. The former two poles with allies and satellites attached to each had been replaced by a diffusion of power. He did not regard the new multipolar world of independent nations, a world essentially pluralistic, as an obstacle to peace. While it might produce irritations and vexations—as, for instance, de Gaulle's behavior indicated—more importantly, it could avert the dangers arising out of a rigid polarization.

Aware that the Soviet Union's widening rift with China and the growing burdens on the Russian economy were leading Khrushchev to re-evaluate his position toward the West, Kennedy pressed his advantage. A month after his American University address he succeeded in effecting the first move toward a détente with the signing of a nuclear test ban treaty. It was a limited agreement which excluded underground testing, but it was the first significant breakthrough. The President had abandoned earlier insistence on inspection, as it was not particularly important in view of advances in technology and instruments of detection. Some months later, in a continuing effort at a thaw, Kennedy urged the sale of surplus wheat to Russia.

Of global problems, which succeeded one another at a dizzying pace—the Congo, Laos, Vietnam, Berlin—there was no lack. The President also had little respite from domestic problems. Most immediate and crucial was civil rights, the struggle of the Negro for full equality. President Kennedy may have moved too slowly, waiting until his hand was forced by violence in the South. But once he took action, he made a total commitment as no previous President had done. He had earlier dealt with the issue in terms of constitutional principles, but later he unequivocally put it to the nation as a *moral* issue— the first chief executive to do so. Equal opportunity should be given the Negro people not only because the fundamental law provided for it, but because it was right, and he submitted to

Congress the most far-reaching measure for civil rights ever presented.

While Kennedy took office at a time of unprecedented prosperity, he did not shut his eyes to the large pockets of dry rot and despair in the nation. He was probably the only American President to insistently uncover these sores during a period of boom and compel the public to view them. Arthur M. Schlesinger, Jr. relates that Kennedy "could never understand the complacent rich who, so long as they had everything they needed for themselves, were content to starve schools, medical services and social services for their less fortunate citizens." In one of their last talks, Schlesinger said, the President, musing about the legislative program for the following year, told him, "The time has come to organize a national assault on the causes of poverty, a comprehensive program, across the board."

His ideal was a civilized America which would be concerned with the cultivation of mind and spirit, with an appreciation of excellence. He and his wife set an example by transforming Washington into the most cultivated capital in the world, where poets, artists, writers, scholars came not merely for "command" performances, but where they were genuinely esteemed for their gifts. He was one of the few American Presidents who could talk on poetry with grace and felicity and in character, as in the address at the dedication of the Robert Frost Library at Amherst College in October, 1963. A profound and eloquent tribute to the artist, "the deepest source of our national strength," a brilliant commentary on the value of poetry, it also proclaimed his hopes for the future of his country.

The men who create power, Kennedy said, contribute to the nation's greatness, but the men who question it make just as indispensable a contribution, "for they determine whether we use power or power uses us. . . . When power leads men toward arrogance, poetry reminds him of his limitations. When power narrows the areas of man's concern, poetry reminds him of the richness and diversity of his existence. When power corrupts, poetry cleanses, for art establishes the basic human truths which must serve as the touchstones of our judgment." Nothing was more important to the future of the nation and of civilization itself than the full recognition of the place of the artist. Art was not a form of propaganda but a form of truth, and in a free society it was not a weapon for polemics or ideology. The artist who served his own vision of truth served his country best. "And the nation which disdains the mission of art invites the fate of Robert Frost's hired man—the fate of having 'nothing to look backward to with pride, And nothing to look forward to with hope.'" He looked forward, he said, to a future for America when the country would match its military with its moral strength, its wealth with its wisdom, an America which would reward artistic achievements equally with achievements in business or statecraft, which would enlarge cultural opportunities for everyone, which would command world-wide respect not only for its strength but for its civilization as well. "And I look forward to a world which will be safe, not only for democracy and diversity but also for personal distinction."

This speech gives an insight into that mysterious quality called the "style" of John Fitzgerald Kennedy, of which people became more conscious after his death than they had been while he was still alive. It was compounded partly of the charismatic quality of the youthful President, of his wit, his humor, his intelligence, his sophistication, of the brilliant young men with large, expansive views with whom he surrounded himself, of the things he said, and the projects, like the Peace Corps, which he initiated. While he was in office, the nation sensed rather than comprehended a heightened feeling of life, of excitement, of expectation; overseas, especially among the younger generation, he infused a new feeling of hope. When that glow, that vitality was suddenly and so appallingly extinguished, the world darkened. The inexplicable grief that pierced men everywhere was probably unprecedented for depth and breadth in the history of any country. Kennedy's magnetism alone, great as that was, could not have evoked this international reaction. He had achieved, as no other statesman, acceptance as a global leader and the respect of his adversaries. The day before he was assassinated, Fidel Castro told the foreign editor of *L'Express* of Paris that Khrushchev regarded Kennedy as "a man you can talk with." When the Cuban leader heard the terrible news, he exclaimed, "Everything is changed." The President's death, he said, affected millions of people in every corner of the globe. "The cold war, relations with Russia, Latin America, Cuba, the Negro question . . . all will have to be rethought."

To friends of the United States, the calamity was a personal blow. The co-editor of the British magazine *Encounter* commented that not only had Kennedy comprehended the national necessities of his own country, but also the hopes for independence, freedom, equality, and dignity of different and distant peoples, and, above all, the world's longing for peace. "In all of Europe, and also in the Afro-Asian world, there was . . . a feeling . . . that a leader of their own had been foully murdered."

This, then, was the essence of John Fitzgerald Kennedy's achievement: that he elevated the presidency to the highest eminence it had ever reached. Prematurely terminated, his leadership cannot be judged on the basis of policies fulfilled. He will be remembered not for his actual accomplishments, which were few, but for the ideas he generated, the forces he set in motion. The strength and the limitations, the tremendous prestige and potential of the presidential office, but above all, the immutable factor of world leadership, were brought into sharp focus during his tragically brief tenure.

Conclusion

23. Paradoxes of Presidential Leadership

IN 1791, Secretary of State Thomas Jefferson wrote in exasperation to the American Chargé d'Affaires at Madrid, "Your letter of May 6, 1789, is still the last we have received and that is now near two years old. A full explanation of the causes of this suspension of all information from you is expected to my letter of August 6, 1790. . . ." Without telephone or cable and in the days when ships had to rely on favorable winds to sail them across the waters, when couriers on horseback had to struggle over tortuous dirt roads that a heavy rain would turn into quagmires, communication was frustratingly slow. At a time when it would take Benjamin Franklin thirty-eight days to reach France, and even later, when a treaty signed with China would not reach Washington for six and a half months, diplomacy was forced to proceed at a jog trot.

For the President the time lag frequently presented a serious problem. It was difficult for him to establish a fixed policy, since unforeseen developments might require a different response before orders could be received abroad in time to change the original instructions. Policy, accordingly, had to be highly flexible and considerable latitude allowed to subordinates. At the same time, the early chief executives were more than compensated by the nation's meager involvement in foreign affairs, by its freedom from the perilous and recurring crises which keep the contemporary world in a state of constant tension, and demand from the President an incessant alertness. As late as 1913, on the eve of the first world conflict, Woodrow Wilson could omit any reference to international relations in his inaugural address. Even in 1933, when the world was beginning to slide toward disaster, Franklin D. Roosevelt at his inaugural made only a passing reference to external relations. But when John Fitzgerald Kennedy took office, his address was concerned exclusively with the nation's responsibilities in a world community.

Modern technology makes lightning-swift aggression possible. Armies and planes can cross borders in a few hours, the hydrogen missile in minutes. What were once vast moats protecting the security of the United States have shrunk to mere ditches. Instantaneous world-wide communication is available via the telephone. The President has only to pick up a receiver to be in immediate and direct touch with the Kremlin.

Global diplomacy in the nuclear age demands that the White House assume the initiative for major decisions as Congress is not structurally equipped to do so. Only the presidential office has the requisite qualities of flexibility and quick response. Problems have greatly increased in complexity and dimension, requiring technical information available solely from specialists, which even as it is being assembled may be outdated, so swiftly do events move. Only the President is answerable to a nationwide electorate, can base his policies on the widest area of agreement, and has at his disposal a vast institutional apparatus to provide him with any assistance he may require for making responsible decisions. Moreover, as secrecy is imperative in many areas, Congress is dependent on the President for information to evaluate the merit of his policies or for scientific and technical information to which he alone has access, as, for example, on the issue of nuclear disarmament.

The nation has come to look to the White House for an immediate answer to any and all significant problems. Yet, ironically, in a period when the presidency is at the very peak of its influence, probably nowhere in the world is executive leadership more hemmed in, more limited by political considerations, more vulnerable to pressures from within and without than in the United States. For one, Congress by no means has been relegated to a minor position in foreign policy. Far-flung commitments involve the Senate in treaty-making functions, and both Houses in appropriating funds for the vast operational programs overseas. In foreign economic assistance, mutual security aid, national defense, military installations abroad, Congress can obstruct the President and has done so. As George Kennan put it, "A few powerful men—such as some leaders of the House Ways and Means Committee—tie up foreign policy. Some have strong notions about what the Government should be doing; others fear attacks from the extremists; some speak for special interests or jealously hug their prerogatives as holders of the nation's purse strings." The ponderous governmental bureaucracy, which delays and sometimes prevents implementation of policy, is another check on the President's freedom.

Limitations on presidential power come also from the opposing party, from his own party, from the press, and from various organs of public opinion. All of these make his job the most difficult and complicated balancing act on earth while he tries to lead the nation through global agitations that, beyond his capacity to subdue, he can only try to prevent from erupting disastrously.

At the beginning of the twentieth century, the United States still possessed considerable freedom to pursue its own course. Theodore Roosevelt could brandish his big stick at scheming European powers, and his warning sufficed. Or Taft could send Marines into a Caribbean country, and only the invaded nation would make an ineffectual protest. When in 1917 "a little group of wilful men" in the Senate filibustered to death a White House proposal to arm merchant vessels, Wilson proceeded to arm them by executive order. Franklin D. Roosevelt's conviction that the survival of Great Britain was essential to American security led him to assist her even to the point of war. Succeeding Presidents, however, could not consider the use of force to strengthen the nation's security or its diplomatic position in the same manner.

The entangled web of modern international life combined with the nature of military technology have drastically altered the President's perspective. His titanic military power—the authority to order the use of nuclear weapons—ironically limits his freedom to act in a way unknown to his predecessors. No longer are there any simple panaceas, nor can there be any easy or decisive military victories such as were possible in the past. The Cuban Bay of Pigs episode illustrates the complexities of the problems with which the modern President is confronted. Kennedy had to consider the American-Soviet power relationship, the impact of Cuba's social revolution on the peoples of Central and South America, and the views and reactions of the other sovereign members of the Organization of American States. Another example is the direct physical confrontation between Americans and Russians in Berlin which prohibits the President from risking a military engagement; he can only continue to negotiate. For the first time in history, the President of the United States must consider the safety not only of his own nation but of the entire world.

At home the President has always been responsible to several constituencies: the national electorate, the party, the government bureaucracy. He has to balance the national interest or welfare against sectional and local interests of one kind or another. Now vast international constituencies with competing and conflicting needs are part of the equation. The requirements of leadership in world affairs exact a growing emphasis on cooperation and coalition in contrast to the traditional unilateralism and abstention from binding commitments. Franklin D. Roosevelt learned how difficult it was to lead an alliance of nations even when engaged in a common military cause. His successors have found that in peacetime, although exercising a commanding influence over an international community, they are subject to still greater restrictions.

The series of military alliances with which the United States is linked, the re-emergence of Western Europe as a vital political and economic force, the adherence of the Afro-Asian nations to a policy of non-alignment, the independent position of the Latin-American republics—each factor in its own way circumscribes the President's authority. He is frequently impelled to consult with one or more nations before deciding on some issues, and yet sometimes he must refrain from action after a consultation.

Finally, there is the United Nations—the world's security structure, its forum, the bar of world public opinion. A President who exercises wise and sound leadership can use it as an effective instrument of American policy to reach and influence peoples all over the world. The representation which he or his ambassador makes to this body directly affects the prestige of the nation abroad. When popular reactions are a significant element in international power, when the result of the rivalry between Communist and democratic ideologies for the allegiance of the underdeveloped nations may be crucial, the American image is of cardinal importance. Obligations under the United Nations Charter require from the United States joint undertakings with other member states in a variety of political and humanitarian endeavors. To win support from the many constituent members in a particular situation involves the nation in a continual process of negotiation and accommodation.

Americans, who have come to regard their nation as almost omnipotent, are frequently baffled and frustrated when the President does not take action that they consider desirable. Their inability to accept fully that this is a revolutionary age of continuing crises, of a deadly and uniquely complex power struggle, and that force can never again be employed as it has been in the past, hobbles the President's leadership. To jolt the people out of their traditional views, to make them aware of the intangible realities of international power is far more arduous than it has ever been before.

The twentieth-century President must inculcate an awareness of the new and bewildering fact that the dichotomy between foreign and domestic policy has been all but obliterated. In previous eras, the nation's economy was considered purely an internal affair; today, its economic health has direct repercussions on the ability to maintain leadership. Full employment, gross national product, international trade balance, all directly affect the position of the United States in the world arena.

Education, at one time purely a matter of local concern, is

now very much the President's affair. Competition with the Soviet Union requires an acceleration, in quality and quantity, of professional and technical personnel and higher educational standards for the training of intellectual leaders.

Civil rights for minority groups have similarly become involved with the country's world position, and here the United States is perhaps most vulnerable. Whereas at one time the wide gulf between the profession of equal rights and the performance, especially as regards the Negro citizen, deeply troubled thoughtful Americans and embarrassed them when they were abroad, it did not impinge on foreign policy. Today, this explosive internal matter is crucial in the relationship with the millions of Afro-Asians whose friendship and support is vital.

The President's maneuverability is circumscribed also by the ideological conflict. Years of suspended peace and the cold war have created issues that involve doctrinal convictions passionately held. Irrationalities born of fear and frustration have infected segments of the population. Individuals and groups have resorted to the shorthand of slogans and shibboleths—"soft on communism," "better dead than red," "appeasement"—as substitutes for sober discussion and calm analysis. To a considerable extent, rigid views have stifled free inquiry about alternative solutions to certain international problems. Assuming, for instance, that a fundamental change in the China policy would have been advantageous to the national interest in 1962, could the President have felt free to advocate it? Would he not have been pilloried by members of both parties in Congress, to say nothing of a large section of the population, and have risked the loss of his political leadership if he had done so?

To guide public opinion in these troubled times requires the gift of a Pericles, of whom Thucydides said, "Certainly when he saw that they were going too far in a mood of overconfidence, he would bring back to them a sense of their dangers; and when they were discouraged for no good reason, he would restore their confidence." The irony of the President's situation is that while he has instruments of mass communication at his disposal which early leaders would have envied, his task of communicating is far more difficult.

An additional limitation on the President's autonomy is the new military and space technology which has made him heavily dependent on the scientific experts. President Eisenhower formally acknowledged this development when he appointed a scientific adviser. Many of the issues for which the President is responsible are so technical that the layman, even the layman occupying the highest office in the land, must bow to the judgment of the professionals.

Since World War II the decision-making process has been complicated by the vast institutional apparatus created by Congress to assist the President. Even before the many agencies, commissions, and councils began to proliferate in Washington, Harold Laski, a careful observer of the American presidency, commented on the problems arising out of the inevitable expansion of the office. One of the fundamental qualities a President should possess, Laski said, is the ability to coordinate. He must also be able to delegate and put his trust in his appointees since, for the most part, he can be concerned only with the outlines, and "details of the picture must be filled in by subordinates." In his opinion, the President's role was far more exacting than that of a Prime Minister, for the latter, in view of his control of the House of Commons, is free, once policy has been settled, to leave its implementation alone. "But a President may lose a bill in Congress if his subordinates proceed untactfully. . . . Every delegation of power is therefore a risk to be taken, and this makes his judgment of men a matter of supreme importance. He must know that the men he uses will see things through his eyes. . . . He must delegate, too, knowing that at best he is bound to make mistakes, both in men and in things. This is, above all, the case in matters of foreign policy."

The significant position of such groups as the Joint Chiefs of Staff, the Council of Economic Advisers, the Atomic Energy Commission, the Central Intelligence Agency, the National Security Council, and half a dozen other agencies does not detract from the President's pre-eminent position, but it does place a premium on his ability to work out flexible formulas and to remain in control of the situation. The massive institution of which he is the center will continue to restrict even as it assists.

Presidential power, then, is a paradox. The Constitution and the force of custom have made the chief executive the most powerful figure on the domestic scene; the status of the nation has made him the most influential man in the world. But the circumstances of the age have subjected his leadership both domestically and internationally to many limitations. While the President remains the pivotal figure in the affairs of mankind, he is circumscribed by the nature of the nuclear age in ways that were unknown to Presidents of more placid times who had less power.

What qualities must a man possess to fulfill the exacting requirements of presidential leadership in this era?

Almost six decades ago, in a more tranquil time, Professor Woodrow Wilson wrote, "Men of ordinary physique and discretion cannot be President and live if the strain be not somehow relieved. We shall be obliged to be picking our chief magistrate from among wise and prudent athletes—a small class." Although the office has since undergone administrative reorganization to reduce the claims on the time and energy of the chief executive, he still must possess more than the ordinary amount of stamina if he is to exercise real leadership. He must approach the position with zest and thrive on its manifold duties and responsibilities. Self-confidence will enable him to make the weighty decisions which are his alone. At the same time, he should possess the humility that will prevent him from becoming intoxicated with power.

Imagination is an indispensable quality for breadth of vision, for creative innovation, and for a flexible approach to problems. While the Constitution provides for three equal and coordinate branches, it remains for the President to take the initiative in charting new courses for the nation, to bend or break traditions that would stifle growth. The President must have not only the courage of his convictions but also the courage to change his convictions. He must be pragmatic so that he does not become imprisoned by principle or enslaved by doctrine. His objectives should transcend the shifting nature of temporary issues and be motivated by tenets of enduring value.

It is desirable for the President to have a background in both executive and legislative departments to aid him in dealing effectively with politicians and the public. Skill in the art and artfulness of politics is almost indispensable. If the President aspires to be solely a statesman, disdaining the battles of the political arena, he can be only partially successful as a leader. Political amateurs could function in the past without too many unfortunate results; in the nuclear age they are a luxury the nation cannot afford.

The spiritual bond which unites the head of state and the people, clearly demonstrated by the reaction of a deep sense of personal loss to the sudden death of Franklin D. Roosevelt and the tragedy of John F. Kennedy's assassination, together with the mystique that surrounds the office endow the President with unique powers of influence. With the nation turning to the chief executive for guidance and direction, the character of his leadership will greatly affect the public temper. Drift in the White House will be reflected in the country, as will complacency, mediocrity, and parochialism. On the other hand, a profound commitment toward increasing the material resources and strengthening the moral values of the country will spark a similar impulse in the populace.

Americans should look for leadership that will be wise, humanitarian, courageous. They should seek a President with the capacity to perceive the direction of the times and capable of guiding the nation in that direction; a man forthright in enunciating principles and ends, able to diagnose contemporary maladies and offer possible means for their solution, and, above all, capable of illuminating the profound issues that confront the nation. As citizens of a democracy, however, the Presidency belongs to them. In the words of John F. Kennedy, "In your hands, my fellow citizens, will rest the success or failure of our cause." The people must be prepared to make their own commitment.

Chapter Notes

INTRODUCTION

Page 5. ADAMS: Quoted in Clinton Rossiter, *The American Presidency* (Washington, D.C., 1960), p. 73.

6. LINCOLN: Quoted in Norman J. Small, *Some Presidential Interpretations of the Presidency* (Baltimore, 1932), p. 35.

7. WASHINGTON: James D. Richardson (ed.), *A Compilation of the Messages and Papers of the Presidents, 1789-1902* (10 vols., Washington, 1904), I, pp. 222-223.

8. ADAMS: Washington C. Ford (ed.), *The Writings of John Quincy Adams* (7 vols., New York, 1917), VII, p. 49.
JEFFERSON: Andrew A. Lipscomb (ed.), *The Writings of Thomas Jefferson* (20 vols., Washington, 1903), XV, p. 477.

9. ADAMS: See Dexter Perkins, *A History of the Monroe Doctrine* (Boston, 1951), pp. 42-43.

10. ADAMS: Quoted in Edward Howland Tatum, Jr., *The United States and Europe, 1815-1823* (Berkeley, Calif., 1936), p. 244.
SUMNER: Quoted in Foster Rhea Dulles, *America's Rise to World Power* (New York, 1955), p. 13.
BUCHANAN: Richardson, V, p. 435.
SEWARD: Quoted in Charles A. Beard and G. H. E. Smith, *The Idea of National Interest* (New York, 1934), p. 362.

11. CLEVELAND: Richardson, VI, p. 366.
Ibid., VIII, p. 301.

Theodore Roosevelt

2. THE MAN AND THE TIMES MEET

Page 17. ROOSEVELT: Quoted in Howard C. Hill, *Roosevelt and the Caribbean* (Chicago, 1927), p. 21.

18. TAFT: See Howard K. Beale, *Theodore Roosevelt and the Rise of America to World Power* (Baltimore, 1956), p. 63.

Page 18. ROOSEVELT: Quoted in Edward Wagenknecht, *The Seven Worlds of Theodore Roosevelt* (New York, 1958), p. 248.
           JAMES: Quoted in Beale, pp. 37-38.
      19. Theodore Roosevelt, *An Autobiography* (New York, 1924), p. 357.
      20. To TREVELYON: Elton E. Morison (ed.), *The Letters of Theodore Roosevelt* (Cambridge, Mass., 1951), IV, p. 807.
           ON ROOSEVELT: Quoted in James Burns, *Roosevelt: The Lion and the Fox* (New York, 1956), p. 26.
           NATIONAL JOURNAL: Quoted in Steffan Lorant, *The Life and Times of Theodore Roosevelt* (New York, 1959), p. 457.
           Finley Peter Dunne, "Mr. Dooley's Friends: Teddy Roosevelt and Mark Twain," *Atlantic Monthly*, vol. 212 (Sept., 1936), p. 77.
      22. ROOSEVELT: Quoted in Beale, p. 455.
           CANNON: Quoted in Wilfred E. Binkley, *President and Congress* (New York, 1962), p. 240.
      23. *Autobiography*, p. 282.
           Letters, VIII, p. 1114.
           ROOSEVELT: Quoted in Wagenknecht, p. 203.
           Autobiography, p. 386.
           ON PERSONAL DIPLOMACY: Tyler Dennett, *Theodore Roosevelt and the Russo-Japanese War* (New York, 1925), p. 22.

Theodore Roosevelt

3. EXTENDING THE NATION'S POWER

Page 26. ROOSEVELT: Quoted in Beale, p. 80.
      27. *Letters*, II, pp. 1067-68.
           ROOSEVELT: Quoted in Beale, pp. 173, 253.
      28. Theodore Roosevelt, *Works* (20 vols., New York, 1926) XV, pp. 113, 118.
           ROOSEVELT: Quoted in John Morton Blum, *The Republican Roosevelt* (Cambridge, 1954), p. 126.
           To CECIL SPRING-RICE: Dennett, pp. 89-90.
      29. Theodore Roosevelt, *An Autobiography* (New York, 1924), pp. 548-550.
      31. ROCKHILL: Quoted in Beale, pp. 187-88.
           To MAHAN: Quoted in Hill, p. 203.
           Selections from the Correspondence of Theodore Roosevelt and Henry Cabot Lodge, 1884-1918 (2 vols., New York, 1925), I, pp. 485, 486.
           ON CANAL: Quoted in Hill, p. 68.
      32. To HANNA: *Ibid.*, p. 57.
           COUNCIL OF WAR: *Ibid.*, pp. 61-63.
           PANAMA PRESIDENT: Quoted in Lorant, p. 405.
      34. VENEZUELA AFFAIR: Seward W. Livermore, "Theodore Roosevelt, the American Navy and the Venezuelan Crisis of 1902-03," *American Historical Review*, LI (April, 1946), pp. 452-55, 470-71.
           Works, XV, p. 257.

Page 35. *Autobiography,* p. 509.

37. ROOSEVELT: Quoted in Beale, pp. 270-71.
ROOSEVELT'S ACCOUNT OF HIS DIPLOMATIC EFFORTS: *Letters,* IV, pp. 1221-33.

39. To JUSSERAND: Quoted in Beale, pp. 366-67.

41. To VON ECKARDSTEIN: *Ibid.,* p. 447.
Letters, V, pp. 18-20.

42. To ELIOT: *Ibid.,* p. 421.
To ANDREW CARNEGIE: *Ibid.,* pp. 345-46.

43. *Ibid.,* p. 475.

44. CHRONICLE: Quoted in Wagenknecht, p. 238.
ROOSEVELT: Quoted in Foster Rhea Dulles, *Imperial Years* (New York, 1956), p. 284.

45. To HALE: *Letters,* V, pp. 473-75.
ON JAPAN: Quoted in Thomas A. Bailey, *Theodore Roosevelt and the Japanese-American Crisis* (Stanford, 1934), p. 321.

46. ON RUSSIANS: Quoted in Wagenknecht, p. 240.
ON BRITAIN: Quoted in George E. Mowry, *The Era of Theodore Roosevelt, 1900-1912* (New York, 1958), p. 148.
To MAHAN: Quoted in Charles S. Campbell, Jr., *Anglo-American Understanding, 1898-1903* (Baltimore, 1957), p. 347.
ANGLO-AMERICAN FRIENDSHIP: Quoted in Mowry, p. 196.

47. To WHITE: Quoted in Beale, p. 254.

48. To CECIL SPRING-RICE, SEPT. 17, 1908: Quoted in Mowry, pp. 226-227.

49. VIEW OF THE OFFICE: Roosevelt-Lodge Correspondence, II, p. 304.

William Howard Taft

Page 50. To WIFE: Quoted in Henry F. Pringle, *The Life and Times of William Howard Taft* (2 vols., New York, 1939), I, p. 290.
SPEECH MAKING: Quoted in George E. Mowry, *The Era of Theodore Roosevelt, 1900-1912* (New York, 1958), p. 249.

52. To ROOSEVELT: Quoted in Pringle, pp. 400-401.
William Howard Taft, *Our Chief Magistrate and His Powers* (New York, 1916), pp. 139-40.

53. ON EXECUTIVE POWER: William Howard Taft, *The Presidency* (New York, 1916), p. 7.

54. To ROOSEVELT: Quoted in Pringle, I, p. 543.
RELATIONS WITH PRESS: *Ibid.,* p. 415.

55. TAFT AS ADMINISTRATOR: Henry L. Stimson and McGeorge Bundy, *On Active Service in Peace and War* (New York, 1948), p. 495.

56. ARBITRATION TREATIES: Pringle, II, p. 737.
CARNEGIE: Quoted in *Ibid.,* p. 744.
REPLY TO ROOSEVELT: Quoted in *Ibid.,* p. 750.

Page　57.　Archibald W. Butt, *Taft and Roosevelt* (2 vols., New York, 1930), II, p. 804.

58.　ON CANAL TOLLS: Quoted in Pringle, II, pp. 651-52.

59.　DOLLAR DIPLOMACY: Quoted in *Ibid.*, p. 678.

60.　ON TAFT: Mowry, p. 294.

Woodrow Wilson

5. SCHOLAR IN THE WHITE HOUSE

Page　62.　Ray Stannard Baker, *Woodrow Wilson: Life and Letters* (8 vols., New York, 1927-1939), I, pp. 228-29.

63.　CABINET GOVERNMENT: Ray Stannard Baker and William E. Dodd (eds.), *Public Papers of Woodrow Wilson* (6 vols., New York, 1925-27), *College and State*, I, pp. 21-22.
Woodrow Wilson, *Congressional Government* (New York, 1956 ed.), pp. 47, 48, 170.

64.　James Bryce, *The American Commonwealth* (3 vols., London, 1888), I, p. 105.

65.　Woodrow Wilson, *Constitutional Government in the United States* (New York, 1908; Columbia Paperback Edition, 1961), pp. 68-70.

66.　Quoted in Arthur S. Link, *Wilson: Road to the White House* (Princeton, 1947), pp. 130-31.

67.　Quoted in Arthur Walworth, *Woodrow Wilson* (2 vols., New York, 1958), I, p. 183.

68.　Charles Seymour (ed.), *The Intimate Papers of Colonel House* (4 vols., Boston, 1926-28), III, p. 177.
DAVIDSON'S IMPRESSIONS: John Garraty, "Woodrow Wilson: A Study in Personality," *South Atlantic Quarterly*, vol. 56 (April, 1957), p. 176.
Anne W. Lane and Louise H. Wall (eds.), Letters of *Franklin K. Lane* (Boston, 1922), p. 123.

69.　TO FIANCÉE: Quoted in Walworth, I, p. 55.
ON BURKE: Quoted in Baker, III, pp. 301-302.
ON WILSON: Quoted in Arthur S. Link, *Wilson: The New Freedom* (Princeton, 1956), p. 69.

70.　TO FEMALE FRIEND: Baker, III, p. 159.

71.　LANSING: Quoted in Link, *The New Freedom*, p. 67.
RELIGIOUS FAITH: Quoted in Walworth, p. 417.

72.　Burton J. Hendrick (ed.), *Life and Letters of Walter Hines Page* (3 vols., New York, 1924-25), I, p. 122.
TAFT: Quoted in Laurin L. Henry, *Presidential Transitions* (Washington, 1960), p. 59.

73.　TO PALMER: August Heckscher (ed.), *The Politics of Woodrow Wilson* (New York, 1956), pp. 218-19.

Page 75. TIMES: Quoted in Baker, IV, p. 196.
See "President Wilson On His Foreign Policy," *World's Work* vol. 28 (Oct., 1914), p. 493.

76. HOUSE: Quoted in Arthur S. Link, *Struggle for Neutrality, 1914-1915* (Princeton, 1960), p. 428.
Letters of Franklin K. Lane, p. 175.
TO HOUSE: See *Intimate Papers of Colonel House*, II, p. 468.

77. WILSON AND THE PRESS: Baker, IV, pp. 232-235.

Woodrow Wilson

6. ORDEAL OF NEUTRALITY

Page 78. TO FRIEND: Baker, IV, pp. 55-56.
ON PRESIDENT: *Congressional Government* (preface to 15th edition), pp. xi-xii.

79. *Constitutional Government*, pp. 78-79.
WILSON'S WORLD VIEW: Harley Notter, *Origins of the Foreign Policy of Woodrow Wilson* (Baltimore, 1937), pp. 651-54.

80. TO TYROL: Quoted in Herbert Agar, *The People's Choice* (Boston, 1933), p. 298.
Quoted in Howard F. Cline, *The United States and Mexico* (Boston, 1953), p. 141.

82. MEMORANDUM: *Ibid.*, p. 149.
TO JOURNALIST: *Saturday Evening Post*, vol. 186 (May 23, 1914), p. 3.

84. MOBILE: Baker and Dodd, *The New Democracy*, I, pp. 67-69.

86. TO CONGRESS: Baker, IV, p. 415.
WILSON: Quoted in Walworth, I, p. 388.

87. ON LOAN: Ibid., pp. 350-51.

89. ON NEUTRALITY: James B. Scott, *President Wilson's Foreign Policy* (New York, 1918), pp. 66-68.
TO HOUSE: Quoted in Link, *Struggle for Neutrality*, p. 53.

90. *Intimate Papers of Colonel House*, I, p. 417.

91. BRYAN, McADOO, AND LANSING: Quoted in Paul Birdsall, "Neutrality and Economic Pressure, 1914-1917," *Science and Society*, III, (Spring, 1939), pp. 219, 221.

92. TO TUMULTY: Quoted in Walworth, II, p. 5.

94. PLEA TO BRITAIN: Baker, VI, p. 164.
LETTER TO SENATOR: *Ibid.*, p. 169.
Quoted in Walworth, II, p. 48.

96. TO DANIELS: Quoted in John A. Garraty, *Woodrow Wilson* (New York, 1956), p. 109.

97. TO CONGRESS: Baker and Dodd, *The New Democracy*, II, p. 410.

98. *Ibid.*, p. 435.

99. TO COBB: Quoted in Walworth, II, p. 97.

100. WAR MESSAGE: *Ibid.*, pp. 99-100.
BORAH: Quoted in Williams, p. 596.

Woodrow Wilson

7. LIBERATOR IN EUROPE

Page 103. To House: Baker, VII, p. 180.

105. Baker, VIII, pp. 142-43.

106. *Ibid.*, pp. 529-30.

107. WILSON: *Ibid.*, pp. 412-13.

108. APPEAL TO VOTERS: Baker and Dodd, *War and Peace*, I, pp. 286-87.
ROOSEVELT: Quoted in Richard W. Leopold, *Growth of American Foreign Policy* (New York, 1962), p. 361.

109. HOUSE: Quoted in Walworth, II, p. 208.
COBB: Quoted in Herbert Hoover, *The Ordeal of Woodrow Wilson* (New York, 1958), p. 62.

110. Quoted in Walworth, II, p. 206.

111. OBJECTIONS: Quoted in Leopold, p. 362.

112. WILSON IN EUROPE: See Ray Stannard Baker, *What Wilson Did At Paris* (New York, 1919), pp. 6-7.

113. Joseph Grew, *Turbulent Era: A Diplomatic Record of Forty Years, 1904-1945* (Boston, 1952), p. 343.
LLOYD GEORGE: Quoted in Hoover, p. 254.

114. Quoted in George Creel, *Rebel at Large* (New York, 1947), p. 214.
David Lloyd George, *Memoirs of the Peace Conference* (2 vols., New Haven, 1939), I, pp. 96-97.

115. Edith Bolling Wilson, *My Memoir* (New York, 1939), pp. 245-46.

117. SCHEDULE: Walworth, II, p. 296.
CLEMENCEAU: Quoted in *Ibid.*, p. 332.

118. George Herron, Preparatory Remarks to the Herron Papers, II, Hoover Library.
ON TREATY: Quoted in Walworth, II, p. 319.

119. CABLE: Baker and Dodd, *War and Peace*, I, pp. 523-24.
LEDGER: Quoted in Thomas A. Bailey, *Wilson and the Peacemakers* (2 vol. in one, New York, 1947), pp. 305-306.

Woodrow Wilson

8. TRIUMPH AND TRAGEDY

Page 121. WORLD ORGANIZATION: See Link, *Struggle for Neutrality*, p. 51. *Intimate Papers of Colonel House*, II, p. 295.

122. MEMORIAL DAY ADDRESS: Quoted in Walworth, II, p. 39.
To STRACHEY: Baker, VIII, p. 74.

123. Baker and Dodd, *War and Peace*, I, pp. 256, 258.

124. Quoted in Walworth, II, p. 260.

Page 125. MEMO TO WHITE: Quoted in Allan Nevins, *Henry White: Thirty Years of American Diplomacy* (New York, 1930), pp. 353, 355; see also John A. Garraty, *Henry Cabot Lodge* (New York, 1953), pp. 348-49.
LODGE: *Congressional Record*, Vol. 57, Pt. 1, p. 724.
Henry Cabot Lodge, *The Senate and the League of Nations* (New York, 1953), pp. 348-49.

126. Baker and Dodd, *War and Peace*, I, pp. 438-39.

127. OPERA HOUSE ADDRESS: Quoted in Thomas A. Bailey, *The Lost Peace* (New York, 1944), pp. 207-208.

129. Quoted in Walworth, II, p. 361.

130. WILSON'S WARNING: *Ibid.*, p. 372.

131. Edith B. Wilson, p. 290.
Letters of Franklin K. Lane, p. 330.
Lodge, p. 145.

133. Quoted in Edith B. Wilson, pp. 296-97.
HOUSE: Quoted in Stephen Bonsal, *Unfinished Business* (New York, 1944), p. 279.

134. TAFT: Quoted in Garraty, *Lodge*, p. 379.

135. LODGE: See Walter Johnson, "Senatorial Strategy, 1919-1920," *Antioch Review*, III (Winter, 1943), pp. 512-526.
LODGE TO BORAH: *Ibid.*, p. 518.
Quoted in James E. Watson, *As I Knew Them* (Indianapolis, 1936), p. 200.

137. WILSON: Quoted in James Kerney, *Political Education of Woodrow Wilson* (New York, 1926), pp. 469-70.
Quoted In Garraty, *Lodge*, p. 423.

Harding and Coolidge

Page 140. *World's Work*, XLI (November, 1920), p. 9.
New Republic, XXIII (June 23, 1920), p. 99.
MC ADOO: Quoted in Karl Schriftgeiser, *This Was Normalcy* (Boston, 1948), p. 34.

142. To PEACE CRUSADER: Quoted in Robert H. Ferrell, *Peace in Their Time* (New Haven, 1952), p. 35.

143. NATIONAL PRESS CLUB: Quoted in Samuel H. Adams, *Incredible Era: Life and Times of Warren G. Harding* (Boston, 1939), pp. 7-8.
To SECRETARY: Quoted in William Allen White, *Autobiography* (New York, 1946), pp. 616-17.
Quoted in Merlo John Pusey, *Charles Evans Hughes* (2 vols., New York, 1952), I, p. 408.

145. No CRUSADE: Quoted in Don W. Driggs, "The President as Chief Educator on Foreign Affairs," *Western Political Quarterly*, XI (Dec., 1958), p. 814.

146. Quoted in Claude M. Fuess, *Calvin Coolidge* (Boston, 1940), p. 285.
Ibid., pp. 113, 134.

Page 147.   Quoted in William Allen White, *Puritan in Babylon: The Story of Calvin Coolidge* (New York, 1938), p. 433.

148.   COOLIDGE: Quoted in Fuess, p. 348.

149.   ON WORLD COURT: Quoted in Schriftgeiser, p. 233.

150.   ACCLAIMS KELLOGG PACT: *New York Times*, August 16, 1928.

151.   Fuess, p. 497.

Herbert Hoover

Page 154.   Anne W. Lane and Louise H. Wall (eds.), *Letters of Franklin K. Lane* (Boston, 1922), p. 334.
Mark Sullivan, "President Hoover in International Relations," *The Yale Review*, LXI (Dec., 1939), p. 219.

155.   Henry L. Stimson and McGeorge Bundy, *On Active Service in Peace and War* (New York, 1948), p. 196.
TO SECRETARY OF STATE: Herbert Hoover, *The Memoirs of Herbert Hoover* (3 vols., New York, 1952), *The Cabinet and the Presidency, 1920-1933*, II, p. 223.
DANGERS OF WAR: *Papers Relating to the Foreign Relations of the United States, 1929* (Washington, 1943), I, p. 241.

157.   BORAH: Quoted in William A. Williams (ed.), *The Shaping of American Diplomacy* (Chicago, 1956), p. 719.
Hoover, p. 182.

159.   DEFENSE OF EXECUTIVE PREROGATIVE: William Starr Myers (ed.), *The State Papers and Other Public Writings of Herbert Hoover* (2 vols., Garden City, N.Y., 1934), I, pp. 357-58.

161.   See Richard N. Current, "The Stimson Doctrine and the Hoover Doctrine," *American Historical Review*, LIX (April, 1954), pp. 513-42.

163.   ROOSEVELT: Quoted in Hoover, *The Great Depression, 1929-41*, III, p. 179.

Franklin D. Roosevelt

11. SHAPING OF A LEADER

Page 167.   Franklin D. Roosevelt, "Our Foreign Policy: A Democratic View," *Foreign Affairs*, VI (July, 1928), p. 577.

168.   GRANGE: *New York Times*, February 3, 1932.
Walter Lippmann, "The Candidacy of Franklin D. Roosevelt," New York *Herald Tribune* (Jan. 8, 1932), p. 19.
SCRIPPS-HOWARD: Quoted in Arthur M. Schlesinger, Jr., *The Crisis of the Old Order* (Boston, 1957), p. 291.

169.   TO WILSON SUPPORTER: Quoted in Frank Freidel, *Franklin D. Roosevelt: The Triumph* (Boston, 1956), p. 253.

Page 169.   Samuel I. Rosenman (ed.), *Public Papers and Addresses of Franklin D. Roosevelt* (13 vols., New York, 1938-1950) XII, p. 368. (Hereafter cited as *Public Papers.*)

170.   Schlesinger, p. 410.

171.   DEMOCRATIC CONVENTION: Franklin D. Roosevelt, *The Happy Warrior* (Boston, 1928), p. 27.
ON PRESIDENCY: *New York Times*, November 13, 1932.

173.   Raymond Moley, *Twenty-Seven Masters of Politics* (New York, 1949), p. 37.

174.   PITTMAN: Quoted in Thomas H. Greer, *What Roosevelt Thought* (Ann Arbor, 1958), pp. 107-108.

175.   CLEARING HOUSE: *Ibid.*, p. 101. . . . .

176.   Quoted in James E. Pollard, *The President and the Press* (New York, 1947), p. 781.
Public Papers, I, p. xiii.

Franklin D. Roosevelt

12. RETREAT TO THE STORM CELLARS

Page 179.   "BOMBSHELL": *Public Papers*, II, p. 264.
DELEGATE: Quoted in Arthur M. Schlesinger, Jr., *The Coming of the New Deal* (Boston, 1959), pp. 226-27.
Franklin D. Roosevelt, *On Our Way* (New York, 1934), pp. 123-24.

181.   Elliott Roosevelt (ed.), Franklin D. Roosevelt: *His Personal Letters, 1928-45* (2 vols., New York, 1950) I, pp. 463-64. (Hereafter cited as *Personal Letters.*)

182.   To DAVIS: Quoted in James M. Burns, *Roosevelt, The Lion and The Fox* (New York, 1956), p. 250.
BORAH: Quoted in Williams, p. 724.
Roosevelt's Foreign Policy: Franklin D. Roosevelt's Unedited Speeches and Messages, 1933-1941 (New York, 1942), p. 41.

184.   WELLS: Quoted in Edward D. Gerrant, *Roosevelt's Good Neighbor Policy* (Albuquerque, 1950), p. 104.
Public Papers, V, pp. 604-605.

185.   To STIMSON: Quoted in Burns, pp. 251-52.

186.   REPORTS ON DANGERS ABROAD: *New York Times*, Jan. 6, 1943, reprinted from *Peace and War—United States Foreign Policy, 1931-1941* (Washington, D.C., 1943).

187.   To HOUSE: *Personal Letters*, I, p. 472.
Ibid., pp. 506-507.

190.   WARNING MESSAGE: *Roosevelt's Foreign Policy*, p. 76.
Personal Letters, I, pp. 555, 571.
STRAUS: Quoted in Williams, p. 768.

191.   On Welles's proposal, see Sumner Welles, *Seven Decisions That Shaped History* (New York, 1950), **pp. 16-24.**

Page 192. To BERLIN AMBASSADOR: *Personal Letters*, I, p. 606.
           CHICAGO ADDRESS: See *Public Papers*, VI, pp. 408-411.
     193. PRESS CONFERENCE: *Ibid.*, p. 423.
           PEABODY: *Personal Letters*, I, p. 719.
     195. Harold L. Ickes, *The Secret Diary of Harold L. Ickes* (3 vols.,
           New York, 1945), II, pp. 390, 570.
           PERSONAL APPEAL: *Public Papers*, VII, p. 532.
     196. *Personal Letters*, II, pp. 810, 816.
     197. RADIO ADDRESS: *Public Papers*, VII, pp. 564-65.
     198. ANNUAL MESSAGE: *Roosevelt's Foreign Policy*, pp. 155-57.
           CUDAHY: *Personal Letters*, II, pp. 862-63.
     200. Quoted in William L. Langer and S. Everett Gleason, *Challenge
           to Isolation* (New York, 1952), p. 143.
           FOREIGN RELATIONS COMMITTEE: *Public Papers*, VIII, pp. 428-29.
     201. RADIO ADDRESS: See *Ibid.*, pp. 460-64.
     202. To CONGRESS: *Ibid.*, pp. 516, 518.
     203. To LORD TWEEDSMUIR: Quoted in Burns, p. 396.

Franklin D. Roosevelt

13. ARSENAL OF DEMOCRACY

Page 205. ROOSEVELT: Quoted in Langer and Gleason, p. 330.
           Cordell Hull, *Memoirs of Cordell Hull* (2 vols., New York, 1948)
           I, p. 743.
     206. To WHITE: *Personal Letters*, II, p. 968.
           STATE OF UNION ADDRESS: *Public Papers*, IX, p. 2.
     208. SPECIAL MESSAGE: See *Ibid.*, pp. 198-205.
     209. VIRGINIA ADDRESS: *Ibid.*, p. 259 ff.
     210. SENATOR PITTMAN'S COMMENT: Langer and Gleason, p. 517.
     211. Winston Churchill, *Their Finest Hour* (Boston, 1949), p. 402.
           Personal Letters, II, pp. 1050-51.
     212. BULLITT: President's Secretary's File, Box 69, Roosevelt Library.
           See *New York Times*, August 20, 1940.
           Chicago Tribune, August 6, 1940.
           SENATOR WALSH: Quoted in Langer and Gleason, p. 760.
     213. MESSAGE TO CONGRESS: *Public Papers*, IX, p. 391.
           REACTION TO DESTROYER DEAL: *New York Times*, Sept. 4, 1940.
           To SECRETARY: Quoted in Grace Tully, *F.D.R.: My Boss* (New
           York, 1949), p. 244.
     214. WILLKIE: Quoted in Samuel I. Rosenman, *Working With Roose-
           velt* (New York, 1952), p. 235.
     215. Robert Sherwood, *Roosevelt and Hopkins* (New York, 1948),
           p. 191.
           ROOSEVELT: *Public Papers*, IX, p. 517.
           Merlo Pusey, *Charles Evans Hughes* (2 vols., New York, 1952),
           II, p. 786.

Page 216.   CHURCHILL: *Public Papers,* IX, p. 607.
            CABINET MEETING: *Ibid.,* pp. 633-644.

      218. Arthur N. Vandenburg, Jr., and J. A. Morris (eds.), *Private Papers of Senator Vandenburg* (Boston, 1952), p. 10.
            Quoted in Joseph Grew, *Ten Years In Japan* (New York, 1944), pp. 361-63.

      220. DEFENSE BUILD-UP: Basil Rauch, *Roosevelt from Munich to Pearl Harbor* (New York, 1950), p. 320.
            BARBAROSSA DIRECTIVE: William L. Langer and S. Everett Gleason, *The Undeclared War* (New York, 1953), pp. 145, 336-37.
            STIMSON: Quoted in *Ibid.,* p. 528.
            U.S. Department of State Foreign Relations, 1941, I, pp. 766-67.

      221. See Winston Churchill, *The Grand Alliance* (Boston, 1950), p. 369.
            To OURSLER: President's Personal Files 2993, Roosevelt Library.
            To LEAHY: *Personal Letters,* II, p. 1177.

      222. JUSTICE MURPHY: Quoted in Raymond H. Dawson, *The Decision to Aid Russia* (Chapel Hill, 1959), p. 232.
            TAYLOR: *Personal Letters,* II, p. 1205.

      223. To AMBASSADOR OUMANSKY: Quoted in Langer and Gleason, p. 797.

      224. To HARRIMAN: Quoted in Dawson, pp. 260, 262.
            Sherwood, p. 384.

      225. ON RUSSIA: PPF 5476, Roosevelt Library.

      226. Grew, p. 416.
            Public Papers, XIII, p. 441.

      227. FIRESIDE CHAT: See *Roosevelt's Foreign Policy,* pp. 470-75.

      228. Quoted in Nelson M. Blake and Oscar T. Barck, *The United States and Its World Relations* (New York, 1960), p. 669.

      231. MEMO TO HULL AND WELLES: *Personal Letters,* II, pp. 1247-48.
            Stimson and Bundy, p. 393.

      233. STIMSON DIARY: U.S. Congress, *Hearings before the Joint Committee on the Investigation of the Pearl Harbor Attack* (Washington, D.C., 1946), Pt. XI, p. 5433.

Franklin D. Roosevelt

14. THE GRAND COALITION

Page 236.   Stimson and Bundy, p. 564.
            Hull, II, pp. 1109-10.

      237. To STALIN: Quoted in Sherwood, pp. 3, 4.
            To WILLKIE: Quoted in *Ibid.,* p. 3.

      239. LEAHY: Quoted in Rexford G. Tugwell, *The Democratic Roosevelt* (New York, 1957), p. 575.

      241. WILLKIE: Quoted in Eric Goldman, *Rendezvous With Destiny* (New York, 1958), p. 396.

      243. To LEAHY: *Personal Letters,* II, p. 129.

Page 244. OBSERVER: Quoted in Richard W. Leopold, *The Growth of American Foreign Policy* (New York, 1962), p. 595.

    246. To A FRIEND: *Personal Letters*, II, pp. 1365-66.
          To GENERAL STILWELL: Quoted in Willard Range, *Franklin D. Roosevelt's World Order* (Athens, Ga., 1959), p. 181.
          Public Papers, XIII, p. 99.

    247. UNCONDITIONAL SURRENDER: Quoted in Sherwood, p. 696.

    248. Elliott Roosevelt, *As He Saw It* (New York, 1946), p. 117.

    249. JOINT CONFERENCE: *Public Papers*, XII, p. 39.
          CHURCHILL: Quoted in Sherwood, p. 696.
          Personal Letters, II, p. 1535.
          ADDRESS: *Public Papers*, XII, pp. 557-58.

    250. Winston Churchill, *Closing the Ring* (Boston, 1951), p. 56.
          BROADCAST: Quoted in Herbert Feis, *Churchill, Roosevelt, Stalin* (Princeton, 1957), p. 157.

    251. To STALIN: *Personal Letters*, II, p. 1422.
          Hull, p. 1238.

    253. TEHERAN: Quoted in William H. McNeill, *America, Britain, and Russia: Their Co-operation and Conflict, 1941-1946* (New York, 1953), p. 367.
          AMERICAN PARTICIPANT'S VIEW: Feis, p. 275.
          ON STALIN: *Public Papers*, XII, p. 558.

    254. To CHURCHILL: Quoted in Chester Wilmot, *The Struggle for Europe* (New York, 1952), p. 138.
          WITH STALIN AT TEHERAN: *Public Papers*, XIII, p. 161.

    255. *Ibid.*, pp. 197-98.
          To HAMILTON HOLT: President's Personal File, No. 345, Roosevelt Library.

    256. POLITICAL ADDRESS: Quoted in Sherwood, p. 821.

    257. MEMORANDUM: Quoted in McNeill, p. 490.

    258. ON GERMANY: *Public Papers*, XIII, pp. 352-53.

Franklin D. Roosevelt

15. EXPECTATIONS AND REALITIES

Page 261. KENNAN: Quoted in Stephen Borosody, *The Triumph of Tyranny* (New York, 1960), p. 189.
          Stimson and Bundy, pp. 618-19.

    262. HARRIMAN: Quoted in Raymond J. Sontag, "Reflections on the Yalta Papers," *Foreign Affairs*, vol. 33 (July, 1955), p. 617.

    263. POLISH GOVERNMENT: Quoted in James F. Byrnes, *Speaking Frankly* (New York, 1947), p. 30.
          ROOSEVELT: Quoted in McNeill, p. 564.

    265. REPARATIONS ISSUE: Byrnes, pp. 26-33.

    267. WAR DEPT. MEMO: Quoted in Joseph C. Grew, *Turbulent Era: A Diplomatic Record of Forty Years, 1904-1945* (2 vols., Boston, 1952), II, p. 145.

Page 269. Winston Churchill, *Triumph and Tragedy* (Cambridge, 1953), p. 401.
To CONGRESS: *Public Papers*, XIII, p. 573.
Sumner Welles, *Seven Decisions That Shaped History* (New York, 1950), p. 172.

271. ROOSEVELT: Quoted in Hull, II, pp. 1688-89.

272. KENNAN: Quoted in Feis, p. 436.

273. Edward Stettinius, *Roosevelt and the Russians* (New York, 1949), p. 296.
Sherwood, p. 877.

274. HARRIMAN: Quoted in Feis, p. 598.
ROOSEVELT: Quoted in Byrnes, p. 54.

275. To STALIN: Quoted in Blake and Barck, p. 697.
To CHURCHILL: Quoted in Albert Z. Carr, *Truman, Stalin, and Peace* (New York, 1950), p. 48.
LAST MESSAGE: Quoted in Byrnes, p. 59.

276. To WHITE: *Personal Letters*, II, p. 967.

277. POSTWAR PEACE: PPF, Franklin D. Roosevelt to Walter Lippmann, Nov. 8, 1943.
ADDRESS TO ILO: *Public Papers*, XIII, pp. 128-29.
Eleanor Roosevelt, *This I Remember* (New York, 1949), p. 253.
ANNUAL MESSAGE: *Public Papers*, XII, p. 32.

278. To PEABODY: *Personal Letters*, II, p. 1471.
Technical assistance, *Public Papers*, XIII, p. 585.
Henry Morgenthau, Jr., "The Morgenthau Diaries," *Colliers*, vol. 120 (Oct. 18, 1947), p. 156.
Elliott Roosevelt, pp. 38-39; see also Foster Rhea Dulles and Gerald E. Ridinger, "The Anti-Colonial Policies of Franklin D. Roosevelt," *Political Science Quarterly*, LXX (March, 1955), pp. 1-18.

279. See Edgar Snow, "Fragments from F.D.R., Part I," *Monthly Review*, VIII (January, 1957), pp. 316-321.
William D. Leahy, *I Was There* (New York, 1950), p. 313.

280. PRESS CONFERENCE: *Public Papers*, XIII, p. 70.

281. INAUGURAL ADDRESS: *Ibid.*, p. 524.

Harry S. Truman

16. THRUST INTO POWER

Page 284. Harry S. Truman, *Memoirs of Harry S. Truman* (2 vols., New York, 1955), I, p. 19. (Hereafter cited as *Memoirs*.)

285. John Fischer, "Truman: A Little West of Center," *Harper's*, vol. 141 (Dec., 1945), p. 482.

286. *Memoirs*, I, p. 25.

287. HOPKINS CABLE: Quoted in *Ibid.*, p. 287.

288. Churchill, *Triumph and Tragedy*, pp. 573-74.

Page 289. Press and Radio Conference, No. 11, Truman Library.
Press and Radio Conference, No. 29, Truman Library.

290. *Memoirs*, I, p. 258.
HARRIMAN: Quoted in *Ibid.*, p. 263.

291. AT POTSDAM: *Ibid.*, pp. 359-60.

292. Walter Millis (ed.), *Forrestal Diaries* (New York, 1951), p. 78.

293. SCIENTISTS' REPORT: Quoted in Norman Cousins and Thomas K. Finletter, "A Beginning for Sanity," *Saturday Review of Literature,* XXIX (June 15, 1946), pp. 6-7.
Official File 692-A, Truman Library.
PPF 6068, Truman Library.

294. ATTLEE: Quoted in *Memoirs*, I, p. 523.
JOINT CHIEFS: Quoted in *Ibid.*, p. 528.
Henry L. Stimson and McGeorge Bundy, *On Active Service in Peace and War* (New York, 1948), p. 528.

295. VANNEVAR BUSH: Quoted in *Memoirs*, I, p. 527.

296. To CONGRESS: OF 692, Truman Library.

297. FOREIGN POLICY ADDRESS: Louis W. Koenig, *Truman Administration* (New York, 1956), pp. 262-63.
Press and Radio Conferences Nos. 53 and 61, Truman Library.

298. James F. Byrnes, *Speaking Frankly* (New York, 1947), pp. 390-91.

299. Press and Radio Conference, No. 61, Truman Library.
WALLACE MEMORANDUM: *Memoirs*, I, pp. 555-56.

300. Henry A. Wallace, *Towards World Peace* (New York, 1948), p. 9.
Press and Radio Conference, No. 80, Truman Library.
Press and Radio Conference, No. 81, Truman Library.
Arthur N. Vandenburg, Jr., and J. A. Norris (eds.), *Private Papers of Senator Vandenburg* (Boston, 1952), p. 301.

301. Press and Radio Conference, No. 83, Truman Library.
ON BYRNES: Quoted in Jonathan Daniels, *Man From Independence* (Boston, 1960), pp. 309-310.

301. Byrnes, pp. 237-38.

302. *Memoirs*, I, p. 551.

303. FULBRIGHT PROPOSAL: Daniels, p. 293.
TRUMAN'S STATEMENT: PPF 1-F, Truman Library.

304. CONTINUE WITH PROGRAM: *Memoirs*, II, p. 187.
Ibid., p. 208.

305. *Ibid.*, p. 211.
Time, Nov. 8, 1948.
POLLS: *Memoirs*, II, p. 177.

306. PRESS ATTACKS: PPF 9-G, Truman Library.
ONE PARTY PRESS: PPF 1-F, Truman Library.

307. *Memoirs*, II, p. 196.
VETO: PPF 1-F, Truman Library.

308. PRESIDENTIAL POWER: OF 419, Truman Library.
STEEL MILLS: *Memoirs*, II, p. 196.
CABINET MEMBER: *Ibid.*, I, p. 329.

309. MEMO TO SECRETARY OF STATE: OF 20, Truman Library.
Memoirs, II, p. 1.

Harry S. Truman

17. COLD WAR STATESMANSHIP

Page 311. ADDRESS TO CONGRESS: See John C. Campbell, *The United States in World Affairs, 1947-1948* (New York, 1948), p. 48.
New York Times, March 12, 1947.

312. O'MAHONEY: OF 386, Truman Library.

313. See X (George F. Kennan), "The Sources of Soviet Conduct," *Foreign Affairs*, XXV (July, 1947), pp. 574-82.
New York *Herald Tribune*, April 5, 1947.

314. ACHESON: See William A. Williams, *The Shaping of American Diplomacy* (Chicago, 1956), pp. 1005-1008.
MARSHALL: See *In Quest of Peace and Security, Selected Documents on Foreign Policy, 1941-51.* Department of State Publications 4245. General Foreign Policy Series. (Washington, D.C., 1951), pp. 93-95.

318. ON BERLIN: Quoted in Millis, p. 454.
Memoirs, II, p. 128.

320. FOR VARIOUS ACCOUNTS OF THE VINSON EPISODE: *Memoirs*, II; Daniels; Albert Z. Carr, *Truman, Stalin, and Peace* (New York, 1950); H. Bradford Westerfield, *Foreign Policy and Party Politics* (New Haven, 1955).

321. INAUGURAL ADDRESS: *New York Times*, Jan. 21, 1949.
WHITE HOUSE AIDE: Files of Charles S. Murphy, Truman Library.

322. To RAYBURN: *Ibid.*, (Aug. 25, 1950).

324. REPUBLICAN VICTORY: PPF 1-F, Truman Library.

326. A. N. Vandenburg, Jr., and J. A. Norris, pp. 560-61.
OF 386, Truman Library.

327. HOOVER: *New York Times*, Dec. 21, 1950.

328. TAFT: *Congressional Record*, vol. 97, pp. 58-59.
STATE OF UNION ADDRESS: *New York Times*, Jan. 9, 1951.
WHERRY: *Congressional Record*, vol. 97, p. 94.

Harry S. Truman

18. COUNTERING AGGRESSION

Page 331. WEDEMEYER: Quoted in *Memoirs*, II, p. 63.
MARSHALL: *Memoirs*, II, pp. 67-68.

332. WEDEMEYER: *Hearings before the Committee on Armed Services and the Committee on Foreign Relations*, United States Senate, 82 Congress, 1st Session (Washington, D.C., 1951), pp. 3238-42.

333. MESSAGE TO CONGRESS: PPF 1-F, Truman Library.
SENATOR McMAHON: Quoted in H. Bradford Westerfield, *Foreign Policy and Party Politics: Pearl Harbor to Korea* (New Haven, 1955), p. 268.

334. *Hearings, Committee on Armed Services.*

335. POLICY STATEMENT: PPF 1-F, Truman Library.
ACHESON: Quoted in Williams, p. 1060.

Page 336.   ACHESON: *New York Times,* Jan. 13, 1950.

337.   *Memoirs,* II, p. 333.

338.   PRESS RELEASE: *New York Times,* June 28, 1950.
ACHESON: *Department of State Bulletin,* XXIII (July 10, 1950), p. 46.
CHOU EN-LAI: Quoted in John W. Spanier, *Truman, MacArthur and the Korean War* (Cambridge, 1959), p. 86; see also Allen S. Whiting, *China Crosses the Yalu: The Decision to Enter the Korean War* (New York, 1960), p. 108.
MACARTHUR: Quoted in *Memoirs,* II, pp. 365-66.

339.   TRUMAN: *Ibid.,* p. 382.
GENERAL BRADLEY: Quoted in Spanier, p. 261.
KREMLIN: *Memoirs,* II, pp. 420-21.

340.   ATOM BOMB: *Ibid.,* p. 395.
To MACARTHUR: *Ibid.,* pp. 435-36.

341.   Quoted in *Ibid.,* p. 354.

342.   DIRECTIVE: *Ibid.,* p. 383.
BRITISH FEARED: *The Observer* (London), April 8, 1951, as quoted in Spanier, p. 206.

343.   *Memoirs,* II, pp. 442, 444.
MACARTHUR LETTER: *New York Times,* April 6, 1951; also, OF 471-B, Truman Library.
DRAW THE LINE: OF 471-B, Truman Library.

345.   LIPPMANN: New York *Herald Tribune,* August 24, 1956.

346.   MCCARTHY: *New York Times,* Feb. 9, 1950.

347.   Press and Radio Conference, No. 221, Truman Library.
WOMAN'S LETTER: OF 471-B, Truman Library.

348.   ALISTAIR COOKE: Quoted in Norman A. Graebner, "Dean G. Acheson," Norman A. Graebner (ed.), *An Uncertain Tradition: American Secretaries of State in the Twentieth Century* (New York, 1961), pp. 268, 270.

349.   To BRIDGES: OF 419-K, Truman Library.

351.   BEFORE CONVENTIONS: *Memoirs,* II, p. 511.
EISENHOWER'S RESERVATION: *New York Times,* August 15, 1952.
MESSAGE: *Memoirs,* II, p. 505.

352.   PRIVATE CONVERSATION: *Ibid.,* pp. 514-15.
TRUMAN AND EISENHOWER: Quoted in Laurin L. Henry, *Presidential Transitions* (Washington, 1960), p. 487.
PRESS CONFERENCE: *New York Times,* Dec. 19, 1952.

Dwight D. Eisenhower

19. HERO IN POLITICS

Page 353.   EISENHOWER: Quoted in Marquis Childs, *Eisenhower: Captive Hero* (New York, 1958), p. 111.

357.   To AIDE: Quoted in Emmett Hughes, *Ordeal of Power: A Political Memoir of the Eisenhower Years* (New York, 1963), p. 41.

Page 357. TRUMAN: Quoted in *U.S. News and World Report,* vol., 28 (Jan. 2, 1950), p. 75.

360. DESCRIBED SYSTEM: Hughes, p. 153.
PRESIDENT-ELECT: Quoted in Sherman Adams, *Firsthand Report: The Story of the Eisenhower Administration* (New York, 1961), p. 5.

362. ADAMS: *Ibid.,* p. 50.
Louis Koenig, *The Invisible Presidency* (New York, 1960), p. 338.

364. *Public Papers of the Presidents of the United States: Dwight D. Eisenhower* (8 vols., Washington, D.C. 1953-1961), 1953, pp. 701-702.
Ibid., 1956, p. 884.

365. *Ibid.,* 1957, pp. 640-41, 646.
New York Times, July 18, 1957.

366. OBSERVATION BY FRIEND: *U.S. News,* vol. 43 (Nov. 22, 1957), pp. 51 ff., 69.

367. "Eisenhower on the Presidency," CBS Telecast with Walter Cronkite, Part II, Nov. 23, 1961.
PRESS CONFERENCE: *Public Papers,* 1957, p. 591.

368. HAGERTY: Quoted in *New York Times Magazine* (Feb. 13, 1955), p. 62.
PRESS INTERVIEWS: *Public Papers,* 1960, p. 559.

370. PRESS STATEMENT: Quoted in Robert J. Donovan, *Eisenhower: The Inside Story* (New York, 1956), p. 373.
Quoted in Adams, p. 228.

371. *New York Times,* March 1, 1956.
RADIO AND TV ADDRESS: Quoted in Eric F. Goldman, *The Crucial Decade and After: America, 1945-60* (New York, 1961), p. 223.

Dwight D. Eisenhower

20. POLICY BY SLOGANS

Page 373. FOR VIEWS ON LIBERATION: John Foster Dulles, "A Policy of Boldness," *Life,* vol. 32 (May 19, 1952), pp. 146-160; Republican Platform 1952; *Hearings Before the Committee on Foreign Relations,* U.S. Senate, 83rd Congress, Jan. 15, 1953 (Washington, D.C., 1953), pp. 5-6.
STATE OF UNION ADDRESS: *New York Times,* Feb. 3, 1953.

377. ON McCARTHY: *Public Papers,* 1953, pp. 153-54.

378. DARTMOUTH ADDRESS: *Ibid.,* pp. 415, 417.

379. CABINET MEETING: Quoted in Hughes, pp. 143-44.

380. To KNOWLAND: Quoted in Donovan, p. 239.
MEETING WITH CONGRESSIONAL LEADERS: *Ibid.,* p. 241.

382. *Public Papers,* 1953, p. 329.

383. To SYNGMAN RHEE: Quoted in Adams, p. 100.

384. PRESS CONFERENCE: *Public Papers,* 1956, pp. 1100-01.

Page 385. DULLES'S ADDRESS: *Department of State Bulletin*, XXX (Jan. 25, 1954), pp. 107-108.

GUARDIAN: Quoted in Hans J. Morgenthau, "John Foster Dulles," Norman A. Graebner (ed.), *An Uncertain Tradition* (New York, 1961), p. 295.

386. DULLES'S STATEMENT: Quoted in *Ibid.*

REACTION TO NIXON: Adams, p. 122.

To CONGRESSIONAL LEADERS: Quoted in *Ibid.*, p. 123.

387. *Economist*: Quoted in Morgenthau, p. 296.

EISENHOWER ON RECOGNITION: *Public Papers*, 1953, p. 296.

388. MEETING WITH SENATE LEADERS: Donovan, pp. 133-34.

389. Adams, p. 130.

To RAYBURN: Quoted in *Ibid.*, p. 135.

391. To REPORTERS: *Public Papers*, 1957, p. 498.

393. LEADERS' COMMENTS: Quoted in Childs, pp. 210-211.

394. RADIO ADDRESS: *New York Times*, Nov. 1, 1956.

395. PRESS STATEMENT: *Public Papers*, 1957, pp. 86-87.

396. BROADCAST: *New York Times*, July 16, 1958.

397. To KHRUSHCHEV: *Public Papers*, 1958, p. 177.

Dwight D. Eisenhower

21. SUMMIT DIPLOMACY BEDEVILED

Page 400. Adams, p. 415.

401. ADDRESS TO NATION: *New York Times*, Nov. 9, 1957.

402. OUTER SPACE: Quoted in Adams, p. 417.

PRESS CONFERENCE: *Public Papers*, 1960-61, p. 152.

403. *Ibid.*, p. 135.

404. PRESS CONFERENCE: *Ibid.*, p. 622.

405. ON DULLES: *Ibid.*, 1959, p. 327.

DULLES: Quoted in Adams, p. 89.

406. OBSERVER: Quoted in Morgenthau, p. 305.

JACKSON: Quoted in Walter Johnson, *1600 Pennsylvania Avenue* (Boston, 1960), p. 297.

407. BRINKMANSHIP: James Shepley, "How Dulles Averted War," *Life*, XL (Jan. 16, 1956), p. 78.

Adams, p. 123.

409. EISENHOWER: *New York Times*, May 12, 1960.

410. BROADCAST ADDRESS: *Public Papers*, 1960-61, p. 439.

Quoted in Adams, pp. 445-46.

411. George E. Allen, "My Friend the President," *Saturday Evening Post*, vol. 232 (April 9, 1960), p. 54.

412. Quoted in Cabell Phillips, "New Look of the President," *New York Times Magazine* (August 16, 1959), p. 17.

Page 412. Eisenhower: Quoted in Norman A. Graebner, "Eisenhower's Popular Leadership," *Current History*, vol. 39 (October, 1960), p. 236.

413. Major problems: *Public Papers*, 1960-61, p. 169.

414: Aide records: Hughes, p. 101.
CABINET MEETING: *Public Papers*, 1960-61, p. 153.

415. Washington address: See *Ibid.*, 1953, pp. 186-88.
Farewell address: *Ibid.*, 1960-61, pp. 1038-39.

A Selected Bibliography

The literature dealing with the Presidents and the Presidency is prodigious. In addition to the sources cited in the notes, the titles listed below provide useful and interesting background material for the theme of this book and its related aspects.

THE PRESIDENCY

Acheson, Dean, *A Citizen Looks at Congress.* New York, 1956

Agar, Herbert, *The People's Choice: From Washington to Harding.* Boston, 1933

Binkley, Wilfred F., *The Man in the White House.* Baltimore, 1959

Chamberlain, Lawrence H., *The President, Congress, and Legislation.* New York, 1946

Corwin, Edward S., *The President: Office and Powers.* 4th ed., New York, 1957

Driggs, Don W., "The President as Chief Educator on Foreign Affairs," *Western Political Quarterly,* XI (December, 1958), 813-819

Fenno, Richard F., Jr., *The President's Cabinet.* Cambridge, 1959

Finer, Herman, *The Presidency: Crisis and Regeneration.* Chicago, 1960

Hart, James, *The American Presidency in Action.* New York, 1948

Herring, Pendleton, *Presidential Leadership.* New York, 1940

Hobbs, Edward H., *Behind the President.* Washington, D.C., 1954

Hyman, Sidney, *The American President.* New York, 1954

Hyman, Sidney (ed.), "The Office of the American Presidency," *Annals of the American Academy of Political and Social Science,* vol. 307, (September, 1956)

Koenig, Louis W., *The Presidency and the Crisis*. New York, 1944

Laski, Harold J., *The American Presidency: An Interpretation*. New York, 1940

Lorant, Stefan, *The Presidency*. New York, 1951

May, Ernest R. (ed.), *The Ultimate Decision: The President as Commander-in-Chief*. New York, 1960

Neustadt, Richard E., *Presidential Power*. New York, 1960

Patterson, C. Perry, *Presidential Government in the United States*. Chapel Hill, 1947

Pollard, James E., *Presidents and the Press*. New York, 1947

Rankin, Robert S. (ed.), "Presidency in Transition," *Journal of Politics*, II (February, 1949)

Rossiter, Clinton L., "The American President," *Yale Review*, vol. 37 (Summer, 1948), 619-37

————, *The American Presidency*. New York, 1956

————, "The Constitutional Significance of the Executive Office of the President," *The American Political Science Review*, vol. 43 (December, 1949), 1212-1217

————, *The Supreme Court and the Commander-in-Chief*. Ithaca, 1951

Rusk, Dean, "The President," *Foreign Affairs*, Vol. 38 (April, 1960), 353-69

Seligman, Lester G., "Developments in the Presidency and the Conception of Political Leadership," *American Sociological Review*, XX (December, 1955), 706-712

Small, Norman J., *Some Presidential Interpretations of the Presidency*. Baltimore, 1932

Smith, Merriman, *A President is Many Men*. New York, 1948

Sorensen, Theodore, *The Olive Branch or the Arrow: Decision Making in the White House*. New York, 1963

Truman, David B., "The Presidency and Congressional Leadership: Some Notes on our Changing Constitution," *American Philosophical Society Proceedings*, vol. 103 (October, 1959)

Tugwell, Rexford G., *The Enlargement of the Presidency*. Garden City, 1960

Warren, Sidney, "How Powerful is the Presidency?" *Saturday Review* (July 21, 1962), 12-15

————, "The President in the Constitution," *Current History*, XXV (September, 1953), 133-137

FOREIGN RELATIONS

Acheson, Dean, *Power and Diplomacy*. Cambridge, 1958
Beard, Charles A., and G. H. E. Smith, *The Idea of National Interest*. New York, 1934
Burns, Edward McNall, *The American Idea of Mission*. New Brunswick, 1957
Cheever, Daniel S., and H. Field Haviland, *American Foreign Policy and the Separation of Powers*, Cambridge, 1952
Cook, Thomas I., and Malcolm Moos, *Power Through Purpose: The Realism of Idealism as a Basis For Foreign Policy*. Baltimore, 1954
Earle, E. M., "A Half-Century of American Foreign Policy—Our Stake in Europe, 1898-1948," *Political Science Quarterly*, LXIV (June, 1949), 168-88
Graber, Doris A., *Crisis Diplomacy: A History of U.S. Intervention Policies and Practices*. Washington, D.C., 1959
Graebner, Norman A. (ed.), *An Uncertain Tradition: American Secretaries of State in the Twentieth Century*. New York, 1961
Halle, Louis J., *Dream and Reality: Aspects of American Foreign Policy*. New York, 1959
Immerman, Robert M., "The Formulation and Administration of U.S. Foreign Policy," Foreign Service Journal, Vol. 37 (April, 1960)
Kennan, George F., *American Diplomacy, 1900-1950*. Chicago, 1951
———, *Realities of American Foreign Policy*. Princeton, 1954
Lippmann, Walter, *U.S. Foreign Policy: Shield of the Republic*. Boston, 1943
Markel, Lester (ed.), *Public Opinion and Foreign Policy*. New York, 1949
Osgood, Robert E., *Ideals and Self-Interest in America's Foreign Relations*. Chicago, 1953
Perkins, Dexter, *A History of the Monroe Doctrine*. Boston, 1955
———, *The Evolution of American Foreign Policy*. New York, 1948
———, *The Monroe Doctrine, 1867-1907*. Baltimore, 1937
Rippy, J. Fred, and Angie Debo, "The Historical Background of the American Policy of Isolation," *Smith College Studies in History*, IX (April-July, 1924), 71-165
Rostow, Walt W., *The United States in the World Arena*. New York, 1960
Weinberg, Albert K., *Manifest Destiny*. Baltimore, 1935

Williams, William A., *The Tragedy of American Diplomacy*. Cleveland, 1959

THEODORE ROOSEVELT

Anderson, Eugene N., *The First Moroccan Crisis, 1904-1906*. Chicago, 1930

Blake, N. M., "Ambassadors at the Court of Theodore Roosevelt," *Mississippi Valley Historical Review*, XLII (September, 1955), 179-206

Harbaugh, William Henry, *Power and Responsibility*. New York, 1961

Jessup, Philip C., *Elihu Root*. 2 vols. New York, 1938

Lodge, Henry Cabot, "Our Blundering Foreign Policy," *Forum*, XIX (March, 1895), 8-17

May, Ernest R., *Imperial Democracy: The Emergence of America as a Great Power*. New York, 1961

Millis, Walter, *The Martial Spirit*, Boston, 1931

Mowry, George E., *The Era of Theodore Roosevelt, 1900-1912*. New York, 1958

————, *Theodore Roosevelt and the Progressive Movement*. Madison, 1946

Padelford, Norman J., *The Panama Canal in Peace and War*. New York, 1942

Pratt, Julius W., "The 'Large Policy' of 1898," *Mississippi Valley Historical Review*, XIX (September, 1932), 219-42

————, *Expansionists of 1898*. Baltimore, 1936

Pringle, Henry F., *Theodore Roosevelt*. New York, 1931

Puleston, William D., *Mahan: The Life and Work of Captain Alfred Thayer Mahan, U.S.N.* New Haven, 1939

Rippy, J. Fred, "Antecedents of the Roosevelt Corollary of the Monroe Doctrine," *Pacific Historical Review*, IX (September, 1940), 267-79

Roosevelt, Theodore, "How the United States Acquired the Right to Dig the Panama Canal," *Outlook*, XCIX (October, 1911), 314-318

Van Alstyne, Richard W., *The Rising American Empire*. New York, 1960

WILLIAM HOWARD TAFT

Hechler, Kenneth W., *Insurgency: Personalities and Policies of the Taft Era*. New York, 1940

Taft, William Howard, *Our Chief Magistrate and His Powers*. New York, 1916

WOODROW WILSON

Baker, Ray Stannard, *Woodrow Wilson and World Settlement*. 3 vols., Garden City, 1922

Bartlett, Ruhl J., *The League to Enforce Peace*. Chapel Hill, 1944

Bell, Herbert C. F., *Woodrow Wilson and the People*. Garden City, 1945

Binkley, Robert C., "Reactions of European Public Opinion to Woodrow Wilson's Statesmanship from the Armistice to the Peace of Versailles," Doctoral Dissertation, Stanford University, June, 1927

Birdsall, Paul, *Versailles Twenty Years After*. New York, 1941

Blum, John M., *Joe Tumulty and the Wilson Era*. New York, 1951

————, *Woodrow Wilson and the Politics of Morality*. Boston, 1956

Borchard, Edwin, and W. P. Lage, *Neutrality for the United States*. 2d ed., New Haven, 1940

Buehrig, Edward H., *Wilson's Foreign Policy in Perspective*. Bloomington, 1957

————, *Woodrow Wilson and the Balance of Power*. Bloomington, 1955

Corwin, Edward S., "Woodrow Wilson and the Presidency," *Virginia Law Review*, XLII (October, 1956) 761-783

Curti, Merle, *Bryan and World Peace*. Northampton, 1931

Daniels, Jonathan, "The Long Shadow of Woodrow Wilson," *Virginia Quarterly Review*, XXXII (Autumn, 1956) 481-493

Daniels, Josephus, *The Wilson Era*. 2 vols., Chapel Hill, 1944, 1946

Davidson, John W. (ed.), *Crossroads of Freedom*. New Haven, 1956

Fleming Denna F., *The United States and the League of Nations, 1918-1920*. New York, 1932

Greene, Theodore P. (ed.), *Wilson at Versailles*. Boston, 1957

House, Edward M., and Charles Seymour (eds.), *What Really Happened at Paris*. New York, 1921

Houston, David F., *Eight Years with Wilson's Cabinet*. 2 vols., Garden City, 1926

Kennan, George F., *Soviet-American Relations, 1917-1920*. 2 vols., New Jersey, 1956, 1958

Keynes, John Maynard, *The Economic Consequences of the Peace*. New York, 1920

The Lansing Papers, 1914-1920: Papers Relating to the Foreign Relations of the United States. 2 vols., Washington D.C., 1939, 1940

Lansing, Robert, *War Memoirs of Robert Lansing, Secretary of State.* Indianapolis, 1935

Latham, Earl (ed.), *The Philosophy and Policies of Woodrow Wilson.* Chicago, 1958

Lederer, Ivo J. (ed.), *The Versailles Settlement: Was It Foredoomed to Failure?* Boston, 1960

Leopold, Richard W., "The Problem of American Intervention, 1917: An Historical Retrospect," *World Politics,* II (April, 1950), 405-25

Link, Arthur S., *Wilson the Diplomatist.* Baltimore, 1957

———, *Woodrow Wilson and the Progressive Era, 1910-1917.* New York, 1954

Mantoux, Etienne, *The Carthaginian Peace: Or the Economic Consequences of Mr. Keynes.* Fair Lawn (N.J.), 1946

Martin, Laurence W., *Peace Without Victory: Woodrow Wilson and the British Liberals.* New Haven, 1958

May, Ernest R., *World War and American Isolation, 1914-1917.* Cambridge, 1959

Morrissey, Alice M., *The American Defense of Neutral Rights, 1914-1917.* Cambridge, 1939

Nicholson, Harold, *Peacemaking, 1919.* Boston, 1933

Seymour, Charles, *American Diplomacy During the World War.* Baltimore, 1934

———, *American Neutrality: 1914-1917.* New Haven, 1935

———, *Woodrow Wilson and the World War.* New Haven, 1921

Shotwell, James T., *At the Paris Peace Conference.* New York, 1937

Smith, Daniel M., "Lansing and the Wilson Interregnum," *The Historian,* XXI (February, 1959), 135-161

———, "Robert Lansing and the Formulation of American Neutrality Policies, 1914-1915," *Mississippi Valley Historical Review,* XLIII (June, 1956), 59-81

———, *Robert Lansing and American Neutrality, 1914-1917.* Berkeley, 1958

Tansill, Charles C., *America Goes To War.* Boston, 1938

Watson, R. L., Jr., "Woodrow Wilson and His Interpreters," *Mississippi Valley Historical Review,* XLIV (September, 1957), 207-236

Woolsey, Lester H., "The Personal Diplomacy of Colonel House," *American Journal of International Law,* XXI (October, 1927), 706-15

WARREN G. HARDING—CALVIN COOLIDGE

Bagby, Wesley M., *The Road to Normalcy: The Presidential Campaign and Election of 1920.* Baltimore, 1962

Buell, Raymond L., *The Washington Conference.* New York, 1922

Coolidge, Calvin, *The Autobiography of Calvin Coolidge.* New York, 1929

Cornwell, Elmer E., "Coolidge and Presidential Leadership," *Public Opinion Quarterly,* XXI (Summer, 1957), 266, 275, 276-78

Ellis, Lewis E., *Frank B. Kellogg and American Foreign Relations, 1925-1929.* New Brunswick, 1961

Faulkner, Harold U., *From Versailles to the New Deal.* New York, 1950

Feis, Herbert, *The Diplomacy of the Dollar: First Era, 1919-1932.* Baltimore, 1950

Fleming, Denna F., *The United States and the World Court.* Garden City, 1945

———, *The U.S. and World Organization, 1920-1933.* New York, 1938

Hicks, John D., *Republican Ascendancy, 1921-1933.* New York, 1960

May, H. F., "Shifting Perspectives on the 1920's," *Mississippi Valley Historical Review,* XLIII (December, 1956), 405-427

Nevins, Allan, *The United States in a Chaotic World: A Chronicle of International Affairs, 1918-1933.* New Haven, 1950

Perkins, Dexter, *Charles Evans Hughes and American Democratic Statesmanship.* Boston, 1956

Scott, James B., "President Harding's Foreign Policy," *American Journal of International Law,* XV (July, 1921), 409-411

Slosson, Preston W., "Warren G. Harding: A Revised Estimate," *Current History,* XXXIII (November, 1930), 174-79

———, *The Great Crusade and After, 1914-1928.* New York, 1930

Stoner, John E., *S. O. Levinson and the Pact of Paris.* Chicago, 1942

Warren, Sidney, "Harding's Abdication from Leadership," *Current History,* XXXIX (October, 1960) 203-207

HERBERT HOOVER

Current, Richard N., *Secretary Stimson: A Study in Statecraft.* New Brunswick, 1954

DeConde, Alexander, *Herbert Hoover's Latin-American Policy.* Stanford, 1951

Ferrell, Robert H., *American Diplomacy in the Great Depression.* New Haven, 1957

Langer, Robert, *Seizure of Territory: The Stimson Doctrine.* New York, 1947

Myers, William S., *The Foreign Policies of Herbert Hoover, 1929-1933.* New York, 1940

Smith, Sara R., *The Manchurian Crisis, 1931-1932.* New York, 1948

Stimson, Henry L., *The Far Eastern Crisis: Recollections and Observations.* New York, 1936

Wilbur, Ray L., and Arthur M. Hyde, *The Hoover Policies.* New York, 1937

Wolfe, Harold, *Herbert Hoover: Public Servant and Leader of the Loyal Opposition.* New York, 1956

FRANKLIN D. ROOSEVELT

Adler, Selig, *The Isolationist Impulse: Its 20th Century Reaction.* New York, 1957

Alsop, Joseph, and Robert Kintner, *American White Paper: The Story of American Diplomacy and the Second World War.* New York, 1940

Bateman, Herman E., "Observations on President Roosevelt's Health during World War II," *Mississippi Valley Historical Review,* XLIII (June, 1956), 82-102

Beard, Charles A., *American Foreign Policy in the Making, 1932-1940.* New Haven, 1946

————, *President Roosevelt and the Coming of the War, 1941.* New Haven, 1948

Blum, John M., *From the Morgenthau Diaries: Years of Crisis, 1928-1938.* Boston, 1959

Borg, Dorothy, "Notes on Roosevelt's 'Quarantine' Speech," *Political Science Quarterly,* LXXII (September, 1957), 405-433

Briggs, H. W., "Neglected Aspects of the Destroyer Deal," *American Journal of International Law,* XXXIV (October, 1940), 569-587

Carmichael, Donald Scott (ed.), *F.D.R. Columnist: The Uncollected Columns of Franklin D. Roosevelt.* Chicago, 1947

Cole, Wayne S., *America First: The Battle Against Intervention, 1940-1941.* Madison, 1953

———, "America's Entry into World War II: A Historiographical Appraisal," *Mississippi Valley Historical Review*, XLIII (March, 1957), 595-617

Daniels, Jonathan, *The End of Innocence*. New York, 1954

Davies, Joseph E., *Mission To Moscow*. New York, 1941

Dodd, William E., Jr., and Martha Dodd (eds.), *Ambassador Dodd's Diary, 1933-1938*. New York, 1941

Donovan, John C., "Congressional Isolationists and the Roosevelt Foreign Policy," *World Politics*, III (April, 1951), 299-316

Drummond, D. F., *The Passing of American Neutrality, 1937-1941*. Ann Arbor, 1955

Einaudi, Mario, *The Roosevelt Revolution*. New York, 1959

Farley, James A., *Jim Farley's Story: The Roosevelt Years*. New York, 1948

Feis, Herbert, *The Road to Pearl Harbor*. Princeton, 1950

———, "War Came at Pearl Harbor: Suspicions Considered," *Yale Review*, XLV (March, 1956), 378-90

Ferrell, R. H., "Pearl Harbor and the Revisionists," *The Historian*, XVII (Spring, 1955), 215-33

Flynn, Edward J., *You're the Boss*. New York, 1947

Freidel, Frank, *Franklin D. Roosevelt: The Apprenticeship*. Boston, 1952

———, *Franklin D. Roosevelt: The Ordeal*. Boston, 1952

———, *Franklin D. Roosevelt: The Triumph*. Boston, 1956

Gosnell, Harold F., *Champion Campaigner, Franklin D. Roosevelt*. New York, 1952

Gunther, John, *Roosevelt in Retrospect*. New York, 1950

Hammen, Oscar J., "The 'Ashes' of Yalta," *South Atlantic Quarterly*, LIII (October, 1954), 477-484

Hassett, William D., *Off the Record with F.D.R., 1942-1945*. New Brunswick, 1958

Hooker, Nancy H. (ed.), *The Moffat Papers*. Cambridge, 1956

Johnson, Gerald W., *Roosevelt: Dictator or Democrat?* New York, 1941

Johnson, Walter, *The Battle Against Isolation*. Chicago, 1944

Kilpatrick, Carroll (ed.), *Roosevelt and Daniels: The Friendship in Politics*. Chapel Hill, 1952

Langer, William L., "Political Problems of a Coalition," *Foreign Affairs*, XXVI (October, 1947), 73-89

———, *Our Vichy Gamble*. New York, 1947

Moley, Raymond L., *After Seven Years*. New York, 1939

Morison, Elting E., *Turmoil and Tradition*. Boston, 1960

Morison, Samuel E., "Did Roosevelt Start the War—History Through a Beard," *Atlantic Monthly*, vol. 182 (August, 1948), 91-97

Neumann, William L., *Making of the Peace, 1941-1945*. Washington, D.C., 1950

Nevins, Allan, *The New Deal and World Affairs*. New Haven, 1950

Perkins, Dexter, "Was Roosevelt Wrong?" *Virginia Quarterly Review*, XXX (Summer, 1954), 355-372

Range, Willard, *Franklin D. Roosevelt's World Order*. Athens (Ga.), 1959

Rauch, Basil, *Roosevelt: From Munich to Pearl Harbor*. New York, 1950

Robinson, Edgar, *The Roosevelt Leadership, 1933-1945*. New York, 1955

Roosevelt, Franklin D., *Whither Bound?* Lectures at Milton Academy, May, 1926. Boston, 1926

Rosenau, James N. (ed.), *The Roosevelt Treasury*. Garden City, 1951

Rossiter, Clinton L., "The Political Philosophy of F. D. Roosevelt," *The Review of Politics*, II (January, 1949), 87-95

Schlesinger, Arthur M., Jr., "Roosevelt and His Detractors," *Harper's Magazine*, CC (June, 1950), 62-68

Snell, John L. (ed.), *The Meaning of Yalta: Big Three Diplomacy and the New Balance of Power*. Baton Rouge, 1956

Sobel, Robert, *The Origins of Interventionism: The United States and the Russo-Finnish War*. New York, 1960

Stettinius, Edward R., *Lend Lease: Weapon for Victory*. New York, 1944

———, *Roosevelt and the Russians: The Yalta Conference*. Garden City, 1949

Tansill, Charles C., *Back Door to War*. Chicago, 1952

U.S. Department of State, *Foreign Relations of the United States: The Conferences at Malta and Yalta, 1945*. Washington, D.C., 1955

Wecter, Dixon, *Age of the Great Depression*. New York, 1948

Wheeler-Bennett, John W., *Munich: Prologue to Tragedy*. New York, 1948

White, Theodore H. (ed.), *The Stilwell Papers*. New York, 1948

Willkie, Wendell L., *One World*. London, 1943

HARRY S. TRUMAN

Amrine, Michael, *The Great Decision*. New York, 1959

Bundy, McGeorge (ed.), *The Pattern of Responsibility*. Boston, 1952

Byrnes, James F., *All in One Lifetime*. New York, 1958

China White Paper, *United States Relations with China: With Special Reference to the Period 1944-1949*. Washington, D.C., 1949

Congressional Hearing, *The Military Situation in the Far East*, 82nd Congress, 1st Session, Washington, D.C., 1951

Crabb, Cecil V., Jr., *Bipartisan Foreign Policy, Myth or Reality?* New York, 1957

Dahl, Robert A., *Congress and Foreign Policy*. New York, 1950

Davison, Walter P., *The Berlin Blockade: A Study in Cold War Politics*. Princeton, 1958

Feis, Herbert, *Between War and Peace; The Potsdam Conference*. Princeton, 1960

————, *China Tangle*. Princeton, 1953

————, *Japan Subdued: The Atomic Bomb and the End of the War in the Pacific*. Princeton, 1961

Goldman, Eric F., *The Crucial Decade—and After: America, 1945-1960*. New York, 1961

Graebner, Norman A., *The New Isolationism*. New York, 1956

Higgins, Trumbull, *Korea and the Fall of MacArthur: A Précis in Limited War*. New York, 1960

Jones, Joseph M., *The Fifteen Weeks*. New York, 1955

Kennan, George F., *Russia, the Atom and the West*. New York, 1957

Latourette, Kenneth S., *The American Record in the Far East, 1945-1951*. New York, 1952

Lippmann, Walter, *The Cold War*. New York, 1947

Mosely, Philip E., "Dismemberment of Germany: The Allied Negotiations From Yalta to Potsdam," *Foreign Affairs*, XXVIII (April, 1950), 487-98

Public Papers of the Presidents of the United States: Harry S. Truman, 1945, 1946, 1947. Washington, D.C., 1961, 1962, 1963

Rovere, Richard H., and Arthur M. Schlesinger, *The General and the President and the Future of American Foreign Policy*. New York, 1951

Stimson, Henry L., "Decision to Use the Atomic Bomb," *Harper's Magazine*, vol. 194 (February, 1947), 97-107

U.S. Department of State, *A Decade of American Foreign Policy, Basic Documents, 1941-1949.* Washington, D.C., 1950

——, *United States Relations with China, 1944-1949.* Washington, D.C., 1949

Vinacke, Harold M., *The United States and the Far East, 1945-1951.* Stanford, 1952

Wedemeyer, Albert C., *Wedemeyer Reports.* New York, 1958

Willoughby, Charles A., and John Chamberlain, *MacArthur, 1941-1945: Victory in the Pacific.* New York, 1954

DWIGHT D. EISENHOWER

Beal, John R., *John Foster Dulles: A Biography.* New York, 1957

Bell, Jack, *The Splendid Misery: The Story of the Presidency and Power Politics at Close Range.* Garden City, 1960

Eisenhower, Dwight D., *Mandate for Change: The White House Years, 1953-1956.* Garden City, 1963

Gould-Adams, Richard, *John Foster Dulles: A Reappraisal.* New York, 1962

Hyman, Sidney, "The Failure of the Eisenhower Presidency," *The Progressive*, XXIV (May, 1960), 10-13

Lear, John, "Ike and the Peaceful Atom," *The Reporter*, XIV (January 12, 1956), 11-21

Lukacs, John, *A History of the Cold War.* Garden City, 1961

Murphy, Charles J. V., "The Eisenhower Shift," *Fortune*, vol. 53 (January, 1956), 83 *ff.*, vol. 53 (February, 1956), 110 *ff.*, vol. 53 (March, 1956), 110 *ff.*

——, "The White House Since Sputnik," *Fortune*, vol. 57 (January, 1958), 98 *ff.*

Nixon, Richard M., *Six Crises.* Garden City, 1962

Pusey, Merlo J., *Eisenhower the President.* New York, 1956

Rovere, Richard H., *Affairs of State: The Eisenhower Years.* New York, 1956

——, "Eisenhower Over the Shoulder," *American Scholar*, XXXI (Spring, 1962), 176-179

Shannon, William V., "Eisenhower as President: A Critical Appraisal of the Record," *Commentary*, XXVI (November, 1958), 390-398

Smith, A. Merriman, *Meet Mr. Eisenhower.* New York, 1955

——, *President's Odyssey.* New York, 1961

Tobin, James, "The Eisenhower Economy and National Security:
    Defense, Dollars, and Doctrines," *Yale Review*, XLVII (March,
    1958), 321-334
Wise, David, and Thomas B. Ross, *The U-2 Affair*. New York, 1962

JOHN F. KENNEDY

Burns, James MacGregor, *John Kennedy: A Political Profile*. 2d ed.
    New York, 1961
David, Paul T. (ed.), *The Presidential Election and Transition, 1960-
    1961*. Washington, D.C., 1961
Fuller, Helen, *Year of Trial: Kennedy's Crucial Decisions*. New
    York, 1962
Johnson, Haynes, *The Bay of Pigs*. New York, 1964
Meyer, Karl E., and Tad Szulc, *The Cuban Invasion: Chronicle of a
    Disaster*. New York, 1962
Nevins, Allan (ed.) *President John F. Kennedy: The Burden and
    The Glory*. New York, 1964
Pachter, Henry M., *Collision Course: The Cuban Missile Crisis and
    Coexistence*. New York, 1963
*Public Papers of the Presidents of the United States: John F. Ken-
    nedy, 1961, 1962*. Washington, D.C., 1962, 1963
Sidey, Hugh, *John F. Kennedy, President*. Toronto, 1963

Index

471

DATE DUE

DATE DUE			
AP 1 '65			
AP 15 '65			
AP 27 '65			
AP 26 '66			
FEB 19 '70			
IN			
FEB 19 '85			
FEB 11 '85			
APR 28 '87			
MAY 13 '87			
AP 23 '98			
GAYLORD			PRINTED IN U.S.A.